Development and the State in the 2

Development and the State in the 21st Century

Tackling the Challenges Facing the Developing World

Natasha Ezrow

Erica Frantz

Andrea Kendall-Taylor

First published 2016 by
PALGRAVE

Palgrave in the UK is an imprint of Macmillan Publishers Limited, registered in England, company number 785998, of 4 Crinan Street, London, N1 9XW.

Palgrave Macmillan in the US is a division of St Martin's Press LLC, 175 Fifth Avenue, New York, NY 10010.

Palgrave is a global imprint of the above companies and is represented throughout the world.

Palgrave® and Macmillan® are registered trademarks in the United States, the United Kingdom, Europe and other countries.

ISBN 978–1–137–40712–2 hardback
ISBN 978–1–137–40711–5 paperback

This book is printed on paper suitable for recycling and made from fully managed and sustained forest sources. Logging, pulping and manufacturing processes are expected to conform to the environmental regulations of the country of origin.

A catalogue record for this book is available from the British Library.

A catalog record for this book is available from the Library of Congress.

Printed in China

Contents

List of Boxes and Tables

Boxes

Tables

Acknowledgements

This book was inspired by my students in the Government Department at the University of Essex. After many years of teaching classes in Development Studies, I found students constantly asking me when, if ever, countries would drive themselves out of poverty. In other words, with so many readings about poverty and despair, were there any success stories? Though this book focuses much attention on the challenges that face the developing world, the aim is to provide hope for what states can do to overcome these challenges.

I would also like to thank our editor Stephen Wenham (and the team from Palgrave) for being so patient while various drafts and proposals were being worked on and for providing us with clear guidance to help us improve upon the earlier versions.

This book would not have been possible without the help of Erica and Andrea who worked so hard to organize all of the research and make it clear and readable. Both are exceptional in how quick and easy they are to work with, all the while managing full-time jobs and five children between them. I would also like to thank my parents, Jeff and Yvette, for their constant support and enthusiasm. I would finally like to thank my two daughters, Annika and Karolina, for being adorable.

NATASHA EZROW

Part I

Understanding Development

Chapter 1

Setting the Stage: What Is Development?

Why are some countries richer than others? What explains disparities in the quality of life both across countries and within them? How can countries create conditions conducive to economic growth? These are the enduring questions that scholars and policymakers in the field of international development seek to address and answer. Although the development community has made enormous strides in addressing important issues like poverty and inequality, there are a number of challenges that lie ahead.

Let's start with some good news. According to the World Bank (2013b), the percentage of people in the developing world living on less than $1.25 per day has decreased considerably in the past 30 years (from 50% in 1981 to 21% in 2010). Remarkable success stories in states like China, India and Brazil, all of whom have made great strides in growing their economies and reducing the number of their citizens living in poverty in the past few decades, highlight the advances the development community has made. In 1981, the percentage of the population living on less than $1.25 per day was 84% in China, 60% in India and 17% in Brazil. By 2005, these numbers declined to 16% in China, 42% in India and only 8% in Brazil (The Economist, 2009). These are considerable transformations.

Yet, significant challenges for the development community remain. The absolute number of the world's people who live in poverty is still all too high. According to the World Bank (2013b), there are 1.22 billion people who live on less than $1.25 per day, a third of whom live in Sub-Saharan Africa (unless otherwise noted, from here on we will refer to Sub-Saharan Africa as Africa). And for many of the world's poor, their quality of life continues to deteriorate. The endless cycles of political instability, outbreaks of disease and episodes of famine that plague this part of the world continue to prevent reforms that would enable growth to take root (Collier, 2008).

Take the Democratic Republic of Congo (DRC). According to the World Bank (2013a), the DRC has the potential to be one of the wealthiest states in the African continent due to the abundance of agricultural and mineral resources there. Yet, it has been plagued by an endless cycle

3

of conflicts since the 1990s. There are now over two million displaced persons and refugees inside the DRC's borders, and humanitarian emergencies in various parts of the country have become the norm. Its institutions are weak, damaged by the violence and instability, and the standard of living experienced by citizens is among the lowest in Africa, if not the world. In sum, the problems in the DRC are many and there appears to be no end to them in sight.

As the case of the DRC underscores, addressing the world's development needs is no easy task. In this book we seek to shed light on many of the critical issues in the field today and to draw attention to the key challenges that lie ahead. But in order to fully understand why today's development landscape looks the way it does and to better prepare the field's future leaders to confront tomorrow's challenges, we also seek to take stock of where the development community has been in the past. By analysing the evolution of key development theories, and highlighting the many factors that scholars have found to affect development outcomes, we hope to provide a solid foundation on which future practitioners can build.

What is the developing world?

The central goal of the field of development is to improve the quality of life for more of the world's population. Though there is consensus on this point, there is disagreement on most other issues in the field. For one, observers disagree about the set of states that should be the subject of inquiry. Few argue that the United States, Canada, Western Europe, Australia, New Zealand and Japan need development assistance, but from there things get quite contentious. Should states like Qatar, where citizens are often wealthy but lack many basic political rights and liberties, be included in the sample? Should states like Cuba be included, whose citizens, though poor, have better access to a variety of public goods, like education and health care? These are not easy questions and the answers often depend on the specific goals one seeks to achieve.

Observers also disagree about the specific terminology that should be used to refer to the sample of states that warrants our attention. During the Cold War, scholars and policy practitioners referred to this group of countries as the 'Third World' where countries in the West comprised the First World, the countries associated with the USSR and communism made up the 'Second World', and the 'Third World' referred to everywhere else. After the end of the Cold War, however, the term 'Third World' has become less relevant and has decreased in prominence accordingly.

The terms that have since emerged to fill the void are admittedly imperfect. Some observers, for example, use the term 'underdeveloped' to reference the sample of states under inquiry, yet this implies that these states are in some way backward. Others use the term 'less developed', which suffers from a similar drawback. Some observers instead use the term 'Global South', but this term is misleading. For example, Afghanistan, a state that nearly all observers agree warrants the attention of the development community, lies in the Northern Hemisphere, while Australia lies in the Southern. Other observers use the term 'developing', which has also been criticized because it implies that states classified as such are all in the process of achieving, and will eventually achieve, a (development) goal, which is an overly optimistic assumption.

We acknowledge that there are drawbacks to all of these terms. For consistency, we use the term 'developed' to refer to the West and Japan and 'developing' to refer to everywhere else. By the West, we mean Europe, the United States, Canada and Australia. Japan is also included due to its history as a colonial power and current status as an economic power. Though there are drawbacks to grouping these countries together in our analysis, these countries are the most predominant members of the major international financial institutions and organizations, such as the Organisation for Economic Cooperation and Development (OECD). They are also some of the largest donors of foreign aid.

What is development?

There are also disagreements with respect to what we mean by development. Is it political development (implying a focus on democracy), social development (implying a focus on social conditions) or economic development (implying a focus on poverty reduction)? All three of these types of development are intertwined, making matters even more complex.

Political development consists of building governments that are responsible and representative, with some form of mass participation and universal laws. Definitions from the 1950s and 1960s assumed that political development entailed an 'increased differentiation and specialization of political structures and the increased secularization of political culture' (Almond and Powell, 1978, 20). For Samuel Huntington (1968), political development includes the institutionalization of political organizations and procedures, which then improves government performance. Additionally, political development is also associated with creating a national identity (Rustow, 1970).

Social development generally speaking encompasses a process of planned social change that is designed to promote the well-being of the population as a whole (Midgley, 2014, 13). Social development is concerned with projects and progressive policies, which may entail improving education, health care and removing barriers that prevent social inclusion

(Midgley, 2014, 14, 17), with the prime focus on the structural changes to society.

Economic development may include many issues that concern social development, but in essence, economic development is concerned with structural changes in the economy. Economic development constitutes not only economic growth, economic growth per capita, savings and investment but also socio-economic improvements such as increases in living standards, improvements in health care and education, and quality of life – which all provide more choices and opportunities. In this way economic development coincides closely with social development. Economic development can also constitute building infrastructure, ensuring environmental sustainability and improving security and chances for employment (Sen, 1983).

Thus, development can mean many different things, but broadly speaking development encompasses change, growth, progress or some sort of evolution of the human condition. Development is supposed to promote the well-being of the population as a whole, improve the quality of life, reduce the spread of disease and mitigate its effects, reduce poverty and increase life expectancy (Stiglitz, 1998, 77). Development may imply that massive societal shifts have taken place such as moving from a rural/agricultural to an urban society, or changes in class structure. Development may also indicate a large shift away from traditional relations, cultures and social mores (Stiglitz, 1998, 77). Development may also entail a move towards scientific ways of thinking.

After World War II, early meanings of development were focused on rebuilding economies in the developed world as a way of preventing the rise of communism. Early conceptions of development focused entirely on economics and growth. Early on the World Bank focused on promoting foreign private investment, and raising productivity as a means of raising the living standards of countries. By the 1970s, the Bank started to emphasize the importance of social development. When Robert McNamara became World Bank president in 1968, the World Bank became more committed to improving the productivity levels of the developing countries. He also recognized that development had a social objective that was aimed at eliminating poverty and global injustices. He paid particular attention to issues such as overpopulation, urbanization, land reform, income redistribution, health care and the environment. The Bank started to use social indicators to measure development, which went beyond just looking at economic growth. Overall, there was an emphasis on the quality of growth, which incorporated broader criteria of development.

Noted scholar and Nobel Prize-winning economist Amartya Sen (1983) expanded on the definition of development, advocating a human-centred approach to development. Going beyond economic growth, Sen argued that freedom was crucial to development since it enhanced individuals' well-being. Sen highlighted five basic freedoms, which included political and participative freedoms such as civil rights, freedom of speech and elections; economic opportunities to help people work to pay for what they may need to consume such as food, clothing and housing; social opportunities such as education and health care; transparency guarantees such as an open government and societies with high levels of social trust; and protective security such as law and order and social safety nets for the unemployed and to prevent people from living in abject poverty. Development, as he sees it, is the process of 'enlarging people's choices' (Human Development Report, 1995) and expanding freedoms and capabilities enables people to live the types of lives that they would value (Sen, 1999, xii, 1, 18). For Sen, all of these freedoms are crucial to development. Only states that provide a host of different freedoms will enable individuals to pursue trade and other productive endeavours. Ideas of development started to emphasize that development could be achieved through education, meeting nutritional needs and health-care needs (Schultz, 1962).

Heavily influenced by Sen, in 1990 the United Nations Development Programme (UNDP) began to publish its annual Human Development Report. This reflected another shift towards human development. This shift was also reflected in the World Bank's definition of economic development, which according to the World Development Report of 1991 was defined as improving living standards, improving education, health care and environmental protection.

Inequality and development

Scholars started to focus on development that took into account how growth and wealth was distributed both between countries and within. Though growth was taking place, not all developing countries were catching up to the growth that had taken place in the developed world. For example, using data from the World Bank's World Development Indicators (2014) from 1960 to 2010, we see that in the developed world, life expectancy is 79 years, infant mortality rates are seven deaths per 1000 infants and nearly all adults over 15 years of age are literate. Compare this to the developing world, where life expectancy is only 57 years, 135 infants die out of every 1000 and just two-thirds of adults (61%) can read. These are fairly dramatic differences. On a number of fronts, the data indicate that the quality of life of citizens in the developing world is inferior to that of citizens in the developed world. Another difference is that the gap between women and men in terms of earning power, political power and education is much larger in the developing world than in the developed world. Women are more impoverished, less likely to be a member of parliament and have much lower literacy rates. For more on *women and development*, see Box 1.1.

Additionally, though growth had taken place in developing countries, it was very unevenly distributed. There was little evidence that growth within one country would trickle down. Instead, there was more support that meeting the needs of the poor through social development would create conditions that were positive for economic growth (Newman and Thomson, 1989, 469). Dudley Seers (1969) aimed to redefine how development was defined and measured by focusing on reducing poverty and inequality. He claimed that development that was not accompanied by social improvements to address inequalities was meaningless. Much of development was uneven, and development planning needed to address the problems of unbalanced development. Hollis Burnley Chenery et al. (1975) argued that rapid economic growth would not by itself spread the benefits of development widely to raise living standards for all. For this reason, measures that directly reduce income and wealth inequality are needed.

In 2010, high-income countries, which account for 16% of the world's population, were estimated to generate 55% of the global income. Low-income countries created only 1% of the world's income though they constitute 72% of the world's population. There also continue to be growing gaps between rich and poor within countries. China, Russia and India are seeing their inequality levels rise. Billionaires in Russia and India are responsible for 18.6% of Russia's GDP and 11% in India. These disparities are obvious in Africa as well. Those living under $2 a day account for 60.8% of the population but hold only 36.5% of the income, while those living on $20 a day account for 4.8% of the population and hold 18.8% of the total income. In some countries these disparities are even greater. In Mozambique the average share of income of the lowest 20% of the population is 5.2% while the richest 20% have a share of 51.5% (African Development Bank Group). In Namibia, the situation is even worse. The poorest 10% of households command just 1% of the country's total income whereas the wealthiest 10% control more than 50% (UNDP).

Inequality (for more on this, see Box 1.2) has major implications for both social and economic development. Countries with low levels of inequality sustain higher growth rates for longer periods of time (Alesina and Rodrik, 1994; Berg et al., 2012). In contrast, countries with high levels of inequality have less stable and efficient economic systems, which can stifle economic growth (Stiglitz, 2012). One reason for this is that countries with high levels of inequality have lower levels of aggregate demand, which slows down economic growth. Low wages make it difficult for the poorest segments of the population to consume. All of the wealth being concentrated in the hands of the few does not generate enough demand to stimulate the economy (Goldberg and Pavcnik, 2004).

Inequality also perpetuates poverty traps. It slows the pace of poverty reduction because it limits opportunities for social mobility and access to health care and education. Much of the population in countries with high levels of inequality will see their potential go untapped. Inequality usually means that there are fewer people working, and also more people working only part time, resulting in fewer total working hours.

Inequality in health care can affect long-term development. Health outcomes are important to mobility since adults in poor health will find it more difficult to attain and hold a good job, which leads to lower wages (Case and Paxson, 2006). Additionally, children in poor health have greater difficulty learning and leave school earlier than healthy children. Nutrition is an area where inequalities remain very high. In Latin America, survey data shows that there are high disparities in countries such as Bolivia, Honduras and Peru, where child stunting is nine times higher among children from poor households compared to children from rich households (United Nations, 2013, 48). Though life expectancy disparities have decreased across most regions, this has not been the case in Africa. In Africa, life expectancy was 14 years lower than the world average in 1980–1985. From 1995 to 2000, life expectancy was 16 years lower than the world average.

All regions have made improvements in increasing access to education. In developed countries the average number of years of schooling increased from 6.1 to 11.3 years, while the average number of years of schooling in developing countries increased from 2 to 7.2 years. Nevertheless, within countries there still remain high levels of inequality in education. A report from 63 developing countries between 2005 and 2011 found that children from poor households were three times more likely to be out of school than children from rich households. Additionally, rural children were twice as likely as urban children not to be enrolled in school. The poor–rich divide is still striking in countries like Chad. In 2004 only 9% of children from the poorest households were attending primary school compared to 63% of those from the richest households (United Nations, 2013, 53–54). Studies have found that countries with high levels of secondary school enrolment are better able to tackle the major issues of development such as reducing poverty, improving infant mortality rates, improving life expectancy, reducing maternal death rates and stimulating economic growth (Hertz et al., 1994; Tilak, 2007).

Generally speaking, while poor countries are more likely to have conflict, countries with high levels of inequality are especially prone to conflict (Collier, 2007). Areas with low income compared to the national average are more likely to see conflict (Buhaug et al., 2011). Additionally, inequalities taking place along ethnic lines produce situations that are particularly conducive to conflict (Cederman et al., 2011).

Box 1.1   Women and development

The UNDP concluded in its 1997 Human Development Report that no country treats its women better than its men. The report claimed that in the developing world women still continue to face numerous injustices and fare worse on a number of indicators including life expectancy, wealth and education. Previous policies to deal with the plight that women faced in the developing world focused on welfare-oriented policies that made the assumption that the most important role for women was motherhood. The welfare approach believed that welfare provisions needed to be targeted towards women, who along with the disabled were identified as 'vulnerable groups'. The approach assumed that women were passive recipients of development, rather than actively participating in the development process. It also assumed that the only important role for women in society is motherhood and that raising children was the most important contribution of women in development (Moser, 1989, 1807). Thus the welfare approach consisted of top-down handouts of free goods and services. Training for women was only offered in areas that were deemed appropriate for non-working mothers (Moser, 1989, 1808).

Eventually, new approaches examined the role for women in the development process. Researchers moved away from only examining the role of women within their own families, and moved more towards understanding the challenges for women in employment. Women were now viewed as an untapped resource that could contribute to development. Women should be

$\rightarrow$

In many developing countries the distribution of land ownership is very uneven, which helps to explain why inequalities persist. In Latin America, the ownership of land still remains concentrated in the hands of the few (Volrath, 2007). This highly unequal distribution of land creates social and political tensions leading to conflicts. Inequalities in land distribution also have implications for economic growth. Small landowners often do not have access to credit or resources, which could help them increase their productivity levels.

Countries that have seen their inequality levels decline have done so by expanding education and by making public transfers to the poor (United Nations, 2013, 31). It may be especially important to provide more social protection coverage for informal workers to prevent poverty traps and to increase the minimum wage for formal workers. Latin America was able to make small improvements in income inequality by increasing public spending on education, which led to higher primary and secondary school enrolment and completion rates (Lopez-Calva and Lustig, 2010).

more involved in the development process. It was acknowledged that men and women have different needs in society, and that policies should identify what these needs are in order to implement policies that cater to women better (Moser, 1989, 1800). In low-income families, women are responsible for childbearing and rearing and often work as secondary income earners. They are usually involved in the agricultural sector in rural areas, and the informal sector in urban areas. When the state fails to offer housing, and basic services such as water and health, it is women who suffer the most but are also forced to figure out how to allocate limited resources to ensure the survival of their households (Moser, 1989, 1801).

Approaches that followed shifted from looking at women in isolation and more towards gender and how social relationships between men and women kept women systematically subordinated. These gendered approaches examine how ideological, historical, religious and cultural differences shape the social relationships between men and women. Yet, most policymakers involved in development planning have not recognized the role of gender. Decisions are male dominated (Moser, 1989, 1801). These approaches also emphasized the need to increase equity and participation for women in the developing world.

Women's contributions to development are still devalued, though women are indispensable to economic development. Studies have also shown that women are not only important to improving economic growth but are also key to democratic transitions, conflict resolution and reducing corruption (Jaquette and Wolchik, 1998; Dollar et al., 2001; Swamy et al., 2001; Ramsbotham et al., 2011).

Countries in East Asia reduced inequality by ensuring that the quality of education was as uniform as possible, with high primary and secondary school enrolment rates (Birdsall et al., 1995). Countries can make significant inroads into reducing inequality by making long-term investment in human capital.

Social inequalities

The UNDP 1995 report on human development claimed that 70% of the 1.3 billion people living in absolute poverty are women. Environmental disasters, economic crises, structural adjustment programmes and armed conflicts have all resulted in the 'feminization of poverty' (Food and Agricultural Organization of the United Nations. In some countries in the developing world, for example Lesotho, women still lack the right to own land. All deeds must include a man's name and if the man on the deed is to die, the woman has no legal claim to the land that she may have lived on her whole life. In countries where women cannot own land, this also makes it more difficult to secure credit since land is a major factor in securing loans. This makes it difficult for women to upgrade equipment and expand production.

Women are also more likely in developing countries to die before men, though life expectancy for women is higher than men in developed countries. In developing countries, one of the major causes of death is childbirth and complications during pregnancy, something that is often preventable given an adequate public health-care system. In 2013, 289,000 women died worldwide due to complications during pregnancy and childbirth, with almost 800 women dying a day (World Health Organization). In developing countries, among women of reproductive age, the second leading cause of death after HIV/AIDS is complications during pregnancy and childbirth, and constitutes the number-one cause of death among girls aged 15–19 (Food and Agricultural Organization of the United Nations). Women are also more likely to be malnourished than men. In developing countries, they often serve the family first and then eat whatever food is left. This is especially problematic when women are pregnant or breast-feeding (FAO).

There are also huge discrepancies in terms of education. In developing countries, 41% of women are illiterate while only 20% of men are. Girls are forced to leave school earlier, particularly in rural areas to help out with other responsibilities. The lack of public transport also disproportionately affects women's attendance rates, as parents may be more cautious about the safety of their daughters travelling long distances to go to school. Yet girls who complete their education are less likely to marry young, and more likely to have a smaller family, live a longer life and earn higher salaries (Food and Agricultural Organization of the United Nations).

Women are mostly still concentrated in low-salary fields in the developing world. A strict gendered division of labour still exists. There are still few women occupying key positions in large companies, working in the ministries of finance and budget and heading the central banks (Food and Agricultural Organization of the United Nations). Women hold only 15.6% of elected parliamentary seats in the world. Women involved in policymaking are more likely to allocate funds towards family and community resources, health, education and eradicating poverty. Men, in contrast, are more likely to invest in the military. At the household level, women are also more likely to spend income on their own families.

In the aftermath of a natural disaster (see Chapter 10), women are also more likely to suffer long-term consequences then men. After a disaster, consumption levels decrease, which may negatively affect women more than men. For example, in India, because there are biases in the allocation of food among household members, women are more likely to suffer from malnutrition than men after a natural disaster. Moreover, in the aftermath of a natural disaster, women also will have less access than men to reconstruction jobs and credit (Charvériat, 2000, 28).

In addition to women, indigenous people are worse off on most social and economic indicators compared to non-indigenous populations. Indigenous people are among the poorest groups in the world, and account for 10% of the world's poor. As many as one-third of all indigenous people live in poverty. In developing countries, poverty rates of indigenous people are almost five times higher than among the rest of the population (UN, 2013, 89). Though inequalities have been reduced in many countries in Latin America, poverty rates have not improved much among the indigenous populations.

There are also economic and social inequalities between persons with disabilities and the general population. Around 20% of the world's poor are disabled (Elwan, 1999). The disabled are more likely to be poor because they are often excluded from work and educational opportunities. Disabled people in developing countries are often unable to access cash transfer programmes due to physical and social barriers that surround them (Mitra, 2005). On the flip side, poverty also increases the risk of being disabled due to malnutrition, and poor living and working conditions. Disabilities also affect the family members of the disabled. For example, households that had at least one member with a disability had lower assets (Mitra et al., 2011). The burden of earning income falls on the shoulders of one family member, which perpetuates poverty traps.

Thus, by the early 1970s, definitions of development emerged to include ideas of meeting basic needs, and many scholars have conceptualized economic development in very comprehensive terms. Economic development now entails improving the economic and social well-being of people, by developing human capital, infrastructure, environmental sustainability, social inclusion, health care, security, literacy and employment (Sen, 1983).

Another major shift occurred with the rise of *sustainable development* approaches. By the 1980s it became more widely understood that development needs to be sustainable. This definition of development refers to development that can meet the needs of the present without compromising the ability of the future to meet its own needs (World Commission on the Environment and Development, 1987, 43). Sustainable development approaches were the result of a growing awareness of the global links between environmental problems, poverty, inequality and well-being. The term was first used in 1980 at the World Conservation Strategy. It was later more clearly expressed in the Brundtland Report, which was published by the United Nations World Commission on Environment and

Development in 1987, which recognized the dependency of humans on the environment to meet the needs and well-being in a much wider sense than merely exploiting resources.

The Brundtland Report, while emphasizing the significance of poverty and inequality (the report was especially critical of past growth models for not reducing poverty or narrowing the gaps between rich and poor), warned that environmental destruction would limit forms of economic growth. This approach recognizes that ecology and the economy are becoming 'more and more interwoven, locally, regionally, nationally and globally', (World Commission on the Environment and Development, 1987, 35). Humanity depends on the environment both for now and the future. This approach argues that the globe is interconnected, and environmental problems are not only local but global. Local actions can have an international effect. Pollution can cross boundaries. Meanwhile, environmental problems threaten people's health and livelihood, and can threaten future generations. Thus, this approach offers a definition of development that looks at environmental, cultural and social factors. It also sees increasing participation and eradicating poverty and inequality as key elements of development (World Commission on Environment and Development, 1987, 49).

In the following section we illustrate how development is often measured and how measurement of development has changed over time.

How is development measured?

Now that we have established that there are many different ways of looking at development, how can we measure it? Development indicators have evolved since the 1960s. Growth in GDP was first used to measure development. For many years, economic development was typically measured by per capita rates of gross domestic product (GDP per capita). GDP refers to the total goods and services produced by a state in a given year. This number is then divided by a state's total population to obtain the state's GDP per capita. To take into account differences in the costs of living across states, some observers also adjust this number by calculating differences in the total cost of the same basic goods, referred to as purchasing power parity (PPP).

The process of transitioning from a developing state to a developed one requires (at a minimum) significant and sustained increases in levels of economic development. These changes in levels of economic development from one year to the next are referred to as economic growth rates and are measured as the annual percentage change in a state's GDP per capita. Most fast growing developing countries experience growth rates substantially greater than those seen in the developed world. The United States, for example, has a long-term growth rate of about 2–5%. A fast growing developing country can achieve growth rates around 10%. These differences are explained, in part, by a country's starting position. Afghanistan and Sierra Leone, for example, logged the highest economic growth rates in 2012, growing at 15.2% and 14.4%. While such rates of economic growth are positive for those countries' development trajectories, it is important to put such figures in perspective by considering the levels from which a country is growing.

The focal point of this book is how states can develop and improve the standard of living they provide for their citizens by growing their economies. Some argue that focusing solely on economic growth, however, misses the boat. They point to developing states like Cuba, which have poor growth records, but offer their citizens a host of social services. Though it is true that the Cuban government has not required strong economic performance to bestow such public goods on its citizens, the state would be able to provide a larger array of services by growing the economy.

At the same time, a drawback of focusing on economic growth is that it reveals very little about societal distributions of wealth. One could easily imagine two scenarios with the same high rate of economic growth: in one, economic gains are distributed equally to a state's citizens and all are better off, while in the other, economic gains are distributed to a small elite who prosper and pad their bank accounts while the rest of the citizenry languish in poverty, finding themselves either the same or worse off than they were before. Economic growth rates, in other words, can tell us whether the size of a state's economy is increasing (or decreasing), but not how those economic gains (or losses) are affecting individual citizens. For this reason, throughout much of this book we will highlight economic growth as the desired outcome, but also include discussions of inequality (see Table 1.1) and other issues related to income distribution.

GDP per capita (regardless of whether it is adjusted for PPP) is often criticized as a proxy for economic development because it does not always offer a full picture of a state's developmental landscape. For example, some countries that are abundant in natural resources, particularly in small or sparsely populated countries, rank higher in terms of their GDP per capita than the poor quality of life enjoyed by many of their citizens would suggest. Just by observing the GDP per capita rankings of Azerbaijan and Kazakhstan, two oil and natural gas abundant countries in the former Soviet Union, one would probably have an inflated sense of the true levels of development present in these countries.

For this reason, some observers have turned to alternative indicators to capture quality of life. Several academics such as Seers (1972) and

Sen (1999) questioned whether or not per capita income was adequate to measure development. Sen argued that development could not be based on GDP per capita because it did not take into account what an individual's capabilities are. Though income may help in providing a means for achieving other freedoms, Sen argued that there has been too much emphasis placed on this dimension. Sen was influential in formulating a new measure of development that took into account many different dimensions to development, known as the Human Development Index (HDI).

The HDI continues to be a prominent measure of development. There are three dimensions to this index: health (measured by life expectancy), education (measured by average and expected years of schooling) and living standards (measured by GDP per capita). Using the HDI, states like Azerbaijan and Kazakhstan that typically have higher levels of wealth but poorer social services and educational opportunities receive lower rankings than they would solely using GDP per capita. Similarly, states like those in the former communist bloc that typically have greater social services and educational opportunities but lower levels of wealth typically receive higher rankings than they do just using GDP per capita. We agree that the HDI offers a more nuanced picture than GDP per capita.

Other indices that examine development have also tried to go beyond just looking at growth rates. The Human Poverty Index looks at the probability at birth of not living to 40, the adult literacy rate, the percentage of the population without sustainable access to water sources and the percentage of children that are underweight for their age. The Gender Development Index looks at male and female life expectancy rates, male and female literacy rates, male and female school enrolment rates and female and male earned income shares. Sustainable development approaches may examine figures such as calorie consumption, environmental degradation (such as deforestation and desertification), water and sanitation access and statistics on energy usage.

For the practitioners within the development community such as international development agencies and the donor community, development is concerned with clear goals and targets. Recently the most common way of measuring development is through the achievement of Millennium Development Goals (MDGs), which are a set of indicators and outcomes that can be measured and compared. The MDGs were launched in September of 2000 after a series of international conferences and agreements that were led by UN agencies. The MDGs consist of eight goals, 18 targets and 47 indicators. The eight goals are focused on eradicating extreme poverty and hunger; achieving universal primary education; promoting gender equality; empowering women; reducing child mortality rates; improving maternal health; combating HIV/AIDS, malaria and other diseases; ensuring environmental sustainability and developing a global partnership for development. Critics claimed, however, that the MDGs were created exclusively by the industrialized countries without much consultation and that the approach has been mostly top-down (Saith, 2007, 1174, 1184).

In this study, when we refer to development, we mean economic development. By economic development we are referring to the most basic aspects that are measureable such as life expectancy, infant, child and maternal mortality rates, literacy rates and primary school enrolment rates, the percentage of the population living under $2 a day, GDP/ capita increases, calorie consumption, investment rates, unemployment rates, income inequality (including landlessness) and male/female earned income shares, corruption levels and *GDP growth rates*. These measures are chosen because they are often available for a wide set of countries that compares facilitating comparative inquiries. It is important to note that when examining relationships that are important to development studies, the bulk of studies still focus on *economic growth*. Because of this, our analysis is mostly limited to showing this relationship. Thus, unless clearly specified, our investigation of development will examine economic growth as the primary dependent variable. Where possible, however, we highlight studies that have examined other aspects of economic development as the dependent variable, such as access to water, electricity, sanitation, health care and social safety nets and the repression of labour.

Box 1.2   Gini index

Inequality is often measured using the Gini coefficient, developed by Italian statistician Corrado Gini in 1912 (Gini, 1921). The Gini coefficient measures the extent to which the distribution of income (or in some cases consumption spending) among individuals or households diverges from a perfectly equal distribution. Perfect equality, where everyone has the same income, is a 0 and perfect inequality, where one person has all the income and everyone else has none, is a 100. The data in Table 1.1 is based on the World Bank Development Research Group, which looks at primary household surveys obtained both from government statistical agencies and World Bank country departments. The Gini index is also not additive across groups, meaning that the total Gini for a society does not equal the sum of the Gini for its sub-groups (Galbraith, 2012). An additional problem with the Gini is that it is difficult to compare inequality across different countries because the years when the surveys were conducted vary considerably from country to country. Nevertheless, the Gini index can be used to measure income inequalities over time. For example, in Nigeria the Gini index was 43 in 1985 and now stands at 48.83 in 2010, illustrating that in spite of economic growth, inequalities in Nigeria continue to rise.

1. Namibia: 63.9 (2004)

2. South Africa: 63.14 (2009)

3. Botswana: 60.96 (1994)

4. Haiti: 59.2 (2001)

5. Angola: 58.6 (2000)

6. Honduras: 57 (2009)

7. Central African Republic: 56.3 (2008)

8. Bolivia: 56.3 (2008)

9. Colombia: 55.91 (2010)

10. Guatemala: (55.89)

11. Brazil: 54.7 (2009)

12. Zambia: 54.63 (2006)

13. Belize: 53.1 (1999)

14. Suriname: 52.9 (1999)

15. Lesotho: 52.5

16. Paraguay: 52.4 (2010)

17. Chile: 52.1 (2009)

18. Panama: 51.9 (2010)

19. Papua New Guinea: 50.9 (1996)

20. Swaziland: 51.5 (2010)

21. Rwanda: 50.8 (2011)

22. Costa Rica: 50.7 (2009)

23. Zimbabwe: 50.10 (1996)

24. Ecuador: 49.26 (2010)

25. Nigeria: 48.83 (2010)

Table 1.1 *Most unequal countries with populations over one million*

Source: Data from World Bank, available at: http://data.worldbank.org/indicator/SI.POV.GINI?page=3

We also often examine how specific challenges affect economic growth because it can be a strong predictor of a variety of other outcomes that capture the quality of life. In summary, it is true that economic growth is not a panacea for a developing state's problems. Economic gains may be distributed unequally or, even worse, squandered by government officials. Nevertheless, while growth is not a sure-fire means for improving the lives of the poor, without it the alternatives are often worse. Simply put, improvements in the quality of life experienced by the world's people are unlikely to come without growth (Collier, 2007).

That being said, the limitations of this book reflect the need for more research in areas that examine other aspects of development. Though we can agree that economic growth is a useful starting point, more studies are needed that explore the relationships between specific challenges and a wider range of indicators of development.

What is the role of the global forces?

The importance of global forces in development has been well documented (Crafts, 2000; Dreher, 2003; Vietor, 2005; Rodrik, 2008). There has been a massive divergence in income levels and growth performance across countries, especially between the developed and the developing countries (Crafts, 2000, 4). Though the study does not focus on the effects of globalization in depth, it acknowledges that global forces play an important role in development. More than ever, rules are being dictated by international institutions (see Box 3.1 in Chapter 3) and multi-national corporations (see Box 12.1 in Chapter 12). International non-governmental organizations (INGOs) and international donor agencies also have a significant impact on the developing world. Globalization puts pressure on countries in the developing world to allow market forces to rule and globalization also puts tremendous strain on the state in the developing world. The book also explains how states in the developing world have become more and more interdependent, sensitive and vulnerable to states not only in their own region but globally as well. For more explanation of what globalization is, when and how it emerged, and how it affects states in the developing world, see Chapter 12.

Bringing in the state

Improving the quality of life for the 1.2 billion people in the world who live in poverty remains the critical challenge for the development community and governments in the developing world. Yet a number of key traps and hurdles stand in the way. In some cases, these challenges dis-incentivize the selection and implementation of sound economic policies, while in others they work to limit or distort their impact. This book emphasizes traps and hurdles to development, including the difficulties posed by disease, instability and corruption and so on.

To tackle this challenge and overcome these hurdles requires a *state-centred* approach. But the 'state' is a fuzzy term that often serves as a catch-all for many concepts. So what is the state? According to the philosopher Max Weber, it is a 'human community that (successfully) claims the monopoly of the legitimate use of force within a given territory' (1994, 309). In essence, statehood involves the legitimization of violence. Though this is conceptually abstract, the central tie between a state and its citizens is the former's right to use physical force to offer security to the latter and the latter's permission of this behaviour in return for guarantees of protection.

The concept of statehood emerged in the 16th and 17th centuries with the Peace of Westphalia, which codified external sovereignty between political entities (Milliken and Krause, 2002, 755). The process of state formation was long and complex, intermittently interrupted by wars. In the early stages of this process, even the most powerful states lacked full control over their territories, and the strong states quickly absorbed their weaker rivals. By the 20th century, statehood was the norm, however. In 1933, the Montevideo Convention of the Rights and Duties of States solidified matters, setting the international legal criteria for what constitutes statehood. These include: a defined territory, a permanent population, an effective government and the capacity to enter into formal relations with other states (Chesterman et al., 2005, 15).

State institutions evolved out of the process of state formation, serving to help states to meet these criteria and, more importantly, provide security for their citizens and generate revenue. Though state institutions have existed for centuries, the emphasis on their role in development is more recent. Early studies of development alluded to the importance of state institutions for economic growth, but it was not until the 21st century or so that this has become the mainstream argument. Today most observers agree that the development of strong institutions is critical for lifting states out of poverty, and strengthening human capabilities. This reality underscores the importance of advancing perspectives on development that emphasize the role of state institutions.

This book builds off the rise in prominence of the role of institutions in development and examines how state institutions can be moulded and reformed to improve economic performance and reduce poverty. The United Nations' Department of Economic and Social Affairs claimed in its 2013 report that there is a 'growing social consensus on the need for governments to serve as the engines of development, providing social protection as well as public infrastructure' (31). Scholars have also noted that the state can play an important role in coordinating, steering and persuading economic agents to accomplish things. It is 'the only agency capable of this task on a national basis' and is the 'only entity that has the structure and capacity to do so' (Leftwich, 2000, 7). Nobel Prize-winning economist Joseph Stiglitz notes that for economic development to take place, technical solutions focused on 'getting prices right' were not enough. It is important to 'strengthen the capacity of the public sector' (Stiglitz, 1998, 91). It is also necessary to strengthen judicial institutions in order to provide the legal infrastructure and regulatory framework needed to encourage economic growth (Stiglitz, 1998, 90). Economies need an 'institutional infrastructure' in order to work (Stiglitz, 1998, 80). Yet states in the developing world are often criticized for being part of the problem instead of being part of the solution.

This book offers an in-depth explanation of how institutions work in the developing world and the specific challenges states face in structuring their institutions in ways that encourage positive economic performance and increased well-being. To offer a more nuanced picture of state institutions, we emphasize where possible how *specific types* of state institutions affect development. This approach enables the formulation of more precise policy advice tightly grounded in existing empirical research on development.

Of course, a focus on state institutions can introduce a chicken-and-egg problem. State institutions influence the decisions that political actors make (by constraining choices or incentivizing behaviour, for example) and the outcomes that result. But these same actors and outcomes also influence the development of state institutions. Some studies address this problem (referred to as endogeneity, or a loop of causality between two variables of interest) but others do not. Though our primary interest in this book is examining how institutions can improve economic performance, it is possible that the causal arrow runs in the other direction. Though substantively interesting, this is not the focal point of this study. We leave it to researchers to sort out the persuasiveness of the methods used in existing studies to take this endogeneity into account.

We acknowledge that building institutions to coordinate does not happen in a vacuum. Building strong institutions requires societal input. We also note that a state-centred approach does not mean that other actors play no significant role. Societal actors are incredibly important to development and institutions and society can work in tandem. Technocratic approaches that do not rely on society or participation from civil society in the decision-making process have been unsuccessful. There is a need for inclusion and consensus building. Reforms will be more successful if there is a perception of fairness and a sense of ownership about the process (Stiglitz, 1998, 89). Societal involvement also helps to better understand what the primary needs of the communities and individuals are.

For example, sustainable approaches to development argue that development needs to be more closely related to specific conditions, and this requires more inclusion and cooperation of local actors. Sen claimed that local people may have more appropriate information about the conditions that they are dealing with. Local knowledge and participation can also be used to ensure that economic and social institutions work more effectively. Decision-making should also incorporate local participation, and participation should be open to everyone (World Commission on Environment and Development, 1987, 49).

Thus we recognize that building institutions in the developing world is no easy task; there is no one-size-fits-all solution. At best, we devote Chapter 4 of this book to understanding the key characteristics of high-quality institutions and low-quality institutions. Understanding what the key features are of high-functioning institutions serves as a loose conceptual framework for institutional reform and for building and strengthening agencies of the state. We also try to specify what institutions of the state are most helpful for tackling each specific obstacle that states face. The main focus of the book is on the numerous challenges that developing countries face and on the ways in which the state can be helpful in overcoming these challenges. In doing so, the book underscores the importance of the state in the developing world.

A roadmap

This book is organized as follows. Chapters 1–3 address debates over the age-old question of why some states are rich but others are poor. We begin in Chapter 2 by offering an overview of the key theories in the study of development since the 1960s, which seek to both identify and explain disparities in wealth in the global system. Throughout this discussion, we highlight where possible the role that the state plays in these approaches and assess their central contributions and limitations. Early theories like Modernization Theory, for example, exposed the differences in the quality of life between the developed and developing world, but provided little guidance for how the state could affect development. The theorists in the Dependency School, on the other hand, advocated that the state should play a greater role in protecting the economy, but neglected to explain how the state could be more efficient in ensuring economic growth and alleviating poverty. Chapter 3 summarizes the key debates about the role of the state. In doing so, it provides a summary of the key economic approaches that modern states have relied on to inform their economic policies. It first discusses the economic implications of neoliberalism as an economic guide and the tenets proposed by the Washington Consensus. The chapter then compares and contrasts this approach with state-led approaches to development.

Even well-intentioned states can have poor growth records, of course. This is because there are hurdles that states confront that limit the effectiveness of growth-promoting policies and make it difficult for states to pursue them. This is where state institutions come in. With the right types of state institutions in place, developing states can overcome the myriad of hurdles to development; when institutions are poorly designed or are too weak to actually structure behaviour, however, the hurdles become insurmountable. Chapter 4 of this study offers insight into how researchers conceptualize institutions, as well as theories about their origins and impact on development. The chapter delves into what we mean by state institutions and their role in development. It discusses how state institutions have been compared and the challenges in doing so. It provides an in-depth theoretical overview of institutions. The chapter then breaks down state institutions into functional domains: administrative, judicial, political and security. It discusses what high-quality institutions in each of these domains look like, weaving numerous examples from the developing world throughout to illustrate these points. The purpose of this chapter is to provide a starting point for thinking in more specific ways about how state institutions can be moulded to produce better development outcomes.

Chapters 5–13 examines what the major development traps and hurdles are, how they make growth so difficult, and how state institutions can be tailored to surmount them and ultimately improve economic outcomes. Chapters 5–13 are organized in the following way: a thorough definition and background on the specific developmental trap or hurdle is provided. Each chapter then explains the relationship between each of these major challenges and development, and more specifically how these challenges may affect the state. This is followed by an explanation of what states can do to overcome this trap or hurdle.

We begin by focusing on the most important challenges to development, which must be tackled in order to make inroads towards economic development: poverty, instability and corruption. In other words, it is nearly impossible to have high rates of education, equality, life expectancy and growth rates if a country is poor, unstable and/or corrupt. Poverty, instability and corruption are not just challenges to development; they are major barriers that cannot be ignored. We refer to these challenges as 'development traps'.

Chapter 5 examines poverty traps and the solutions to overcoming them. The chapter offers a special focus on the importance of agriculture and explains why agriculture is important to reducing poverty and what the state can do to assist in this process. Chapter 6 addresses the problem of intractable instability, namely civil war and coups. It examines why instability is often difficult to break free from, how recurring episodes of instability hurt states' economies and the severity of the problem across the developing world. It then gives insight into how states can reform their security institutions to reduce levels of instability. In Chapter 7, we look at how corruption affects state institutions. We discuss different types of corruption and detail how each can hamper economic performance. We also point to ways in which states can combat corruption.

Chapters 8–13 examine historical, geographic, environmental and international factors that may challenge states in the developing world. States have no control over their colonial histories, geographical locations, environment or the power of international forces, but these factors have an impact on economic development. Nevertheless, this is not to say that these factors *determine* economic outcomes or that states are powerless in affecting change. Indeed, while it is true that these hurdles also pose challenges for institutional development, a number of developing states, which we highlight here, have had the capacity to turn things around.

Chapter 8 begins by looking at the impact of colonial histories and geographical circumstances. States such as Botswana and Costa Rica have faced similar historical and geographical circumstances as the Democratic Republic of Congo and Haiti, and yet the former two countries have been able to overcome those circumstances by developing sound economic institutions. This chapter examines the origins of institutional variation across states. Though the consensus is that state institutions are important to understanding variations in economic growth, why some states have 'better' institutions than others is an important question. Here, we discuss the influence of resources, geography and colonialism. This chapter first reviews historical experiences with colonialism and the legacies that colonial empires left for states upon independence. While some colonial empires (such as Japan) invested heavily in institution building, which created the foundations for strong records of development, other colonial powers (such as Belgium) invested very little, creating an uphill battle for these newly independent states. This chapter also discusses the effect of geography on state institutions and contemporary levels of development, showing, for example, that states that are closer to the Equator typically are poorer than those that are farther from it.

Chapter 9 discusses the problems associated with debt and financial crises. What caused these crises to occur, how do crises affect development and how have they been handled? What can states do to lift themselves out of debt? What can the international community do? Chapter 10 tackles environmental curses, the most famous of which is the natural resource curse. It offers background on how abundant natural resources can negatively affect economic performance, and examines other environmental challenges states face, like repeated earthquakes and hurricanes. It then points out ways in which states have successfully managed to deal with these curses. Chapter 11 examines the problem of disease, which is often recurrent in the world's poorest states. It shows how disease outbreaks negatively affect development and offers examples of how states have overcome their vulnerabilities to them. Chapter 12 goes over the challenges posed by globalization with particular attention to the ways in which global forces restrict the capacity of the state. The chapter then explains how states can best take advantage of globalization and work to attract sustainable investment. Chapter 13 addresses the challenges posed by international institutions, other states, non-governmental organizations (NGOs) and donors. In particular, we discuss the literature on foreign aid, highlighting when aid works and when it does not. We also offer some explanation of how international actors can be helpful to institution building and development, showcasing some examples of successful partnerships to provide insight into ways to effectively approach development assistance. We conclude this study in Chapter 14 by offering a brief summary of the key points raised and the challenges that remain.

What we emphasize is that instead of viewing the state as bloated, incapable and inept on the one hand, or the panacea for all problems of development on the other hand, a more nuanced approach is needed. Gerald Meier and Joseph Stiglitz emphasize that 'the future is likely to witness a reaction to the minimalist state that was advocated' previously (2001, 34). Are there instances where the state can assist in overcoming the challenges that face developing countries? What are the ways that the state can be most helpful? What are the specific institutions of the state that can assist in achieving development goals? Though the road ahead may not be an easy one, by identifying the ways in which states can shape their institutions to help them overcome development hurdles and how external actors can encourage this, one finds reasons to be optimistic. Development in even the poorest places is possible, but just pursuing the right policies is not enough. Though policies are very important, the process of achieving lasting development is not possible without building effective state institutions.

Questions

- What are the different ways of defining development?
- What does Amartya Sen mean by a human-centred approach to development?
- In what ways does inequality impact social and economic development? What is the most commonly used measurement of inequality?
- What issues are emphasized by sustainable development approaches?
- What is the most common way of measuring development? What are some alternative ways of measuring development?

Facts

- In the 1970s, the World Bank first started to focus on using social indicators to measure development.
- There is a huge gap in terms of life expectancy between the developed and developing world. Life expectancy is 79 years in the developed world whereas it is only 57 years in the developing world.
- In the developing world, after HIV/AIDS, the second leading cause of death of women of reproductive age is complications during pregnancy, according to the World Health Organization.
- The Brundtland Report published in 1987 highlighted the link between environmental problems, poverty, inequality and well-being.
- The Human Poverty Index looks at the probability at birth of not living to 40, the adult literacy rate, the percentage of the population without sustainable access to water sources and the percentage of children that are underweight for their age.

Chapter 2

Theories of Development: Why Are Some Countries Underdeveloped?

Most states in the world were poor when they gained independence. This applies to countries ranging from the United States in 1776 to Kenya in 1963. Despite this common beginning, the ability of states to grow their economies has varied dramatically from one case to the next. For example, using data from the World Bank's World Development Indicators (2014), the GDP per capita of Japan and Ghana in 1950 was comparable, at $1,873 and $1,193, respectively. By 2010, however, Japan's GDP per capita skyrocketed to $34,000, while Ghana's stayed about the same at $1,576. In those 60 years, Japan experienced major economic gains while Ghana saw little to no economic improvements for its citizens. The different experiences of these two states raise the question, why is Japan rich and Ghana poor? Is it Ghana's fault that it remains poor? Or is Ghana the victim of an unjust system?

Early theories of development sought to take a stand on these questions. Global disparities in wealth became fairly obvious by about the 1960s when most of the world's colonial empires were beginning to fall apart. Scholars of the time sought to explain these economic disparities and the reasons they existed. Their arguments varied dramatically based on whether they viewed external factors falling outside of a state's control or the state itself as the primary driver of diverging outcomes.

This chapter offers an overview of these early theories. It centres the discussion on two of the most influential theories of development: modernization theory and the ideas of Structuralism and the Dependency School. After summarizing the major tenets of these theories, this chapter assesses the limitations of these theories and the lessons we have learnt from them. Understanding these theories is important because they largely influenced the policy choices made at the time. Moreover, the often negative consequences of the policies suggested by these theories yield important lessons that have shaped contemporary economic approaches to development.

Modernization theory

Modernization theory was the first major theory seeking to explain wealth disparities across states and potential approaches for mitigating them. At its core, modernization theory was optimistic about development. It assumed that all states follow the same linear pathway to development and that less developed countries would eventually develop just by virtue of adopting the economic and social structures found in the developed world. In this way, modernization theory viewed the causes of 'underdevelopment' as internally driven, but surmountable. Modernization theorists also believed that growth was tightly related to a country's political development. These theorists argued that as states develop economically, democracy would follow (Lipset, 1963).

According to modernization theorists, growth was the result of a state's transformation from a traditional to a modern or industrialized society. Traditional societies are characterized as having a number of distinct characteristics, including an attachment to the local sphere, little social mobility, a focus on primary economic activities (like agricultural), a hierarchical structure of authority, and little focus on achievement. Modern societies, by contrast, feature a nuclear family structure, the ability to think beyond the family or village, opportunities for social advancement and change, differentiated and complex occupational systems, universalistic standards (where individuals are judged based on their abilities as opposed to their ethnicity or caste), a belief in change and the value of science and technology, economic diversification and citizen involvement in politics. According to modernization theorists, the evolution from a traditional to a modern society could be achieved through education (to engender modern values), urbanization (moving peasants to cities to encourage the diversification of the economy), the spread of mass media (to provide citizens with access to information) and the diffusion of modernity from modern societies to traditional ones (through organizations like the Peace Corps and the distribution of foreign aid). For example, the works of David Apter (1967) argued that the process of industrialization, commercialization and urbanization would cause society to be more individualistic, secular and committed to the findings of science. By transforming a given society from its traditional to a more modern form, growth and development would result. (For more on this, see Box 2.1 *Kuznets Curve*.)

Walt Rostow was one of the first scholars to advocate modernization theory. In his seminal work, *The Stages of Economic Growth: A Non-Communist Manifesto* (1960), Rostow argued that economic development requires that society pass through five evolutionary stages – traditional society, preconditions for take-off, take-off, drive to maturity and age of mass high consumption – when evolving from traditional societies to the modern stage. In the first stage, states are traditional societies, characterized by extended kinship ties, engagement in primary economic activities, a hierarchical structure of authority and little focus on achievement. In the second stage, or the 'preconditions for take-off stage', traditional societies begin to commit themselves to secular education, which encourages capital mobilization (or the ability to move money, labour, or raw materials to other locations where it can be used more efficiently). Greater capital mobility supports the emergence of an entrepreneurial class, which is needed to launch a manufacturing sector, and facilitate the shift away from primary economic activities, which have a lower economic return than the manufacturing sector. This leads to a 'take-off' stage (the third stage), in which other economic sectors begin to sprout and society morphs into one driven more by economic processes than by traditions. Norms of economic growth become well established. The fourth stage is called the 'drive to

---

Box 2.1 Kuznets curve

Scholars argued in the past that economic growth would not only lift the poor out of poverty but also dampen income inequalities. Simon Kuznets claimed that industrialization would lead to increased inequality initially, but this would decline as more workers joined the high-productivity sectors of the economy (Kuznets, 1955). Though there would be short-run social costs of development, they would reach a place where growth and inequality reduction go hand in hand and where poverty rates would eventually drop significantly, following an inverse U shape. Development would lead to moving from low-income rural agriculture to high-income urban industrialized sector. The graphical representation of this phenomenon is known as Kuznets curve. Kuznets curve can be simplified to: income distribution must get worse before it gets better. Capitalism would cause a significant gap between rural and urban areas, and rural areas would decrease in size as urban populations increased. More people migrating to urban areas for jobs would eventually cause income inequalities to subside.

The predictions made by Kuznets never fully came to fruition. The problem was that a number of countries never passed the initial stage of industrialization and inequalities rose instead of tapering off (Piketty and Sanz, 2006). Inequality levels increased in China as the country opened itself up to the world economy. The income share of the poorest quintile decreased from 8% to 7% while the share of the richest quintile increased from 30% to 45% (Banerjee et al., 2006, 90). In India after many decades when inequality levels remained stable, the liberalization years led to an explosion of inequality, particularly in urban areas (Banerjee et al., 2006, 90). Inequality can also be sufficiently high to result in rising poverty despite good underlying growth prospects (Ravallion, 1997). Thus the promise that all boats would be lifted with development was incorrect. While economic growth is important, it is not sufficient to lessen inequalities.

maturity'. Here, the economy starts to diversify, in turn reducing poverty rates and enhancing standards of living. Once society arrives at this stage, it no longer needs to endure the sacrifices it did in the past. This then leads to the final stage, in which there is mass consumption of durable consumer goods and services and increased spending on welfare.

Modernization theory acknowledges the role of institutions, but only briefly and tangentially. Modernization theorists acknowledged that institutional reforms, particularly in the political and judicial sectors, can encourage development by protecting property rights and establishing the rule of law. They argued that political structures need to be differentiated to achieve this and that legal sources of authority must be rational. Those points aside, however, modernization theorists generally advocated that the state stay out of the modernization process to allow the market to drive growth and resource allocation.

Modernization theory has been criticized on numerous grounds. First, the focus on traditional values and the characterization of traditional societies as somehow 'backward' is viewed as ethnocentric. This depiction treats values associated with the West as superior to those espoused elsewhere. Second, accounts of Western development as linear and rapid are not fully accurate. Development in the West did not happen overnight, and there were indeed setbacks in the process. Third, the theory anticipated that convergence would occur, meaning that all states would eventually reach a developed status. This prediction did not match the reality years later: in many states, despite the rise in globalization and the spread of Western values, levels of development remained the same or even became lower than they were at independence.

The Dependency School was at the forefront of these criticisms of modernization theory. It offered an alternative to the theory's Western-centric accounts of universal and linear modernization processes and emphasized the failure of the theory's policy prescriptions to improve the lives of citizens in the developing world. Dependency theorists argued that the very developed states from which modernization theorists emerged were actually responsible for exploiting developing states and perpetuating an international system that kept them poor. The following section explains these arguments in more detail.

Structuralism and the Dependency School

Structuralism and the Dependency School provided an alternative approach to the study of development. Largely based on the experience of Latin America in the 1950s and 1960s, both schools attacked previous theories, which neglected wider global inequalities and ignored the role of history. Before going into detail about these approaches, we first highlight the influence of Marxism.

Marxism brought attention to the relationships between capital and labour, arguing that class conflict was inevitable in capitalist societies. Capitalism divided society into those who owned the means of production (what is needed to produce goods such as tools, equipment, land, crops and minerals), known as the bourgeoisie, and those who have to sell their labour for a wage, known as the proletariat. Those who had to sell their labour were not only labouring for themselves but also for the bourgeoisie. The profits would be reinvested into more factories or land, which created more wealth for the bourgeoisie. Marx viewed capitalism as a necessary stage towards socialism but inherently unstable and vulnerable to crises. Eventually, revolutionary political change would end private ownership and make way for a classless society with socialist forms of organization and production.

Though socialist forms of organization did not cover the globe, by the 20th century scholars started drawing from Marxist ideas (for more on this, see Box 2.2 *Communist Economic Philosophy*). Scholars who were applying Marxist thought to mid-20th-century conditions were given the loose label of being neo-Marxist. These theories were often dismissed in mainstream development circles but they did draw attention to the issue of global inequality. Historical factors, which are largely outside the control of the developing world, account for the inability of developing states to catch up to developed countries. They viewed colonialism and imperialism as the cause of underdevelopment, rather than traditional cultures and values as modernization theorists believed (for more on this, see Box 2.3 on *Colonialism in Haiti*). We first highlight Structuralism and follow that with an overview of dependency theory.

Structuralism, which emerged before dependency theory, was primarily associated with Latin American scholars who were mostly concentrated in the United Nations' Economic Commission in Latin America (ECLA). The ECLA was formed in 1948 in Santiago, Chile, and was headed by Argentine scholar Raúl Prebisch. Scholars at the ECLA argued that the path to development for the developed world could not be replicated by developing countries because these states faced an entirely different set of circumstances from those countries that had already developed. Countries in the developing world endured a colonial heritage, which led to a high concentration of wealth in the hands of the few, and low levels of productivity in every sector but primary exports. This structural problem (non-market) could not be dealt with just by relying on market forces.

Structuralists (and later dependency theorists) claimed that the international system could be divided into two types of states (often referred to as dominant/dependent, centre/periphery or metropolitan/satellite). The

Box 2.2   Communist economic philosophy

Communist ideas first gained prominence in the mid-19th century with Karl Marx's *Communist Manifesto*. The motivation for Marx was the unfair division of society into classes, with the poorest classes caught in a cycle of exploitation by the richest. In his view, this was caused by capitalism: an economic system in which private individuals or corporations control investment and ownership. For this reason, Marx supported a state-controlled economic system in which the government plans the economy. In theory, this would entail a society in which there was no private property, no competition, and no class differences. In its purest form, supply and demand would not exist. Production and distribution would be 'from each according to his ability; to each according to his need' (Marx, 1875, 27). The state drives the production process, encouraging self-sufficiency; trade with other states is unnecessary. A communist economic philosophy, therefore, advocates full state ownership and control of the economy and the abolishment of the private sector. Marx believed that such a radical reordering of the economic sphere would allow for the elimination of all other major social problems including class conflict, political oppression, racial discrimination and gender inequality.

Few states have ever fully pursued a communist economic agenda, though some have come close. Even in states that profess to be communist, the elite still maintain a higher standard of living than the bulk of society. The most famous example of a communist state is the Union of Soviet Socialist Republics (USSR). During the Cold War, the USSR spread its communist agenda to many parts of the world, most notably Eastern Europe. Since its collapse in 1991, however, the number of communist states has declined considerably. Today, there are five states that claim to support a communist agenda – China, Cuba, Laos, North Korea, and Vietnam – though the extent to which they do it in practice varies.

One of the reasons for the collapse of the USSR and the ensuing decreased popularity of communism as an economic philosophy is that its policy prescriptions produced suboptimal outcomes. There are a number of explanations for this, a few of which we will review here. First, the lack of competition lowered productivity by removing the incentives for innovation and efficiency. Second, the high government spending that was required to sustain full state ownership of business and industry was difficult to maintain. Making matters worse, the lack of emphasis on trade robbed governments of potential income through exports. The discouragement of trade also meant that the government became the sole producer of many goods. Yet, it was difficult for a single state to produce everything its citizens needed in an efficient fashion, leading to poor-quality products and frequent shortages. Since the end of the Cold War, the consensus position is that communist economic policies lead to inefficiency, government debt and economic stagnation. For this reason, states like China, though communist in theory, no longer advocate communist economic policies.

dominant states were the advanced industrial nations, such as those in the Organisation for Economic Co-operation and Development (OECD). The dependent states were those states of Latin America, Asia and Africa that had low per capita GNPs and that relied heavily on the export of a single commodity for foreign exchange earnings. Both structuralists and dependency theorists contended that the divisions between the centre and periphery stemmed from the period of colonization during which the colonial powers extracted raw materials from their colonies for use in the production of manufactured goods, which were then sold back to the colonies. The 'value addition' in manufacturing a usable product always makes the product costlier than the primary products used to create it. Therefore, poorer countries would never be earning enough from their exports to pay for their imports.

The relationships formed between these two groups were entrenched and bad for growth of the periphery. The explanation is as follows. Economies reliant on the production of primary products and raw materials are vulnerable to fluctuations in the global price of these goods and a downward trend in relative value in the long term. Studies by Hans Singer (1982) documented, for example, a deterioration in the terms of trade of Latin American countries, whereas Presbich can be credited for explaining the factors underlying this downward trend. Known as the Prebisch–Singer thesis, these scholars argued that barring major changes in the structure of the world economy, the gains from trade will continue to be distributed unequally (and unfairly) between nations exporting mainly primary products and those exporting mainly manufactured goods. Moreover, inequality of per capita income between the centre and periphery states will be increased by the growth of trade, rather than being reduced. In other words, if the Singer–Prebisch analysis was right, participation in the world trade regime was a losing proposition for many developing countries.

Developed countries' access to cheap primary products and raw materials enabled these countries to produce manufactured and high-value goods that enriched them but came at the expense of the developing countries. The developed nations took advantage of these economic structures to lock developing states into such trade relationships that prevented them from industrializing themselves. These trade relationships made it difficult for developing states to generate enough revenues to free themselves from their dependence on the developed world. Developing countries were too poor to pursue technological innovations and were dependent on the developed countries for technology. Developing countries were forced to borrow capital and technology to grow their economies, causing dependence on others that was difficult to sever. Any efforts they did pursue to play catch up and produce high-end goods domestically were thwarted by the fierce competition these goods faced from industrialized states, which had become more efficient at producing them since they had already created

Box 2.3   Colonialism in Haiti

Haiti is currently one of the poorest countries in the world with a per capita income of less than $500 and 77% of the population living on under $2 a day. Only around half of the population is literate, while more than half lack access to water and are malnourished. Surprisingly, Haiti was not always the poorest country in the Americas (Schifferes, 2004). On the contrary, Haiti was one of the richest colonies in the Americas, having been colonized by the French in the early 1700s. By the late 1700s Haiti was producing more sugar than all of the British colonies in the Americas combined, and was the largest sugar exporter in the world. It was also a leading producer of indigo, cotton and coffee. In order to produce vast volumes of agricultural goods a plantation system was introduced, slaves were brought in from Africa and what was left of the indigenous population (most died of smallpox, were forced to flee or were killed) was enslaved. Haitians lived under one of the most brutal slave colonies. In addition to suffering from the brutality of colonial rule, one-third of Africans who had been brought over to Haiti died within a few years, often due to smallpox or typhoid fever. Those brought over died so quickly that at times France had to import 50,000 slaves a year to keep up the numbers and profits. Eventually, many Haitians were released from slavery and by 1804 Haiti had revolted against France and gained independence.

Though Haiti gained independence earlier than many developing countries, scholars still point to France's role as a source of Haiti's economic

→

economies of scale. This process creates a vicious cycle of dependence that prevents developing states from joining the developed world.

The key solution for mitigating the gap between the rich and poor states was import substitution industrialization (ISI). ISI policies called on developing states to close their economies off from most foreign economic influences such as foreign investment to protect their domestic industries from foreign competition. In order to reduce foreign dependence, governments sought to promote the local production of industrialized products by subsidizing the production of strategic substitutes, erecting trade barriers such as tariffs, and manipulating local currencies in order to help manufacturers import capital goods such as heavy machinery more cheaply. ISI was touted as the key means through which developing states could industrialize and catch up with the developed world in light of the disadvantages they confronted. The state would play an important role in ensuring long-term economic growth and capitalist development. Structuralists argued that capitalist development is possible in the periphery through industrialization and comprehensive reforms, such as land reform.

decay (Dupuy, 1976; Edmonds, 2011). Haiti's colonial institutional framework was discarded much earlier in Haiti than in most countries in Latin America. Furthermore, Haiti was also destabilized by France's retaliatory policies. France did not recognize Haiti's independence until 1825 and in return demanded that Haiti pay France 150 million gold francs or the equivalent of five times the country's annual export revenue. Additionally, after Haiti's revolution the French destroyed 800 sugar plantations and imposed a trade blockade. By 1900 around 80% of the Haiti's budget was still taken up by debt repayments (see Chapter 9). By the time that Haiti finally paid off its debt, its economy had become distorted (MacIntyre, 2010).

Dependency theorists point to Haiti's dependent relationship with core countries during the colonial period as culpable for Haiti's poor economic performance. The repercussions of being a cash crop colony for so many years were severe. Wages were eventually introduced by the mid-19th century but it was difficult for workers to leave agricultural employment since there was no urban option. No investment in manufacturing had been permitted and thus Haiti lacked an industrial base. Haiti's entire economy was structured around supplying sugar and other primary products to developed countries. As a result, though more than half of the population works in the agricultural sector, Haiti still has to import more than half of its food needs. Though Haiti's leadership has been corrupt, dictatorial and inept, it is hard to ignore the role that historical factors have played in undermining Haiti's chances for economic development.

The Dependency School (advocates of which are often called 'dependistas') was much more critical of capitalism in the periphery. As they saw it, backwardness in the periphery was not due to their lack of capitalist development. Instead, dependency theorists argued that much of the underdevelopment of the peripheral countries was due to the global capitalist system that the periphery had been incorporated into in the late 15th century. The core countries grew due to colonialism, plunder and subordination of the periphery, subjecting it to different types of dependence.

Paul Baran was one of the key thinkers in the Dependency School. Baran and Robert Sutcliffe (1957) challenged modernization theorists by arguing that the developed world did not guide development through aid, investment and expertise, but instead retarded economic growth and progress. In his view, developing states are characterized by dual economies: a large agricultural sector and a small industrial sector. This is troublesome because there is very little potential to generate economic surpluses from such heavy reliance on agricultural exports. Even today, over one billion peasants in the developing world contribute only 13% to total world trade (Keet, 2002). Baran emphasized that class relations and the utilization of economic resources are crucial barriers to development. The bourgeoisie and traditional landed elites in the developing world do not have a vital interest in promoting industrialization because this shift would threaten their wealth. To confront these challenges, Baran advocated that the state play a strong role in the industrialization process to rupture these traditional class relations and ways of doing business (Martinussen, 1997, 87).

Andre Gunder Frank (1969) further popularized the Dependency School, extending Baran's central ideas. While Baran emphasized dual economies, Frank's work focused on the exploitation of developing states both before and after colonial rule. Developing states (or satellites) are incorporated in the global capitalist system and taken advantage of by developed states (or metropoles). In Frank's view, satellites exist solely for the purpose of fulfilling the needs of metropoles, which extract resources from satellites through unfair trade relations. Capitalism in the centre was not progressive but was parasitical on the periphery. Frank used the example of northern Brazil, once one of the richest regions of Brazil, to highlight the problems of dependence on exporting a single commodity. Once global demand for sugar decreased, northern Brazil became impoverished. Frank argued that in order to break free from the detrimental relationship with metropoles, satellite states needed to de-link from the global market. Frank also emphasized that underdevelopment in the satellite states was not just a transitional stage through which countries must pass. It was a condition that plagued regions involved in the international economy in a subordinate position. Dependent capitalism does not lead to development. Countries in the global periphery were doomed to be exploited and marginalized forever.

In contrast to Frank, the world-systems theory approach developed by Immanuel Wallerstein (1979) was not quite as pessimistic. Wallerstein linked the idea of dependency but suggested that there are opportunities for development because the international system was more fluid. Instead of there being a core of developed states and a periphery of developing states, there was also a semi-periphery of states that fell somewhere in between. Though countries do not follow a linear path to development, categories were not fixed over time. Countries could move in and out of these categories if they grew or when the global economy changed.

Fernando Henrique Cardoso and Enzo Faletto in their famous book *Dependency and Development in Latin America* (1979) also acknowledged that development was taking place but argued that the type of development was dependent. They emphasized how dependence created social structures *within* the periphery where the ruling class would exploit the locals on behalf of the core countries. Thus, the elites at the centre and the periphery had coinciding interest that perpetuated dependence. Cardoso and Faletto write,

> of course, imperialist penetration is a result of external social forces (multinational enterprises, foreign technology, international financial systems, embassies, foreign states and armies, etc.). What we affirm simply means that the system of domination reappears as an 'internal' force, through the social practices of local groups and classes which try to enforce foreign interests, not precisely because they are foreign, but because they may coincide with values and interests that these groups pretend are their own. (xvi, 1979)

In order to confront the challenges facing developing countries, some of the more radical dependency theorists advocated completely delinking from the global economy. For writers such as Frank, the periods in which the developing world grew the most was when it was not engaged in the global system. For others promoting ISI was the more pragmatic solution, and these policies seemed to enjoy a good deal of success up until the 1970s. Real per capita income nearly doubled between 1950 and 1970. But the enormous state investments in nascent industries, subsidies to help these industries keep their prices low and state protection from foreign-made competitors that ISI policies required eventually took their toll. By the 1980s, many developing states were mired in debt. Previous gains were lost and per capita incomes and investment levels were declining. The ideas promoted by both the Structuralists and the Dependency School quickly lost favour in development circles as a result.

The poor performance of ISI policies was just one of the reasons – albeit a major one – for the downfall of dependency theory. Other criticisms include the theory's conceptual fuzziness, as well as methodological and measurement errors in studies that advocated it. Critics also alleged that the theory failed to examine internal causes of underdevelopment and economic stagnation (Harrison, 2003). For example, Argentina and Chile share similar historical backgrounds. Yet, Argentina's economic performance in the 1970s and 1980s was underwhelming given its potential largely because of the policies pursued by its populist leadership. Chile's economy, by contrast, boomed during the same period because its government invested in research and infrastructure using the economic surpluses it secured from the boom in copper prices (Harrison, 2003). Dependency theory, with its denial of state agency, could not explain these different outcomes.

Similarly, the fact that dependency theory's central claim of the impossibility of development within the global economic framework was largely contradicted by events of the late 20th century further led to its demise.

The evolution of at least four economies – South Korea, Singapore, Taiwan and Hong Kong, also known as the 'Asian Tigers', – showed two things radically at odds with dependency tenets: first, that attaining economic progress is very much possible; and second, that it is feasible via enhanced integration with the world economy. Take the case of Taiwan, for instance (Barrett and Whyte, 1982). Taiwan was a Japanese colony and hence in a condition that would qualify it as experiencing economic dependence. After World War II and the Chinese Civil War, Taiwan received massive amounts of American aid. When US aid was gradually phased out in the 1960s, large amounts of foreign investment poured into Taiwan in its place, and Taiwan became extraordinarily dependent on foreign trade. Counter to the expectations of dependency theory, however, Taiwan had one of the highest sustained growth rates of any country for the period from the early 1950s to the early 1970s, averaging around 9%. As a result of that growth, some dependency-oriented writers of the time advocated that Taiwan be upgraded from peripheral to semi-peripheral status. In addition to Taiwan, four other Asian candidates have often been mentioned as examples of countries pursuing rather successful development strategies (the late 1990s' Asian financial crisis notwithstanding) within this global framework. These are the so-called Asian tiger cubs: Philippines, Thailand, Malaysia and Indonesia.

Indeed, inattention to the role that a state's policy choices play in influencing development was perhaps the biggest problem with Structuralism and dependency theory. As indicated above, some states in the developing world grew economically in spite of the penetration of foreign capital or their late insertion into the global economy. In addition, Structuralism and dependency theory argued that the state needed to play a strong role in guiding the industrialization process, but it did not consider that the state could misuse economic resources or promote inefficiencies. Overall, the economic strategy suggested by dependency theory (ISI) was largely a failure for those states that sought to implement it in the post–World War II era.

Theories of growth in practice

The following three cases offer insight into how theories of growth may unfold in practice. The first case of Tanzania demonstrates how focusing on self-reliance with little planning or flexibility plunged Tanzania further into poverty. The state was heavy handed but not necessarily able to stimulate economic development. In Brazil, the state's implementation of ISI policies was initially helpful encouraging the computer industry, but this protectionism eventually led to inefficiencies. The final case of China illustrates a successful dual-track strategy of protecting those who needed the state, while exposing other economic agents that had the potential to adapt to the laws of the market.

Case study: Tanzania's failed experiment with socialism

By the time Julius Nyerere (1964–1985) of Tanzania stepped down from power on his own volition in 1985 (only the second African head of state to do so), the economy was in an acute crisis (Southall, 2006, 235). The country was deeply indebted, on the brink of famine, suffering from high inflation and low rates of productivity. Tanzania's average growth rate was only around 1%. Per capita income levels were nearly the same in 1985 when Nyerere stepped down as they had been at independence in 1961 (Ndulu and Mutalemwa, 2002).

Decades before Tanzania had reason for optimism. Immediately after taking power Nyerere lectured on the importance of self-reliance, comparing socialism to a vaccine (Meredith, 2005, 258). Heavily influenced by traditional African values and dependency theory, Nyerere focused on how Tanzania could carve out its own independent course of development (Ibhawoh and Dibua, 2003, 63). Several years later the country embarked on a socialist path that emphasized improving literacy rates and eradicating poverty and disease. Some impressive gains were made. Literacy rates increased from 10% in 1964 to 59.1% by the time Nyerere left power (World Bank, 2013). The government was also able to provide tap water for four in ten villages. Nearly a third of all villages had a health clinic and life expectancy rose from 41 to 51 years of age.

But Nyerere's policies on economic production ended up overshadowing the gains made. The programme of self-reliance urged nomadic people to move to planned development villages. The 'villagization' policy involved very little planning, however. Bureaucrats were given orders to cram as many peasants as possible into villages giving them little direction. The state demonstrated little knowledge of the local regions affected. By the early 1970s, collectivization was forced after much of the population refused. There were many reports of brutality and anyone who resisted was denied food (Meredith, 2005, 255). In the process of creating planned development villages, much of the infrastructure and land was destroyed or abandoned. The villages created by the government contained 90% of the rural population but only produced 5% of the output (Meredith, 2005, 257).

In the past Tanzania had been able to feed its people and was one of the largest exporters of food in Africa. This changed when the government primarily invested in tobacco and tea farming. Though outputs for both of these products increased as farmers were educated to use modern irrigation techniques, food production plummeted. As a result, Tanzania had to import large amounts of food. Most pressing was the deficit in grains. Food imports helped, but this exhausted Tanzania's foreign exchange reserves. Tanzania was given 200,000 tons of food and forced to take out loans and grants from the World Bank and the IMF in 1975 to prevent a complete catastrophe (Meredith, 2005, 256).

Debt also accumulated because the government had become the largest employer of the country but lacked a plan for development that understood local needs and properly utilized its workforce. The size of the government only delayed productivity and undermined the small and powerless business community. The private sector was crowded out, facing cumbersome bureaucratic procedures and high tax rates. The multiple permits needed allowed officials to collect bribes at every juncture. Public funds rapidly disappeared. Nyerere tried to curb the corruption, but made little impact. Even though the widespread corruption made it more difficult to implement his plans, this may not have mattered; Nyerere's policies were misguided and not well thought out. Though well-intentioned, most of the improvements in Tanzania's economy (per capita income levels more than doubled) took place after it abandoned its socialist experiment.

Case study: Brazil's computer industry

Dependistas saw the state as critical to protecting young industries from competition as a means of encouraging development. While it is true that some protectionism is often necessary for infant industries to get their feet off the ground, it is also true that shielding industries from competition for too long can be troublesome. Brazil's experience in the early days of its computer industry illustrates these problems and some of the problems with the Dependency School more generally.

Brazil's computer industry grew out of a national development project directed by the state. The key initiators were middle-level technocrats, but the Brazilian Economic Development Bank (BNDE) and the Coordination Commission for Data-Processing Activities (CAPRE) also played a large role. The Brazilian government worked to redefine the interests of local capital and shift the position of local industry in the international division of labour (Evans, 1986, 805). In June of 1977, it barred the leading multinational corporations in the computer field from manufacturing minicomputers in Brazil, with the goal of protecting five recently formed local firms. The government wanted to limit linkages between local and foreign firms to enable local companies to develop capabilities on their own. Local firms were given the space to grow and mature free from the competition posed by foreign firms.

Meanwhile, by the end of the 1960s and the beginning of the 1970s several research centres and universities in Brazil had started to acquire technological capacity, and soon after there were many talented engineers that emerged from these programmes ready to work in the information technology (IT) industry. The state-guided computer field provided jobs for many of these individuals. The government also invested in industrial infrastructure. As a result, by the end of the 1980s, Brazil had a diversified set of IT companies with a strong presence in the local market (de Melo et al., 1993, 386).

All was not perfect, however. Though Brazil had a large and techno-logically advanced computer industry by the 1990s, it was operating in isolation of foreign firms (Dedrick et al., 2001, 1203). Local companies could not acquire foreign technology unless they received government per-mission (causing some to resort to pirating it). Yet, during this time the global computer industry was advancing rapidly in the face of significant technological innovations. Brazil's computer industry could not adapt and adjust to these innovations because of the state's protectionism. It did not take long for Brazilian computers to become outdated in comparison to those manufactured outside of Brazil.

In addition, because local firms faced few competitors in local markets, they behaved as if they would forever be in business. Low prices and high quality standards were therefore not prioritized (de Melo et al., 1993, 386). Brazilian consumers could buy locally made computers, but they were often far more expensive and lower in quality than they would have been had they faced foreign competition (Dedrick et al., 2001, 1203).

Later in the 1990s, the Brazilian government pursued a liberalization strategy, which meant that it opened its doors to foreign computer firms. Suddenly, Brazilian consumers had access to lower cost and higher quality computers produced by foreign firms. While consumers benefitted from the policy change, local firms were blown away by foreign competition. The protectionist policies that enabled them to gain their footing had been allowed to linger for too long, leading to complacency in the industry and ultimately its demise.

Case study: China's dual track to development

In the 1950s through the mid-1970s, China was deeply impoverished and growth rates were negative. In 1976, after Chairman Mao Zedong died, China experienced growth rate of −1.6%. Under the leadership of Deng Xioaping (1976–1997), massive changes were made in economic reform to help boost the country's economic output and lift millions of people out of poverty.

In the late 1970s, China began to pursue a dual-track approach to eco-nomic reform that combined elements of central planning with free mar-ket principles. The goal was to encourage economic reform that would eliminate the inefficiencies introduced from purely communist principles without creating losers. The basic principle of the dual-track approach is as follows. Under the 'plan' track, economic agents are assigned rights and obligations to produce a fixed quantity of goods at fixed plan prices as specified in the pre-existing plan. In addition, a 'market' track is introduced under which economic agents participate in the market at free-market prices, provided that they fulfil their obligations under the pre-existing plan. The introduction of the market track provides the opportunity for economic agents who participate in it to be better off, whereas the maintenance of the plan track protects those who would potentially not thrive in the free market by guaranteeing their share of production under the pre-existing plan.

The plan was first applied to the liberalization of the agricultural sector, where liberalization occurred only in part, while keeping the plan system intact. Farmers were allowed to sell surplus crops freely at a market-determined price only after they had fulfilled their obligations to the state under the state system. Researchers have referred to this as an ingenious system that generated efficiency without creating any losers (Lau et al., 2000). In particular, it was a shortcut that neatly solved a conundrum inherent in wholesale liberalization: how to provide microeconomic incentives to producers while insulating the central government from the fiscal consequences of liberalization. The dual-track approach was eventually employed in other areas as well, such as industrial goods (like coal and steel) and labour markets (with employment contracts). Many view the system as critical in China's ability to achieve political support for the reform process, maintain its momentum and minimize adverse social implications (Lau et al., 2000).

The result of China's dual-track approach to development was impressive. China has sustained near-double-digit growth rates for several decades. In 1981, 59.3% of the people were living under $2 a day. By 2009, this number had fallen to 9.1%. Per capita income levels in 1962 were $69.80. By 2011, this number had jumped to $5,444.80.

Along the way, China also invested heavily in agricultural research, infrastructure, agricultural irrigation methods and human capital (Fan et al., 2002). Impressive gains were made in education and health indicators. Primary school enrolment was only 30% in 1949. Today 100% of students are enrolled in primary school. In 1982 the literacy rate was 65.5%. By 2010, the literacy rate had increased to 94.3%. Life expectancy was only 43.5 years in 1960. By 2011, the average person lived to 73.5 years.

Though the path to liberalization increased inequalities in China and the road to success was predicated on the work ethic of a highly oppressed labour force, China managed to lift 400 million people out of poverty with its more piecemeal approach to development. China's dual track to development also illustrates that even though the expansiveness of the state needed to be dismantled, the state's ability to support market forces instead of stifling them was another critical factor behind China's success.

Conclusion: where we stand today

Modernization theory and the ideas proposed by the Dependency School sought to identify disparities in the world between rich and poor states and assess what to do about it. Though both theories have serious flaws, they do contain some partial truths.

For example, modernization theorists are correct that greater human capital (through things like universal education) does encourage economic growth and that the state does play a role in development (though they underemphasized in what ways the state can drive development). And, as the theory implies, strong economic performance often requires a society that is willing to pursue it. While modernization theorists did not emphasize this point, some states remain underdeveloped because they persistently make bad policy choices. States that waste resources, spend beyond their means, and close their economies, for example, are not going to experience stellar growth.

At the same time, dependency theorists are right that the developed world has taken advantage of the developing world and the playing field is unequal. It is also true that the same policies that spurred the growth of the developed world's economies will probably not work for the developing world given dramatic changes in the world economy that have occurred since the West developed. Moreover, some states simply do not have the same resources as others do and have greater obstacles to overcome to advance their economies.

In the end, perhaps the key contribution of these early theories of development was the identification of the problem: the world was bifurcated into rich states and poor states and the quality of life experienced by citizens in each was dramatically different. Although modernization and dependency theorists were able to draw attention to the issue, the answers they generated were not sufficient. Indeed many developing states remained mired in debt in the 1980s and were searching for solutions to their development needs. Yet, economists of the time themselves did not have a firm grip on the types of policies that were ideal for improving human welfare, and policies focusing on the role of women were completely neglected (for more on this, see Box 2.3). In the chapter that follows, we review more recent approaches to development: neo-liberalism and state-led approaches. In doing so, we highlight how these approaches differ in terms of how they view the role of the state.

Questions

- According to modernization theory, what causes underdevelopment to persist? What is the solution?
- In what ways was modernization theory overly optimistic about growth in the developing world? What explained the rise of the Dependency School?
- In what ways are dependency theorists critical of the global capitalist system? What is the primary solution to dealing with the challenges posed by the global capitalist system for countries in the developing world?
- What are the key criticisms of the Dependency School? In what ways did the Asian tigers discredit dependency theory?
- Though well intentioned, in what ways were Tanzania and Brazil's economic policies detrimental to economic growth?

Facts

- For modernization theorists, the path to development was a linear process, mostly unaffected by historical experiences.
- The Dependency School argued that growth in the global capitalist system would only increase inequalities even further, as developing countries would become more badly exploited and poorly developed.
- Revised dependency theorists such as Fernando Cardoso and Enzo Faletto argued that social structures within the periphery (developing world) led the ruling class to exploit the locals on behalf of the core countries (the developed world).
- Though Tanzania's government under Julius Nyerere had good intentions, its policies of self-reliance and collectivization led to only 1% growth rates.
- China's dual-track approach to development led to impressive gains, with a reduction in those living under $2 a day from almost 60% in 1981 to 9% in 2009.

Chapter 3

Debates on the State and Development

Early theories of development highlighted the gap between the world's rich and poor countries. Figuring out how to narrow that gap, however, proved difficult. Modernization theorists anticipated that states would eventually develop just by virtue of the modernization process, particularly if assisted by Western aid and other capital investments. That, of course, did not happen. Dependency theorists thought, by contrast, that development required insulation from the developed world and an inward focus on industrialization. This policy advice did not help matters either. Many developing states found themselves worse off after following the policy prescriptions implied by the dependency theorists than they were previously.

The failure of many states in the developing world to lift themselves out of poverty led to the emergence of new philosophies on how to make this happen. New debates surfaced that put the state central to the analysis, either by arguing that it needed to play a minimal role in development or by claiming that the state should be a central figure in the path to development. Neo-liberal perspectives argued forcefully that states should stay out of the economy and that policies that emphasized the market would encourage economic growth and improve the welfare and living standards of the world's population. Statist perspectives argued the opposite, that strong and capable states were necessary to pull countries out of poverty and spur on economic development.

In this chapter, we summarize the key debates on the role of the state in the last several decades. We first provide an overview of neo-liberalism: Which scholars have influenced its formation? When did it gain political traction and why? What has been the experience of developing states who have implemented neo-liberal programmes? Why did it come under attack? We then provide an overview of the rise of statist approaches and how international financial institutions have evolved in terms of how they view the role of the state in development, namely through the emphasis on the importance of 'good governance'. We close by briefly highlighting what the term 'good governance' means in practice.

Government intervention in the economy

Economic philosophies typically differ in their views of the ideal extent of government intervention in economic markets. During the Great Depression, John Maynard Keynes published *The General Theory of Employment, Interest and Money* in 1936. In it, he criticized the free market as an engine of growth on its own. Instead he advocated that the state play a positive role in promoting economic growth. States should deliberately spend more than they could take in as revenues through their tax system in order to increase demand and boost their economies. The state could invest in infrastructural projects, which would have a positive effect on job creation and further wealth generation. Governments could also intervene in shaping interest rates, but the most important objective was to keep employment levels high, even if that meant heavy government spending. During the post-war period, Keynesian economics was the basis of growth theories, leading to policies that were widely adopted by the West and many governments in the developing world. Keynes provided a rationale for the state's involvement in economic planning. States should prioritize high levels of employment above all else and government expenditure to prevent the onset of crises.

Development economics was initially influenced by the Keynesian traditions of state involvement in the economy. Though there were many vocal critics of state-led development plans and protectionism during the 1960s and 1970s, many development advisers believed that states in the developing world used the state to promote capital accumulation, protect domestic industry from competition, build infrastructure, schools and hospitals, often creating a large and bloated bureaucratic apparatus. Overall many development economists were confident that development would take place and that the state should have an extensive role for governments in development planning (Meier and Stiglitz, 2001, 15). Due to growing debt and economic stagnancy, by the 1970s Keynesian economics was under attack.

Neo-liberal ideas gained popularity as a panacea to all of these economic problems facing countries in the developing world. Highlighting the importance of efficiency and productivity, relying on markets instead of the state was hailed as the solution. This 'counter-revolution' in development theory of the 1970s and 1980s was generally opposed to Keynesianism, Structuralism and dependency theories and state intervention in general. The following section details the early influences of neo-liberal philosophy and then provides an overview of some of the well-known economists associated with this school. The chapter then explains why neo-liberalism became so popular in both academic and policy circles and demonstrates the role of neo-liberalism in practice.

Neo-liberal economic philosophy: early influences

One of the earliest influences of neo-liberal thought came from the works of Adam Smith (1723–1790) with his foundational piece, *The Wealth of Nations* (1776). Here, Smith provided in-depth detail of the industrial development of Europe. He emphasized the key role that competition played in encouraging productivity and innovation. Smith's insights led to the emergence of laissez-faire economic prescriptions, meaning that the government should not intervene in the economy but should let the 'invisible hand' of the market determine supply and demand. If people look out for themselves, the competition created by free markets will paradoxically lead to the best outcome for all involved. Markets would set prices, wages and so on. Smith envisioned a minimal role for government in economic affairs, meaning little government spending on social services like health or education, deregulation, limited subsidy provision and taxation, and privatization of public enterprise. The primary responsibility of the state, therefore, was to provide the basic infrastructure to advance the rule of law with respect to property rights and contracts. At the international level, neo-liberalism translates into free trade without restrictions, the free movement of capital and the ability to invest.

Another early influence on neo-liberal philosophy was David Ricardo (1772–1823), who was most noted for developing the theory of comparative advantage and advocating free trade. Besides enabling competition to take place between states, free trade leverages the concept of *comparative advantage*, which refers to products that a state can produce at a lower opportunity cost than other products. To have a comparative advantage in the production of a product does not mean that a state is the best at producing it (referred to as an *absolute advantage*). It simply means that it is less costly for the state to produce that product than to produce something else. States should focus on producing the products they have the comparative advantage in to reap the most profit. This will lead to greater specialization and efficiency, which will then lead to more profits and economic growth. An example will help us to illustrate this. The professional golfer Jack Nicklaus is known to be one of best golfers to have played the game. It is very likely that with his knowledge of golf he also could have been one of the best caddies ever, had he chosen to dedicate his time to being a caddy. Yet, Nicklaus did not spend his career as a caddy. Because he would earn more as a golfer than as a caddy, the opportunity costs of being a caddy were too high to have made that a reasonable choice. Nicklaus, therefore, had a strong comparative advantage in golfing as opposed to caddying, even though compared to others he is one of the best at both. The concept of comparative advantage helps to explain why free trade is, in theory, always good for everyone. If every state concentrates on producing and exporting the product they have a comparative advantage in, it is always in every state's interest to trade.

The rise of neo-liberalism in the 20th century

As development policies based on heavy state involvement in the economy were failing to yield positive results, a neo-liberal counter-movement was initiated by various economists who championed a market-led approach to development. Economic stagnation, low growth rates, high unemployment and high inflation were attributed to development policies that relied too much on the state. Huge bureaucracies and endless state regulations were actually suffocating private investment, distorting prices and making economies more inefficient. The cost of maintaining protectionist policies, in some cases, amounted to 6% or 7% of GDP (Peet and Hartwick, 1999, 50). In spite of tremendous government planning, many countries were still in poverty and economists became disenchanted with state-led development programmes.

The works of a host of scholars gained traction in policy circles by the early 1980s, though their writings took place much earlier. Milton Friedman (1912–2006), from the University of Chicago, was especially influential. Friedman (1962, 1982, 2009) highlighted the benefits of relying on the market over the state, and argued that inflation and debt was due to excessive government spending. Friedman's work as a professor at the University of Chicago would later inspire a group of Chilean economists who would help implement these ideas in Chile in the 1970s.

Friedrich von Hayek (1899–1992) also argued that too much state involvement in the economy was detrimental to growth. Hayek and others doubted the ability of the government to intervene optimally within the economic system, let alone manage the economy effectively. Hayek argued that centrally planned economies could not allocate goods and productive resources reliably because planners never had enough information to do so. Economies could never be planned but rather emerged spontaneously. He warned that social planning could be so invasive that it was likely to lead to dictatorships.

Subsequent neo-liberal scholars also criticized the role of the state in the economy. Harry G. Johnson (1923–1977) argued that development planning did little to improve society because it required unnecessary government intervention into the economy. Johnson countered the notion that colonialism was to blame for underdevelopment in the developing world. Instead, misguided development policies were problematic. For P.T. Bauer (1972), the negative legacy of colonialism was that the developing world had inherited large and inefficient European bureaucracies. As a result, constant state interference led to economic stagnation. He also criticized the concept of necessity of central planning. He thought that governments should stop restricting the talents and energies of their citizens.

Deepak Lal (1983) argued that the neo-classical ideas about growth in developed countries should be applied to developing countries. He criticized state intervention because it led to too much development planning. Markets should set prices and wages in order to ensure that resources would be allocated most efficiently.

Hernando De Soto (1989) argued that the state had a negative role in development in Latin America due to constant regulations. With a particular examination of the role of overbearing regulations that Peruvian entrepreneurs faced, he claimed that reducing the role of the state was necessary for development and economic growth. Any progress that took place was due to the efforts of the enterprising millions who worked hard to spur on the economy.

Neo-liberalism in economic policy

By the 1980s, the role of the state in development was under attack as a new economic orthodoxy influenced public policy (Harvey, 2005). Many states in the West turned away from the state and ideas and policies that emphasized free markets triumphed. At the heart of the neo-liberal paradigm is the idea that 'imperfect markets are better than imperfect states' (Colclough, 1993, 7). In practice these economic policies were associated with the likes of Margaret Thatcher of the United Kingdom and Ronald Reagan of the United States.

One of the first neo-liberal experiments in the developing world occurred in Chile after Augusto Pinochet's overthrow of Salvador Allende in 1973. A group of economists that had studied at the University of Chicago, and were influenced by the works of Milton Friedman, who was then a professor there, were summoned to help rebuild the Chilean economy. Working with the IMF, these economists reversed the nationalizations that had taken place under Allende. Social security was privatized, foreign direct investment was encouraged, tariffs and other non-tariffs barriers were dismantled. Export-led growth was encouraged. The labour market was freed from regulations. Some neo-liberal reforms also took place in Argentina and Uruguay.

Development policies from both the IMF and the World Bank also focused on a market-based approach. After World Bank president Robert McNamara retired in June of 1981, this approach ushered in a new era in the lending policies of the World Bank. More representatives of the business community were promoted to leadership positions within the World Bank.

These views were reflected in World Bank Development Reports. By 1983, the World Development Report from the World Bank was also focused on the role of the state in economic growth rates. The report argued that countries that had the least involvement from states distorting

Box 3.1   What are IFIs?

IFIs are the primary organizations responsible for managing the global economy and assisting countries experiencing financial difficulty. The major IFIs include the International Monetary Fund (IMF), the World Bank (WB) and the World Trade Organization (WTO). These organizations (known as the Bretton Woods institutions) were originally established to help the major powers prevent the recurrence of the economic hardships that took place during the Great Depression. In efforts to increase economic inter-dependence, the IMF was established in 1945 to give out loans to deeply indebted countries of the developed world. The World Bank was created in 1944 to provide development loans and administer projects for states in the developing world, with the goal of reducing poverty. Finally, the General Agreement on Tariffs and Trade was formed in 1947 with the task of reducing tariffs and trade barriers in efforts to facilitate global trade, eventually becoming the World Trade Organization in 1995.

The initial objective of the IMF was to oversee the fixed exchange rate agreements between countries, help countries manage their exchange rates and provide short-term capital to assist with balance of payments. After countries allowed their exchange rates to float in 1971, the IMF's role shifted significantly. The IMF started to take a bigger role in shaping states' economic policies, not just their exchange rates.

The IMF also shifted focus from primarily providing loans to countries in the developed world to structuring debt repayment to highly indebted countries in the developing world. In order to help with economic recovery, the IMF was committed to examining the economic policies and researching what types of policies would be best in ensuring an economic recovery. These loans, known as Structural Adjustment Programmes (SAPs), were not delivered without conditions. Aid recipient countries had to adopt free market policies. National industries were privatized. Much of the policies espoused by the IMF were equally championed by the World Bank. Recipients of

$\rightarrow$

the market also had the most rapid rates of economic growth. In the years that followed, subsequent reports also emphasized that growth would take place if public spending commitments were reduced. A World Bank Report of 1989 omitted the role of the state in development, but blamed poor governance instead as a major reason for economic stagnation in Africa. The World Development Report of 1991 again emphasized the need for states to direct development in ways that would allow for more reliance on the market.

During the same period, other developing states, and particularly those pursuing isolationist policies advocated by dependency theorists, were experiencing economic hardship in the form of a debt crisis. Though much of the developing world was in trouble, Latin American states were development loans were encouraged to pursue neo-liberal policies such as privatization, deregulation and scaling down the government.

One of the negative effects of the SAPs was that state capacity was severely limited. Public spending was curtailed. The number of civil servants was reduced. But because aid was not tied to bureaucratic reform, such as improving meritocratic recruitment and offering pay raises, the result was an even more poorly performing public sector with an underpaid and unqualified staff (Fritz and Menocal, 2007, 542).

IFIs were also critiqued for promoting policies that did not lead to growth but that distorted the structure of economies of countries in the developing world, triggering a *fallacy of composition*. By encouraging the production of single commodities, this created a decline in prices due to the excess of supply and the inelasticity of demand. For example, in Africa, countries were encouraged to focus on the production of commodities such as coffee. Unfortunately, this led to overproduction and a decline in coffee prices, rather than leading to a comparative advantage.

IFIs have been repeatedly criticized by those in the developing world for serving the interests of the developed world. One of the biggest criticisms of the IFIs is that they are governed by a small number of economically powerful countries, though they claim to represent over 180 countries. And it is these most powerful countries that dictate the policies of the IFIs. For example, the United States has 18% of the votes in the IMF, while Mozambique only has 0.06%.

Critics have also claimed that the IFIs have paid little attention to issues of equity, employment and how privatization actually takes place. The overemphasis on gross domestic product (GDP) growth has ignored sustainable development and improving living standards. Nevertheless, by the 1980s, the IFIs began to admit that the SAPs were not enhancing the lives of those most impoverished. Both the World Bank and the IMF introduced Poverty Reduction Strategy Papers in 1999 to replace the conditional loans, though these reduction strategies have been criticized for reinforcing the same problems of equity (Stone and Wright, 2006).

perhaps in the worst situation. The debt crisis of the 1980s was largely due to the combination of excessive state spending among developing states in an effort to encourage industrialization with extensive borrowing, primarily from *international financial institutions* (IFIs), to fund it. In Latin America, borrowing rose steadily throughout the early 1970s (for more on this, see Chapter 10). The dramatic rise in oil prices that began in 1973 only accelerated such borrowing as oil and other imported goods became more expensive. The increasing price of imports caused serious balance of payments problems for developing nations, which these countries needed to finance through borrowing. Western financial institutions (for more on IFIs, see Box 3.1) such as the International Monetary Fund (IMF) were the primary lenders.

A second spike in oil prices in 1979 only exacerbated the problem. The record-high interest rates in the United States of the early 1980s, caused by the Federal Reserve's efforts to curb the oil-based inflation of the 1970s, brought on a global recession and helped to trigger the overall crisis. Because most of the debt incurred in the developing world was linked to interest rates in the developed world, the cost of debt for the developing nations rose to record levels. Finally, in 1982, the Mexican finance minister indicated that his nation could no longer meet interest payments. By year-end 1982, approximately 40 nations were in arrears in their interest payments, and a year later 27 nations – including the four major Latin American countries of Mexico, Brazil, Venezuela and Argentina – were in negotiations to restructure their existing loans. Many economists at the time targeted the fiscal irresponsibility of developing states – specifically overspending and reckless borrowing – as the trigger for the crisis, and as a result, advocated in favour of a neo-liberal approach to get out of it.

The most widely advocated way out of the debt crisis of the 1980s was what came to be referred to as the Washington Consensus (so named because the major institutions advocating these policies such as the IMF, the World Bank and the Inter-American Development Bank were all based in Washington DC), a term coined by John Williamson in 1989. Proponents of the Washington Consensus prescribed less government spending and economic intervention and argued that neo-liberalism was the key to economic prosperity. They believed that development could only take place if markets were given the freedom to operate without intervention. Government intervention, in their view, only works to create opportunities for rent seeking (rent seeking refers to actions by individuals and groups to alter public policy and procedures in ways that generate more income for themselves without reciprocating any benefits back to society through wealth creation), which leads to greater inefficiency and waste of resources (Brinkerhoff and Goldsmith, 2002, 13). Due to the Washington Consensus, many developing states were advised to privatize state industries, dramatically reduce government spending, float their exchange rates, and open up their economies to trade and foreign investment.

A number of developing states were so indebted to IFIs that they were forced to implement these policies as part of their loan repayment negotiations. The IFIs imposed SAPs as a way to ensure debt repayment and economic restructuring. Based on the neo-liberal economic agenda, the main objective of the SAPs was to modify the structure of a state's economy to foster high growth rates while also lowering debt by reducing the role of the state. The SAPs consisted of stabilization and adjustment measures. Stabilization measures were about decreasing government spending such as wages, cutting government programmes, introducing user fees for health care and schools, laying off civil servants and devaluing the currency so that exports would be more attractive. Once the economy was stabilized, adjustment measures consisted of opening up the economy to foreign investment, improving tax collection, reducing tariffs and non-tariff barriers on imports, and privatizing industry. The combination of stabilization and adjustment would maximize government efficiency.

To ensure that these measures were taking place, the IMF and the World Bank placed their staff in the ministries of finance or national planning agencies for countries receiving loans. National Development plans were completely discarded. The first SAP was implemented in Turkey in 1980, but by the end of that decade there were 187 SAPs implemented in 64 developing states (Dickenson et al., 1996, 265). As a result, in many parts of the developing world, states cut spending and social welfare programmes, privatized industries, and reduced the size of government by laying off public employees and/or cutting their salaries.

The results of these significant policy changes, however, were not necessarily as hoped. To illustrate, global per capita income growth was 3.1% from 1960 to 1980. The application of neo-liberal policies generally took place between 1980 and 2000 and saw growth per capita of 2%. Growth of per capita income in developing countries decelerated from 3% to 1.5% between these two periods. Moreover, most of the growth that did take place in developing countries is accounted for by China and India. Without including these two countries the growth rate would be reduced to 1%. For Latin America, growth rates have stalled from 1980 to 2000 and for Africa, growth was negative (Chang, 2003, 2). Thus, economic performance was far from stellar and those economic gains that were made often came at a high societal cost. The government's retreat from the economy typically happened rapidly – large numbers of state employees found themselves without a job seemingly overnight. And yet at the same time, due to cuts in government social welfare programmes, basic social services like unemployment assistance ceased to exist. Levels of inequality dramatically intensified leading to serious social unrest. In the case of Chile, the implementation of neo-liberal policies led to some short-term gains, but everything fell apart when the Latin American debt crisis took place in 1982 (for more on this, see Chapter 9). In a number of states in Latin America, such as Argentina and Brazil, incumbent governments were overthrown due to mass pressures and frustrations, creating further instability.

It was also noted that the effects of orthodox stabilization packages were not gender neutral, affecting women much worse than men (for more on scholarship on women and development, see Box 3.2). Adjustment policies affect women because they form the majority of the world's poor. The shrinking of public enterprises and traditional industries that employ women affect women's wages directly. SAPs also focus on the productive

Box 3.2   Modernization and women

The informal slogan of the United Nations Decade of Women (1975–1985) was that women do two-thirds of the world's work, receive 10% of the world's income and own only 1% of the means of production (Robbins, 2007, 354). One of the first scholars to draw attention to this injustice was Ester Boserup, who published *Woman's Role in Economic Development* in 1970. Prior to this development, modernization theorists argued that economic growth and women's incorporation into the labour force would take place simultaneously. Contrary to the assumptions made by modernization theorists, the initial stages of development actually caused women's participation in the work force to decrease. Urbanization and industrialization with male-dominated factory production supplanted female-dominated home-based production. Thus the emergence of the factory system led to a decrease in women's participation in the economy. It is only that once development goes into a later stage the need for women in the labour force might increase as well. This, coupled with more education for women, will lead to falling fertility rates and give rise to more female participation in the work force (Çağatay and Özler, 1995, 1884). However, for many women in the developing world, this transition has not taken place. In other words, though women are essential to development, development does not always immediately improve the conditions for women (Moser, 1989, 1813).

Boserup's pioneering work argued that both the process of development and development policies have been biased against women. Women have been consistently marginalized in economic development. Men have had access to new technology and education, which has led to a decline in women's share of the labour force. Using empirical evidence to support her arguments, Boserup demonstrated that women made major contributions to agricultural and industrial development. One of the more notable revelations was that in Africa almost all of the tasks connected to producing food are left to women. In the rest of the developing world, women also play an important role in the small farming sector, producing 60–80% of the food. Women play an important role in producing secondary crops, gathering forest products, fuel wood and water and processing and conserving food. They do this even though they have much less access to information and farm support services (FAO).

economy while ignoring the impact of the reproductive economy, or what is needed to sustain human beings, which is mainly sustained by female labour (Sadasivam, 1997, 636). Thus, cutbacks in areas such as health care, food subsidies and social security programmes may affect women indirectly. Women are often expected to make ends meet with much fewer resources, such as working longer hours or taking in fewer calories.

Thus, the experiment with neo-liberalism made IFIs like the IMF unpopular throughout much of the developing world, as citizens associated them with the economic hardship they were experiencing.

At the time, the Cold War was in full swing and many development scholars during the Ronald Reagan and Margaret Thatcher era in particular, viewed neo-liberalism as a counterweight to communism and as the solution to the economic troubles prevailing in many states with interventionist approaches. These scholars viewed the failures of countries that had pursued protectionist agendas as evidence of the benefits of neo-liberalism. The following section illustrates a recent experiment with neo-liberalism in the developing world.

Neo-liberalism in practice

Neo-liberalism in practice has led to economic growth in many cases, but this growth has often been accompanied by greater inequalities. Countries that have implemented neo-liberal reforms have achieved high growth rates, such as Mozambique and Ghana, which have seen economic growth rates of 7.5% and 8.5%, respectively. Yet poverty rates in such countries remain high. Chile's experience with neo-liberalism has been marked by contention over how to interpret the results. Neo-liberals claim that Chile's experience with slashing tariffs and privatization has led to impressive levels of economic growth and high levels of foreign direct investment. Critics claim, however, that Chile remains one of the most unequal countries in the world. Moreover, one of Chile's most profitable companies, the National Copper Corporation of Chile, is state-owned.

We turn now to look at Ecuador. Ecuador implemented neo-liberal policies under pressure from the IMF, but found some success only after the state became more proactive in guiding the state's development.

Case study: Ecuador and the Washington Consensus

Many states in the developing world pursued the Washington Consensus agenda without much success. In Latin America, for example, though export rates more than quadrupled from 1980 to 2005, the average per capita income growth rate was 0.43%, the lowest in decades (Solimano and Soto, 2005). Inequality rates also increased to some of the highest in the world. To shed light on this experience, we detail the case of Ecuador.

Ecuador pursued IMF-led structural adjustment policies and export promotion from 1982 onwards. It liberalized its markets, reduced protectionism, floated its exchange rate, partially deregulated its labour markets, dismantled many subsidies, and decreased public spending.

Despite these dramatic changes, poverty rates saw little improvement. In 1995, for example, the poverty rate was 56% (with poverty levels as high as 76% in the countryside). Just five years later, however, the poverty rate increased to 69%. In addition, real wages decreased by 40% and urban unemployment rose to 17% (Larrea, 2006, 12). More than one in four children suffered from chronic malnutrition. And the education system was rated among the worst in Latin America.

Liberalization also left Ecuador vulnerable to international crises. The panic from the Asian financial crisis, for example, led to a massive withdrawal of short-term capital from Ecuador, which ended up costing it 22% of its GDP. Massive protests in Ecuador became commonplace as local populations voiced their frustrations with the neo-liberal agenda (Kennemore and Weeks, 2011, 8).

In the last decade, however, Ecuador has experienced a complete turnaround and become one of Latin America's success stories. The key to these successes has been increased attention to lessening inequality through the strategic use of government spending. Since the election of Rafael Correa in 2007, Ecuador's economy has grown at an average of 5% each year. Poverty rates have fallen by one-third, inequality has decreased, and free health care and education were introduced.

Ecuador was able to increase spending due to a combination of properly managed natural resources and increased tax collection. In terms of resources, the National Assembly approved a mining law in 2009, which allowed foreign companies to explore and extract from Ecuador's mines, but entitled the state to more than half of the profits. This law replaced the prior policy written under the neo-liberal model, which favoured foreign investment over all else. The Ecuadorian government stated that with the new law it was breaking from the neo-liberal policies of the past and trying to recapture lost surpluses (Kennemore and Weeks, 2011, 10). Regarding tax collection, Ecuador increased the tax rate for foreign companies, as well as the royalty tax on profits (Kennemore and Weeks, 2011, 9). The Correa government then used these revenues to double poverty assistance and make it easier for citizens to access credit for housing loans. Electricity was also subsidized for low-income consumers.

The state has also dedicated resources towards improving its information technology (IT) sector. Due to government policies, by 2011 there were 500 companies specializing in IT services. The government even set up an agency, the Software and Technology Sector for ProEcuador, to implement policies that support national investment in Ecuador's software industry (Biggerstaff, 2011).

Ecuador increased its human capital by investing in education, as well. Public spending on education increased from 1% of GDP in 2001 to nearly 5% of GDP in 2010. As a result, literacy rates increased from 84%

to 91% and secondary school enrolments from 63% to 96%. The success of these policies largely explains Correa's re-election in 2013 (Neuman, 2013).

The case of Ecuador illustrates that, for many in the developing world, the Washington Consensus agenda led to poor results. Developing states that pursued it learned the tough lesson that neo-liberal policies often bring with them social and economic inequalities that eventually cannot go ignored.

State-led growth in practice

The 1980s was generally a disastrous decade for Latin American and African economies. Critics of neo-liberalism argued that the policy advice being given to developing states was leading to poverty and instability. Yet the debate on the effects of neo-liberal policies raged on due to the success of states in East Asia. In the 1980s a number of states in East Asia were growing their economies by integrating themselves into the world economy. These states came to be known as the East Asian tigers; they included Singapore, Taiwan, South Korea and Hong Kong. Each saw record rates of economic growth, achieved through a focus on exports of high-value goods to industrialized nations. By emphasizing exports, and specifically high-valued ones, these states generated revenues that led to a favourable balance of trade, stable prices and ultimately economic transformation. The works of economist and World Bank consultant Bela Balassa (1971) examined growth rates in some of the East Asian tigers and demonstrated that countries that adopted a non-protectionist approach such as Japan, Korea and Singapore were best able to grow. Neo-liberal observers hailed the East Asian tigers' export-led model of growth as a testament to the benefits of neo-liberalism.

By the 1990s, it became more apparent that the economic success experienced by the East Asian tigers was not due to a purely neo-liberal approach. While it is true that those states emphasized trade, their governments were not absent from the process. Governments in East Asia took an active role in identifying the specific export industries to prioritize and structured their economies to ensure that those industries prospered. This occurred through large fiscal and financial incentives such as tax holidays, preferential access to capital and foreign exchange for exporters, credit offered at low interest rates and tariffs to protect selected industries. Special export processing zones were created to facilitate trade, and currencies were devalued (below market values) to make exports even more competitive overseas. In addition, the East Asian tigers invested their revenues from exports heavily in infrastructure, improving transportation networks such as roads and railways, as well as networks for telecommunications and electricity. Sizable investments were also devoted to education at all levels, leading to accumulation of human capital, which in turn improved the quality and quantity of the labour force. In other words, though the successful policies pursued by the East Asian tigers appeared to be neo-liberal on the surface, a deeper analysis revealed a heavy government hand.

Bringing the state back in: achieving good governance

As the previous section discussed, by the 1970s the role of the state was increasingly questioned. This all changed with the success of the Asian tigers and the renewed interest in the state in academic circles. Theda Skocpol's work 'Bringing the State Back In' (1985) highlighted the importance of the state in policymaking. At the same time, the idea of the developmental state gained popularity as a model for state-led development. The concept of a state that strategically intervenes in the market, facilitating industrial transformation and economic growth, has preceded the growth of the East Asian tigers, however. Friederich List (1789–1846) and Alexander Gerschenkron (1904–1978) highlighted the extent to which nationalist government policies that distorted market forces were responsible for economic development in Europe. Max Weber (1864–1920) had also emphasized the role of the bureaucratic efficiency (for more on this, see Chapter 4).

Gunnar Myrdal (1898–1987) was a noted Swedish economist who believed that state intervention was necessary to help reduce inequalities that were inherent in free market economies. In his book *Economic Theory and Underdeveloped Regions* (1957), he argued that planning was a solution to development problems. Though he acknowledged that many states in the developing world were 'soft' and therefore unable to achieve developmental objectives, he was critical of leaving development to the free market (1970). Other scholars such as Seers (1969), and Streeten (1989) have argued that states have the means and power to promote social development. Governments have the capacity to mobilize their populations as well as international resources and other governments. They can regulate and direct markets to ensure that they work for society and are able to allocate and distribute resources.

Thus, in contrast with neo-liberal perspectives, statist approaches see that the state is a key factor in stimulating development. Though the state has long been looked down upon by neo-liberals, scholars such as Nobel Prize winning economist and former head of the World Bank, Joseph Stiglitz, have also emphasized the importance of institutions for development. Strong institutions may be necessary to make policies effective.

Universal principles of good economic management don't map uniquely into particular institutional arrangements or policy prescriptions. While Stiglitz argues that markets are the engine for growth, he adds that when 'they are not supported by sound institutions and good governance they can stall or fail' (viii). Other critics charge that the reforms advocated by the Washington Consensus will not work properly if not accompanied by investment in roads, schools and infrastructure, something that is almost unachievable without functioning administrative institutions.

As Chapter 9 will explain in further detail, the Asian financial crisis further discredited neo-liberalism by exposing the vulnerabilities of developing economies to the global economy. The Asian financial crisis began in July 1997 in Thailand, but spread rapidly through the region. The states that were hardest hit were Indonesia, South Korea and Thailand. What happened? The Thai economy found itself in serious trouble. Investors lost confidence in the Thai currency, the *baht*, and decided to pull their money out virtually overnight. A herd mentality took over, leading to a mass exodus of capital out of Thailand (often referred to as capital flight) and the *baht* quickly became worthless. Unexpectedly, events in Thailand produced a contagion effect, such that investors not only took their money out of Thailand but out of other countries within the region. Money left quickly, and domestic economies plummeted.

The disaster was largely attributed to the neo-liberal view that states should not put in place controls that can limit the movement of capital. The IMF in particular advised states to encourage foreign investment by allowing the free flow of capital in and out of their borders. Though such a policy does make it easy for investors to put their money into an economy, it also makes it easy for them to take it out. The Asian financial crisis was devastating for a number of states in the developing world and caused many in the development community to rethink their advice, including the IMF.

Because of these experiences in the developing world, economists now support a more measured approach. Free trade is still heralded as critical. Free trade helps growth by reducing opportunities for corruption in the form of rent seeking while leveraging a comparative advantage. Exports should also be promoted, specifically in the form of a diversified export industry, as opposed to one reliant on a single agricultural product. At the same time, nascent export industries must receive some government protection in their early stages to buffer them from more advanced competitors. And though states should create domestic conditions amenable to foreign investment, including the rule of law and property rights protection, they need to have at least minimal capital controls in place to ensure that this investment cannot be taken out overnight. Governments also cannot ignore the needs of their citizens.

Safety nets must be in place to help citizens weather the storm of economic changes. And sizeable investments need to be devoted to public goods like education and health to develop the human capital required to propel the economy forward.

By the late 1990s, the role of the state was more positively redefined by the major international financial institutions. Development thinking had changed considerably from placing the blame on getting policies and prices right, to getting 'institutions right' (Meier and Stiglitz, 2001, 3). In 1997 the World Bank produced a report called *The State in a Changing World*, which admitted that the state was important to development. The study was the consequence of a compromise among Japanese sponsors who were ideologically at odds with the policy recommendations being issued by the World Bank's technocratic writers. The report admitted that some countries went too far in trying to create a minimalist state in the 1980s. Though the World Bank accepted no blame for why countries had adopted orthodox economic policies, the report appeared to be an indication that the Bank's fundamentalist commitment to orthodoxy may be wavering.

This change of heart did not usher in an attack on market-led approaches, however. The World Bank's 1997 report was still very cautious about states trying to do things that markets could do better. Weak states were also cautioned against doing anything at all. Nevertheless, there was some recognition that a lean but effective state might be necessary to help states interested in capitalist development. In addition to this shift, there was now a major emphasis on 'good governance'.

Good governance is a term that is commonly used in policy circles but is often difficult to define in practice. Though the World Bank did not specify how states achieve good governance in great detail, the implication is that good governance cannot be achieved without an efficient and professional bureaucracy, though its size and scope may vary according to the needs of each country. In vague terms, good governance refers to accountability, transparency and efficiency. More specifically, good governance assumes that officials are responsible for the actions. Rules and laws are clearly stated and provide predictability and stability. Rules are also fairly applied to all and provide the basis for conflict resolution through the help of an autonomous judicial system. As a result, corruption levels are low. The government works to enhance and consult with private interests over the best paths to achieving development. Early conceptions of good governance argued in favour of a minimal state with reduced public intervention in the economy with markets being used to deliver public services. This may work perfectly well in certain settings. However, other countries may be better assisted by a state that is more involved in delivering public services and ensuring high levels of human capital.

Case study: good governance in Botswana

Good governance has become a major concern for international development agencies. Botswana offers an excellent example of how strong state institutions can bring about positive outcomes for developing states. Botswana gained independence from the British in 1966. At that time, it was one of the poorest states in the world and landlocked to boot. Only 12 km of its roads were paved, there were only two secondary schools, and only 80 students that year obtained a secondary-level education in the entire country (compare this latter statistic to Zambia, which had ten times that number of graduates and Uganda, which had 70 times it) (Esterhuyse, 2012). Botswana emerged from independence, in other words, with few assets and very little infrastructure.

Yet, in the three decades that followed, its economy grew at an average annual rate of 7.7%, an incredible number to maintain for such a long time period. For this reason, Botswana is often touted as a development success, specifically one that illustrates the criticality of good governance. From the start, Botswana had some advantages that perhaps some of its neighbours did not. Its decolonization process was better planned than many others, for one. In addition, the tribal institutions that existed encouraged broad-based participation and constraints on the leadership. This set the stage for the development of high-quality institutions later.

Though Botswana is not considered democratic by many observers, it has had remarkable political stability. The Botswana Democratic Party (BDP) has led the state since independence and remains in power today. The party successfully incorporated a host of elites, ensuring that they did not feel threatened and try to overthrow the regime. The party apparatus also limited the powers of individual leaders and the types of policies they can pursue. The BDP has been able to integrate itself with traditional rural structures as well, and incorporate them into the BDP coalition. Over time, the BDP passed legislation that progressively stripped tribal leaders of their remaining powers, including their control over the land allocations. The Chieftaincy Amendment Act of 1970, for example, enables the president of Botswana to remove a chief. Steps like these were critical to ensuring the primacy of the state.

At independence, the government also resisted the temptation to indigenize the state's administrative institutions. It opted to wait until locals had sufficient skills to take these positions. For example, only 25% of all civil servants in Botswana were natives in 1966. International advisors and consultants were used instead, who were phased out by 1991. In other words, the government did not lower its standards in its hiring practices just so that it could hire more locals. In addition, promotions and salaries were based on merit. At the time, the government advocated this approach because it believed that the success of its development plans depended on having a talented and competent staff that could implement them. This strategy helped to nurture the relative autonomy of Botswana's bureaucracy and led to administrative institutions that were higher in quality (Esterhuyse, 2012).

The bureaucracy was also held accountable by the state's political institutions. At the same time, it was given enough autonomy so that it could develop internal coherence, discipline and strong integrity (Samatar, 1999, 10–11). Politicians and bureaucrats had clear divisions of labour and jurisdiction. They cooperated, but as two separate entities (Samatar, 1999, 9–11).

To deter corruption, the government also created an Auditor General, a position independent of the government. The Auditor General has the power to ensure that all public funds are accounted for and used for the public's benefit. An Internal Audit Unit in the Ministry of Finance and Development Planning was also established to ensure that the government did not commit any transgressions (Sebudubudu and Molutsi, 2008, 56).

This institutional foundation paved the way for the success of Botswana's economic policy choices down the road. Botswana's government implemented and adopted a series of development plans that emphasized investment in infrastructure, health care and education. Government expenditures, for example, are around 40% of GDP. The plans have emphasized long-term goals, as opposed to short-term successes (Esterhuyse, 2012, 67). This development strategy has by and large yielded excellent results.

In the field of education, adult literacy rates have more than tripled from 1966 to 2005 and now stand at more than 90%. Primary school enrolment has skyrocketed, as has university enrolment, which increased from only 22 students at independence to nearly 5,000 by the turn of the century (Samatar, 1999, 3).

With health care, even before the outbreak of the HIV/AIDS pandemic in the mid-1980s, the government had a comprehensive institutional framework for health-care provision. When the HIV/AIDS outbreak hit, Botswana increased the health-care budget from 5% to 7% in the 1980s and about 15% in the 2000s (Sebudubudu, 2010, 254). The state has been very responsive to HIV/AIDS and has ensured the widespread provision of anti-viral medication to the victims of the disease, particularly pregnant mothers. By the end of the 1990s, the majority of citizens (85%) had a health facility within 15 km walking distance.

Botswana also has substantial natural resources, but it has been careful in its management of them. In 1967, it passed the Mines and Minerals Act that gave sub-soil mineral rights to the state. The state also was able to negotiate with diamond companies so that it receives half of all diamond profits. It has used these revenues to fund its public investments. It also created the Revenue Stabilization Fund (RSF) and the Public Debt Service Fund to ensure sound fiscal management (Matshediso, 2005).

To ensure that the manufacturing sector stayed afloat despite the resource abundance (for more on the resource curse, see Chapter 10), Botswana introduced the Botswana Development Corporation in 1970 and created the Financial Assistance Policy to subsidize industrial ventures in 1982 (Sebudubudu, 2005). Though Botswana has not had large-scale industrialization, its manufacturing sector contributes about 5% of its GDP, which is an achievement in light of its abundant resources (OECD, 2010).

Botswana has some of the highest government spending in Africa, yet most state programmes are based on the needs of citizens, as opposed to patronage (Fombad, 2001, 59). Programmes such as the Arable Lands Development Programme (ALDEP I, II and III), the Accelerated Rainfed Agricultural Programme (ARAP) and Small Livestock Owners in Communal Areas Programme (SLOCA), for example, all provide assistance to those living in rural areas and individuals who work in the arable and livestock sectors of the agriculture industry (Sebudubudu, 2010, 254).

As a result of Botswana's strong institutional framework, and consequently its prudent policy choices, Botswana's economy grew at a rapid rate. By 1972, it was no longer dependent on aid from the British to balance its budget. As such, Botswana is a classic example that instead of focusing on policies or outcomes, 'reform should focus on the structure of state institutions and how they can be altered to form a national state' (Robinson, 2009, 12).

Conclusion

Economists to the left and to the right differ in terms of what role the government should play in development. Economists of the left attribute the underlying problems of development to market failures. As they see it, the state should guide development. Economists of the right assumed by contrast that the government was the problem and once governments got out of the way, markets would drive growth. Governments were simply trying to do too much. Yet successful development strategies in developed countries *did* require an active role for the government (Stiglitz, 1998, 6). Moreover, capitalist economies before the era of greater government involvement were very unstable and had widespread social and economic problems.

Even in the developing world states maintain ownership of at least a few industries (like defence and education), they use taxation to fund public goods projects (like roads and clean water access), and nearly all states distribute some form of subsidies to their citizens, typically in the areas of energy and agriculture.

While the experience of communism (see Chapter 2) may cast doubts on full government intervention in the economy, lack of any government involvement is also problematic. Joseph Stiglitz writes that 'there is no consensus except that the Washington Consensus did not provide the answer' even though most of its policies 'made sense for particular countries' (2007, 1). Thus, a more balanced approach to the state is required. Stiglitz further argues that development plans need to include a focus on building and transforming institutions in order to create new capacities (1998, 16). He adds that development strategies need to pay close attention to the public sector and identify where the state can be helpful to development. There are many areas of development where the public sector and the private sector can complement each other.

In sum, the one-size-fits-all approach to development does not yield favourable results. Though there are some basic good practices that states should pursue, the precise application of those tenets and the efficacy of particular policies are context dependent. Moreover, the particular types of institutions in place explain a great deal of the variation in economic performance across countries. Different institutional arrangements can alter the expected effect of economic policies on economic outcomes and may play an important role in achieving more optimal outcomes. To help to gain a better understanding of these relationships, Chapter 4 explains in more details what we mean by institutions.

Questions

- How does neo-liberal philosophy view the state? In what ways can the reliance on market forces lead to greater efficiencies?
- What factors explained the rise in popularity of neo-liberalism?
- Why did neo-liberal reforms fail to meet expectations in the developing world?
- What explains why the role of the state was more positively redefined by the late 1990s?
- What is meant by good governance? How does Botswana offer an example of good governance in the developing world?

Facts

- Early influences on neo-liberal philosophy emphasized that the invisible hand of the market should determine supply and demand.
- Chilean economists who would help implement neo-liberal ideas in Chile were influenced during their studies at the University of Chicago by professors such as Milton Friedman.
- The Washington Consensus (a name coined by John Williamson in 1989), which comprised of major institutions such as the IMF and the World Bank, advocated neo-liberal policies.
- In Ecuador, increased use of strategic government spending (such as spending 5% of GDP on education instead of 1%) led to higher growth rates of 5% per year since 2007.
- The World Bank first mentioned the role of the state and good governance in its report *The State in a Changing World* in 1997.

Chapter 4

Institutions and Development

This chapter offers insight into how researchers conceptualize institutions, as well as theories about their impact on development. We start by explaining what state institutions are and how state institutions have been theorized and compared. We then try to break down the study of institutions into more easily understandable categories. State institutions are often lumped into one broad category, but this tells us little about what the specific functions are of each institution of the state. This chapter breaks down state institutions into functional domains: administrative, judicial, political and security. It discusses what high-quality institutions in each of these domains look like, weaving numerous examples from the developing world throughout to illustrate these points. The purpose of this chapter is to provide a starting point for thinking in more specific ways about how state institutions can be moulded to produce better development outcomes.

Institutions in theory

What are institutions?

As the study of institutions has become widespread, the term 'institutions' is increasingly used in ways that lack meaning or conceptual clarity. What do institutions actually refer to? Douglass North offers one of the most frequently used definitions in the rational-choice institutionalist literature: 'Institutions are the rules of the game in a society or, more formally, are the humanly devised constraints that shape human interaction' (1990, 3). The expansiveness of this definition underscores the fact that institutions are extremely varied in nature. That said, all institutions do share a common characteristic: they are rules and procedures that structure social behaviour.

It is important to note that though the terms 'institution' and 'organization' are often used interchangeably, but they are distinct concepts. North helps clarify the distinction: 'If institutions are the rules of the game, organizations and their entrepreneurs are the players. Organizations are made up of individual rules bound together by some common purpose to achieve certain objectives' (1994, 361; Hodgson also offers a helpful summary of how North conceptualizes institutions versus organizations). In other words, organizations are a subset of institutions, which are far broader in nature. Some institutions, like political parties and schools, are organizations; others, like elections, are not.

Institutions under this conceptualization can be formal and informal. Formal institutions are fairly straightforward: they are legal rules that are subject to third-party enforcement (Rodrik, 2008, 510). Things like constitutions and bureaucracies fall into this category. Informal institutions are a bit trickier to define and identify. They typically refer to norms and established patterns of behaviour. Examples here would include social conventions and moral codes (North, 1994, 360; Rodrik, 2008). The institutionalist literature has primarily focused on formal institutions (Leftwich, 2006, 2), not because researchers doubt the importance of informal institutions, but simply because the former are easier to recognize and measure. Informal institutions also help to explain behaviours and outcomes but are far more difficult to research in methodologically sound ways.

In this study, we look exclusively at a subset of formal institutions: institutions of the state. These refer to institutions that are either created or supported by a government. An institution does not have to be government run to qualify as a state institution, but it does have to be part of a state's legal or constitutional structure. A political party that is legal but does not have ties to the government, for example, would be considered a state institution using this definition. We focus on state institutions given this study's emphasis on how state structures can pave the way for or impede development, a subject to which we now turn.

Why institutions matter

'Institutions rule'. Those are the title words of a 2002 study by Dani Rodrik, Arvind Subramanian and Francesco Trebbi. The authors argue that state institutions are the critical factor in predicting income levels across the world. In their study of the causal factors that account for differences in states' economic performance, the quality of institutions 'trumps everything else' (Rodrik et al., 2002, 4).

Theirs is just one of a multitude of studies in recent years showing that institutions matter for development. Economists Daron Acemoglu and James Robinson, for example, assert in their 2012 book, *Why Nations Fail*, that economic development is almost entirely dependent on a state's institutions. The right set of institutions leads to higher incomes and improved human welfare in the long term, while the wrong ones lead to prosperity for a small group of elites, but poverty for virtually everyone else. Though what classifies as the 'right' institutional structure is less agreed upon among researchers, the overwhelming message that has emerged is clear: state institutions have to be contoured appropriately to enable positive economic performance.

States with poorly designed or absent institutions (for more on states with failed institutions, see Box 4.2 on Failed States) will lack incentives to pursue the right economic policies for growth. Indeed, as renowned economist Williams Easterly writes, 'The consensus among most academic economists is that destructive governments... explain the poverty of nations' (Easterly, 2009). The second is that even with the right economic policies for growth in place, poorly designed or absent institutions will limit their efficacy, the so-called 'governance-policy gap'. Too much state corruption and bureaucratic red tape, for example, will prevent even the most open economies from attracting investment. World Bank economist Daniel Kaufmann emphasizes this reality, asserting that despite 'significant strides' in improving developing states' economic policies, 'improvements in governance are not keeping pace' (Kaufmann, 2004, 25).

Within political science, there is a virtual consensus that institutions are an important feature of the state. Samuel Huntington puts it well: 'the most important political distinction among countries concerns not their form of government but their degree of government' (1991, 28). Researchers point to institutions and differences in their make-up as a critical factor in explaining a range of political outcomes.

Institutions in practice

The previous section makes clear that state institutions matter for economic development. It has become a common adage in development circles to say, 'get institutions right' (Meier and Stiglitz, 2001, 27). We defined state institutions as those institutions that are created or supported by a government. But this is a broad definition encompassing a wide spectrum of organizations and functions. How can we better understand what this institutional landscape actually looks like? To get a more precise picture of what state institutions refer to in practice, we break them down into four functional categories – administrative, judicial, political and security – which, taken together, provide a comprehensive overview of those state institutions that affect a country's economic development (Debiel, 2006, 104). The purpose of this exercise is not to offer an exhaustive review of all of the functions of the state, but rather to provide a useful starting point for thinking in more specific ways about how state institutions can be altered to improve development prospects.

There are a number of reasons why greater specificity is desirable. The first is that different state institutions affect economic development in different ways. For example, some types of institutions affect levels of corruption within a state, but are not relevant to property rights protection, both of which influence economic growth. Understanding the specific pathways that link institutions to growth can enable policymakers to prioritize where limited resources should be allocated to mitigate or solve a state's specific obstacles to growth.

Moreover, different states have different administrative and political challenges that constrain their development. Colombia, for example, has developed institutions that effectively protect private property, but is lacking institutions that help preserve public order. In other cases, countries such as South Africa and Botswana may be competent at collecting taxes (which require sophisticated administrative institutions, at a minimum), but has experienced greater difficulty in dealing with the HIV/AIDS crisis. In other words, different states confront dramatically different challenges when trying to enhance their prospects for economic growth and development. Thinking in concrete terms about specific types of institutions and the specific ways in which they affect economic development, therefore, is helpful for developing context-specific policies to promote growth and development.

In this study, therefore, we focus on identifying how specific features of state institutions affect economic performance. In most instances, researchers have yet to use a more nuanced approach to examining how institutional spheres influence growth. Existing research often concludes with the message that institutions matter for development, but does not go into greater detail in terms of which ones and how. In this chapter and those that follow, we review the broad messages that have emerged in the development literature, but we also disaggregate institutions and their links to development. The primary goal is to provide a foundation for a more critical approach to the study of institutions and their role in development and to highlight the key focal points for reforms that can spur growth and improve economic outcomes.

It is important to emphasize that the institutional domains that we review in this chapter are not mutually exclusive. Some institutions may serve functions falling in more than one of our four categories, and institutions from more than one category may be necessary for upholding policies necessary for growth. For example, the Ministry of Defence in many states have elements that could be classified as both security and judicial institutions. And both security and judicial institutions are key to ensuring the rule of law within a given state. The four types of institutional domains we discuss here are simply intended to be a starting point for engaging in a more specific discussion about state institutions and how they affect development rather than a rigid disaggregation of their roles and functions.

In this chapter, we define administrative, judicial, political and security institutions. Here, is a brief summary:

- *Administrative institutions:* Institutions of the state engaged in policy implementation and the regulation and delivery of services. Examples include: state ministries, bureaucratic agencies.
- *Judicial institutions:* Institutions of the state engaged in law interpretation and enforcement, the distribution of punishments and conflict mediation. Concepts such as property rights and the rule of law are components of judicial governance. Examples include: the courts.
- *Political institutions:* Institutions of the state engaged in decision-making, articulation of policy and the selection of public officials. Examples include: political parties, legislatures, elections.
- *Security institutions:* Institutions of the state engaged in law enforcement, border control, citizen protection and defence. Examples include: military and police forces.

In the sections that follow, we discuss each of these institutional domains in more detail. We identify the criteria that distinguish high- from low-quality institutions and summarize existing research on how each institutional domain affects economic development.

Administrative institutions

Administrative institutions can be thought of as encompassing the 'bureaucratic' functions of the state (despite this conceptual overlap, we use the term 'administrative institutions' rather than the term 'bureaucracy' because the latter in the Weberian sense refers to a set of well-organized administrative institutions; see also Evans and Rauch 1999, 749). Doing so also enables us to maintain a consistent terminology throughout the book. These are the institutions that administer state policy, which can entail policy implementation and the regulation and delivery of services. Administrative institutions include both bureaucratic agencies and state ministries. They are important because 'societies need a capable administration to keep order, collect revenue, and carry out programs' (Goldsmith, 1999, 531). They execute and enforce government-mandated regulations and provide basic goods and services to citizens, including health care, infrastructure development and education (Schneckener, 2006, 24). The responsibilities of administrative institutions can range from mail delivery to garbage collection to the provision of utilities. As such, administrative institutions are extremely important for the translation of policies into actions and outcomes. Beyond this, administrative institutions are also responsible for collecting revenue for the state (through taxes). Most states require tax revenues to function (although the availability of natural resource wealth such as oil reduces a state's need for taxation – a topic that we discuss in Chapter 10); well-functioning administrative institutions are required to effectively fulfil this task.

It is important to note that officials in administrative institutions are not directly responsible for policy formulation – those decisions ultimately rest with officials in a state's political institutions. Administrative institutions, rather, function to ensure that the policies that have been selected are executed in the desired manner. In other words, even the most effective administrative institutions can be inadequate to stimulate development on their own if poor policies, such as complex taxation systems or low public goods allotments are in place. Of course, poor state policy choices often come in tandem with incompetence in other institutional domains, but in this section we review the features of high-quality administrative institutions assuming that the policies selected are consistent across states. In addition, officials employed in the state's administrative apparatus (often called civil servants) are not elected to their posts. They typically obtain their positions either through appointments or a traditional hiring process. This contrasts with officials in political institutions, who are usually elected.

Administrative institutions can vary dramatically in their ability to carry out the tasks demanded of them and do so efficiently. Here we review the features that distinguish high- from low-quality administrative institutions.

High-quality administrative institutions

High-quality administrative institutions are often referred to as Weberian administrative institutions, after Max Weber's (1978) foundational work on the ideal bureaucracy types. In *Economy and Society,* Weber argues that administrative institutions play a pivotal role in providing the state with the appropriate structure to encourage capitalist growth. In his view, administrative institutions should consist of a formalized, standardized, hierarchical and specialized structure. The staff should comprise professionals who are promoted based on merit rather than political affiliations, loyalty or other clan or ethnic networks. Their behaviour should be predictable, transparent and objective, driven by a standard set of procedures (Brinkerhoff and Goldsmith, 2002). To reward such officials, the state should offer adequate compensation, including competitive salaries and long-term career rewards. Doing so ensures the retention of employees, which fosters the establishment of consistent norms and reduces the temptation of corruption. These features lead to an administrative structure that is capable and competent in fulfilling its responsibilities and the mandates of the state.

High-quality administrative institutions, therefore, have three key features (Dahlström et al., 2011):

1. *Meritocratic recruitment and promotion*: civil servants are hired and promoted based on their qualifications and competence, not their political ties.
2. *Salary competitiveness*: civil services receive competitive compensation to reduce incentives for corruption.
3. *Autonomy*: civil servants have stable careers, lifelong tenure and special laws that protect the terms of their employment.

Administrative institutions that have all three of these features are high in quality. In practice, many states have some, but not all of them.

Low-quality administrative institutions

Low-quality administrative institutions essentially lack the three key features above. According to Weber, low-quality administrative institutions feature 'personal relations of subordination... instead of bureaucratic impartiality' (Hutchcroft, 1991, 415). In such an environment, personal favours and considerations and political ties dominate. For these reasons, they are often referred to as patrimonial institutions.

There are a number of key indicators of low-quality administrative structures. First, there is limited separation between private and official spheres of activity because the administrative apparatus is politicized. The state's administration is viewed in this context as a 'purely personal affair of the ruler, and political power is considered part of his personal property which can be exploited by means of corruption and fees' (Weber, 1978, 128–129).

Second, hiring and promotion decisions are driven by personal relationships. Loyalty and kinship trump experience and qualifications. Because these systems reward loyalty rather than competence, they tend to underperform. A 1988 study in Egypt, for example, demonstrated that one in ten civil servants obtained their job through a personal connection (Palmer et al., 1988, 26).

Third, low-quality administrative institutions are often very large in size and frequently consume a significant proportion of a state's budget. This is because political leaders often use administrative institutions to supply jobs and distribute patronage to loyal supporters. In Brazil, for example, jobs were allotted based on connections rather than competence for many years (Evans, 1992, 167). The state came to be known as a *cabide de emprego* (source of jobs). In another example, in Belarus,

President Alexander Lukashenko has used widespread employment in the state apparatus to maintain popular support for his authoritarian rule; the state employs approximately 50% of the work-age population, according to national statistics.

Fourth, low-quality administrative institutions feature underpaid civil servants who are subject to dismissal for little reason. As a result, turnover among employees is high, limiting the experience and knowledge the staff can acquire. Brazil, again, offers an example of this. In the 1980s, civil servants changed agencies on average every 4–5 years (Evans, 1992, 167).

Lastly, because of low salaries and job insecurity, civil servants in low-quality institutions are susceptible to bribery, increasing the levels of corruption. Indeed, large cross-national studies have documented a strong negative relationship between measures of corruption and civil service salaries (van Rijckeghem and Weder, 2001). In Ukraine, for example, an academic study found that public sector employees received around 25% less wages than their private sector counterparts. Yet, workers in both sectors had essentially the same level of consumer expenditures and asset holding, indicating that public sector employees were able to make up the difference through non-reported compensation (i.e. bribes) (Gorodnichenko and Peter, 2007).

Administrative institutions and development

Research on administrative institutions indicates that a high-quality administration facilitates economic development. Though this research is not abundant, the overall message is fairly consistent. Weber's study of states' administrative apparatus was one of the first to underscore the relationship between capitalism and high-quality administrative institutions. Weber writes, 'Capitalism and bureaucracies have found each other and belong intimately together' (Evans, 1989, 567). Other researchers have built on this argument, emphasizing the importance of administrative institutions for supporting markets and capital accumulation (Evans, 1992, 146). And according to the World Bank, poor administrative performance leads to declines in overall welfare (1997, 30).

High-quality administrative institutions are important for development because they give civil servants longer time horizons by providing strong incentives to stay (like competitive salaries and other benefits), providing lifelong tenure, and/or because arbitrary dismissals are uncommon. Because civil servants have long time horizons and can expect to reap the benefits of longer-term decisions, they are more likely to pursue policies that are in the long-term interest of the state (rather than less prudent decisions that yield immediate personal payoffs). For example, officials with long-term horizons may be more likely to advocate for higher public infrastructure investment, which is helpful for growth, while officials who are less certain of their career tenure may advocate for greater consumption spending, which yields more immediate benefits but is harmful to growth (Evans and Rauch, 1999, 752). Moreover, long time horizons increase the internal cohesion of the administrative staff. This means that investments in infrastructure are more likely to yield high returns because they are more likely to be widely and deeply implemented as opposed to more arbitrarily executed (Evans and Rauch, 1999, 752).

High-quality administrative institutions also tend to experience lower levels of corruption, which creates an environment more conducive to economic development (we return to the relationship between corruption and growth more fully in Chapter 7). As we discussed above, officials in high-quality administrative institutions tend to receive salaries that are competitive with their private sector counterparts, which reduces incentives for corruption. Moreover, studies have identified a link between the size of a state's bureaucracy and corruption (Goel and Nelson, 1998). Because high-quality administrative institutions tend not to be those that are used to supply jobs and distribute patronage to loyal supporters, they tend to be smaller in size, and therefore less prone to corrupt practices.

In addition, high-quality administrative institutions indirectly foster economic growth because they increase levels of private investment. Investors are often deterred by 'red tape', or excessive regulations and time required for conducting normal functions necessary for doing business in a given state. The World Bank created the 'Ease of Doing Business' index, which measures some of these regulations and hurdles to doing business in 189 countries. Although the index measures functions that cross into some of the other institutional domains (such as the extent of regulations, number of taxes paid or other juridical functions), the index also reflects the efficiency of a state's administrative institutions to execute many of the core functions associated with doing business, such as procedures and time to open a new business, time to obtain permits, number of documents and time necessary to import and export, and procedures and time to obtain a permanent electricity connection. The World Bank has shown that there is a strong relationship between improvements in these indicators and economic growth.

Additional studies that have sought to test the relationship between administrative institutions and economic development have found that high-quality administrative institutions are indeed correlated with better economic performance. According to Peter Evans and James Rauch (1999), for example, states with administrative agencies that use meritocratic recruitment and offer employees long-term and predictable careers have higher growth rates than those without them. Other studies in the literature support these findings (see Hydén et al., 2003, for a review of them).

Of course, it is possible that the causal arrow runs in the other direction: economic growth may encourage the emergence of high-quality administrative institutions. After all, it takes economic resources to be able to develop the human capital required for a well-qualified group of civil servants and to adequately compensate them. Alberto Chong and Cesar Calderon (2000) offer some indications that this is true: they find that the quality of administrative institutions both affects and is affected by the performance of the economy.

In sum, the evidence indicates that high-quality administrative institutions, which feature meritocratic recruitment and promotion, salary competitiveness, and autonomy, are associated with positive economic performance. Future research is needed for better identification of the particular ways in which each of these features shapes economic outcomes.

Judicial institutions

Judicial institutions are state institutions responsible for interpreting and enforcing laws, doling out punishments and mediating conflicts. Courts are the primary judicial institutions. Judicial officials can be both elected and appointed. Judicial institutions are important because they help arbitrate conflicts that arise between citizens, citizens and the state and different state institutions. They also help ensure that punishments for breaches of the law are appropriate. Without judicial institutions, state policies have no bite as citizens would likely ignore or manipulate rules and regulations when in their interest. Without an arbiter, conflicts could also easily escalate into violence (World Bank, 2002b). Judicial institutions help ensure that laws are not arbitrarily enforced, that punishments are fair, and that society is orderly.

It is important to note that in this study we only look at formal judicial institutions. Informal judicial institutions, such as tradition, customary norms and practices, community relations and religious law, operate in many developing states, particularly in those that do not have formal mechanisms to resolve disputes. The United Nations notes that in developing countries, and particularly in rural and poor urban areas, around 80% of cases are resolved through informal systems of justice. In informal systems, decision-making is usually based on consultation not by lawyers or jurists but by local, tribal or religious leaders, either individually or in groups. Informal justice systems tend to address issues similar to those of their formal counterparts, including protection of land, property and livestock; resolution of family and community disputes; and protection of entitlements, such as access to public services. In some instances, these informal judicial institutions may work better than their formal counterparts (Kaufmann et al., 1999; Chang, 2006). We recognize the importance of informal judicial institutions, but keep our focus on formal state institutions.

In addition, as with other administrative institutions, judicial institutions are not responsible for the types of policies that they are tasked with enforcing. For example, state policies may be contradictory or unclear, or unfair and discriminatory. Regardless, judicial institutions are simply staked with ensuring that laws are interpreted and enforced in an equitable fashion.

As a final point, we group law enforcement groups (like the police forces) with security institutions, though there is some overlap. These groups are primarily concerned with enforcing state policies and less so with interpreting them.

The quality of judicial institutions varies markedly across developing states. We review the key criteria used to differentiate those institutions here.

High-quality judicial institutions

High-quality judicial institutions deliver fair and impartial decisions and their judges make decisions free from the pressures of political actors. Officials are protected from retaliation for their choices, while also held accountable for unethical behaviour. The case system is managed in a clear and transparent fashion so that citizens understand the reasoning behind decisions. Moreover, the system is accessible, such that it is not overly difficult for citizens to gain access to the courts and other institutions. In high-quality judicial institutions, the staff is well trained and are appointed or selected because of their qualifications. Judges are assigned specific cases based on merit, rather than their political ties or leanings, and case assignments are transparent. The expenditures in proceedings are also made public and easy to monitor. High-quality judicial institutions are also adequately funded with enough resources to enable them to efficiently deal with caseloads and appropriately compensate staff. Citizens trust the judicial system and its ability to fairly arbitrate cases.

In summary, there are four key features of high-quality judicial institutions (this list is drawn from the United States Agency for International Development, 2009, 4).

1. *Independence*: The government and other society sectors do not determine how cases are decided. Judgments are based on the deliberations of well-qualified judges. Budgets are not politicized and officials are protected from retaliation for their decisions.
2. *Integrity and accountability*: Ethical standards and codes of conduct are in place and enforced.

3. *Transparency and efficiency*: Sophisticated case management systems are used to ensure that standards are adhered to in terms of how judges are assigned cases, how financial resources are distributed and how judgments are determined. The process is quick and cost effective.
4. *Equal access*: Citizens have equal access to the judicial system; it is available to them regardless of their income or location.

States with judicial institutions that have these features engender their citizens' trust in the system. Citizens believe that laws are interpreted and enforced in a transparent and consistent fashion.

High-quality judicial institutions and the rule of law

The term 'rule of law' is frequently used in development and policy circles and is touted as a key factor in encouraging development. As Thomas Carothers put it, 'one cannot get through a foreign policy debate these days without someone proposing the rule of law as the solution to the world's troubles' (1998, 95). Organizations like the United Nations, the World Bank and others argue that the rule of law is critical to economic performance. It is often conflated with high-quality judicial institutions, and for this reason it is important to discuss what the rule of law means and how it differs from the quality of a state's judicial institutions.

The United Nations defines the rule of law as follows:

A principle in governance in which all persons, institutions, and entities, public and private, including the State itself, are accountable to laws that are publicly promulgated, equally enforced and independently adjudicated, and which are consistent with international human rights norms and standards. It requires, as well, measures to ensure adherence to the principles of supremacy of the law, equality before the law, accountability to the law, fairness in the application of the law, separation of powers, participation in decision-making, legal certainty, avoidance of arbitrariness and procedural and legal transparency. (United Nations, Rule of Law, www.un.org)

Though there are a variety of definitions of the rule of law, most share similar features with this one. Most of these definitions underscore that while high-quality judicial institutions are necessary for the rule of law, their presence alone cannot guarantee it. The above definition highlights, for example, the importance of laws that conform to international human rights norms and standards. Yet, the judicial system is not responsible for the content of laws, simply that they are enforced and interpreted in a fair and impartial manner. The same is true with respect to the emphasis on participative decision-making, which is up to the state's political apparatus to ensure, not its judicial institutions.

High-quality judicial institutions and property rights

The concept of 'property rights' is viewed as a critical driver of a state's development, largely because they are seen as integral to the development of the rule of law (Hoff and Stiglitz, 2005). There are two essential elements of property rights. First, individuals must possess the exclusive right to use their resources as they see fit as long as they do not violate someone else's rights. Second, individuals must have the ability to transfer or exchange those rights (to delegate, rent or sell those rights) on a voluntary basis (O'Driscoll and Hoskins, 2003). In other words, individuals must have the exclusive right to use their resources as they see fit (Alchian, 2008). Though the distinction is often not emphasized, the term is most frequently used to reference private as opposed to government property rights.

A state's judicial institutions are not solely responsible for building strong property rights systems. The state's political institutions play a primary role in the extent of property rights' protections. Although democratic forms of government are not a guarantee of strong property rights (property rights have been strongly protected in dictatorships), the strongest property rights systems tend to occur in wealthy, established democracies (O'Driscoll and Hoskins, 2003). A state's judicial institutions, however, do play a role in the enforcement of property rights. Property rights enforcement is frequently viewed as an indicator of a high-quality judicial system, and of judicial independence specifically (Moustafa, 2003). The idea is that judicial institutions are better able to protect private interests when they do not face political interference. We see the enforcement of property rights, therefore, as an indicator of high-quality judicial institutions (of which judicial independence is a key feature), rather than a direct measure of judicial quality. It is possible, for example, that a state's judicial institutions may face little interference when it comes to property rights enforcement, but may be subject to meddling in other domains.

Low-quality judicial institutions

When low-quality judicial institutions are present, citizens face difficulty accessing the court system, the process of issuing judgments if often lengthy and arbitrary, and it is difficult for citizens to determine why particular decisions were made. Officials may be punished if they issue decisions that are unpopular with political actors, and they are able to violate procedures with impunity due to the absence of accountability.

In states with low-quality judicial institutions, political interference in the judicial process is commonplace. If officials deliver decisions that are unpopular, they are likely to face retaliation, leading to decisions based on politics rather than the law. Political officials may be habitually in contact with judges to ensure that they issue decisions that are favourable to their interests. If judges decline to do so, they may lose their positions. They have little job security and can be fired at any time. At the same time, if judges or other officials engage in unethical behaviour, it is likely to go unpunished. When similar cases are heard, the judgments issued are likely to be very different. In Ukraine, for example, reducing the extent of political interference in the judiciary is a top priority for the government of President Petro Poroshenko, who came to power in June 2014 following the departure of Viktor Yanukovych after months of protests. During deposed president Viktor Yanukovych's rule, courts were often merely tools for punishing political opponents and increasing Yanukovych's own power. Such widespread judicial corruption led to the public's dismally low trust in the courts (Popova, 2014).

In low-quality judicial systems, case management systems are often non-existent or unsophisticated. It is unclear to the public how judges are assigned to cases, how resources were spent and the logic underlying judgments. Citizens come to view the system as biased and ineffective, given its arbitrariness and inaccessibility. Laws, in turn, are rendered insignificant in the public eye. Citizens use the courts only when they have no other options.

Low-quality judicial institutions typically are under-funded or erratically funded. Political interference in budgetary decisions is also commonplace. Benefits (like housing allowances and tuition fee reductions) are commonly extended to judicial officials at the discretion of the executive branch. The judicial institutions lack independence from other branches of government.

Judicial institutions and development

As Daniel Webber wrote, 'There has been increasing recognition in recent years by the World Bank and other development institutions that, to be successful, the development process must be comprehensive and supported by an effective judicial system' (2007). That being said, few empirical studies have looked at the relationship between the underlying features of a state's judicial institutions and economic performance.

Instead, most research in this area has focused on the economic impact of property rights and/or the rule of law. These studies argue that when property rights are insecure, citizens fear that the government will step in and expropriate their assets, which limits the extent to which individuals are willing to invest in their assets to make them more productive. This in turn hurts economic growth (Barro, 2000). The same is true with the rule of law: when citizens fear an absence of law and order, they are less likely to invest in the economy (Barro, 2002). A number of studies have tested these arguments and found supporting evidence: when property rights are enforced and there is law and order, economic performance is improved (North and Thomas, 1970; North, 1981; Knack and Keefer, 1995; Engerman and Sokoloff, 2002; we should note that a few researchers have questioned these relationships, such as Hewko, 2002). In one study on the impact of property rights on growth, O'Driscoll and Hoskins (2003) find that nations with the strongest protection of property – defined in terms of the transparency, independence and efficiency of the judicial system – have a GDP per capita (measured in terms of purchasing power parity) that is twice as high as that in those providing only fairly good protection.

Property rights enforcement and the rule of law are not synonymous with high-quality judicial institutions, as mentioned above. Yet, there is some overlap, given that both require at least some independence of the judicial apparatus. For this reason, it is reasonable to expect that the quality of judicial institutions will affect economic performance, as well. There are two mechanisms through which this could occur: (1) high-quality judicial institutions lead to property rights enforcement, checks on abuses of power in government and the rule of law; in turn increasing economic growth; and (2) high-quality judicial institutions make it easier for private actors to engage in economic exchanges, which also increase growth (Messick, 1999). In terms of the latter, for example, many studies have highlighted the importance of contract enforcement, which enables parties to enter into contracts without fear that they will be revoked when it suits one of the parties (Rodrik, 2000). In all of these cases, a system of laws and courts to make markets function efficiently is necessary for economic growth.

There is some evidence to indicate that these arguments are true (Collier and Gunning, 1999; Widner, 2001; Feld and Voigt, 2003; Moustafa, 2003; Rugege, 2006; Chemin, 2009). However, many of these studies face challenges in measuring the institutional quality of the judicial system (Messick, 1999), often relying on small-scale surveys of public perceptions of how well the judicial system is functioning. The consensus opinion, therefore, is that though the evidence suggests that high-quality judicial institutions help development, more research is needed to increase the certainty of existing findings (Prillaman, 2000; Court et al., 2003).

Political institutions

A state's political institutions refer to those institutions responsible for decision-making, policy articulation and the selection of public officials.

In many ways, political institutions are the most important for development. After all, a state's administrative institutions can only implement public goods if political actors task them to do so, a state's judicial institutions can only maintain independence if political actors refrain from interfering in the judicial process, and a state's security institutions can only train their officers well if they are allocated sufficient financial resources. Low-quality political institutions often negatively affect the other institutional domains; yet, at the same time, political institutions that are high in quality are not sufficient to ensure that all of the other state institutions are the same.

We note that political institutions are not synonymous with 'the government' (as in, the leadership), although the two are largely intertwined. Governments tend to come and go within the same institutional framework. In most cases, governments are not the original architects of the institutions that govern their states. And conversely, governments have the ability to alter their institutional frameworks. For these reasons, governments and their political institutions should be treated as analytically distinct.

There are a wide variety of political institutions – including constitutions, political parties and legislatures – but in this study we emphasize the criticality of elections. Elections are formal, state-run occasions that determine a state's political leadership. They differ across states in terms of who can vote, the types of positions that are contested, the extent of competition and the frequency with which they are held.

Our primary focus is on whether elections are free and fair. In other words, we are mainly interested in the distinction between democracy (where elections are free and fair) versus dictatorship (where they are not). To some researchers, free and fair elections do not guarantee democracy. We use this definition to reference democracy in this study, regardless, due to its clarity and simplicity (see, also, Przeworski et al., 2000).

It is not that other political institutions do not also matter (and we will reference them in this study when they do), but simply that this distinction between democracy and dictatorship often trumps all others. High-quality political institutions, therefore, can take many forms, but in this study we concentrate on the presence of free and fair elections.

High-quality political institutions

In states with high-quality political institutions elections are held on a regular basis, there are few unreasonable restrictions on suffrage, and the process is competitive. In other words, elections are free and fair.

When elections are free and fair, votes are counted in an equitable fashion, and qualified individuals and parties can run for office without having to face government meddling or harassment. During the electoral process, human rights are respected and coercion is not used to determine winners and losers (Goodwin-Gill, 2006). Perhaps most importantly, citizens'

Box 4.1 Populism

For scholars of development, populism is a political strategy that has economic consequences for development. Populism is often referred to as a style of leadership that many leaders in Latin America often embodied, but leaders across the developing world have also exhibited populist styles of leadership. The leadership style is often classified as charismatic, personalistic and paternalistic, but not repressive. Populist leadership aims to please multiple sectors of society, focusing on promoting policies that are largely popular with the population though not necessarily helpful to development. The populist leader seizes the opening created by the institutional vacuum and aims to make direct connections with the population. The problem is that this linkage is formed at the expense of institutions.

With populist leadership, *political institutions* such as political parties and legislatures are often weakened. In Zambia under Michael Sata (2011–2014), the platform of his political party, the Patriotic Front, was devoid of any clear programme. Sata was mainly focused on making promises to multiple sectors of the population while siding differently on a given issue depending on who the audience is.

Populism may also lead to the weakening of *administrative institutions* as well, which has direct consequences on the functioning of the economy and the types of economic policies favoured. The economic policies of a populist regime are focused primarily on distributing patronage (Roberts, 1995, 88). From this perspective populist leaders are not focused on economic growth through stimulating entrepreneurship. Instead, populist leaders may

$\rightarrow$

votes dictate who is elected. In this context, citizens have the power to hold political officials accountable for their behaviour; they can unseat those leaders who they deem to be unfit.

Low-quality political institutions

In states with low-quality political institutions, elections are not free and fair, limiting the ability of citizens to hold leaders accountable and responsive to citizens' policy preferences. Elections, if they are held, may occur infrequently. Even in instances where elections are held on a regular basis, there are major irregularities in how votes are tallied. Ballot-stuffing is rampant, international monitors are prevented from attending polling sites, and there is little transparency in the electoral process. Individuals who oppose the government are barred from competing, harassed or otherwise disadvantaged, and their supporters often face ill treatment. Large swathes of the citizenry are prevented from voting, and there are significant favour nationalization of industries in order to keep employment levels high (Dornbusch and Edwards, 1990). Because the policies are distributional, there is no urgent need for an effective bureaucracy. The bureaucracy becomes a large resource that the populist leader can use to distribute patronage to his or her constituents and main support groups. For example, in Pakistan Zulfiqar Bhutto (1971–1977) weakened the state by appointing a large number of loyal cronies to top government and party positions (Ellner, 2003, 149). The populist leader also tries to circumvent the administrative institutions in order to deliver goods directly to people; as a result, the linkages between the leader and his or her constituents also become stronger. All of the strategies of the populist leader have the effect of elevating the popularity of the populist leader at the expense of the state's institutions.

Populist leaders may also try to weaken the *judicial institutions* by packing the courts with judges that are politically pliable. The courts are another source of patronage for the populist leader to deliver goods to his supporters. In the case of Egypt under Gamal Abdel Nasser (1952–1970), the courts were undermined by his deliberate selection of politically loyal judges. This ensured that court rulings were always friendly towards his regime. As a result, the rule of law was weakened, and a host of government abuses took place with impunity.

The populist leader wants to ensure that everyone is content; he or she will never initiate policies that may have difficult short-term consequences, and institutions are deliberately weakened in order to maintain power. Though everyone's interests are appealed to, there are few winners under populist leadership in the long term.

resources dedicated to ensuring that the incumbent stays in power. In many cases, although the political opposition is allowed to contest elections, the playing field is often so heavily slanted in favour of the incumbent that the opposition has no real chance of winning, such as was the case of Hugo Chávez of Venezuela (for more on Populism, see Box 4.1).

States that lack free and fair elections range from what researchers term 'hybrid regimes' to outright autocracies. In such states, there are few means through which citizens' views are represented by the political system. This makes it impossible (or at least quite difficult) for citizens to hold their leaders accountable for their actions.

Political institutions and development

The relationship between democracy (our focus here) and development has been the subject of intense inquiry ever since modernization theorists pointed out in the mid-20th century that the two tend to go hand in hand.

Most of the world's rich states appeared to be democratic, while most of the world's poor states tended to be governed by autocrats. Modernization theorists posited that this was because development was required to enable democracy (Lipset, 1963). Lipset suggested that wealthier countries possess populations that are educated and urbanized, which engenders a citizenry with tolerance and a willingness to compromise – qualities that facilitate a more stable democracy. The lack of such values in poorer countries, by contrast, undermines democratic development. Similarly, other modernization theorists such as Barrington Moore (1966) focused on class dynamics and democratization. He argued that economic development created larger and more powerful middle or working classes that provide a strong social base for dispersed political power. In these views, development *causes* democracy.

Modernization theorists were correct in that democracy and development are highly correlated. Although there are exceptions to this relationship, most of the world's democracies are rich, and most of the world's dictatorships are poor. Those countries that tend to buck this trend include many of the oil-rich dictatorships like Qatar and other anomalies like authoritarian Singapore, as well as some stable democracies that remain poor such as India. Some observers view these anomalies as evidence that autocracies are better suited for promoting growth. The inability of citizens to vote their leaders out of office, the argument goes, may insulate autocrats from public backlash triggered by unpopular but necessary economic reforms. Although this may be valid in some cases, by and large the relationship between regime type and level of wealth is robust.

Other studies have suggested that the causal arrow could run in the other direction arguing that democracy *causes* development. In this view economic development can only occur under a democratic system in which policymakers are held accountable for their policy decisions and can be voted out of office if they plunder their economies. The strong institutions that tend to occur in democracies provide a basis for sound economic policies and growth.

The above arguments aside, democracy may be conducive to positive economic performance because democracy leads to a number of other outcomes that are amenable to growth. A large body of literature has shown, for example, that democracies lead to better human rights outcomes for citizens than do dictatorships, meaning that incidences of state-sanctioned repression are more infrequent in the former than in the latter (Davenport and Armstrong, 2004). Free and fair elections, therefore, lead to very real differences in the violence experienced by citizens at the hands of the state, which may in turn be reflected in their propensity to invest in their economies. In addition, democracies are also shown to invest more in public goods. Public goods are important to the state's economy for a number of reasons, such as making trade easier and increasing human capital (Knack and Keefer, 1995). Because democracies feature electoral accountability, political leaders who do not invest in public goods can be voted out of power. Aspiring politicians and incumbents, therefore, often have to accede to citizen demands for public goods. A number of studies have shown that the evidence is consistent with this argument: democracies are more likely to provide public schooling, roads, safe water and public sanitation than are dictatorships (Deacon, 2009). Democracies also have higher life expectancy rates and lower infant mortality rates than do dictatorships (Przeworski et al., 2000). Democracies also have an advantage over dictatorships in reducing corruption (Linz and Stepan, 1996; Rose-Ackerman, 1999; Lederman et al., 2005), which is shown to harm economic growth (Mo, 2001). Democracies have lower rates of corruption on average than do dictatorships, largely because their officials are monitored and punished through the exercise of elections.

The potential for reverse causality has made empirically testing arguments about democracy and development difficult, though not impossible, to execute. In his extensive study on this issue, Adam Przeworski and his colleagues (2000) find that democracy is correlated with high levels of wealth and dictatorship is not, though average growth rates actually do not differ between the two regime types. On average, growth rates are the same in democracies as they are in dictatorships. This is true even when taking into account the endogeneity of this relationship, as well as other factors that might distort the relationship. A different picture emerges, however, when we look at how growth rates vary from one year to the next in democracies versus dictatorships. Though growth rates are comparable on average, the variance is quite a bit higher in dictatorships than in democracies. This means that the states with both the highest as well as the lowest growth rates are ruled by dictatorship. Economic miracles, like China's amazing performance in recent years of double-digit growth, as well as economic disasters, like Chad's far-from-stellar economic performance, are more likely with dictatorship. This means that democratic leaders take fewer risks but also do less to destroy their economies than do their authoritarian counterparts. The fear of losing office is enough to incentivize democratic governments to use a more measured economic approach. Regardless, neither type of political system, on average, has an advantage when it comes to economic performance.

The question of why we continue to observe the correlation between democracy and development remains. Przeworski et al. (2000) argue that economic development does not itself promote democratization. Instead, high levels of economic development create more stable regimes. Thus, in contrast to poorer countries, when rich countries become democratic, they stay that way. Przeworski summarized his argument in 2011 stating, 'I do not think that economic development necessarily leads to democracy but only that, once established, democracy survives in developed countries' (Afronline interview).

The relationship between democracy and development is clearly a complex one and the direction of causation is likely to remain a topic of debate for some time.

Security institutions

Security institutions encompass the police, military, paramilitary forces, militias and, in some instances, the intelligence apparatus. These institutions are dedicated to defence, citizens' protection, border control and law enforcement. Any organization or agency that has the authority to threaten or use force to protect the state and its citizens is a security institution (Pion-Berlin, 1992; Ball and Brzoska, 2002). They have a 'formal mandate to ensure the safety of the state and its citizens against acts of violence and coercion' (Ghani et al., 2005, 9). This means that their primary focus is on guaranteeing external and internal security (Wulf, 2004). They protect the state from attacks from other states, as well as provide order within the state's borders.

Security institutions tend to span across several of the institutional domains discussed above. For example, security institutions work in tandem with judicial institutions to enforce laws. While judicial institutions interpret laws and issue judgments, security institutions are responsible for enforcing decisions. Similarly, security institutions complement administration institutions to implement laws and ensure that state policies are executed appropriately. In each of these examples, the key factor that differentiates security institutions from other institutional spheres is their ability to threaten or use force to carry out their mandate. Security institutions are the only segment of the state that has the authority to use force.

As in the other institutional domains discussed above, security institutions rely on the decisions of the state's political institutions to determine the scope and nature of their mandate. Decisions to limit political and civil liberties or use force against citizens in ways that violate human rights are largely political decisions and security actors are often just following orders to implement such decisions. Creating policy is the responsibility of the state's political institutions, not of the security apparatus.

We note that though law enforcement organizations, like the police, are also part of the security apparatus, most of the literature on security institutions focuses on the military. For this reason, we do so as well. We now turn to a discussion of the dimensions on which security institutions vary in quality across states.

High-quality security institutions

High-quality security institutions create a sense of internal order, while also protecting the state from external threats (MacDonald, 1997). At the same time, when security institutions are high in quality, their officials do not try to interfere in politics. Instead, they concentrate on enforcing policies and heeding the directives of the state's political institutions (Lee, 2005). The size of the security sector is unimportant; what matters is its structure and function (Janowitz, 1988).

A critical feature of high-quality security institutions is professionalization, meaning that the security apparatus has well-trained officials, promotions are based on merit rather than clan or political loyalties, and it is well funded and internally cohesive (Huntington, 1957; Brzoska, 2003). When security institutions are professionalized, the military is more effective in war fighting and protecting state borders, as are police in protecting citizens from internal violence and security threats. Protocols and standards are adhered to, and policies dictated by the state's political institutions are enforced in unbiased fashion.

Another important feature is a centralized command structure, meaning that there is a well-organized security apparatus that does not have competing interests or groups, like personal armies or security units. The internal chain of command within each organization must also be clearly defined.

High-quality security institutions also feature civilian accountability, which protects citizens from abuses of power. This means that the security apparatus is restricted from entering the political sphere. This is important because when security institutions involve themselves in civilian activities, it weakens the apparatus as a whole by distracting security officials from their key responsibility: protecting the state and its citizens. It is also critical that security institutions never enter the political domain because there is always the risk that they will abuse their coercive abilities and force the government out of power by staging a coup.

In summary, the key features of high-quality security institutions are as follows:

1. *Professionalization*: There are sufficient budgets, rigorous training requirements, and merit-based promotions. This makes political interference less likely, improves the efficacy of law enforcement activities and makes for a better-performing military force in combat.
2. *Centralized military command structure*: A centralized military force controls the use of force and does not have to contend with parallel armies or security units. The internal chain of command is clear and hierarchical.

3. *Civilian accountability*: The security apparatus is subordinate and accountable to the state's political institutions, lessening the chances that it will use its weaponry and training to overthrow the government or otherwise try to influence policy.

States must possess all three of these features in order to create high-quality security institutions. The absence of any one feature can easily lead the security apparatus to overstep its bounds in ways that create suboptimal outcomes. For example, a professionalized military force is likely to be better equipped to stage a coup. A professionalized military in the absence of civilian accountability, therefore, may have detrimental effects on development. Similarly, a security apparatus that is accountable to civilians but lacks professionalization exposes citizens to internal and external threats. Moreover, if the command structure is not centralized, rival security groups may turn against one another, lowering the capacity of the state's security institutions to fulfil their responsibilities.

Low-quality security institutions

When states have low-quality security institutions, citizens lack protection, both from each other and from aggressive actions of other states or non-state actors. The state's borders are poorly guarded, making the state vulnerable to breaches of its territorial integrity. Beyond the security apparatus' inability to ensure the security of the state's citizens, its officials frequently do not heed political orders. They engage in behaviour that breaches the separation between political and security domains. In some instances they try to influence policy, while in others they seek the government's overthrow. Low-quality security institutions interfere frequently in politics, staging coups on a whim, and creating instability.

Security institutions and development

By and large, the vast majority of studies that have examined security institutions have looked at their impact on coups and other forms of political instability. The overall message to emerge from this literature is that greater professionalization deters coups: states with professionalized militaries, specifically, are less likely to experience coups. While coups are an important indicator of political instability and, like all manifestations of political stability, can be economically disruptive, the relationship between security institutions and development appears to be indirect. No studies to our knowledge have examined directly how the quality of a state's security institutions affects development.

These points aside, we include security institutions in the discussion here because they are critical to ensuring stability, which is also critical

Box 4.2   Failed states

This book in particular has emphasized the role that a strong and capable state can play in stimulating development. Many states in the developing world, however, are failing, and as such are mired in poverty and plagued by instability. Failed states are states that are no longer able to function or provide services for their citizens. The Organisation for Economic Co-operation and Development (OECD) argues that state failure constitutes the incapacity of the state to 'provide the basic functions needed for poverty reduction, development and to safeguard the security and human rights of their populations' (Jones and Chandran, 2008).

The first responsibility of the state is to ensure a monopoly over the legitimate use of force. In strong states the security institutions, namely the military and the police, are professionalized, and exercise control over the territory. In contrast, failed states are often characterized by ongoing conflict and enduring violence. Failed states often have armed revolts and insurgencies, civil unrest, dissent, internal communal ethnic conflict and religious strife. In some cases, warlords control vast swathes of territory. Criminal violence and gangs have taken over. The police force is often paralyzed. There is also no control over borders.

The administrative institutions and their various agencies also do not provide citizens with adequate education and health care. There is no water management, electricity or infrastructure. The state is unable to process passports, visas or birth certificates, let alone guide the economy and help provide industrial support for businesses. The roads are riddled with potholes with no repairs taking place. The state is unable to extract taxes from its citizens and any revenues to the state are often acquired through foreign aid or external rents.

Corruption and wastefulness flourishes on a destructive scale. Kickbacks and bribes take place over anything from medical supplies to textbook supplies to construction of infrastructure. Judicial institutions are so weak that impunity is the norm. Unnecessary licenses exist for non-existent activities. The bureaucracy is not rule bound, but bound by personal bonds. A huge patronage system develops that flows from the top to the bottom.

In failed states the political institutions are also not working. The legislatures are flawed or non-existing. There is an absence of debate and representation. The state lacks legitimacy. Elections are fraudulent. Political parties are simply vehicles of power-hungry leaders. The courts also fail to function. Judicial decisions are for sale. Judges are in the pockets of a dictatorial leader, drug kingpins or warlords. There is a complete absence of the rule of law.

It should come as no surprise that failing and weak states do not perform well on any development indicators. Some of the poorest countries in the world are also those that are ranked the worst on various failed state indices. Therefore, one of the contributions of the failed states literature is that it highlights the importance of state capacity for development, something that the development literature should continue to focus on as well.

to ensuring positive economic performance. We discuss in Chapter 7 how security institutions can be moulded to pave the way for better development outcomes.

Conclusion

State institutions mould the behaviour of political actors who are responsible for determining political and economic outcomes. A wide body of research has underscored the importance of state institutions for economic development. Yet, simply asserting that state institutions matter for growth is not very informative. To offer a more detailed picture of the relationship between institutional landscapes and development, we reviewed four institutional domains of the state in this chapter: administrative, judicial, political and security. This disaggregation is not intended to be a rigid roadmap for divvying up the state, but rather a starting point for thinking about how specific features of state institutions impact development outcomes. We argue that a specific approach, like this one, should improve our understanding of the key developmental challenges encountered in the developing world and the ways in which institutions can be shaped to overcome them.

Some developing states have high-quality institutions, but many do not. In the chapter that follows, we review some of the historical and contextual reasons why we see this type of institutional variation.

Questions

- What are institutions and why do they matter? What are the different types of institutions that constitute the state?
- What are the key features of high-quality versus low-quality administrative institutions?
- In what ways are high-quality judicial institutions important to establishing the rule of law?
- In what ways are high-quality administrative and judicial institutions important to development?
- What is the relationship between political development and economic development? Why is it difficult to argue that autocracies don't encourage economic development?

Facts

- Scholarship has emphasized that the quality of a state's institutions has an impact on economic development.
- A Weberian bureaucracy refers to a very well-organized set of administrative institutions with merit-based recruitment.
- Independent and accountable judicial institutions are important to implementing the rule of law.
- Although there are exceptions, democracy and development are highly correlated.
- The key factor that differentiates security institutions from other institutional spheres is their ability to threaten or use force to carry out their mandate.

Part II

Development Traps and Hurdles

Previous chapters in this study looked at the economic philosophies and theories that have been proposed to explain and understand development. Economists have argued that development will take place as long as the appropriate policies are in place (such as free trade, exporting and encouraging foreign investment). Though these policies may be growth enhancing, they may not lead to economic development. Part of the reason for this is that there are major challenges to development, which propel a cyclical behaviour, or as Paul Collier puts it, 'development traps' (2007, 3–16). Development traps make it more difficult to create and maintain high-quality state institutions, which are in turn vital to overcoming these obstacles and improving economic performance.

Chapter 4 emphasized the importance of institutional reform. Though we are well aware that institutional reform is difficult to execute in the face of these development challenges, we argue that it is an appropriate first step. The right institutional changes can have a cascading effect that leads to positive outcomes in a number of arenas. In other words, institutional reform tackles the 'big picture' problem. Though it is difficult to engender, dedicated politicians, particularly when coupled with effective international assistance, can make it happen. For this reason, we acknowledge that the relationship works both ways, but subsequent chapters of this study focus on the ways in which institutions can be altered to help states rise above development hurdles, as opposed to the reverse causal arrow.

Chapter 5

Poverty Traps

As Chapter 1 stated, 1.22 billion people live on less than $1.25 a day and 2.6 billion live on less than $2 a day (World Bank, 2015). This is an improvement from 1.91 billion in 1990 and 1.94 billion in 1981 (World Bank). Nevertheless, these improvements don't erase the fact that billions of people are still deeply impoverished, most of whom will never ever be lifted out of poverty.

In this chapter, we discuss the challenges of alleviating the *poverty trap*. After first explaining how poverty is measured and defined, the chapter offers the dominant perspective for approaching poverty. The chapter then details what poverty traps are and why they are so difficult to overcome both for individuals experiencing chronic poverty and for states with large numbers of chronically poor people. Thus the chapter explains how poverty and development are connected, as well as how poverty affects the state. The chapter then explains what can be done to deal with poverty, with a special focus on tackling rural poverty, both for the state and for international and local organizations as well.

Poverty

Poverty is defined and measured in many different ways. There is absolute poverty and relative poverty. Absolute poverty measures poverty in relation to the amount of money necessary to meet basic needs such as food, clothing and shelter. With absolute poverty incomes are so low that even a minimum standard of nutrition, shelter and personal necessities cannot be maintained (World Bank, 1975, 19). Absolute poverty was often defined as living on less than one dollar a day, adjusted by taking into account local purchasing power, and the current figure stands at $1.25 a day.

In contrast, relative poverty examines relative deprivation or observable disadvantages relative to the local community or nation to which an individual group belongs (Townsend, 1993). Relative poverty focuses more on inequality and social exclusion. Relative poverty refers to poverty that takes place when people fall below prevailing standards of living, known as a poverty line. A poverty line is a level of income or expenditure below which a recipient (expressed as household, individual or per capita) is said to be poor. The headcount ratio is the fraction of all recipients who fall below the poverty line, usually estimated as 50% of the country's average income (Fields, 1980). The poverty line is an arbitrary measure, providing an estimate of what it is required for an individual to meet the most basic necessities.

The relative poverty line is set at a constant proportion of the mean or median income of a country that is either 25%, 50% or even 100% of the median income. Each country would have a different relative poverty line, expressed in dollars – and each country's relative poverty line also changes as income increases. Thus, comparing the United Kingdom and Mozambique, those with incomes equal to the median in the United Kingdom would be much higher than those living with incomes equal to the median in Mozambique.

Sometimes poverty is distinguished by the severity and duration. Abject poverty, or severe poverty is defined by the United Nations as 'a condition characterized by severe deprivation of basic human needs, including food, safe drinking water, sanitation facilities, health, shelter, education and information. It depends not only on income but also on access to services, (UN declaration at World Summit on Social Development in Copenhagen in 1995).

Structural poverty consists of poverty that is long term and due to personal and social circumstances such as lack of land or labour. Conjunctural poverty is poverty that takes place during a time of a crisis and is caused by a specific economic shock or a period of political instability (Gray and Moseley, 2005).

Measurements of poverty

There are different approaches to measuring poverty. The monetary approach is the most common option and it looks at income. Monetary approaches would also look at the percentage of people that live under $1.25 a day, which would denote abject or extreme poverty and the amount of people living in moderate poverty is $2 a day. It is important to note that the World Bank uses purchasing power parity to measure poverty rather than exchange rates. PPP takes into account differences in relative prices. It takes into account the differences in relative prices and differences in purchasing power in different countries. One dollar in Bangladesh can buy much more than one dollar in the United States. The purchasing power parity figure takes these differences into account. This method tries to factor in local variations in the purchasing power of particular goods, a laudable aim, but one that is particularly difficult when measuring poverty. This is because the basket of goods that is used to make the comparison include goods, which are unlikely to be consumed by the poor, and which measures average income. This underestimates the number of people living in poverty as consumers with rising incomes above poverty level spend a decreasing proportion of their income on food, and an average rise in income over time will therefore translate into smaller comparisons of those goods that the poor actually consume, and whose price differentials may be far more significant.

One of the problems with this approach is that policy outcomes are focused on the formal economy but this may overlook those who don't participate much in the formal economy. In addition, though consumption patterns may be more constant, income can be more variable. Moreover, calculating who lives on less than $1.25 a day is not easy. It is based on consumption per capita and the income comes from household surveys, using a random sample of households and asking about incomes and expenditures. The quality of these surveys will vary, which affects the results.

Another way of calculating poverty is to look at calorie consumption rates. Calorie-based approaches are used because most impoverished people spend most of their incomes on food. Food is also an essential good without which no one can survive. Many countries look at how much it costs to obtain 2,000 calories a day. The problem is that some people who work as agricultural labour may need as much as 4,000 calories a day. Calorie consumption rates in countries like India are also down because fewer people are involved in manual labour (Basu and Basole, 2012). People also need protein as well as just calories. There are other specific aspects of one's diet that are also important such as iodine. Iodine deficiency can lead to mental retardation, goitre and problems during pregnancy. The other issue is that the minimum amount needed to maintain a diet of 2,000 calories may lead to a very boring diet (Stigler, 1987, 6).

A basic needs approach examines poverty by not only looking at whether or not they have money but whether or not they have food, shelter, education, sanitation, safe drinking water and health care. A basic needs approach sets a minimum standard for each of these necessities. Poor people are then classified according to those that have access to less than a minimum allowance. The poorest nations are not based on per capita income levels but based on those who cannot satisfy the basic needs of their people. Sri Lanka is ranked 120 in the world in terms of GNP per capita but satisfies basic needs better than this ranking would indicate.

In contrast to the basic needs approach, the capabilities approach, most notably conceptualized by Amartya Sen (1983, 1999), argues that poverty has to do with well-being and opportunities. Sen claims that well-being is something unrelated to the possession of a commodity. Instead, well-being is what a person can do with the commodity. Poverty is seen as consisting of low levels of functions and capabilities. Thus for Sen, poverty is more than inadequate incomes, but also entails the lack of access to education and participation. Functions include physical elements such as being adequately fed and sheltered and more complex social achievements such as taking part in a community (Sen, 1992, 110). These capabilities include nutrition, education, clothing and housing needs, which are preconditions for participating in labour and credit markets, and functioning as a social and political citizen.

The capabilities approach asks questions such as: how healthy are people, how much freedom do they have, how many people have access to water, how many children are underweight? Sen also argues that it is important to examine what a person can command in society, what opportunities are open to them. The capabilities approach is multidimensional but is much harder to measure. It is also harder to find accurate data for many of these factors, especially access to water. Nevertheless, it may tell us more about how well an impoverished person can recover from a crisis. Recovering from a crisis, such as a famine, depends on not only asset levels but also social networks, something that is often not measured by survey data on income (Davies, 1996).

As stated in Chapter 1, the Human Development Index is one of the more well-known indices that looks at development. It ranks states based on how they measure on a composite score that comprises life expectancy, literacy rates and per capita income levels. To gain a better understanding of poverty, the Human Poverty Index takes into account several other factors that indicate more about how impoverished a nation is. The Human Poverty Index looks at the percentage of people that are likely to die before the age of 60, the percentage of adults who are illiterate, the percentage of the population without access to water and the percentage of children who are underweight for their age. The last two indicators are especially important to providing a more complete picture of the challenges the poor face in the developing world.

Theories on poverty reduction

The predominant poverty reduction strategies of the last several decades have emphasized the promotion of market forces (Banerjee et al., 2006, xxi). As explained in Chapter 3, the Washington Consensus's approach to reducing poverty is to focus on economic growth. Many economists have argued that market-friendly policies are the only effective way of raising growth rates. Though there have been some studies that have shown that there is no statistically significant correlation between economic development and poverty (see Ravallion, 2001; Deaton, 2003), a host of scholars (such as Sachs and Warner, 1995; Frankel and Romer, 1999; Bhagwati and Srinivisan, 2002; Dollar and Kraay, 2002) have done studies to demonstrate how economic growth is the principal driver of poverty reduction (known as the Bhagwati hypothesis). These studies claim that developing countries will not decrease poverty unless they integrate quickly into the global economy, engage in free trade and encourage direct investment. One of the most cited works is David Dollar and Aart Kraay (2002), who argued that more open economies are associated, on average, with more economic growth and thus, less poverty. The primary examples of this argument are China and India. China had poverty rates of 28% in 1978, but these rates fell to 9% in 1998. India's poverty rates fell from 51% in 1977 to 27% in 2000. In India's case, growth rates had remained very low for a long time and poverty rates remained very high at 55%. It was not until India achieved higher growth rates that poverty reduction also took place.

Market-based poverty reduction strategies operate under the premise that that overall economic growth would trickle down and reduce poverty. Many studies have noted the positive relationship between growth and poverty reduction, not only across countries but also within countries over different periods of time (Banerjee et al., 2006, xviii). Studies demonstrated that poverty rates in countries in the developing world increased during recessions and decreased during economic upswings. Where growth occurs for countries with millions of poor people, some of the poor are bound to benefit. Nevertheless, growth at the bottom is never as impressive as overall growth. For example, though growth can occur in low-income countries such as Uganda and Mozambique, this growth may be driven by foreign companies, and may not lead to lower levels of poverty (Hulme and Shepherd, 2003, 413).

Though Uganda and Mozambique have achieved impressive levels of economic growth, they have not been as successful in achieving other aspects of economic development. This highlights that economic growth and economic development are not one and the same. Growth refers to the total volume of goods and services produced in a country during a year. However, economic growth rates say nothing about the composition of how growth is distributed. Though growth is a necessary and important condition for real income to rise per head, it is not a sufficient condition on its own to help economic development take place. Economic development is a much more comprehensive term. As stated in Chapter 1, it entails improving economic and social well-being of people, by developing human capital, infrastructure, environmental sustainability, social inclusion, health care, security, literacy and employment. According to Sen, economic growth is just 'one aspect of the process of economic development' (1983, 748).

One of the problems with approaches that assume that economic growth will reduce poverty rates is that most of the very poor meet their needs through subsistent methods such as farming, hunting and bartering.

Their standard of living may not go up just because the national income has increased. In many countries growth could take place, yet millions of people may still be stuck in ruts of poverty, or poverty traps. The next section explains in more detail what poverty traps are and why they persist.

Poverty and development: poverty traps

For many people in the developing world, poverty is a lifelong condition. With few opportunities and options, the impoverished get stuck in a poverty trap. The poverty trap refers to any self-reinforcing mechanisms that cause the poor to stay poor (Bloom et al., 2003, 355). Poverty traps reinforce chronic poverty, which affects as many as 580 million people (Hulme, 2003, 411). Chronic poverty is conceptualized as poverty that is transmitted from one generation to the next. Children of impoverished households are more likely to remain in poverty. With chronic poverty 'an individual experiences significant capability deprivations for a period of five years or more' (Hulme, 2003, 405). In other words, they are chronically poor if they are living under the poverty line for more than five years. The poverty line is the minimum asset threshold below which families are not able to educate their children, and build up their productive assets (Carter et al., 2007,836). For those living in abject poverty, measured as less than $1.25 a day by the monetary approach, poverty is almost always enduring. The next sections explain why poverty traps endure.

Low levels of education

Investment in human capital is important to breaking this cycle of poverty. But human capital is extremely low in developing countries. Literacy rates (see Table 5.1) in the developing world still have room for improvement. In 2011, there were 774 million illiterate adults, a decline of only 1% since 2000. Of those 774 million, over 750 million illiterate people live in the developing world. Illiteracy makes an impact at both the macro and micro levels of development. At the macro level, countries with high illiteracy rates cannot progress or improve their output substantially, and living standards remain low as a result. At the micro level, illiterate and less educated individuals or households are less productive, earn less money and have low standards of living.

Many studies have shown that education and poverty are inversely related in that countries with populations with higher levels of education have less poor people, because knowledge and skills are gained with education that are associated with higher wages (Fields, 1980; Tilak, 2007). Until 1979, economic growth rates in India and China were similar (Herd

Literacy rates	1950	1960	1970	1980	1990	2000–2004	2005–2011
World	55.7%	60.7%	63.4%	69.7%	75.4%	81.9%	84%
Developing Countries			47.7%	58.0%	67.0%	76.4%	80%
Developed Countries			94.5%	96.4%	98.6%	99%	99%
Africa			27.8%	37.8%	49.9%	59.7%	60%
Middle East		18.9%	28.8%	39.2%	50%	62.7%	77%
East Asia and Pacific			57.5%	70.3%	81.8%	91.4%	95%
South and West Asia			31.6%	39.3%	47.5%	58.6%	63%
Latin America			73.7%	80%	85%	89.7%	92%

Table 5.1 *Literacy rates*
Source: UNESCO 2014

Box 5.1   Fertility rates and development

Fertility rates are directly related to development and therefore getting a hold on fertility rates is important for development for many reasons. Population growth skews income distribution against the poor. Countries that have population growth rates of more than 2% a year suffer economic problems; in turn, wealthier populations have lower fertility rates compared to poorer countries. A 10% increase in a country's GDP per adult is associated with a 13% lower fertility rate (Schultz, 2007). The link between fertility and poverty is clear. Lowering fertility rates is more than just increasing a woman's access to birth control. Decreasing fertility rates only takes place when parents have more incentives to have fewer children. Thus there are many things that the state can do to tackle this problem.

States can implement policies that can ensure that women have more autonomy, which has a direct effect on the number of children women have. These policies include ensuring that women's wages are closer to men's, mandating better inheritance practices, eliminating forced marriages, creating more opportunities for women in the workforce and easing access to credit for women. In particular, ensuring that women have access to education has an important effect on fertility rates. Not only does education decrease fertility rates, but it also reduces infant mortality rates (which in turn reduce fertility rates). Education gives women more voice in making household decisions so that they can better protect the needs of small children and help them benefit. In India, women's education is the most important correlate of declining fertility rates (Eswaran, 2006). The case of Kerala in India illustrates these points. Women are much more empowered in Kerala than in other parts of India. Women in Kerala are not excluded from inheritance and the female literacy rate is 92% compared to 65.5% in the rest of India. As a result, fertility rates in Kerala are also the lowest in the country (Eswaran, 2006, 157). In addition, when women are more empowered, their children are not only healthier but have more access to education.

States also need to step in to provide better national security systems, retirement plans and elderly health care. Entwisle and Winegarden (1984) found strong evidence that state-sponsored pension programmes reduce

→

and Dougherty, 2007) but China has invested much more in education than India has. Literacy rates in China are much higher (95.1% compared to 74% in India), while poverty rates continue to be higher in India. However, a standout case is the Indian state of Kerala, where rural poverty declined from 59% in 1973–1974 to 12% in 1999–2010. Meanwhile literacy rates in Kerala steadily improved and now stand at 91.9%, the highest in the country.

fertility. By providing pensions, it is no longer important to have a large family so that the grown children provide care for their elderly parents. Retirement plans have a similar effect. In very poor countries there are few financial assets to transfer incomes from working to retirement. Parents therefore see children as essential to helping with security once they get older. For example, in the case of Malaysia, it was only after couples satisfied their perceived old age security needs that they opted to use contraception (Eswaran, 2006, 149).

The number of children born per woman has fallen by half in most countries. More opportunities for education lead to a *fertility transition*, which creates a virtuous cycle. Fertility transition is fertility rates becoming lower due to more opportunities for women in education and career advancement. Thus the more developed a country, the lower the fertility rates. The lower the fertility rates, the easier it is for women to enter the workforce and contribute to development.

Country	Fertility rates	GDP/capita nominal
Niger	6.89	$400
Mali	6.16	$700
Burundi	6.14	$300
Somalia	6.08	$600
Burkina Faso	5.93	$700
Zambia	5.76	$1,600
Malawi	5.66	$300
Angola	5.43	$6,600
South Sudan	5.43	$1,000
Afghanistan	5.43	$700
Mozambique	5.27	$600
Nigeria	5.25	$1,700
Ethiopia	5.23	$400
Timor Leste	5.11	$5,200
Benin	5.04	$800

Countries with the 15 highest fertility rates

Source: CIA Factbook 2014, available at: https://www.cia.gov/library/publications/the-world-factbook/rankorder/2127rank.html

The effects of education on wages are significant, particularly for girls (for more on how education is connected to fertility rates, see Box 5.1). One additional year of education leads to high returns for girls (increasing earnings by 12.4%) and for boys (increasing earnings by 11.1%). In Argentina, the ratio of wages for those who have a college degree to those of the average unskilled worker almost doubled for men and almost trebled for women (Banerjee et al., 2006, 89).

Vocational and technical education and training that is directly related to labour market needs is also associated with higher levels of productivity and growth (Tilak, 2007). Poor families are often not specialized enough in one particular field, which further contributes to chronic poverty. They may seek out countless economic opportunities but only work in short bursts and never develop special skills that can offer higher wages. This lack of specialization is costly for the poor. As can be seen later in the chapter, education is also connected to poverty because it has a strong impact on agricultural development (Tilak, 1994).

Education is not only connected to potential earnings, but also to good health. In both developed and developing countries there is a strong correlation between education and good health. Each additional year of schooling for men in the United States is associated with an 8% reduction in mortality rates, which is consistent across European countries as well. In the developing world people with greater levels of education also report that they are significantly healthier as well. Education leads to less risky choices of occupation, more understanding of sanitation and hygiene, more use of health-care systems and improved ability to read labels (Banerjee et al., 2006, 273). Once people learn how to protect themselves against germs, the mortality rates of children fell to 40% of the national average. In turn, healthier people are able to succeed better in the classroom leading to a channel from better health to more schooling.

Malnourishment

In addition to low literacy and primary school enrolment rates, a large portion of the population in the developing world suffer from poor health. As Chapter 11 will demonstrate, diseases, such as HIV/AIDS, malaria and other neglected tropical diseases, have disastrous effects on the poor. Paying for health care can deplete savings and lead to many days of lost productivity and unearned income. The costs of disease are addressed in more depth in Chapter 11. Just as pressing as the prevalence of disease, is the issue of malnourishment. According to the United Nations Food and Agriculture Organization (UNFAO), nearly 870 million people are suffering from chronic undernourishment. Almost all the hungry people, 852 million, live in developing countries. While the number of malnourished people has decreased in Asia and the Pacific from 739 million in 1990 to 563 million in 2012, over the same period Africa has seen a rise in the number of malnourished from 175 million to 239 million. Despite being the second biggest grower of rice and wheat, in India 224.6 million people (or over 20% of the population) are malnourished.

Chronic food insecurity and malnutrition lead to reduced physical capacity and stunting. It inhibits learning, affects future incomes and has long-term health- and productivity-related effects for future generations (Moore, 2001; Banerjee et al., 2011, 31–32). Nutrition is especially important in early childhood and pregnancy. Malnutrition among pregnant women leads to low birth rates for their new-born babies, with one in six born underweight. Proper pre-natal care and nutrition has long-lasting effects on health and economic well-being (United Nations Food and Agriculture Organization). Children who suffer from malnutrition suffer more illnesses, up to 160 days a year. Nutrition affects child mortality rates of at least 50% of the nearly 11 million children under five who die each year. Every disease that children are afflicted with is negatively affected by malnutrition (World Hunger Organization).

Vitamin A deficiencies cause blindness and reduce the body's ability to reduce diseases. As many as 500,000 children in the developing world become blind each year due to Vitamin A deficiencies. More than 32% of children in developing countries face stunted growth issues, caused by Vitamin A deficiencies. Iron deficiencies are also a problem (United Nations Food and Agriculture Organization).

Over 30% of the world's population is anaemic due to iron deficiencies. Iron deficiencies make it more difficult to fight off worm infections and malaria. Iron deficiencies also cause problems with cognitive development and lower school performance. For pregnant women, anaemia is a factor in 20% of all maternal deaths (WHO).

Iodine deficiencies also cause serious problems, such as stillbirths, congenital abnormalities and mental retardation. It affects intellectual abilities and school performance, and affects 13% of the world's population. As many as 50 million people are mentally impaired due to iodine deficiency. In Tanzania, women who did not receive enough iodine while pregnant gave birth to children who would receive 30–50% less schooling compared to their siblings.

Malnutrition is associated with lower levels of economic status as people do not have enough resources to alleviate hunger. In turn, malnutrition affects productivity, making it harder for impoverished people to earn enough to feed themselves. For example, jobs in agriculture that entail working long hours of manual labour require more caloric intake than most jobs. Not surprisingly, undernourished farm workers have lower levels of productivity (Datt and Ravallion, 1998).

Little access to health care

In addition to hosting many people who are malnourished, many countries in the developing world lack an extensive public health-care system that can reach the poor. When health care is needed but is delayed or not obtained, people's health worsens, which in turn leads to lost income and higher health-care costs, both of which contribute to poverty. The relationship between poverty and access to health care can be seen as part of a larger cycle, where poverty leads to ill health and ill health maintains poverty (Peters et al., 2008, 161).

Free and effective primary and secondary health care or effective insurance to enable payment for health care is very important for lifting the chronically poor out of poverty. Studies have demonstrated that the poor are positively affected by public spending on health care (Bidani and Ravallion, 1997). Yet the costs of health care continue to rise for the poor, due to the introduction of user fees (McIntyre et al., 2006). In Nigeria, 70% of health-care payments are paid for out of pocket (Amaghionyeodiwe, 2009, 221). In the developing world, the total economic costs of illnesses for households are above 10% of household income. In Sri Lanka the monthly household costs of health care is 11.5% of income and it's 11% in Nigeria (McIntyre et al., 2006, 861). The total costs of malaria per year are as much as 18% of annual income in Kenya and 13% in Nigeria. In a study in the Ivory Coast, the average household income declines by 52–67% when a household member becomes ill with AIDS and household expenditures on health care quadruples (Aliber, 2003, 482). These costs impose large and uneven costs on households, with the poor bearing the brunt as they are forced to forgo health care altogether. Poor households are also less likely to get medical treatment for themselves or their children (Banerjee and Duflo, 2007). In a 1997 study examining 35 countries, Bidani and Ravallion found that the poor have significantly worse health status than the non-poor (Amaghionyeodiwe, 2009, 223). Thus the inability to pay for health-care costs helps to explain why this is the case.

The reason why the poor forgo health care is that they have few options available to them to pay for it. Coping strategies include reducing food consumption, selling assets such as land or livestock and/or borrowing from family, friends or a moneylender. Tasks are also reallocated among household members, and often children are removed from school to take on the work activities of a sick parent (McIntyre et al., 2006, 862).

A study by David Hulme (2003) of a single chronically poor household in Bangladesh is illustrative of the poverty trap. A woman, whose husband is terminally ill, depleted all of her assets to pay for medical expenses. The situation for her is made worse when her father-in-law seized the land of the household. As a result she is unable to pay for food costs, which affects her capacity to be productive. The lack of health-care provision was a critical factor to blame for her descent into chronic poverty (Hulme and Shepherd, 2003, 408).

Little access to electricity, water and sanitation

The availability of physical infrastructure to the poor like electricity, tap water and even basic sanitation (like access to a latrine) presents another obstacle for the poor to overcome.

In a study in rural Udaipur in India, there is no access to tap water or a latrine for the poor. In rural Indonesia, Papua New Guinea, East Timor and South Africa, less than 6% of poor households have access to tap water. In rural parts of Guatemala, only 36% of the poor have access to tap water. Only 1.3% of rural households have access to electricity in Tanzania, while only 6% have access to electricity in rural Udaipur. For the rural poor in Guatemala, only 30% have access to electricity (Banerjee and Duflo, 2007).

The lack of power, transport and communications services is also critical to development. According to the International Energy Agency, 1.5 billion people do not have access to electricity. This has implications for education and sanitation. This means that there are no classes that can be taken at night, no computers can be used for learning, there are no pumps for safe water well usage, no mills to process food, no refrigeration for food and no medicine storage.

While not having access to electricity is problematic, not having safe drinking water and sanitation also has a wide-reaching impact. Over 1 billion people do not have access to clean water and 2.5 billion people lack access to sanitation (UNDESA, 2014. Not having safe drinking water uses up valuable productive hours of the poor in carrying and collecting water. Unsafe water in turn increases the spread of diseases and poor sanitation exacerbates these illnesses.

No safety nets

The poverty trap is also reinforced by the absence of effective safety nets such as insurance and social security. The poor deal with constant uncertainty and insecurity, as their incomes fluctuate all the time. Poor people have very few buffers against shocks and few poor households have savings accounts (Banerjee and Duflo, 2007). Most people can bounce back from a shock but the poor do so at a rate that is comparably much slower. The absence of effective public social protection means that social networks and private liquid assets are incredibly important. Thus the poor have to rely on their own resources to pursue security, but by doing so they undermine their chances of lifting themselves out of poverty.

Those who are uninsured are unwilling to take any risks even though this behaviour may be costly in the long term. Due to high risks, the poor devote whatever savings they have into non-productive assets as insurance, such as grain stocks, animals or gold and jewellery, reducing their investments in more productive activities. The need for these precautionary savings reduces growth opportunities of the poor and creates poverty traps. For example, poor farmers in rural India are less likely to invest in irrigation equipment than in cattle, though there is a much higher rate of return on the former. Cattle can be sold during times of need whereas pumps cannot. This leads to outmoded agricultural technologies being used simply because they are less risky. Risk causes impoverished people to have high levels of unproductive liquid wealth (Rosenzweig and Wolpin, 1993, 211). The poor use the liquid wealth to protect them so that if there is a sudden drop in income the liquid wealth insures them. The poor also have to avoid taking risks that could be profitable because they have little access to formal insurance (Banerjee and Duflo, 2007). The lack of insurance also leads the poor to underinvest in risky but profitable technologies, such as new seeds (Banerjee and Duflo, 2007).

The lack of social security also reinforces the poverty trap because it undermines the demographic transition from taking place. With little social security available, many impoverished families feel that they must continue to have large families in order to provide some social safety net for themselves when they get older. *High fertility rates*, in turn make it more difficult for the poor to take care of their families, while demographic growth pushes the state further into poverty (Sindzingre, 2004, 18).

Landlessness

The majority of those who are chronically poor in the developing world are landless or near-landless. In South Africa, blacks living in rural areas have the greatest chance of being poor. In 1997 (out of a population of 43 million at the time) there were 900,000 African households that did not have access to arable land and 1.4 million that had no livestock other than chickens. Not having livestock is especially difficult since studies have shown that poor households rely on selling livestock to offset a financial crisis or shock (Ardington, 1988). Though many South Africans live in rural areas, they do not have the land or resources to survive as agriculturalists.

Land records in developing countries are often incomplete. Many poor people who own land do not have titles to their land. Thus, the poor spend a lot of time protecting their claims to their land. When poor do not own the land, they lack incentives to make the best use of the land that they are cultivating (Shaban, 1987). One study found that a reform of tenancy that forced landlords to raise the share of output going to the sharecroppers and also gave them a secure right to the land raised productivity by about 50% (Banerjee et al., 2002).

Many of the rural poor who are landless are stuck in low-wage jobs working long hours, which reinforce chronic poverty. For example, a labourer in India climbs date palm trees every day working 16 hours a day. He risks serious injury every day (since he could easily fall) and earns less than \$.14 a day. The low wages of the casual agricultural worker explains chronic poverty. Not surprisingly, poverty increases and decreases were connected to the wages of rural agricultural workers in India (Mehta and Shah, 2003, 494).

Inaccessibility of the poor

Most of those who are chronically poor live in rural remote areas that are inaccessible. This may be because they are geographically far from an urban area; they live in an area that is physically insecure and/or it is difficult to contact them by phone or email. Being inaccessible makes it more difficult for governments, international agencies and NGOs to reach out.

Living in rural remote areas means that food security may be more erratic as is the government's provision of education and health care. Transportation costs are high due to a lack of infrastructure. Most of Zimbabwe's poorest people live in remote rural areas (Bird and Shepherd, 2003). The cost of reducing poverty for the chronically poor is high and the state often neglects the rural poor simply because it is too costly to reach them (Hulme and Shepherd, 2003, 417).

It is the ranks at the bottom that are in the most need of intervention that are also the hardest to reach. It is not just the state that may have great difficulty reaching the poor, but international agencies and NGOs as well. For example, NGOs may go out of their way to avoid the poorest groups simply because they may see their programmes as less apt to make an impact on them. A study in Bangladesh reported that in the mid-1990s as many as 41% of all eligible households did not have any contact with the NGOs operating in the localities (Husain, 1998). NGO micro-finance programmes were also reported to exclude those that are the most impoverished. Almost 75% of those who experience the deepest deprivation have never received social development services from NGOs. In much of the developing world, most of the NGOs that offer social development services such as health care or basic education do so through structures, which deliver microfinance that are not reaching the poorest groups (Matin and Hulme, 2003).

Poverty and the state

The previous section explained the relationship between poverty and development. Due to all of the aforementioned ways in which poverty challenges development, poverty also places great strain on institutions in the developing world, stretching the state and forcing it to react and respond to a host of hardships. Simply put, the state has much more that it needs to attend to.

No base for taxation

Poverty also affects the state's ability to collect revenues, which in turn makes it near-impossible (unless the state can rely on a steady supply of revenues from resources such as oil and gas) for the state to provide many services or develop administratively. Tax revenue as a proportion of GDP is typically much lower in developing countries than in rich countries (Auriol and Warlters, 2005, 625). For instance, direct taxation represents only 7% of GDP in Africa but 22% in industrial countries (Auriol and Warlters, 2005, 626).

Many states in the developing world that cannot directly tax their citizens and corporations have to resort to gaining a proportion of their revenues from taxes on international trade, which can slow down growth. In Africa almost one-third of all revenues come from international trade compared to almost zero for European countries and 1% for the United States. In Guinea, taxes on international trade represented 77% of its revenue. But given that Guinea is already extremely poor, any volatility in commodities has a huge impact on public revenues. Impoverished countries that cannot extract from incomes and profits from capital gains have to rely on commodities that can fluctuate, causing the fiscal budget to vary by as much as 100% within a fiscal year (Sindzingre, 2004, 13). This makes it difficult to invest in education, health care, infrastructure, electricity, agriculture, business and social security. This in turn has a direct impact on those who are impoverished.

Impoverished countries also have large informal sectors, which further aggravate taxation traps and weaken the state and its institutions. Impoverished countries usually develop a large *shadow economy* (see Box 7.1), which cannot be taxed. A study that looked at 76 countries in the developing world showed that the average size of the shadow economy was 39% of GDP compared to 12% in the OECD countries (Auriol and Warlters, 2005, 626). Because impoverished populations cannot rely on development opportunities, children often work in the informal labour market, contributing to the expansion of the informal sector (Sindzingre, 2004, 18). The ease of entry into the informal market attracts those with few opportunities to pursue education, though in many cases education is not available to them.

A vicious cycle develops where the state is too weak to help lift the impoverished out of poverty, and poor *entrepreneurs are too weak* to start businesses that have too many sunk costs. Official registration is too difficult and costly – beyond the reach of most poor entrepreneurs. Businesses run by the poor also tend to be very small in scale. Many of these businesses operate at too small a scale for efficiency (Banerjee and Duflo, 2007). As a result, no thriving businesses exist that can be taxed by the state to help keep the state's budget healthy (Auriol and Warlters, 2005, 627).

Dealing with poverty: a focus on agriculture

We acknowledge that there are a host of strategies to tackle poverty reduction. Here we focus on the role of *administrative agencies* committed to rural development. Before doing so, we provide an in-depth overview as to why it is so important for developing countries to emphasize agricultural development.

Previous policies have advocated that economic growth will automatically reduce poverty. As stated earlier in the chapter, studies showed that growth that is generated by market-friendly policies would trickle down to positively affect the poor by creating more employment opportunities. Though focusing on economic growth is important, the causal error may not be that growth alleviates poverty, but that poverty reduction stimulates growth. If this is so, poverty reduction should go further than encouraging market forces in poverty reduction.

Past approaches have focused on offering protection to reduce vulnerabilities for the poor by providing single interventions such as handouts like food aid. The 1980s and 1990s saw a global shift away from focusing on protection approaches to promotional approaches such as 'workfare'. This shift was shaped by neo-liberal philosophies that cautioned against the moral hazard of welfare dependency. Promotion approaches emphasized finding a way to help the poor increase their income, productivity and overall prospects. In the sections that follow, we offer ways in which the state can contribute to poverty alleviation as well as NGOs. We focus entirely on the role of agriculture. In a Nobel Lecture, Theodore Schultz highlighted why focusing on agriculture is so important: 'Most of the world's poor people earn their living from agriculture, so if we knew the economics of agriculture we would know much of the economics of being poor' (1980, 639). Over 85% of those in absolute poverty live in rural areas. Thus, the idea that poverty is largely a rural phenomenon should not be surprising (Dercon, 2009). In spite of this, rural poverty still continues to be neglected by states. More recent works note urban biases in contemporary development policy (Rola-Rubzen et al., 2001; The World Bank, 2003; Byerlee et al., 2005).

Scholars now argue that agricultural growth is clearly connected to poverty reduction, and it is much more effective than other sectors at reducing poverty and hunger in both urban and rural areas. In cases where agricultural GDP grew, it contributed positively to poverty reduction in 20 out of 25 countries (Christiansen and Demery, 2007). A 1996 study by Ravallion and Datt concluded that 85% of poverty reduction in India was due to agricultural growth. This is particularly important if there is more equal land distribution (Ravallion, 1997).

Scholars in the past did not always emphasize the importance of agriculture. In the 1960s and 1970s, development scholars and practice neglected agriculture, and emphasized import substitution industrialization and export promotion instead. More often scholars claimed that economic growth was motored by industrialization and manufacturing. It was advised that with economic progress, agriculture as a share of GDP naturally declines (Timmer, 1988; Byerlee et al., 2009; Cervantes-Godoy and Dewbre, 2010). Lewis (1955) argued that agriculture was an area of low productivity with low use of modern technology, while modern industrial sectors were associated with higher levels of productivity. Lewis's theory was used to justify state support for industrialization and protection of domestic industries, while taxing the agricultural sector (Kirkpatrick and Barrientos, 2004). The literature regarding the deteriorating terms of trade for agriculture reinforced these types of policies. Known as the *urban bias*, policymakers often favoured urban areas over rural areas (Lipton, 1977). Manufactured goods are protected while the costs of industrial inputs to agriculture are still kept too high, squeezing out farmers, affecting agricultural production (Eswaran and Kotwal, 2006, 119). The results of these policies were disastrous for growth, however (Ravallion, 1997). Not surprisingly, anti-agricultural price policies are associated with slower agricultural growth (Schiff and Valdes, 1992).

Beginning in the 1960s, a major revision in development thinking argued for a central role for agriculture as a driver of growth, especially in the early stages of industrialization (Johnston and Mellor, 1961; Valenzuela and Anderson, 2008). This view of agriculture's lead role, stimulated in large part by the emerging experience in Asia, was founded on two core contributions. First, it was recognized by leading scholars (such as Schultz, 1964 and Hayami and Ruttan, 1971) that traditional agriculture could be transformed rapidly into a modern sector through the adoption of science-based technology, thereby making a large contribution to overall growth. Second, economists now explicitly identified the strong growth linkages and multiplier effects of agricultural growth to the non-agricultural sectors (Mellor, 1999).

Scholars argued that a large share of manufacturing in the early stages of development is agriculturally related. More importantly, rising incomes of rural households were seen as vital to providing a market for domestically produced manufactures and services (Adelman, 1984). In addition, technological change and productivity growth in agriculture were linked to lower food prices in a closed economic model, which in turn held down urban wage costs and stimulated competitive exports of industrial products (De Janvry and Sadoulet, 2010). It was also emphasized that just focusing on urban-based formal sector manufacturing will not reduce poverty. Formal sector manufacturing growth is very capital intensive and may result in more people migrating to urban areas but not finding employment, leading to higher urban poverty. In China, where land is relatively equally distributed, the reduction in poverty was almost four times higher from GDP growth originating in agriculture than from GDP growth originating in industry or services (Ravallion and Chen, 2007).

Agricultural income growth is so effective in reducing poverty because poverty tends to be highest in agricultural and rural populations, most of whom depend on agriculture for their livelihoods (Christiansen and Demery, 2007; Ravallion and Chen, 2007; World Bank, 2007). Though poverty can be reduced through remittances and some migration from farm to non-farm areas for work, 80% of poverty reduction is due to economic improvements in rural areas including agriculture. Agriculture increases growth rates, directly improves rural incomes, creates employment, provides for cheaper food for both urban and rural poor, generates opportunities in the non-farm sectors and creates more demands.

Agricultural exports can also be a major source of growth. Rapid agricultural development helped Vietnam reduce its poverty rates, as it has had success exporting coffee (van de Walle and Cratty, 2004). Ghana has had success in improving its productivity in cocoa, which has played a role in poverty reduction since 1995. Agricultural productivity also increases employment. The state can also emphasize agricultural products that stimulate demand for agricultural labour (Mellor, 1999). Thus, though agriculture may not contribute to the GDP, it plays an important role in reducing poverty through the labour market.

Agricultural productivity growth also contributes to poverty reduction by stimulating rural non-farm growth, especially where infrastructure and the investment climate are already in place (Hazell and Haggblade, 1991; Barnes and Binswanger, 1986). In India and Indonesia, growth in rural services was estimated 'to contribute at least as much growth in agriculture toward reducing poverty' (World Bank, 2007, 37). Most of the poor are engaged in agriculture in Africa and Asia. A boom in commercial agriculture boosts demand for marketing, transportation, construction and finance. In Africa every $1 a day in the farm sector generates an extra $1.50 in non-farm sector, and an extra $1.80 in Asia. When agricultural productivity increases, consumers can become richer and start to demand different types of goods and services, which are often domestically produced and non-tradable (Eswaran and Kotwal, 2006, 118).

Agricultural productivity also impacts poverty reduction through increasing staple food output (Mellor, 1999). Agricultural productivity growth especially for staple items can improve the nutritional status of many poor households. Better nutritional status improves overall labour productivity rates (Strauss, 1986; Behrman and Deolalikar, 1988). Studies have found that there is a significant relationship between the initial levels of food inadequacy or calorie per capita and overall growth rates (Arcand, 2001). Rising productivity increases rural incomes and lowers food prices, making food more accessible to the poor.

Major success stories in poverty reduction have taken place with investment in broad-based agricultural growth, then leading to spillovers to non-agricultural sectors. In China, the state played a key role in fostering an environment where agriculture had a chance to thrive. Not surprisingly, many scholars (Ravallion and Chen, 2007; Montalvo and Ravallion, 2009) have noted that agriculture was the main engine behind China's spectacular success in poverty alleviation. In China's case, the state's astute handling of the agricultural sector lifted 400 million people out of poverty (Huang et al., 2006).

China relied heavily on agricultural development using broad-based agricultural technological improvements and local infrastructure investments and rural education. Increased rural incomes led to increases in demand for other products that were provided also by the rural-based small-scale but labour-intensive industries. China began its strategy of liberalizing prices on agriculture in 1979. Agricultural communes were then given greater autonomy and incentives. The results were impressive. While agricultural production doubled, the number of poor people declined from 250 million in 1978 to 125 million by 1985, and to less than 100 million in the mid-1990s. The proportion of people living below the poverty line decreased from 28% in 1978 to 9% in 1990 (Asian Development Bank, 2002). Thus, how the state handles agriculture is a critical factor to propel the country out of poverty.

Malaysia has physical agricultural resources that are similar to West Africa, yet it is a success story in terms of agricultural development, which has led to poverty reduction. The agricultural growth in Malaysia came from exporting cash crops like rubber and palm oil rather than food crops. However, Malaysia invested in research and rural infrastructure that led to huge yield increases and induced large income increases from many small producers of these products. Increased rice production increased rural incomes, which translated to increased non-farm employment as well (Mellor, 1999).

Thus for states in the developing world hoping to reduce poverty rates, neglecting agriculture is not an option. The state, namely the administrative agencies dedicated to rural development, can assist agriculture in numerous ways, such as providing access to credit, fertilizers and seeds; investment in education, agricultural research and extension and technology; and access to infrastructure such as transport and storage facilities (Carter et al., 2007, 853).

Providing credit and creating credit institutions is one way that the state can promote agriculture (Eswaran and Kotwal, 2006). Improving access to credit is often regarded as one of the key elements in raising agricultural productivity. The establishment of parastatal institutions with a mandate to channel credit to smallholder farmers is one of the approaches used by governments in developing countries to promote smallholder agricultural development. Credit can be used to purchase machinery needed to be more productive.

The state can also provide access to fertilizer, seeds and manures. Fertilizer access and other inputs such as green manures, crop covers, water harvesting and improved seeds can increase food yields. In spite of this, many small farmers do not make use of these inputs. In Kenya, for example, less than 20% of small farmers use fertilizer (Eswaran and Kotwal, 2006). For small farmers, using fertilizer is an investment because it requires some experimentation. It may lead to some losses in the first few years. Farmers that cannot afford a lot of fertilizer and can only use it on a small scale may consider it to be worthless to try to master the technology (Eswaran and Kotwal, 2006). For this reason, it is important for the government to assist farmers by providing subsidies for fertilizers. In countries such as Cameroon, Mali, Zambia, Tanzania, Pakistan and Vietnam, a reduction in state subsidies for fertilizer had a negative effect on small farmers. This led them to intensify agricultural production by trying to expand on agricultural lands, which accelerated deforestation and soil degradation (Reed, 1996, 314).

A long-term objective to tackle rural poverty is to invest in education, research and extension. The state can provide primary education to everyone so that the entire population is literate. It is also important to provide training to farmers in order to help them understand how to make the most of the technology that is available to them given what their needs are (Eswaran and Kotwal, 2006). Agricultural productivity enhancing measures such as providing infrastructure and new technologies will produce higher returns when implemented in conjunction with improved education. Irrigation equipment was found to be more efficient by better educated farmers in Vietnam (van de Walle, 2000). The human capital and institutional base of smallholder agriculture must be strengthened for long-term growth in this sector and to attack rural poverty in a sustainable manner.

The state also plays a role in increasing the levels of technology in agriculture. The application of scientific research and new knowledge to agricultural practices is known as *agricultural extension*. As farmers gain access to new technology, this in turn creates new demands for intensive inputs, increased need for credit and a steadier water supply. Improvements in technology have thus far benefited richer farmers more so than the poor since rich are more likely to be literate. This then enables them to better understand how the new technology works. Investment in research and development for agriculture tends to have large geographical spillovers, creating high rates of returns for such investments.

The state can also help out with investing in infrastructure. Rural infrastructure, including roads, water supply, electricity, telecommunications and storage facilities, is very important for the development of agriculture, for fostering reliable markets and agro-processing, and especially for realizing the full potential of the growth linkages of agriculture to the entire rural sector. Public expenditure reviews by the World Bank have shown very little shift in emphasis by governments from urban infrastructure to rural infrastructure, and the latter continues to be neglected in government budgets.

The World Bank has begun a major African rural infrastructure initiative which would allocate responsibility for management of construction and maintenance to local government bodies, and use private contractors to undertake most works, yet this has not led to large levels of investment. For many states in Africa, linking rural infrastructure investments with agricultural growth remains the weakest part of the agricultural development strategy. Ethiopia has the world's lowest ratio of roads per person. About 90% of the population lives in the highlands which are inaccessible (Webb and von Braun, 1994). Inadequate physical infrastructure in rural areas, particularly in the former homeland areas, remains a major obstacle to smallholder agricultural growth in South Africa.

The case of Zimbabwe illustrates the impact of the state in providing support for small farmers. In the 1980s, when the state used to provide support to farmers in Zimbabwe through agricultural extension, finance and marketing services, smallholder farmers were able to double maize and cotton production. Smallholder farmers in Zimbabwe tripled maize production between 1980 and 1987 and increased their share of the national marketable maize surplus from 10% in 1980 to 40% in 1987 (Rukuni and Eicher, 1994). By the 2000s this support had dissipated. Zimbabwe went from being the breadbasket of Africa to badly needing food aid for over half of the country in 2002.

Thus, agriculture is an area where the state can utilize promotional strategies to help the rural poor generate income. In the case study that follows, we offer an example of success in what NGOs can do to help lift the rural poor out of chronic poverty.

Case study: Income Generation for Vulnerable Group Development (IGVGD) programme

In countries like Bangladesh many NGOs have moved from offering welfare and social protection to offering micro-finance to encourage self-employment (Matin and Hulme, 2003, 650). Nevertheless, the promotion strategies, just like the protection strategies before, are based on providing a single intervention. With promotion strategies, a single intervention may constitute giving microcredit to a poor person to build their own small enterprise. This should help increase their annual income and eventually lift that person out of poverty. But the provision of a single intervention to solve the issues for the chronically poor has not been a long-term solution. The strategy of providing single interventions assumes that poverty reduction is a one-step process.

The strategy of a single intervention may work for those who are moderately poor, but not for those who live in abject poverty. Thus, while microfinance has been an effective poverty-alleviating tool for many people in Bangladesh, demonstrating how poor people can help themselves, it may not be an immediate panacea for everyone. For those facing constant food insecurity with no way of protecting themselves from shocks, microfinance is not helpful. Microfinance has convinced NGOs to treat the poor as a homogenous group who are ready to serve as entrepreneurs and have businesses ready to make profits from and have the skills ready to take advantage of small loans.

For promotion strategies to work they must be combined with some protection. More importantly, promotion strategies do not work without coupling opportunities with educational training. The success of the work-based programme in Bangladesh illustrates this point.

In 1974 a famine in Bangladesh led the United Nations World Food Programme (WFP) to create a Vulnerable Group Feeding Programme (VGF) to reduce chronic food insecurity for millions by providing the most impoverished and food-insecure population with wheat each month. In 1985 one of the largest NGOs in the world, the Bangladesh Rural Advancement Committee (BRAC), partnered up with the WFP to create a programme that combined food relief with skills training in order to build a foundation for households to earn income in the future. The new programme, which was called the Income Generation for Vulnerable Group Development (IGVGD) programme made it compulsory for any household that participated to save a compulsory amount per month in order to build up a sum to make an investment. After a two-year training programme, 750 women became eligible to access microcredit, health care, legal awareness and other services provided by BRAC. The results of the programme found that women increased their incomes significantly, exceeding the value of wheat donations. In comparison with the VGF programme, many participants were not better off when they left the programme compared to when they started. By 2000, more than 1.2 million households had passed through the programme (Matin and Hulme, 2003, 654).

The approach had three elements combining promotional approaches with protective approaches: food grants, skills training and microcredit. The programme also focuses on meeting those who are most vulnerable. Recipients must meet three criteria: they must be widowed or abandoned female heads of household, they must own less than 0.5 acres of land and earn less than $6 a month (Matin and Hulme, 2003, 654). BRAC also sought to integrate women from the IGVGD programme with other programmes that catered to women from higher income levels to alleviate the issues of social isolation of the poorest groups (Matin and Hulme, 2003).

Promotion will raise incomes while protection will prevent a decline in living standards (such as hunger and starvation). Effective protection makes promotion more likely since the poor will have more confidence to take risks and engage in higher return economic activities to raise income levels. And a rise in income means that there are more resources available for the poor to protect themselves.

Conclusion

Lifting the chronically poor out of poverty (or overcoming poverty traps) does not take place overnight, nor is it a linear process. There will be reversals, which means that a range of measures (such as emergency loans and basic health care) to protect the most impoverished should be available. Poverty reduction is also facilitated by improving social safety nets, such as insurance, social security and access to credit. There are important benefits from institutions that protect people from shocks or provide temporary support for the most impoverished. It is also important to focus on long-term solutions for building human capital. This includes building a more extensive health-care system and providing education, both basic and vocational, that the poor can benefit from to take advantage of opportunities. The state can also play an important role in ensuring that agriculture is not neglected. Agricultural development is critical to ensuring the livelihood of those living in poverty. This coupled with improving the effectiveness of the state to collect revenues can help build up fiscal health of the state so that it is better able to provide more extensive support to its most needy citizens. A final comment is that reaching the chronically poor is very difficult. Programmes need to make one of their priorities reaching the most deeply impoverished instead of deliberately excluding them (Matin and Hulme, 2003).

Questions

- What are the different ways of measuring poverty? What are the strengths and weaknesses of using these different measurements?
- What is meant by a market-based poverty reduction strategy?
- What is a poverty trap? Why are the various reasons why poverty traps endure?
- In what ways does poverty place a strain on the state?
- Why is agriculture so important for alleviating poverty? In what ways can administrative institutions help to alleviate rural poverty?

Facts

- The poverty line is usually estimated as 50% below the country's average income.
- 580 million people are affected by chronic poverty.
- The number of children born per woman has fallen by half in most countries.
- Nutrition affects child mortality rates of at least 50% of the nearly 11 million children who die under the age of five each year.
- Many scholars have argued that agricultural growth is clearly connected to poverty reduction.

Chapter 6

Intractable Instability

Since 1946, Yemen has experienced five coups, a civil war so devastating that from 1968 to 1990 the state was split into two (the Yemen Arab Republic and the People's Democratic Republic of Yemen, the latter of which also experienced its own civil war in 1986), another civil war in 1994, and a revolution in 2011 following clashes with protestors and security forces that killed over 2,000 people. In other words, Yemen has been plagued by instability and violence.

This pattern of repeated episodes of instability that seem to evade resolution are often called intractability. Intractable instability, simply put, is difficult to get rid of. States find themselves mired in an endless cycle of instability, where conflict, tension and violence become commonplace.

Instability, broadly speaking, refers to 'a condition in political systems in which the institutionalized patterns of authority break down and the expected compliance to political authorities is replaced by political violence' (Morrison and Stevenson, 1971, 348). It can occur at the elite level, like with coups, at the communal level, like with civil wars, and at the mass level, like with revolutions. In this chapter, we focus on the first two types of instability – coups and civil wars – because they occur with the most frequency in the developing world.

Instability, of course, takes a toll on development. Take Yemen, for example. Yemen is the poorest state in the Middle East, with 39% of its population living below the poverty line (Country Profile Yemen). Many of its neighbours, like Saudi Arabia and Qatar, have had far fewer episodes of violence and are some of the richest states in the world.

Repeated episodes of instability damage infrastructure, deter investment and decrease productivity. States that are prone to instability experience lower growth rates than those that are not (Londegran and Poole, 1990; Alesina and Perotti, 1996; Blomberg and Hess, 2002; Collier, 1999). And like with all of the development hurdles discussed in this study, the causal arrow runs both ways: not only does instability make poverty more likely, but poverty is also a trigger for instability. Researchers have developed the terms 'coup trap' (Collier and Hoeffler, 2005) and 'conflict trap' (Collier, 2007) due to the cyclical nature in which coups and civil wars occur and the difficulties states encounter in trying to break free from repeated episodes of each.

To break free from the cycle of instability and poverty requires both the will to do so and institutional structures to guide the process. Though all of the institutional domains of the state can play a role, security institutions – the arm of the state with control over the use of force – are particularly important. High-quality security institutions are less likely to stage coups, factionalize into warring opponents, and turn a blind eye to civilian acts of violence on the streets.

This chapter begins by discussing what coups and civil wars are and the ways in which they each harm economic performance. It then looks at approaches that have been used thus far to minimize intractable instability, emphasizing the role that state institutions can play in stopping the cycle.

Instability

There are a number of ways in which instability can manifest itself. Instability can take the form of civil wars, involving separatist movements, revolutionary movements or other types of insurgencies. Instability is also reflected in the high frequency of coups, coup attempts and assassinations. Other indicators of instability are terrorist incidents, assassinations, kidnappings and violent crime (for more information on crime and its effects, see Box 6.1). Finally, riots and violent demonstrations are also signs of instability. We focus on *coups* and *civil wars* because they are frequent occurrences in the developing world and detrimental for development.

Coups

A coup is a quick 'infiltration of a small but critical segment of the state apparatus, which is then used to displace the government from its control of the remainder' (Luttwak, 1979, 26–27). Coups are carried out by individuals, who are part of the state, nearly always members of the military forces. Civilians may back or press for coups, but they are usually not involved in carrying them out. Though they are often spearheaded by members of the military elite, coups carried out by junior officers in the military are not uncommon. Coups often only require a handful of individuals to be successful.

The military is the group that typically levies a coup because coups require proper training and coordination (Luttwak, 1979). To be successful, coup plotters must be able to follow instructions and have organizational unity. These are features of many militaries, which often have established hierarchies and chains of command. Beyond these

Box 6.1 Violent crime and development: Latin America and the Caribbean

Historically, Latin America and the Caribbean have often been considered very violent areas of the world, marked by multiple instances of 'political disappearances, repressive dictatorship, torture, death squads, and revolutions'. Crime is so prevalent that the levels of violence are comparable to periods of war. Latin America has broken from its authoritarian past, but it has not eradicated the violence that continues to mark social and political life in many Latin American countries (Koonings and Kruijt, 2004, 1). Low-intensity internal wars persist and crime remains rampant. Violence in Latin America has occurred between authoritarian regimes and armed groups, illegal economic cartels, corrupt elites and the poor masses. All of this violence perpetuates an uncivil society, weakens institutions and undermines development (Aguirre, 2006).

Latin America is home to several countries with some of the highest homicide rates in the world: Honduras with 87 homicides out of 100,000 people, El Salvador with 71, Venezuela with 67, Belize with 39, Guatemala with 39, Colombia with 33, Dominican Republic with 31, Brazil with 26 and Mexico with 18 (UNODC Homicide Statistics). Latin America experienced a 40% increase in the homicide rate from the 1970s to the 1990s. Latin America has a homicide rate that is four times the rate of other developing regions. A World Bank report claimed that criminal violence situation was so bad that it was 'the single major obstacle to the realization of the region's long-standing aspirations for sustainable economic and social development'. Crime rates have increased each decade for the region as a whole. The absolute number of crimes more than tripled between 1990 and 2003, with homicides, rapes and assaults rising by 460% (Rodgers, 2004, 5).

Violence impacts development in many ways. Crime adversely affects the stock of physical capital by destroying physical infrastructure – roads, public facilities and major installations such as electric power generating facilities. Crime and violence have a negative impact on the overall investment climate. Crime also reduces investment in physical infrastructure. In Colombia for example, high homicide rates have lessened gross capital formation by 38% had they remained at their 1970 level. Jamaica's tourism industry has stagnated because of a lack of new investment in hotels and tourism infrastructure caused by increasing crime and violence.

Crime and violence also erode the development of human capital. Victims of crime and violence are more likely to be absent from work. Violent crime prevents children from attending school. A World Bank poverty assessment survey of Jamaica found that 30% of girls surveyed said that they were afraid to go to school due to threats of crime and violence. The educational quality is affected by an atmosphere of violence. A study of the Caribbean and Latin America assessed that the net accumulation of capital has been cut in half due to an increase in crime and violence over the past 15 years (Ayres, 1998, 7–8).

requirements, the military also has the means to stage a coup: trained troops and weaponry (O'Kane, 1989).

Coups are often associated with violence, but in reality nearly 80% do not involve bloodshed (Zimmerman, 1979, 435). Though violence is not essential for coups to be successful, the threat that it will be used to accomplish the plotters' goals must be credible.

Coups are essentially unconstitutional seizures of power. Rather than let institutionalized rules guide the political process, coups reflect decisions by the military (and in some instances the civilians working with them) to determine who will run the government. They are often a manifestation of dissatisfaction with how the government is working. That being said, the goals of coup plotters vary quite a bit from one case to the next. In some instances, plotters simply want a leadership change, while in others they seek to fundamentally transform the system. Some coups are driven by the preferences of a small group within the military, while others are levied by military actors acting in accordance with the demands of a disgruntled citizenry.

Theories of coups

There is a large and varied literature dedicated to the causes of coups. Here we focus on three key factors that increase the chance of coups: economic conditions, personal ambitions and threats to the military as an institution (Ezrow and Frantz, 2011).

The first factor associated with coup risk is poor economic conditions. Coups are nearly 21 times more likely to happen in a poor state than in a rich one. In fact, 'coups are virtually non-existent in developed countries' (Londegran and Poole, 1990, 151). Compare this to the developing world, where between 1945 and 1985 about half of all states experienced at least one coup (Belkin and Schofer, 2003). One reason for this may be that in poor states, governments do not have the resources to ensure that the military is properly funded, mobilizing the military to voice their dissatisfaction through a coup. Economic downturns also provoke coups. Poor economic performance can lead to societal unrest, including strikes and protests, which can in turn pressure the military into staging a coup to restore order (Welch and Smith, 1974). Economic mismanagement can also trigger a coup because it may cause the military to view the government as incompetent. The military may see itself as more capable of handling the economy than civilians, as in the case of the coup that ousted Salvador Allende in 1973 in Chile.

The second factor that increases the chance of a coup is personal ambitions. According to Samuel Decalo (1973), coups often happen because coup plotters have a lust for power. Though the stated motivation for the coup may be to restore order, the underlying driver is the seizure of the leadership post. There are a number of examples of this. In Dahomey (now Benin), Colonel Christophe Soglo staged a coup in 1963 because Dahomey Unity Party leader Justin Ahomadégbé had humiliated him. In the Central African Republic, as well, David Dacko was ousted by his cousin, Jean-Bedel Bokassa, in 1965, whose ambitions for the leadership post were well known. Idi Amin's 1971 ouster of Milton Obote of Uganda also fits this story. Amin feared that Obote was going to demote him, making this a 'classic case of a personalized takeover caused by a General's own fears and ambitions, within the context of a widespread civic malaise and a fissiparous fratricidal army rife with corporate grievances' (Decalo, 1973, 112).

The third factor that triggers coups is threats to the military as an institution (Welch, 1972; Bienen, 1974; Zimmerman, 1979). When members of the military fear that the government is trying to intervene in their sphere or reduce their influence, they often stage a coup to prevent further meddling down the road. There are a number of government actions that can make the military feel threatened, including cuts to military budgets; interference in military promotions, salaries or other affairs; and the creation of rival security forces (Needler, 1975; Nordlinger, 1977).

A number of examples illustrate this. In Ghana, Kofi Busia's decision to cut the military budget by 10% prompted a coup led by Colonel Ignatius Acheampong in 1972 (Nordlinger, 1977). In Guatemala, as well, Jacobo Arbenz created a new military force as a rival to the regular military, which then opted not to defend Arbenz in the face of the threat posed by invading forces led by Carlos Castillo Armas in 1954 (Needler, 1975). As one researcher puts it, defence of the military's interests is 'easily the most important interventionist motive' (Nordlinger, 1977, 65).

Coup trends

Coups are fairly common in the developing world due to the role of poverty as a trigger, as mentioned earlier. For more on how leaders attempt to prevent coups, see Box 6.2, *coup-proofing*. It is perhaps not surprising then that coups have been particularly frequent in Sub-Saharan Africa, where, as some researchers estimate, nearly 85% of states have experienced either a coup or a coup attempt (McGowan, 2003). Between 1956 and 1984, half of all coups and a third of all attempted coups were in Africa (McGowan and Johnson, 1986; Agyeman-Duah, 1998). Coups were once common occurrences in Latin America, due to the prevalence of military dictatorships in that region during the 1960s, 1970s and 1980s, but since most of that region democratized in the 1980s and on, they have become far less frequent. The 2009 coup in Honduras, for example, shocked most observers. Coups have been comparatively less common in Asia, with the exception of Thailand (which has experienced more coups than any other country); they have also been rare in Eastern Europe. While Iraq, Yemen and Turkey have experienced a number of coups, the frequency of coups is also relatively low in the Middle East.

It is also worth pointing out that since the end of the Cold War, the number of coups in the world has decreased considerably (Marinov and Goemans, 2013; Frantz and Kendall-Taylor, 2014). There are two reasons for this (Marinov and Goemans, 2013). Cold War dynamics led to more coups as many states in the developing world were caught in the struggle for power between the United States and the Soviet Union at that time. With the end of the Cold War, external support for many military regimes declined, undermining their ability to maintain power. The reduction in the prevalence of military regimes affects the frequency of coups because coups have been the primary means of leadership turnover in these regimes. In addition, recent research has also suggested that the end of the Cold War increased Western commitment to defend democracy, for example by punishing those who attempt to bring down elected incumbents. Since 1997, for example, an act of Congress has bound US presidents to suspend foreign aid if a recipient country experiences a coup. The European Union made a similar commitment in 1991. Research contends that these post-Cold War policies have led to a decline in the frequency of coups by lowering the payoffs that would-be coup plotters expect to gain by seizing power.

Coup traps

Research has shown that once a state has experienced a coup, the likelihood of another one occurring increases significantly (Londegran and Poole, 1990; Limongi et al., 1996).This is referred to as the coup trap. As a result, past coups are a good predictor of future coups. The shockwaves and increased coup risk following a coup can last for up to six years (Londegran and Poole, 1990).

There are several reasons why one coup can propel additional ones. The first is that states can develop a political culture in which military interventions become viewed as acceptable methods for transferring power (Londegran and Poole, 1990). In states that have never experienced coups, by contrast, plotters may be more hesitant to stage one to reach their goals. Second, militaries are more likely to view coups as a tool to mitigate disputes once coups have already been used to do so in the past. In many states, coups lead to more coups and the time intervals between them is very short. A number of states in Africa, for example,

Box 6.2 Coup-proofing

States in the developing world often have weak security institutions. Sometimes this is a result of the state being so weak that it is unable to develop a strong security force. However, in other cases, the leader deliberately weakens the security institutions in order to prevent the security apparatus from staging a coup. Better known as coup-proofing, this is a common strategy of leaders in the developing world to maintain themselves in power.

Coup-proofing can include interfering with recruitment and promotion of members of the military. Instead of recruiting the best and most capable members of society to serve in the military, the leader deliberately chooses those who have little potential to serve as a threat. In some cases this includes only recruiting members of a certain ethnic group, clan or religious sect. For example, the Beti tribe of Cameroon were the only ethnic group recruited into the military under Paul Biya. President Gnassingbé Eyadéma of Togo only recruited the Kabre (Howe, 2001, 39). In some cases only family members are promoted to high-level positions within the military. In other instances, foreign mercenaries are used, such as has been the case in many states in the Gulf.

In addition to poor recruitment methods, the lines of promotion and demotion are constantly interfered with by the leader. Leaders may force officers from their same-age cohort into early retirement to increase the status distance separating them from any eventual rivals. In Somalia under Siad Barre, his top military personnel were constantly being shuffled around to prevent any one person from gaining too much power.

Coup-proofing also entails deliberately providing little to no training for the military. For example, Sudan's forces are mainly ill-trained conscripts (Howe, 2001, 45). Some countries in the developing world have turned down opportunities to have their military staff professionally trained to tackle genuine security threats. Nigeria turned down riverine training opting instead to hoard military aid and bribe the military with special perks (Howe, 2001, 42).

Another common coup-proofing strategy is creating parallel military organizations with overlapping responsibilities. The parallel military's main objective is to offset the regular army to prevent it from staging a coup. Parallel militaries are often supplied with better weapons and training. This siphons away funds from the regular army, which renders it less capable of dealing with security challenges effectively. In Gabon, Omar Bongo employed his 'Corsican Mafia' to serve as a counterbalance to his regular army (Howe, 2001, 45). Kenya's General Services Unit was capable of defeating the entire army by itself (Howe, 2001, 44).

→

In addition to a parallel military organization, leaders may create a presidential guard. The presidential guard is often comprised of the most well-trained professionals in the country. In most cases, the members of the presidential guard are recruited from a particular ethnic group or tribe that is close to the leader. But they are not equipped with ensuring national security, only regime security. In Guinea, the presidential guards under Colonel Lansana Conté were said to be mostly Sousou, the same ethnic group as Conté (Kudamatsu, 2009, 8). The army in Mauritania under President Maaouya Ould Sid'Ahmed Taya was no match for the presidential guard, Bataillon autonome de sécurité présidentielle (BASEP). BASEP was an elite battalion that was better equipped and trained. It was recruited from among tribes thought to be loyal to Ould Taya, such as the Smassides and the Terkez (N'Diaye, 2005, 431).

A final tactic is to create multiple security agencies that are charged with informing, monitoring and uncovering coup plots. This includes the creation of both intelligence and counter-intelligence agencies. In addition to the presidential guards and the parallel militaries, these monitoring agencies have a chain of command distinct from the regular military. They are directly in contact with the regime, constantly alerting the leader of potential threats. In Guinea, its leader Ahmed Sékou Touré was constantly being alerted of coup plots. The alleged perpetrators were always dealt with harshly.

Most scholars claim that the biggest problem facing developing states is establishing security and a monopoly over the use of force (Zartman, 1995). Yet coup-proofing strategies prevent the security institutions from being effective, making it more difficult to provide stability. Interfering with recruitment, promotion and assignment procedures discourages the professionalization of the military. Low levels of training, poor supervision and competence of commanders makes it difficult to carry out complex commands and deliver information (Pilster and Bohmelt, 2011). Coup-proofed regimes typically perform poorly in battle, making their citizens more vulnerable. Uganda under Idi Amin (1971–1979) illustrates this. The military under Amin was mostly recruited from one particular district. Training was poor and morale was extremely low. The least qualified individuals were promoted while the most qualified and experienced were purged. When Amin gave orders to invade Tanzania, its incredibly poor neighbour, Uganda was trounced decisively and chaos ensued.

Coup-proofing a regime often leads to a loss of the monopoly over the legitimate use of force in the long term. Moreover, because the security institutions have been deliberately weakened, regime transitions are more prone to disarray and instability (Driscoll, 2008).

'experienced a succession of coups and attempted coups following an initial event' (Wang, 1998, 663). In some states, they are so common (such as Thailand, where the military has staged at least 19 coups, with the most recent one taking place on May 22, 2014) that they are 'analogous to votes of no-confidence in parliamentary democracies' (Geddes, 2004, 24).

Civil wars

Civil wars are violent conflicts that occur between one or more groups and a state government and involve at least 1,000 battlefield deaths (Hoeffler, 2012). Both sides must incur battlefield deaths otherwise the violence is viewed as a massacre or genocide. With a civil war, organized groups seek to 'take power at the center or in a region, or to change government policies' (Fearon, 2007, 3). While coups are events that are rapidly executed, civil wars tend to have long durations. According to some estimates, the average civil war lasts around 16 years (Fearon, 2004).

Since World War II, around 16 million people have died in civil wars (Hoeffler, 2012). Civil wars are therefore very costly in terms of human life. They are also costly in economic resources, taking an enormous toll on the state. Civil wars are estimated to reduce growth by 2.3% a year (Collier, 2007, 27). This means that with a seven-year civil war, the state is 15% poorer than it would have been otherwise (Collier, 2007, 27). Civil wars not only kill a state's citizens through violence, but also through the spread of disease. Because some sectors of the population are often uprooted from their homes during civil wars, they are forced to move from one place to the next as refugees. With the health infrastructure often in a state of collapse (see more on this below), disease often spreads quickly (Collier, 2007). These costs are not inflicted solely upon the state experiencing the instability, but can quickly affect neighbours through refugee flows and the spread of disease. The International Crisis Group estimates, for example, that civil wars cost a state and its neighbours an average of $55 billion. According to Paul Collier, these costs quickly add up: he estimates the global tab of civil wars to be over $100 billion each year (2007, 32).

In their most basic form, civil wars involve at least one rebel group that challenges the central government. Though many states have disgruntled sectors of the population, launching a war effort against government forces requires rebel groups that are well-organized and able to overcome collective action problems: all members of the group will benefit from the group's victory even if they themselves do not take up arms. To levy a legitimate challenge against the government, rebel groups also must have the financing to do so for more on small arms, see Box 6.3.

Rebel groups can be motivated by two factors: greed and grievance (Hoeffler, 2012). Groups that are driven by greed take up arms against the government in order to pad their pockets. Private economic gain is the key goal. Groups that are stirred by grievances, by contrast, levy challenges to the government out of frustrations with discrimination on account of religion, ethnicity or class. Rebel groups may launch their efforts trying to right past government wrongs, but may shift their motivation to greed as the conflict persists. As Anka Hoeffler puts it, justice-seeking can turn into loot-seeking in the course of the war' (2012, 3).

Theories of civil wars

Researchers have pointed to a myriad of triggers for civil wars, with some findings being more robust and consistent than others. There are a few causal factors, however, on which there is consensus. A large body of research indicates that civil wars are more likely in states that: (1) have already experienced one in the past, (2) are poor, (3) have poor economic growth and (4) have large populations (Hoeffler, 2012).

The state's access to revenues may also matter. Some have argued that civil war is more likely when governments cannot defend themselves against rebel groups due to a lack of resources (Collier and Hoeffler, 2006). This is more likely to be the case when states have difficulty extracting taxes from their citizens. Without enough income to invest in defence, governments become more vulnerable to the challenges of rebel groups and conflict can erupt.

Perhaps surprisingly, researchers have found little connection between political regime type and civil war. One would expect that because democracies allow citizens to voice their concerns through elections, rebel groups would be less likely to take up arms as a means of airing their frustrations. The evidence indicates, however, that democracies are not less prone to civil war than dictatorships. As one researcher writes, 'democracy is not a sufficient prerequisite to shield a society against violent threats' (Schneider and Wiesehomeier, 2008, 194).

Civil war trends

According to data provided by the International Peace Research Institute, Oslo (PRIO), following the end of World War II, the number of civil wars in the world remained steady at around 15–20 each year, until the Cold War heated up. Both sides in that dispute funnelled resources into a number of developing states, at times directly provoking conflicts and other times indirectly doing so. Starting in the 1960s, the number increased each year, peaking at more than 50 a year by the time the Cold War ended, with the breakup of the Soviet Union playing a large role in the increase in civil wars experienced at that time. Since the end of the Cold War, the number of civil wars has decreased for the most part, hovering around 30 a year for the past decade.

As with coups, the bulk of civil wars occur in the developing world. Among developing states, Africa typically experiences the most civil wars each year, with Asia being a close second. Civil wars have been comparatively rarer in the Middle East and Latin America. According to one estimate, nearly three out of four citizens in the world's poorest states have recently been in a civil war or are currently in one (Collier, 2007).

Civil war traps

Like coups, the incidence of one civil war can lead to future civil wars or recurrence of the same conflict. Immediately following the resolution of a civil war, the chance of a relapse is very high (Collier, 2007). This is referred to as a civil war trap. Civil war traps are more likely to occur in the developing world, where resources are scarcest and fiercely fought over. As the war progresses, participants on each side manoeuvre to take advantage of the situation, such that inevitably some actors and/or groups stand to profit from the war's continuance, making a resolution difficult to secure (Collier, 2007). As Paul Collier writes, 'the end of a war often is not the end of the conflict; once over, a conflict is alarmingly likely to restart' (2007, 27). The poorer the state, the higher the chances of a relapse.

Instability and development

Both forms of instability discussed here, coups and civil wars, are more common in poor states than in rich ones, which are in turn more likely to see such violence recur. Perhaps most troubling about these traps is that these conflicts also take an alarming toll on the economy, preventing already poor places from getting out of poverty. The overwhelming evidence is that instability leads to lower growth rates, as mentioned earlier. It damages markets, interrupts trade, increases transactions costs and can lead to balance of payment problems, overspending, hyperinflation and significant debt. In this section, we discuss the economic costs of instability and the mechanisms through which such instability harms development.

Instability negatively impacts development through a variety of ways. First, it deters investment, which is a critical seed to grow an economy. Instability signals to investors that their investments may not be secure. The conflict in Chad (1979–1982), for example, led to large decreases in investments in its mining sector (Draman, 2003). According to some estimates, the investment Chad lost could have increased its GDP per capita by 80% (Azam et al., 1999). In states prone to instability, would-be investors opt to take their money elsewhere and existing ones often do the same.

Second, instability reduces human and physical capital. The most educated and entrepreneurial sectors of society flee the country to find a safer haven (Elbadawi, 1999). Civilians are often killed in episodes of instability, particularly in civil wars, decreasing the size of the labour force. Physical capital is also affected, as key infrastructure may be destroyed, such as bridges, roads and communication facilities.

Third, instability lowers productivity levels. Research indicates that output levels plummet amid conflict, while unemployment rates go up (Collier, 1999, 169–170). In Afghanistan, for example, agricultural production came to a halt. Farming was prohibited by the pervasiveness of landmines in the 1990s (Andersson et al., 1995). During the conflict in Mozambique (1977–1992), as well, rebels intentionally targeted vital economic resources, like electricity transmission grids, causing hydroelectricity production to drop, dramatically slowing economic activities (Collier, 2003).The protracted conflict in Sudan (1983–2005) delayed the introduction of modern agriculture and starting of industrial projects as well as gold exploration.

Fourth, instability can increase inequality (Muller and Seligson, 1987; Esteban and Ray, 1994; Østby, 2008). Some regions in a state may be more affected by the instability than others, increasing regional differences in income. In addition, the privatization of security can increase the divide between the rich and the poor: those who have the means to pay for their own security apparatus can ensure that they are safe, while those who do not are vulnerable to the effects of violence. The poor can also be disproportionately affected by instability, as it may entail rebel groups taking over transport routes and blocking food distribution and aid allocations.

Instability and the state

It should come as no surprise that instability puts a great strain on the state. First, instability limits the ability of the state to provide public goods. Governments at risk of coup or civil war may divert state resources to military spending instead of other public good provisions. Governments may also be more likely to hoard the resources. Countries that experience more coups and thus face more threats to their survival are more likely to engage in self-interested behaviour such as rent seeking and other types of predatory behaviour (Bohlken, 2010). For example, for several

Box 6.3   Small arms

The proliferation of small arms has serious consequences for the developing world. Countries that have been flooded with small arms may not only have difficulty maintaining stability but also steady economic development.

Small arms are weapons that are intended for individual use and include pistols, rifles, sub-machine guns, assault rifles and light machine guns. Light weapons are designed for use by two or more people that may serve as a crew and include heavy machine guns, grenade launchers, mortars, anti-aircraft guns and anti-tank guns, which must all be less than 100 mm in calibre (United Nations Institute, 2006). Both small arms and light weapons are readily available, widely produced, cheap, easy to use, easily transportable and diffused, difficult to trace and monitor and have a long shelf life and are easily maintained.

There are over half a billion small arms (640 million) and light weapons available, causing 15,000–20,000 casualties per year. More than 8 million small arms circulate around West Africa alone. Eight million new guns are being manufactured every year by at least 1,249 companies in 92 countries. Producing small arms requires little technical know-how, and due to demand, there are well over 600 suppliers around the world.

Small arms have directly contributed to high levels of casualties in conflicts in the developing world. In 90% of conflicts since 1990, small arms

→

decades Nigeria was constantly under the threat of coups, and a series of leaders dealt with this uncertainty by hoarding. Because of instability the focus of leadership was primarily concerned with 'personal survival rather than national development', (Omololu, 2007, 29). Due to constant coup threat, President General Sani Abacha (1993–1998) engaged in frenetic looting, stealing over a billion (Fagbadebo, 2007, 31).

Infrastructure damage can lead to fewer public services available to citizens, like health care and education. As a result, in states with intractable instability, infant mortality rates are higher and fewer children are enrolled in school. The turmoil can also make it difficult for states to collect revenues, minimizing the pool of resources they have to devote to public goods. For example, in the case of the Democratic Republic of Congo, though the country is mineral rich, public service delivery has been constrained by low revenues since resources are concentrated in areas that are highly unstable (Arieff, 2014).

Instability can also disrupt political and to a lesser extent judicial institutions. Elections may have to be postponed due to constant instability. For example, elections in Lebanon have had to be repeatedly postponed due to constant instability. Instability can interrupt legislative sessions, party meetings and judicial proceedings. Iraq has seen many of and light weapons have been the primary weapons used in fighting, increasing the proportion of civilian deaths in those conflicts (Bourne, 2007). Given the high number of battle deaths due to use of small arms, their role in exacerbating the casualties inflicted during conflicts is important.

The proliferation of small arms has a direct effect on development because they make conflict and banditry more feasible and enduring, the costs of which are incredibly high. Transit routes are blocked, national industries cannot function, businesses screech to a halt and foreign investors leave. Schools cannot operate, basic services are disrupted (for example, a water project that aimed to connect a pump to a nearby school in Kenya was derailed due to bandits in Northern Kenya), health care cannot be provided, food cannot be harvested, the population is displaced, diseases spread and sexual violence is carried out more easily (Alagappa and Inoguchi, 1999, 93).

The prevalence of small arms also perpetuates the war economy, which is the economy that is built around sustaining violence (Le Billion, 2005, 288). The war economy thrives on conflict and impedes the emergence of a flourishing economy. Crime and conflict also interrupt the legal economy because legal industries may be held hostage to lightly armed groups, forcing people to circumvent effective business practices. The state is drained of resources that may go towards dealing with the negative externalities of widespread small weapons.

its parliamentary sessions and elections delayed due to instability. Due to high levels of instability, the parliament has been unable to carry out its oversight role. Constant kidnappings and threats of assassination of members of parliament (MPs) have led many MPs to avoid parliamentary sessions. Additionally, a military operation launched by Iraqi security forces in December of 2013 to break up sit-ins for the Sunni tribes in Anbar led 44 MPs in the Iraqi parliament to resign in protest. The constant instability, therefore, weakens parliamentary performance since MPs are simply unable to vote on laws and enact legislation (Albadry and Abdullah, 2014).

Thus there are many ways in which instability can weaken the state. The following section offers some suggestions of how the security sector can be reformed to help developing countries tackle this challenge.

Dealing with instability

Breaking the state from intractable instability is clearly not an easy task. The causal factors that account for coups and civil wars are complex and varied. In other words, there is no single 'fix' that can prevent them from occurring and, perhaps more importantly, recurring down the road. Though external actions, like military intervention, has been effective in some instances (Collier, 2007), in line with this book's focus on domestic institutions, we concentrate on how institutional reform can make a difference. By and large, the critical institutional sphere for controlling instability is the security sector. This is not to say that other institutional spheres do not matter – indeed, the absence of broad-based political institutions can increase violence (Hendrickson, 1999, 23). We highlight security institutions because even effective political institutions are likely to be vulnerable to instability amid low-quality security institutions. Thus institutional reform of the security sector is critical to preventing instability.

The connection between the security apparatus and coups is fairly direct, given that coups are nearly always staged by members of the military. But in what ways does the nature of the state's security institutions affect the likelihood of coups? Existing research has primarily focused on the role of professionalization. As stated in Chapter 4, professionalized militaries are well trained and use a merit-based recruitment strategy. Professionalized militaries are also well funded and therefore able to support high salaries and budgets for equipment. The idea is that a more professionalized military will be less likely to stage a coup because they are more likely to respect civilian control over the state. And indeed more professionalized militaries are associated with fewer coups. Military budgets appear to be particularly important. Higher levels of military expenditures are correlated with a lower coup risk (Leon, 2012), as are increases in military spending (Powell, 2012). Others find that this relationship only holds among low-income countries (Collier and Hoeffler, 2007), but the overall message is that governments can reduce their risk of a coup if they buy off the military through greater military budget allocations. Additional resources give the military incentive to remain loyal to the government.

There are a number of examples to support this. In Thailand, Cambodia, Indonesia and Myanmar, coups occurred because soldiers were unhappy with their salaries and equipment (Crouch, 1985). In Kenya, as well, the 1982 coup was provoked by soldiers' dissatisfaction with the resources they had been given. They rebelled given the decline in the 'ability or inclination of the government to provide equipment that worked, uniforms that fit, housing that was adequate, or food that was palatable – and pay that would enable the soldiers to live in reasonable comfort' (Dianga, 2002, 48–49).

In light of this relationship, the provision of adequate resources to the military, or when resources are limited, and consultations with members of the military prior to cuts to the military budget are likely to mitigate incentives for coups (Scobell, 1994).

The evidence also indicates that military training decreases the chance of a coup: those militaries whose members have received extensive training have staged fewer coups (Ruby and Gibler, 2010). States with more attendees of the US Professional Military Education programme over a five-year period, for example, experienced fewer coups than states whose officers had not received such training (Ruby and Gibler, 2010). Given the success of training programmes like this one, greater resources should be devoted (both by developing states and the development community) to increasing training opportunities for members of the military in the developing world.

In terms of civil wars, high-quality security institutions are also important. Rebel groups may be more likely to launch an offensive when they think they have a reasonable chance of winning. An un-professionalized and under-funded military force can therefore make the state vulnerable to attack.

Military recruitment patterns can also affect civil war risk. When militaries base promotions on ethnicity, for example, rather than merit, it opens the door for conflict. Research indicates that when militaries that use ethnically exclusive recruitment patterns lose strength, rival groups use the opportunity to take up arms against the state (Goldstone et al., 2010). In addition, militaries that recruit along sectarian, regional or ethnic lines can make rival groups feel insecure out of fears that they lack protection from the state, which can also motivate a challenge (Burton, 1987). Such groups may evolve into guerrilla units to fill the security void, as has been the case in Lebanon and Colombia. In Ivory Coast, minority ethnic groups felt threatened by the Laurent Gbagbo government's decision to fill the police and military units with members of his same ethnic group; groups operating in the north and west of the country instigated a conflict against the government to protect themselves. When military forces are dominated by members of the same sector of society, this generates fear in the minds of other sectors and can lead to violent confrontations (Posen, 1993).

Discriminatory recruitment patterns are also troublesome because in the face of civilian calls for regime change, the military is more likely to violently cling to power. These patterns were largely evident during the Arab Spring in 2011, in which mass protests spread across parts of North Africa and the Middle East. In Syria, the predominantly Alawite military was willing to cling to power and largely remained loyal to orders from Syrian president Bashar al-Assad. This pitted Alawite groups against non-Alawite groups and led to the country's civil war. In contrast, in other places like Tunisia, where military recruitment patterns were less imbalanced, civil war was averted. Efforts to discourage discriminatory recruitment patterns in the military would help mitigate conditions that can precipitate civil wars.

Case studies: success stories of security sector reform

We highlight here a number of 'success' stories, where states that were once prone to serious instability have made progress in bucking the trend through institutional reforms. Because successes are few and far between, they can provide valuable insight into approaches states and the development community can pursue to lower the risk of instability (Hoeffler, 2012).

Sierra Leone has experienced considerable political instability throughout much of its post-independence history. It experienced a coup in 1967, another one in 1968, a state of emergency in 1987, a long and devastating civil war from 1991 to 2002, and three coups during the civil war (in 1992, 1996 and 1997). Since the end of the civil war, however, things appear to be slowly stabilizing. The civil war had virtually destroyed the structure of the state's security institutions. One of the first efforts of reform after the civil war, therefore, was to modernize and improve the state's police force. Police partnership boards were created that comprised representatives of local communities. Special emphasis within the police was placed on protecting the most vulnerable members of society, namely women and children, who had been ruthlessly abused and exploited during a conflict. The state created family support units staffed by female police officers and hired social and medical workers to improve the quality of care offered to victims of abuse. It also restructured the police to increase internal accountability, as reflected in the establishment of a department devoted to handling complaints of misconduct. Though the police in Sierra Leone continue to face challenges, great strides have been made to improve its effectiveness since the civil war's end.

The military in Sierra Leone has also undergone a transformation, growing from a demoralized and ineffective body that relied heavily on the United Nations to execute its core functions to one capable of defending the state (Malan et al., 2002, 100). Its officers have been retrained to improve self-confidence and morale, and competitive exams were introduced to establish more objectivity in the standards for selection and promotions (Malan, et al., 2002, 99). All of these institutional reforms have contributed to the relative stability experienced in Sierra Leone in the more than ten years since the civil war's end.

Indonesia, a state that has experienced repeated coups since its independence, has also pursued a number of reforms in its security sector since the early 2000s that have reaped positive rewards. Members of the military no longer occupy positions in the government and are no longer at the forefront of politics (Sukma and Prasetyono, 2003, 22). The military and the police forces have been separated and are now restricted from taking on civilian positions, reducing the number of security actors with positions in national and local parliaments. Efforts have also been made to disconnect the military from political parties, resulting in elections in which it has played a much more neutral role (Sukma and Prasetyono, 2003, 23).

Turkey has also witnessed a transformation of its security institutions, after having experienced three coups between 1960 and 1980, the latter of which brought into power a military dictatorship. Prior to reforms, the military was not only a security institution, but also a core part of the political system (Sarigil, 2011, 271). Members of the military had a significant impact on political policies. The military had to be re-indoctrinated to reinforce the need for separation between the political and military spheres (Sarigil, 2011, 267).

There have been a number of changes that have taken place since. First, the secretary general of the National Security Council (MGK) was no longer allowed to be a military official, the duties of the council were changed, and it was reduced to serving in an advisory capacity (Sarigil, 2011, 272). The prime minister and president were also given more oversight with respect to the council's leadership. Second, military promotions and appointments are now subject to far more civilian control (Sarigil, 2011, 278). There is more transparency in military expenditures, and a Court of Auditors is now given authorization to audit accounts and transactions that involve the armed forces. The military can also no longer prosecute civilians in military courts (though there are some exceptions to this), and it must receive approval to gather intelligence on societal unrest.

As a sign of the progress that has been made in limiting the military's role in politics, many high-ranking military officers accused of involvement in coup plots in 2007 were detained and put on trial in civilian courts. And retired generals have been arrested for past transgressions.

Ghana is yet another example of successful security sector reforms leading to improved political stability. In the 1970s and 1980s, Ghana was prone to repeated episodes of military intervention. In all but two years, the military ruled Ghana between the years of 1972 and 1992. Ghana has implemented a number of changes to put an end to this. First, it reformed its constitution to place greater restrictions on the military and enable greater parliamentary oversight of the military (BICC, 2006). The Ministry of Defence is now more involved in monitoring the activities of the military and assessing its effectiveness. With the help of the United Kingdom Defence Advisory Team, it launched the Performance Improvement Plan in 2003, with the goal of strengthening the civilian component of the Ministry of Defence (BICC, 2006, 4). Another feature of this plan is to spearhead collaborations between civil society organizations and the Ministry of Defence. In addition, the Security and Intelligence Agencies Act of 1996 ensures greater transparency in the intelligence sector and requires an annual parliamentary report on its operations.

Former president Jerry Rawlings (a military leader himself) initiated a number of reforms to professionalize the Ghana Armed Forces (GAF), including putting in place measures to restore discipline, tighten the chain of command and improve recruitment standards. Rebellious units were purged and their soldiers faced arrest (Hutchful, 1997, 256). Officers were trained to increase their knowledge of democratic rights and given opportunities to train in Europe (Hutchful, 1997, 253).

Civilian authorities in Ghana now maintain much greater control over the military, which has been delinked from popular movements and distanced from the policy process (Hutchful, 1997, 258). Instead, the military has increased its involvement in peacekeeping missions and engaged in joint training sessions with NATO. Such partnerships have also helped soldiers supplement their wages without having to resort to corrupt military entrepreneurship.

The police forces have also been transformed. Community policing has been encouraged to reduce high crime rights, including the creation of neighbourhood watch groups. The government has also launched a weapons-for-rewards programme and established the Ghana National Commission on Small Arms (GNCSA) to retrieve excess and unlicensed weapons from citizens.

The situation is not perfect, of course. There are still accusations of security appointments being made on the basis of ethnicity, for example (BICC, 2006, 2). Regardless, the current security institutions are significantly higher in quality than they were in the 1970s and 1980s, and Ghana has experienced relative stability for the last two decades.

In sum, security sector reforms can elicit great benefits for states that have troubled histories of instability. We do not mean to argue that the security apparatus is the only institutional sphere that matters for instability – far from it. Rather, we seek to highlight the critical role of this often-ignored institutional domain of the state for understanding intractable instability.

Conclusion

Instability in the developing world is both rampant and cyclical. States that are the most vulnerable to manifestations of instability, like coups and civil wars, are among the poorest in the world. Low levels of development make states vulnerable to instability, and instability makes it extremely difficult for these states to pull themselves out of poverty. This creates a vicious cycle that is often difficult to break.

Though breaking out of the cycle is extremely difficult, it can be done, as the handful of success stories that we point to indicate. Externally led strategies can undoubtedly aid in this process, but in this chapter we focus on internal transformations, specifically security sector reform. It is the duty of the security institutions, after all, to ensure that there is internal order and stability to defend the state against external and internal threats. As a reflection of this, high-quality security institutions are associated with fewer coups and outbreaks of civil war. Greater attention to the nature of the state's security sector and its ability to address intractable instability are likely to enhance the prospects that states can break the coup and conflict traps that mire them.

Questions

- What are coup traps? Why do coups take place so often in Africa?
- What are civil war traps? What is the relationship between poverty and civil war?
- Why is instability so damaging to economic development?
- In what ways does instability weaken the state?
- What are some of the reasons why Sierra Leone, Indonesia, Turkey and Ghana have been able to achieve security sector reform?

Facts

- No country has experienced more coups than Thailand.
- Coups and civil wars are much more likely to happen in poorer states than in richer states.
- Instability negatively affects development by deterring investment, reducing human and physical capital, lowering productivity levels and increasing inequality.
- When militaries base their promotions and recruitment patterns on ethnicity rather than merit, it raises the risk of civil war.
- One of the key reforms in the security sector in Indonesia was ensuring that members of the military no longer held positions in the government.

Chapter 7

Corruption

Though corruption has multiple negative consequences for society, it is also a commonly cited obstacle to economic development (here, we focus on state-led corruption, rather than corruption pursued by societal actors). There are a variety of mechanisms through which corruption can drag down an economy. For instance, corruption can increase transactions costs due to the accumulation of bribes, in turn deterring investment. It can also delegitimize the state, making citizens disillusioned with their leadership. It can generate an atmosphere of resentment, as citizens witness the illegitimate acts committed by public officials. In some cases, citizens respond in subtle ways, such as evading their taxes (Pope, 1996). In other cases, they take to the streets to voice their frustrations, resulting in disorder and instability (Rose-Ackerman, 1996). All of these responses are harmful for economic development.

Some states in the developing world are so plagued by corruption that it appears to be a part of their political culture. Corrupt acts in such contexts come to be viewed as accepted and normal. In Russia, for example, the former minister of interior, Vladmir Rushailo, stated in response to allegations that 70% of Russian civil servants were corrupt that 'you should not confuse corruption with bribe-taking' (Eigen, 2002, 47), highlighting the regularity of the practice. In such environments, corruption is endemic and there are numerous challenges to overcoming it.

Yet this does not have to be the case. State institutions can be reformed in ways that reduce corruption and prevent its resurgence. In this chapter, we devote a section to the overall effects of corruption on development. We look at how corruption affects specific state institutions and explain how each can negatively affect development. We weave examples from across the developing world throughout to illustrate our main points. We close by providing insights into how state institutions can be tailored to lessen corruption and its pernicious consequences.

Corruption

Corruption is the use of power by state officials for illegal private gain. According to Transparency International, one of the leading providers of cross-national measures of corruption, corruption refers to the 'misuse of public power for private benefit' (2013). Corruption can take a number of forms, ranging from civil servants accepting bribes to police departments solely hiring relatives and friends to political officials stealing from state coffers.

The classical view of corruption is a society or a state that has lapsed from a 'standard of goodness' (Johnston, 1996). In our definition we focus on the institutions of the state. Given this, corruption takes place when an individual who works for the state violates norms or rules in order to gain a private advantage. Thus corruption is dishonest or fraudulent conduct, such as the manipulation of political decisions to favour private economic gains or cronies or the sale of government services, privileges, exceptions or information. Corruption also involves the illegal appropriation and detour of public funds for personal use. Finally, corruption may entail some form of discrimination according to social proximity, religion, social or political class, caste, tribe, race, sex, ethnicity and political views (Kurer, 2005).

Corruption either takes place on a grand scale, where it is systemic, or corruption takes place on a much smaller scale, known as petty corruption. Systemic corruption is corruption that is integrated into an economic, social or political system, requiring widespread participation to help maintain it. In the case of systemic corruption, the major institutions of the state are all routinely involved. As the state is dominated by corrupt individuals, most people have no alternative to dealing with corrupt officials, which has dire consequences for the state's legitimacy (Rose-Ackerman, 2002).

Petty corruption is small-scale bureaucratic corruption that could take place every day between public officials and the public. It is usually associated with bribery and involves modest sums of money. It affects people in their daily encounters with the public administration. It may involve giving bribes in order receive services such as health care, schooling and licensing to name a few. Petty corruption commonly involves the police, customs officials and tax authorities (Riley, 1999).

Theories of corruption

Many scholars have examined the relationship between corruption and development. Though some studies have focused on the role of culture and religion (see Lipset and Lenz 2000; Treisman, 2000), most corruption studies have focused on the role of institutions (and their origin), human capital, income levels and economic policies.

One of the more notable theories on corruption examines the interplay of disease environments and colonial legacies in shaping institutions that are best able to curb corruption. Some former colonies (see Chapter 8) inherited institutions that were better able to prevent corruption compared to others (Acemoglu et al., 2001). Countries that had high prevalence of deadly diseases were more likely to have few settlers that wanted to set up institutions that could prevent corruption in comparison to countries with high numbers of settlers. Thus, the disease environment shaped what type of colony that emerged: *settler colonies*, which focused on building strong institutions, or *extractive colonies*, which never bothered to invest in strong institutions since there were so few settlers. Other theories focus on the identity of the colonial power and how this may have impacted the types of institutions that emerged (La Porta et al., 1998). In most cases, the colonizer transplanted its legal system to the colony. This colonial inheritance had important implications for corruption. Some legal systems were more prone to corruption simply because they were too cumbersome. French colonies had more regulations, which supposedly led to higher levels of corruption (La Porta et al., 1998).

Other theories argue that improvements in human capital and income will cause institutional development that is important to reducing corruption (Glaeser et al., 2004). Education is important for the courts (and other institutions that serve to check corruption) to function efficiently. Moreover, corruption is more likely to go unnoticed if the population is illiterate. Thus, states with a better educated citizenry have been consistently found to have lower levels of corruption (Adserà et al., 2003).

Many studies have also explored how institutional quality (which reduces corruption) is affected by economic factors such as income levels and strength of the middle class. Economic development creates further demands for good governance which is necessary for growth. Thus institutions that are able to prevent corruption respond to a country's income level and needs (Lipset, 1963).

Finally, other studies have focused on the relationship between economic policies and corruption. Restrictions in the marketplace, such as openness to external competition and the regulation of entry for start-up firms, can help explain why corruption persists (Ades and Di Tella, 1999; Djankov et al., 2002).

In sum, there is a wealth of studies that explore the causes of corruption. We now turn to explain the ways in which corruption impacts development and how different types of corruption corrode the state's ability to function.

Corruption and development

According to the World Bank, without reductions in corruption, 'it will not be possible to lift the 1.2 billion people who still live of $1.25 a day or less out of poverty' (Indrawati, 2013). Indeed, multiple studies have shown that corruption is harmful to a state's economy, hurting growth rates (Ugur and Dasgupta, 2011) and increasing the distance between the rich and the poor (Gyimah-Brempong, 2002).

As a sign of this, corruption is positively correlated with *inequality* (a correlation that holds true for developed states too) (Gyimah-Brempong, 2002). It is associated with a 7.8% reduction in income per year (Gupta et al., 2002). Inequality is a consequence of corruption because the corrupt states often invest little in public goods (Tanzi and Davoodi, 1997), as officials are too focused on padding their own pockets. In addition, poor citizens become even poorer because they lack access to state services given that they cannot afford the cost of bribes. A 2013 Transparency International (TI) report claimed that the poor in India, for example, often have to pay bribes for services that are supposed to be free (Transparency International Annual Report, 2013). Pervasive bribery essentially functions as a regressive tax on needy households, which hurts the poor the most. While the typical Mexican family spends about 8% of its annual income on bribes (as mentioned earlier), this statistic jumps to 20% for those in the poorest income bracket according to a 2013 TI report. Corruption can also limit the services the poor receive from the government. In Indonesia, for example, a 2005 study reported that nearly a fifth of the rice provided by the government for poor households disappeared before it reached its final destination (Olken, 2005). Corruption can therefore limit the effectiveness of social welfare programmes, further hurting the poor (Olken and Pande, 2012, 31). Just as the poor get poorer in a corrupt state, the rich get richer, further extending the gap between rich and poor. Politically connected individuals who benefit from corruption are often already in the higher income brackets. Even if they are not directly receiving rents or kickbacks, they have better access to the most profitable government projects. For more on how the underground economy – or the shadow economy – affects development, see Box 7.1.

Corruption also decreases investment in human capital, which is important for growth. It distorts the decision-making process and affects how government expenditures are allocated. In corrupt states, officials distribute resources based on the opportunities for bribes as opposed to potential returns on human capital (Holmberg and Rothstein, 2011). Here we discuss three areas that are important components of human capital development (education, health care and water access) and how corruption can hurt them.

Education

Basic education is supposed to be free in most parts of the world, but that is often not the case once corruption is taken into account. A 2012

Box 7.1 Shadow economy

The shadow economy constitutes a broad range of economic activities that take place outside of state-regulated frameworks. The key activities of the shadow economy include the drug trade, cross-border smuggling, extraction of natural resources, and aid manipulation. In the developing world, the shadow economy is where much economic activity takes place. For example, it was estimated that in the 1990s the shadow economy represented 75% of the size of the officially recorded economy in Nigeria, Egypt and Thailand (Choi and Thum, 2005, 817).

The shadow economy thrives when administrative and judicial institutions are weak. Countries that lack the rule of law are especially likely to have large unofficial economies. The shadow economy is also facilitated by weak enforcement of laws and regulations. A low probability of being caught makes illicit activity more attractive. It is also provoked by heavy administrative burdens for entrepreneurs but weak enforcement. Highly corrupt countries that require a series of excessive licenses that involve bribe after bribe for businesses to operate may cause entrepreneurs to take the risk and go underground.

Though the emergence of the shadow economy is predicated on the weakness of administrative institutions, the shadow economy, in turn also further weakens these institutions. The state is unable to collect revenues, making it more difficult to provide any sort of public good for its citizens. The state is therefore absent in providing a public good such as order, the rule of law and contract enforcement. The state is also unable to offer any support for industry, loans, infrastructure and information. As the official sector shrinks, so will government revenues, which drive more agents to the shadow economy. All of this has ramifications on the state. The state cannot effectively manage the economy, and the legitimacy of the overall legal and regulatory system is challenged (Fleming et al., 2000, 395–397).

The shadow economy has a mostly negative impact on economic growth and development. Without the rule of law to enforce contract obligations, access to capital is limited. Macroeconomic stability is harder to attain and sustain (Fleming et al., 2000, 395–397). The only winners of the shadow economy are those that have access to wealth and connections. Those who do not have connections are not able to run their business effectively. Businesses may purposely avoid becoming too successful because they do not want to attract attention from the wrong actor, whether it be the state, the mafia or a warlord. Circumventing the state and eschewing successful business practices makes these businesses more inefficient, which increases their transaction costs, which are then passed on to the consumer. Because survival is dependent on the exchange of favours, patron clientelistic relationships predominate. In general the shadow economy is synonymous with corruption, wastefulness and instability, none of which bode well for development.

TI report claimed that in countries like Madagascar, Morocco, Niger, Senegal, Sierra Leone and Uganda, nearly half of all parents report that they have had to pay illegal fees to send their children to school. It also stated that in Cameroon, as well, parents have indicated that if they do not pay illegal fees, they cannot receive their child's report card. In other instances, children are expelled or punished if they cannot afford fees (Transparency International Annual Report, 2012). The high bribes requested of parents in many developing states means that the poor do not have access to education because poor parents cannot afford to pay the bribes and enrol their children in school.

Corruption also hurts education because corrupt states typically spend little on improving it. In fact, there is a negative correlation between levels of corruption and education quality. Government spending on education (as a percentage of GDP) decreases as levels of corruption increase (Mauro, 1998).

Even those programmes geared towards improving education face difficulties when states are corrupt (Suryadarma, 2012). In Bangladesh, for example, a scholarship programme intended to help poor families to send their daughters to school was widely viewed as stymied by corruption. Nearly one in four families reported that they had to pay a bribe simply to enrol in the programme. Ghana also provides an example of this. In 2005, Ghana decided to improve its primary education by eliminating school fees. Yet, despite this change, bribes were demanded in order for students to receive class handouts and other school materials. (It is important to note that in this instance, when the Ghanaian government learned of this situation, it implemented changes to ensure that all school materials were either free or affordable (Quaye and Coombes, 2011).)

Health care

Without a healthy labour force, economic productivity suffers. Many work days are lost due to sickness, and workers suffer because they do not earn wages while out. Access to adequate health care, therefore, is critical to the development of human capital and the growth of the economy as a whole.

States that lack corruption are more likely to invest in health care and offer it at affordable rates to citizens. In corrupt states, by contrast, the opposite is true. Take health-care investments. Corrupt states are less likely to offer basic services to citizens like low-cost immunizations for children and maternity care. The state is too preoccupied with diverting state resources towards state officials to worry about whether its citizens are healthy. As a result, corrupt states have higher levels of both maternal and infant mortality rates. Women are denied access to adequate pre- and post-natal care, and few services exist to help the poor when their children are born. Many newborn babies receive either no vaccinations or delayed vaccinations, increasing their exposure to preventable diseases. Because the health-care system is slow and of low quality, citizens stop relying on clinics for their health concerns (Azfar and Gurgur, 2005).

With low health-care investments, in corrupt states health-care worker salaries are often dismal and wages frequently go unpaid. As a result, absenteeism is common in the health-care industry, as many doctors and nurses simply fail to show up, at times because they are seeking additional employment to make a living. A 2003 study in the Kogi State in Kenya, for example, found that 42% of health-care workers had not been paid their salaries in at least six months of the prior year (Lewis, 2006, 34).

The pervasiveness of bribery does not help matters. Jobs in government hospitals were reportedly bought in nearly one in four instances in Ghana and one in five instances in Uganda, according to a 2006 study (Lewis, 2006, 20). In Bolivia, as well, 40% of respondents in a 2004 survey indicated that they had to pay a bribe to receive health care (Lewis, 2006, 14). That number is even higher in both Ukraine and Vietnam, where a third of the citizens report paying a bribe in return for health services. A 2012 TI report claims that in Morocco, if patients want to be seen by doctors at the hospital, they often must pay a bribe, which can at times be as much as a third of a person's monthly income (Transparency International Annual Report, 2012).

Water

Access to clean water is also important for ensuring that a state's citizens can be productive participants in the economy. Yet, here again, corruption can be a major obstacle. More than a billion people in the world have no way of obtaining clean water and nearly three times that number do not have adequate sanitation facilities. According to some reports, corruption is to blame more often than not. Transparency International, for example, estimates that up to 70% of lost water resources could be recovered if corruption were eliminated (2008). Compounding the problem, lack of clean water has negative spillover effects in the areas of education and health care and can increase poverty and gender inequality.

Most frequently, corruption in the water industry takes the form of bribery. If citizens want clean water, they have to pay for it illegally. Because of the prevalence of bribes, the poorest citizens do not receive clean water. According to some estimates, corruption in the developing world increases the costs of connecting a house to a water network by as much as 30–45%. Because of this, those citizens of Manila who are off the grid end up paying more for water than citizens living in London or New York, two of the most expensive cities in the world. As a result, many simply cannot afford water. In Bolivia, Honduras and Nicaragua, more than half of all citizens do not have the resources to secure water access. In Sub-Saharan Africa, this number rises to nearly 70% of citizens (Sohail and Cavill, 2008, 47). Corruption increases the transaction costs of obtaining clean water for many in the developing world (Pope, 1996).

In Kenya, for example, water scarcity affects nearly four million citizens. The water sector is viewed as being riddled with bribery and the procurement process lacks transparency (Sohail and Cavill, 2008). As a result, nearly 87% of residents of Nairobi reported witnessing the payment of bribes in return for access to the city's water network (Transparency International, 2008). In India, as well, informal payments in exchange for water connections are common. About one in three Indians reported in a survey that they had paid a bribe to speed up repair work or obtain access to the water network (Sohail and Cavill, 2008). Residents in need of a new water connection or sewer repair are often asked to pay a bribe. In turn, residents also pay bribes to get falsified meter readings for water bills (Davis, 2004). An example from Zimbabwe is particularly telling of how serious the problem of corruption in the water industry can be. A woman there was wrongly billed for water over 60 times. Even so, she was asked to pay the full bill and, because she was unable to do so, she was forced to collect water from a nearby church (Sohail and Cavill, 2008, 44).

Corruption can affect various sectors of the state. For this reason, to discuss how corruption works in the developing world, we group its manifestations across the four institutional domains emphasized in this study: administrative, judicial, political and security.

Corruption and the state

Administrative corruption

Corruption in the state's administrative apparatus typically appears in the form of bribery, where low-level civil servants accept bribes from ordinary citizens in return for some sort of political favour (Rose-Ackerman, 1999). When administrative corruption is serious, the use of bribery is an accepted practice and administrators solely provide services to citizens if a bribe is paid. The administrative sphere becomes inactive and its output is severely jeopardized (Ulklah, 2004). Administrative corruption, however, typically takes a more benign form, where citizens have access to basic services (like water, electricity and sanitation), but more specific transitions require the use of bribes if they are to be completed in an expedited fashion.

Experts point to a number of states in Asia to provide telling examples of how administrative corruption works. In Vietnam, for instance, civil servants typically take for themselves a portion of commission for whatever services they provide (Quah, 2006). Unless this amounts to a large sum of money, it is not frowned upon. In Mongolia, as well, citizens frequently give gifts to civil servants to get tasks completed (Quah, 2006). Thailand and Cambodia are no different, where gift giving is a common way to solicit the help of the state's administrative apparatus (Quah, 2006). In the Philippines under Ferdinand Marcos (1965–1986) administrative corruption was also widespread across all bureaucratic agencies, but particularly an issue in revenue collection, customs and licensing. And in Indonesia, the tax system under Suharto (1967–1998) was so confusing that individuals could not assess their own tax rates without assistance. This made tax rates 'negotiable' and forced individuals to attend one-on-one consultations with government officials to barter over what their rate should be. For this reason, working as a tax collector was seen as one of the 'surest roads to riches in the government bureaucracy' (Robertson-Snape, 1999, 594–595). Bribery was in fact so endemic in Indonesia that bribes were reportedly required even to register a baby's birth or apply for a driver's license or marriage certificate. A 1998 survey demonstrated this, showing that nearly 80% of Indonesians had come to believe that bribery was an unavoidable part of dealing with the state's bureaucracy (Robertson-Snape, 1999).

Administrative corruption can appear across all sectors of the state's bureaucracy, but the agencies that interact with the public the most, like revenue collections, customs, border control and licensing are the areas where it emerges most frequently (Quah, 2006). This is simply because these sectors create more opportunities for bribery to occur. Beyond this, the more complexity and ambiguity in the state's procedures, the more likely it is that bribes will be used. Such conditions increase the chances that the procedures can be open for interpretation thereby creating opportunities for officials to accept bribes in exchange for favourable interpretations.

Customs agencies, for example, are responsible for the flow of goods in and out of a country. For this reason, customs officials are frequently in contact with citizens, including those involved in illicit economic activities (like the drug trade) (Buscaglia, 2003). Under Suharto's Indonesia, the entire economy was said to be affected by the 'pervasiveness and extremism of corruption within the customs system which was seen to be one of the main causes of Indonesia's high-cost economy' (Robertson-Snape, 1999, 595). As a sign of this, to get a good passed through customs inspections necessitated nearly 40 signatures and a number of unofficial fees (Robertson-Snape, 1999, 595). In Lebanon, as well, there were reports that customs officials will not process transactions unless bribes are procured forcing both importers and exporters to use bribery to move their goods across the state's borders (Gould, 1980).

This, of course, has negative economic consequences, primarily because it raises transaction costs. Central Asia, a region that is prone to administrative corruption in customs agencies, exemplifies this. Businesses operating in the region estimate that to get a truckload of produce from Kyrgyzstan to Russia crossing through Kazakhstan would cost several thousand dollars in bribes. Small traders in Turkmenistan, Uzbekistan and Kyrgyzstan report that customs agents and border guards repeatedly demand that they pay bribes (Collins, 2009). Bribery is so common that jobs in customs agencies are extremely desirable in Central Asia and are often sold to the highest bidder, as would-be employees know that they can easily get back the money spent on acquiring the position through the bribes they will receive down the road. A report by the International Crisis group, for example, states that jobs in the Ministry of Internal Affairs in Kyrgyzstan are sold for anywhere from $100 to $50,000, based on the rank of the post (Cokgezen, 2004).

Licensing is another arena in which administrative corruption is common. In order to obtain a business, export, import or other form of license, individuals must bribe a state official. In India, for example, the License Raj system, which was intact until 1991, meant that licenses were required for virtually all entrepreneurial activities in that country. This created numerous opportunities for corruption and it soon became difficult to start a business without using some form of bribery. Civil servants even grew habituated to delay granting licenses until an illegal payment had been made. In Ghana, as well, according to a 1983 World Bank Report, the Ministry of Trade used to insist on bribery payments of anywhere from 5% to 10% of the value of the license requested (Gould and Amaro-Reves, 1983, 8). And to invest in a company in Russia, a study from the late 1990s claimed that foreigners must bribe every agency involved in the process, ranging from the finance ministry to the central bank (Drury et al., 2006, 22).

Beyond bribery, administrative corruption can also appear in the form of hiring and promotion decisions based on political loyalties rather than competencies (for more on *clientelism*, see Box 7.2). Because skills do not inform the employment process, qualified citizens may leave the country and seek employment elsewhere, a phenomenon known as 'brain drain'. As an extreme example of this, by the time Equatorial Guinean leader Macias Nguema was killed in 1979, he was thought to be one of the most corrupt leaders in the world (Time Magazine, 1979). According to Sam Decalo, there were no university graduates who remained in the country because they had all gone into exile, amounting to one of the worst cases of brain drain on record (Decalo, 1989, 59; see also Lundahl, 1997, 45).

Box 7.2   Clientelism

Clientelism is a system of social and economic exchanges between patrons and clients that pervades much of the developing world and perpetuates underdevelopment. Patrons distribute favours downwards to clients in return for loyalty and allegiance (Blunt et al., 2012, 67). Favours can refer to monetary compensation, jobs, loans, scholarships or other forms of preferential treatment. Also known as patronage, the distribution of government jobs or other favours to political allies irrespective of their qualifications prevents more competent individuals without connections from succeeding. Patron clientelism negatively affects development because it creates pyramid structures that maintain the unequal power hierarchies at the expense of emphasizing merit and competence.

Patron clientelism only benefits a selective group of loyal clients. This differs from *pork-barrel policies*, which have been commonplace in developed democracies. (Pork-barrel funding involves the appropriation of public funds for geographically targeted projects that do not serve the interests of a large portion of the country's citizenry, often circumventing funding procedures.) With pork-barrel legislation an entire geographic constituency may be the benefactor and the relationship between the legislator and the constituent is less personalized. With patron-clientelism, the number of recipients is fewer and the relationship is much more individualized and particular.

Clientelism is also often linked with countries that have weak administrative and political institutions. In turn, clientelistic practices have

→

Research on administrative corruption has shown consistently that it harms development. Paolo Mauro from the IMF was the first to quantify its economic effects (1995). Looking specifically at when civil servants accept bribes for business licenses, he showed that administrative corruption essentially increases the taxes paid by citizens, but in an inefficient and wasteful manner. Instead of a central revenue collection process, administrative corruption creates countless 'consumers of graft' whom citizens must contend with (Drury et al., 2006, 122).

In Lebanon, for example, public resources to rebuild the state's infrastructure following its civil war were inefficiently used and wasted on corruption. Public resources had to be devoted to paying bribes to get public housing and transportation projects going (Höckel , 2007). Making matters worse, construction contracts were reportedly often given to the allies of Prime Minister Rafik Hariri (1992–1998, 2000–2004). As a result, reconstruction efforts in Beirut, which were estimated to cost around $5 billion at the outset, ended up costing the state about ten times that amount (Höckel, 2007, 7).

undermined state capacity in countries in the developing world because merit-based practices and decision-making are avoided, favouritism and complacency abound. Clientelism has undermined the emergence of a capable state in Indonesia. Within the Indonesian civil service, patron clientelism is pervasive. Officials can accept bribes and kickbacks with impunity. The bureaucracy does not engage in any human resource planning as staffing decisions are made with no concerns for local needs. Appointments are completely non-transparent. Nepotism and favorite are the norm. No expertise is needed as most civil servants are hired without any type of formal selection. Civil servants receive little to no performance appraisal. As such, there is high absenteeism making it more difficult for the state to function (Blunt et al., 2012, 70–71).

Systems based on clientelism lead to a host of problems for development. States in the developing world that are saddled by clientelistic structures underperform because resources, funds and personnel are not used in an optimal fashion. Instead of funds being invested towards development, they are squandered and mostly funnelled towards non-productive handouts to a selective group of people. Jobs are doled out to the selective few that have access to a patron. Employment that came as a source of patronage does not lead to a highly productive or motivated work force. The system is set up so that loyalties subsume merit. Most problematic is the fact that the lucky few who are a part of the pyramid have no interest in changing the status quo. This helps explain why developing countries persistently underperform economically and why corruption is so enduring.

Administrative corruption also undermines development because the use of unqualified individuals in the bureaucracy can lead to poor policy implementation. Administrators in such a context have few reasons to train their employees, because career advancements have little to do with performance. Yet, with an untrained civil service, the quality of work provided will be subpar. An incompetent bureaucracy lowers productivity and efficiency (Gould and Amaro-Reves, 1983). In addition, the brain drain that accompanies this form of corruption prevents the state from benefiting from any human capital it has created, essentially resulting in wasted investments.

Judicial corruption

Judicial corruption involves 'corrupt acts by judges, prosecutors, public defenders, court officials, and lawyers who are intimately involved in the operation of the judicial system' (USAID, 2009, 8). Like administrative corruption, it can entail the use of bribery and unfair promotions and hiring decisions. It can also mean that judges are threatened that they will lose their jobs if they do not issue particular rulings.

While administrative corruption typically involves bribery in return for specific tasks, with judicial corruption bribes and other perks are offered in return for a wide range of favours. Usually these fall into two categories: procedural corruption and operational corruption.

The former (procedural corruption) involves things like requests to alter legal files and discovery material and the acceleration or delay of a case through changes in the order in which it will be heard by the judge. It may also involve embezzlement by court officials of public or private property that is held in court custody.

The latter (operational corruption) is more serious and has to do with requests to alter court rulings. In extreme cases, this means that judges ignore evidence and base their rulings on the highest bidder. As an example of this, in Colombia at the peak of its issues with drug trafficking in the 1980s, drug traffickers were able to buy off judges to avoid punishment (Felbab-Brown, 2009, 15). Such a system disadvantages the poor, however, because they cannot afford to offer bribes. Outcomes end up favouring those who are politically connected or wealthy. A 2006 TI survey reported that 21% of Africans, who had been in contact with the judiciary in the past year claimed that they had to pay a bribe to the courts (Transparency International, 2007, 11). Operational corruption can also mean politically motivated court rulings, where judges issue politically important decisions for financial gain, career advancement or retention. When operational corruption is rampant, court rulings merely reflect the wants of the politically connected and wealthy, who are immune from punishment. In Russia, for example, judges are said to be committed not to the rule of law, but to the directives of politicians (Levin and Satarov, 2000, 131).

The consequence of judicial corruption in its most extreme form is that the judicial system is simply an arm of the most powerful actors of society. The poor are largely ignored, the rule of law is jeopardized and political officials and the wealthy can engage in actions with impunity.

Judicial corruption is a strain on the economy, primarily because it can seriously undermine property rights protections. When there is little certainty that contracts will be honoured unless bribes are paid, few want to invest in the state's economy, lowering trade, increasing capital flight and ultimately hurting growth (Dreher and Herzfeld, 2005). In Russia, for example, a weak legal system (in conjunction with unreliable financial information and poor accounting procedures) is said to cost that state as much as $10 billion per year in potential investments that are lost (Eigen, 2002, 48).

Political corruption

Political corruption is perhaps the most serious form of corruption because it often trickles over into other institutional spheres. Political corruption involves the abuse of elected office for individual gain (Kramer, 1997). This abuse can take a variety of forms, including the provision of benefits to family members or friends of public officials and embezzlement and seizure of state assets for officials' personal bank accounts.

States suffering from severe political corruption are known as kleptocracies, or rule by thieves. In a kleptocracy, political officials essentially steal from the state. The primary beneficiary is typically the leader of the government, who exploits the state for personal enrichment. Leaders of kleptocracies often accept bribes and kickbacks in return for political favours, and the entire system is structured to pad the leader's pockets (and in many instances those of other elites too).

In a kleptocracy, private economic activities are discouraged out of the fear that any assets will simply be taken at the discretion of the ruler or his cronies. In Uganda, for example, Idi Amin (1971–1979) allegedly stripped the Asian community of $400 million in assets on a whim (Lundahl, 1997, 37). In such an environment, legitimate businesses often choose to operate underground instead and capital flees.

Experts have identified numerous examples of kleptocratic behaviour. William Reno reported that Malawian president Hastings Banda (1966–1994), for one, used family trusts to manage the state's commercial activities (Reno, 2000), while Bangladeshi president Hussain Muhammad Ershad (1983–1990) was accused of receiving a fixed percentage of income from business deals and funnelling state funds directly into his own bank accounts (Ulklah, 2004, 433). The president of Kyrgyzstan, Askar Akaev (1990–2005), also allegedly stole from the state, amassing a large personal fortune by misusing foreign aid allocations, as did Saparmurat Niyazov (1990–2006), the president of Turkmenistan, who directly pocketed massive sums of money by siphoning energy rents into offshore accounts (Collins, 2009).

The amount of money reportedly stolen by kleptocratic leaders can be staggering: Liberia's Samuel Doe (1980–1990) accumulated a fortune that amounted to half of that state's annual domestic income (Reno, 2000); Sani Abacha (1993–1998) of Nigeria amassed about $4 billion of state funds (Goldsmith, 2004); and Suharto of Indonesia and his family came to be worth in excess of $15 billion (Quah, 2006). According to TI, Haiti's Jean-Claude Duvalier (1971–1986) reportedly stole about 1.7–4.5% of Haiti's GDP every year that he was in office (Rose-Ackerman, 2007). Family members and other cronies received checks from the state, in some cases for as much as nearly seven million dollars (Lundahl, 1997).

One of the most notorious and economically destructive kleptocrats was Joseph Mobutu (1965–1997) of Zaire (today's Democratic Republic of Congo). In the 1970s, reportedly 15–20% of Zaire's operating budget went straight to Mobutu, and in 1977 alone his family used $71 billion from the National Bank for their own personal benefit (Leslie, 1987, 72). Mobutu allegedly siphoned off income from Zaire's resource exports, eventually acquiring over $8 billion. While Mobutu and his family were getting richer, the people of Zaire were getter poorer. Robert Rotberg sums Mobutu up well: 'What set Mobutu apart from other neo-patrimonial rulers was his unparalleled capacity to institutionalize kleptocracy at every level of the social pyramid and his unrivalled talent for transforming personal rule into a cult and political clientelism into cronyism. Stealing was not so much a perversion of the ethos of public service as it was its raison d'être (2003, 31).

Kleptocracy, of course, is an extreme form of political corruption. There are many other, somewhat less harmful, types of political corruption too. Take electoral fraud, for example. Electoral fraud is illegal interference in elections. Typical methods include vote buying (paying voters to vote for a particular candidate or party) and ballot stuffing (manipulating ballot results to favour a particular candidate or party). In addition to these methods, governments can also manipulate elections by putting allies on electoral commissions that then determine the electoral winners. Bangladesh's Ershad, for example, reportedly personally appointed members of that state's electoral commission, ensuring that it served his interests no matter if it was 'destroying the credibility of the electoral system' (Khan, 1998, 10). Though it is less economically destructive than kleptocracy, electoral fraud can disconnect citizens from their representatives and foster voter apathy.

Nepotism and cronyism are other forms of political corruption. Nepotism refers to the distribution of patronage (such as jobs, economic rents and other favours) solely based on familial ties rather than on merit. Cronyism is a similar concept, except patronage is given to friends rather than family members. Both nepotism and cronyism are common forms of political corruption in the developing world.

In many developing states, for example, family members or friends control key sectors of the economy. Kazakhstan's president Nursultan Nazarbaev (1991–) and his relatives head the media, water and construction industries (Franke et al., 2009) and Kyrgyzstan's Akayev's family led the ministries in charge of gold mining. In the Dominican Republic under Rafael Trujillo (1930–1961), family members allegedly amassed a fortune equal to that state's entire GDP and 'controlled almost 80 per cent of the country's industrial production' (Acemoglu et al., 2004, 172).

Nepotism and cronyism can also manifest themselves in the use of laws to undermine rivals. Marcos of the Philippines, for example, passed a decree in 1975 that imposed a 100% tax on tobacco filler for all companies except his brother-in-law's (Aquino, 1997, 45). Nepotism and cronyism can be seen, as well, in the allocation of political posts to family and friends. Under Trujillo, most family members held government positions. Some estimate that as many as 153 of Trujillo's relatives had government employment, including senatorial posts, diplomatic assignments and leadership positions in the military (Acemoglu et al., 2004). Loyalty was the primary qualification necessary to obtain these positions; competence mattered very little. As a reflection of this, Trujillo's son was appointed colonel at the age of four and promoted to brigadier general at the age of nine (Hartlyn, 1998). Not surprisingly, nepotism and cronyism are harmful to development, as they prevent legitimate and qualified businesses and individuals from being productive participants in state activities while also giving influence, money and power to businesses and individuals who are undeserving.

Political corruption is not only harmful to the state's legitimacy and citizen representation, but also to the economy. When government resources are devoted to kleptocracy, nepotism or cronyism, this prohibits adequate spending on human capital and other productive uses of state funds (Drury et al., 2006). Important fields like health care and education suffer, as funds are diverted to the pockets of the well-connected. At the same time, the gains made through corruption are lost on the state, as they are rarely devoted to productive activities, but rather used to further entrench patron–client relationships or increase balances in overseas bank accounts.

Security corruption

Security institutions encompass both the police and the military and, as such, corruption can appear in both. We begin with police corruption. Bribes are a key issue for law enforcement agencies. In corrupt agencies, police officers may refuse to offer help unless money or other favours exchange hands. In Bangladesh, for example, 90% of citizens polled stated that they could not receive help from the police unless they offered a bribe, and 68% stated that the police approached them for bribes (Ulklah, 2004, 433). As a result, many poor citizens try to avoid the police because they cannot afford to pay for their services.

Often times, police corruption entails officers carrying out arbitrary arrests or detainments to pad their pockets. In Indonesia, for example, citizens complain they are often pulled over for no reason while driving and then asked to pay a bribe to avoid a worse penalty (Robertson-Snape,

1999). Beyond bribes, police corruption can also involve officers using their positions to commit crime.

Mexico is a developing state that has suffered from serious problems with police corruption. A survey conducted in 2002 reported that the average Mexican household spends 8% of its income on paying bribes to the police (Reames, 2003). Police officers are also known to serve as fronts for criminal groups and/or to extort them in return for turning a blind eye to their activities. As a result, drug lords frequently pay off police officers so that they can operate with impunity (Davis, 2006). Police corruption is so rampant in Mexico that 90% of citizens state that they have no trust in the police (Reames, 2003). Citizens live in fear of the police, rather than seeing them as providers of security.

Of course, Mexico is not alone in the severity of its police corruption. Police forces in Central Asia are also notorious for their corruption and susceptibility to bribery. The police in this part of the world have reportedly had a heavy hand in the drug trade; drugs easily make their way there via Afghanistan due to the help of paid-off police (Thomas and Kiser, 2002).

Corruption in the military is also a problem. This type of corruption often takes the form of illegitimate procurement practices, though militaries have also engaged in rent seeking in a number of places, taking a cut out of resource income and agriculture profits, for example (Willett, 2009). With military corruption, the military uses its position of power to procure unnecessary equipment and defence supplies in exchange for kickbacks. In Uganda, for example, since the late 1990s the military has reportedly bought military hardware at an inflated rate using the defence budget in return for cash. According to Susan Willett, in 1998, the military bought four Mi-24 helicopters from Belarus for $12.3 million, even though they were not airworthy and worth far less than that. As a gift for this gesture, Major General Salim Saleh (Ugandan leader Yoweri Museveni's brother) received $800,000 (2009, 346). This type of illegitimate transaction can easily occur because transparency in the defence industry is often lacking, as military budgets typically face little scrutiny.

At the same time, corruption of this sort saps state resources. Nigeria provides another example of this. In 1975, the military there reportedly ordered enough cement to satisfy the needs of the entire continent of Africa, costing the state $2 billion or nearly a quarter of the state's oil revenues that year (Lundahl, 1997, 40). This massive cement order, of course, came with a kickback for the military.

In sum, corruption has a number of negative economic consequences for states, some direct and some indirect. It reduces growth, increases inequality and can prevent citizens from obtaining even the most basic services from the state. In the section that follows, we show how institutional reform can help states combat corruption.

Dealing with corruption

Ridding a state of corruption requires both the desire to do so, as well as the capacity to put in place transparent procedures and assurances that officials are held accountable for their actions. The political will to tackle corruption is often the critical factor. Corruption creates vested interests, as those who are benefitting from it have an interest in maintaining the status quo and will actively pressure the state to do so. Thus reducing corruption requires institutional reform for all of the institutions that are plagued by corruption.

In terms of a state's administrative institutions, increases in pay can dramatically reduce corruption. Bribes are simply less enticing when civil servants are well compensated. A number of organizations, including the World Bank and IMF, have argued that in many places administrators accept bribes simply because if they did not they would not be able to survive on their low wages, a phenomenon known as 'survival competition' (Quah, 2008, 242). Ghana provides an example of this. In the 1960s and 1970s, civil servants' salaries were so low that many employees did not make enough to afford a balanced diet even if their entire incomes were devoted to food (Gould and Amaro-Reves, 1983). Low salaries are also troublesome because they can force civil servants to seek supplementary employment, lessening their abilities to perform their duties and work in a productive fashion (Gould and Amaro-Reves, 1983). In places where civil servants lack job security, this situation is even worse.

Streamlining and reducing the number of rules and regulations is also helpful. Excessive rules and regulations create opportunities for administrative corruption. In Central Asia, for example, there are often a multitude of rules and regulations in place to govern economic transactions. In Uzbekistan, getting a business license can require as many as 16 procedures and take as long as 152 days (World Bank, 2012). As a result, it is fairly common for government officials to receive bribes to cut the red tape for private actors (Franke et al., 2009). With fewer rules and regulations in place, there are fewer chances for civil servants to ask for bribes and private actors to offer them.

Cutting down the number of rules and regulations can also make it easier for officials to enforce those that exist. In Latin America, for example, it is often a problem that administrative officials are so bogged down with paperwork that it is difficult for them to keep up with all of it (Fernandez-Kelly and Shefner, 2005). Their state governments require an endless array of forms to be filled out for transactions to occur, and administrative staff often cannot ensure that all are being completed as stipulated. In Peru, a 1989 study showed that it can take 289 days of full-time work to get a business started. To speed up the process, bribes are typically offered at least on ten occasions during the process (de Soto, 1989, 133). Excessive rules and regulations, in other words, both create opportunities for bribery and weigh the administrative staff down with paperwork, leading to cycles of corruption. Corruption levels can therefore be reduced if states reduce red tape in the administrative sector, and if they use clear language in the rules and regulations to reduce the chances that they can be open to various interpretations.

In cases of extreme corruption, individuals may actually seek out civil service jobs as a way of getting rich (Bratton and van de Walle, 1994). Certain offices can lead to big economic gains due to the pervasiveness of bribery. In such instances, as mentioned earlier, individuals will actually pay bribes just to secure the position (Lenski and Lenski, 1987)! This has been the case in the past in Pakistan, where customs posts often went to the highest bidders (Islam, 1989).

Mitigating this problem requires punishment for officials who take part in administrative corruption. The statistics on prosecution rates reflect this. In Hong Kong, which has low levels of corruption, civil servants who engage in corruption are 35 times more likely to be punished than are their counterparts in the Philippines, which has high levels of corruption (Quah, 2006). And in India, one of the reasons that corruption is thought to persist there is because 'corrupt officials are able to get away without punishment [that is] commensurate with their offence' (Quah, 2008, 244). In contrast, both Hong Kong and Singapore have created anti-corruption commissions and enacted laws that give them extensive powers. If officials are found guilty of corruption, they can be subjected to severe punishments no matter their position or political connections. As a result, 'Graft is seen as a high-risk, low-reward activity' (Quah, 2006, 177).

Independent judicial institutions can also help. Many countries have laws prohibiting bribery, but their effect will be minimal if punishments are rarely distributed. Independent judiciaries that are insulated from other branches can increase the chances that punishments will be given in accordance with existing laws. This is true not just for administrative corruption, but also for other areas, like security corruption, in which bribes and kickbacks are a big problem.

Reducing judicial corruption often requires better pay and working conditions for judicial officials, as well as decentralization of the court system. Research shows that corruption levels are higher when the organizational structure of the court system concentrates power in the hands of a few (Moore and Buscaglia, 1999). This is particularly true in states where the judicial institutions are not subject to oversight and face little accountability. Judicial corruption is also shown to be higher in states where the system is complex, overly ridden with procedures and lacking in transparency (Moore and Buscaglia, 1999). This type of environment makes it easier for judges to act arbitrarily, which can lead to inconsistencies in how law is applied in various cases.

In terms of political corruption, democratic political institutions are of critical importance. As a reflection of this, none of the ten most corrupt states in the world is a democracy. The negative correlation between democracy and corruption levels most likely exists because democracies allow for greater citizen accountability and transparency (Robertson-Snape, 1999). Citizens can simply vote out politicians who have engaged in corruption. This greatly reduces the incidence of kleptocracy, in particular (World Bank, 1997). In addition, democracies are more likely to have a free media that can raise a red flag by publicizing offences when corruption occurs (Brunetti and Weder, 2003; Besley et al., 2002). They are also more likely to have active civil society groups that monitor government activities (Quah, 2006).

Political institutions that provide checks and balances on political behaviour are also important in curbing corruption. Different levels of government can 'effectively patrol each other', (Glaeser and Goldin, 2004, 19). Legislative institutions usually tend to be stronger in democracies, and can keep the executive branch in check. Studies have shown that states with executive branches that are stronger vis-à-vis other branches of power are more prone to corruption (Hochstetler, 2006). Leaders can steal from the state with impunity in such a context. Nicaragua provides a good example of this. Though Nicaragua has struggled with corruption, it was particularly troublesome during the tenure of Arnoldo Alemán from 1997 to 2002. The Nicaraguan constitution already gave considerable power to the executive branch, but upon assuming power Alemán concentrated power even further in the hands of the president (Anderson, 2006). These changes paved the way for corruption under his rule. Transparency International estimates that he looted over $100 million just in the five years of his presidency (Transparency International, 2012).

We now offer a case study to illustrate that cutting the cycle of corruption is indeed possible. In particular Georgia is often cited as a case of successful security sector reform (Light, 2014).

Case study: reform in Georgia

Though corruption is common in the developing world and difficult to get rid of, a few states have been able to buck the trend. Georgia offers one example. After achieving independence following the breakup of the Soviet Union in 1991, Georgia quickly became mired in corruption. The situation was so serious that in the years that followed it was consistently ranked one of the most corrupt countries in the world by Transparency International.

Corruption reportedly pervaded every aspect of Georgian life. Students at the top universities there had to pay bribes for admissions. University funds were embezzled rather than devoted to even the most fundamental repairs. Classroom furniture often collapsed as a result and many facilities lacked heating. The calibre of the university system was so low that when students graduated, they lacked basic skills to secure for themselves gainful employment. Lawyers graduated with little understanding of the law; engineers graduated with little understanding of construction (Shelley et al., 2007, 4).

Criminal groups (see Box 7.3 on *Organized Crime*) took control of various parts of the country, including the Pankisi Gorge region bordering Chechnya. Drug smuggling, abductions and other serious crime became common. The Georgian law enforcement agencies simply turned a blind eye to this (Fairbanks, 2001). The government even colluded with some criminal groups, who had infiltrated many state structures. Many members of former president Eduoard Shevardnadze's cabinet were alleged to be directly involved in organized crime, for example (Kukhianidze, 2009).

Bribes were also needed to secure employment in the government, particularly those that gave officials access to kickbacks. A 1998 World Bank study, for example, found that the prices of 'high rent' public positions were 'well known' among public officials and the general public. The study concluded that corruption was 'deeply institutionalized' (World Bank, 1998).

Corruption reduced the quality of services offered to citizens. In the energy sector, for example, corruption was such that citizens often did not have access to electricity. Blackouts became a daily reality of life, and during the long winter months, it was difficult to have functional heating. Roads were also in disrepair due to corruption, as were transportation networks. The chief administrator of the railroads, for example, had stolen most of the money that would have been used to fix them (Shelley et al., 2007, 6). The health-care system suffered as well. Basic sanitation standards were not regulated and bribes were required to obtain even the most basic services (Sumbadze, 2009).

By the time Mikheil Saakashvili (2004–2013) assumed the presidency, Georgia was knee-deep in endemic corruption. Saakashvili had two main priorities when he came to power: reunify Georgia with breakaway regions in Abkhazia and South Ossetia and eradicate corruption. He believed that the former could not happen without completing the latter. Part of the reason for this was the connection between separatist groups in those regions and the illegal economy. Indeed, by some estimates, the illegal economy was so large that it comprised 70% of Georgia's total economic transactions (Shelley et al., 2007, 6). Separatist groups were able to keep their movement alive through the profits they secured through corruption.

Saakashvili first implemented sweeping reforms of the state's police agency, transforming what was once a corrupt force into a professionalized one (Kukhianidze, 2009). Indeed, the police up to that point were considered the most corrupt state institution. He fired a majority of the police officers and gave those who remained significant pay increases, such that their salary packages were above the national averages (Light, 2014). This reduced the incentive for police officers to seek out bribes. To increase officer morale, he also gave them new police cars and uniforms (Di Puppo, 2010, 2). Several police agencies that were failing were purged, and recruitment and training procedures were transformed (Light, 2014). The training process became extensive, favouring university graduates. Future officers had to pass an exit exam after finishing the Police Academy that was rigorous, so much so that a majority of students did not pass. All of this increased the quality of the officer corps. It also dramatically reduced corruption. Surveys taken five years after these reforms revealed that 77% of the police were less corrupt than they had been. And a 2011 study showed that the police were one of the most trusted institutions in Georgia (Nasuti, 2011).

Saakashvili also sought to reform the state's administrative institutions. He reasoned that attacking graft, at all times, would invigorate the private and public sectors and potentially increase state revenues to bolster the fiscal strength of the state (George, 2009). The reason for this is that corruption in the administrative sector prior to this had been so damaging that the state could barely collect tax revenues. To address this issue, Saakashvili introduced reforms that utilized a merit-based hiring process; family members of politicians were no longer hired in the civil service as they had been in past years. Increased revenues due to these changes enabled additional improvements, including the provision of higher salaries for bureaucrats. The changes were so dramatic that tax collection increased by 400% in just the five-year period after the reforms were enacted (Light, 2014, 326). Saakashvili also simplified the tax system, making citizens more willing to comply with it and pay their taxes. The total number of separate taxes was cut from 22 in 2004, for example, to 6 in 2008 (Light, 2014). Fines were increased for not paying taxes, also helping collection efforts. Individuals who tried to engage in tax evasion were investigated and tried, marking a break from the Shevardnadze era (Shelley et al., 2007, 6).

The reforms in the administrative sector had positive ripple effects in other areas. In the energy sector, for example, many citizens no longer experienced extensive blackouts. Electricity is now delivered without interruption and there is access to heating throughout the winter in many parts of the country. Officials in the energy sector who were corrupt were also replaced (Shelley et al., 2007).

Box 7.3   Organized crime

Organized crime consists of groups that are engaged in illicit activities in order to generate income. Organized criminal groups use violence, threats of violence and bribery to maintain their operations. Organized criminal groups usually have no political goals and are more concerned with profits. These groups are most interested in controlling or subverting legal structures to be able to maintain their operations unbothered. Organized crime often infiltrates the state institutions in order to ensure that policies are enacted that sustain their viability and preclude them from having to adhere to the law.

When the state has been captured by organized crime at every level and in every institution, this has serious implications for development. Policy decisions are made that suit the needs of criminal groups. No long-term investment takes place. Legitimate businesses must operate in a chaotic environment. Corruption is rampant and foreign direct investment plummets.

The strength of organized crime is a clear indicator of the state's weakness. In many cases, the state is no longer able to provide physical safety and to enforce commercial contracts and property rights. This creates a social climate permeated by a lack of trust, and protection and enforcement rackets develop as a substitute. Criminal organizations act as an authoritarian *shadow state* (see Box 7.1). In the absence of anything else, these organizations can be perceived as legitimate by the citizenry (Shelley, 1999; Sung, 2004).

Reforms were also pursued in the education system. Competitive national exams were introduced to determine admissions. This means that bribery was no longer the determinant of student acceptance. In addition, due to more stringent monitoring, students can no longer use bribes to improve their grades and pass courses. Incompetent faculty members were also purged, even at the senior level. These changes resulted in higher quality university graduates (Shelley et al., 2007, 6).

Taken together, the reforms initiated by Saakashvili led to a marked reduction in that state's corruption levels. The approach was multipronged, but addressed nearly all of the key sectors of the state. This case illustrates that with the right institutional changes, states can root out even the most rampant corruption.

Conclusion

Corruption is both common and problematic in the developing world. Across the board, corruption harms economic development, regardless of whether it occurs in the administrative, judicial, political or security spheres. Beyond hurting a state's economic prospects, corruption also reduces citizens' trust in the state. It generates feelings of frustration, impotence and resentment among citizens who lose faith in the state's abilities to adhere to its own laws.

Corruption also disproportionately affects the state's poor, increasing inequality in parts of the world where the poor are already struggling to begin with. Corruption typically improves the well-being of the wealthy, who can afford to pay bribes and are often the recipients of illegal rents and kickbacks. At the same time, it disadvantages the poor, isolating them from state services because they do not have the means to pay for them. As such, the economy as a whole suffers in corrupt states, and the distance between the 'haves' and 'have-nots' increases.

Because corruption creates vested interests – in that those who are benefiting from it have incentives to mobilize and keep the status quo in place – it can be difficult to combat. In many places, corruption is so endemic that it can even feel like part of a state's culture. Breaking free from bad habits of corruption requires a state that has the will and capacity to do so. Subtle changes can reap great rewards, including minimizing rules and regulations, but often the institutional changes required to tackle corruption are larger in scale, like implementing a free and fair electoral process and giving the judicial apparatus greater independence. Greater awareness of the negative economic consequences of corruption, however, may provide states with more incentive to pursue even the toughest changes.

Questions

- In what ways have different colonial heritages impacted corruption levels?
- What explains the correlation between corruption and inequality?
- What are the ways that corruption can undermine education, health care and access to clean water?
- Regarding judicial institutions, what is the difference between procedural corruption and operational corruption? Why is the latter a more serious problem?
- What is a kleptocracy and what are the effects of kleptocratic governments?

Facts

- Some scholarship of corruption has emphasized that settler colonies had lower levels of corruption compared to extractive colonies.
- The agencies of the state that are most likely to be corrupt are revenue collection, customs, border control and licensing.
- Notorious kleptocrat, Mobutu of Zaire, was reportedly responsible for stealing as much as $8 billion from resource exports and foreign aid.
- Corruption in the security sector often entails accepting a kickback for procuring unnecessary military equipment such as when the Nigerian military placed a $2 billion cement order (or enough cement to satisfy the needs of all of Africa) in exchange for a huge kickback.
- In Hong Kong, which has low levels of corruption, civil servants who engage in corruption are 35 times more likely to be punished than are their counterparts in the Philippines.

Chapter 8

Colonialism and Geography

Early theorists seeking to explain why some states are rich and others are poor debated the primary reasons for the observed divergence in wealth. Was the international system responsible for persistent poverty by creating and perpetuating exploitative relationships (as the dependency theorists argued)? Or were states to blame for their own lack of growth because their citizens were not yet ready for development (as modernization theorists implied)? As we discussed in Chapter 2, the evolution of research and scholarship seeking to address these questions has significantly affected the policy advice given to developing states. When ideas from the Dependency School prevailed, the primary advice given to developing countries was to close their economies to foreign investment and protect their domestic industries from foreign competition, which stifled prospects for growth through foreign investment. In contrast as the Washington Consensus and its neo-liberal foundations moved to the forefront, developing states were urged to privatize state industries, dramatically reduce government spending, float their exchange rates, and open up their economies to trade and foreign investment, which exposed developing states to enormous vulnerabilities at the hands of international markets.

Though economists now have a better understanding of the benefits of taking a more moderate approach, we still see large numbers of poor states in the world. The overwhelming consensus is that state institutions are the key intervening factor that explains this persistent variation in levels of wealth. Low-quality state institutions can deter states from implementing sound economic policies and, even when states do implement them, can limit their effectiveness. By this point in this study, it should be fairly clear that state institutions matter for economic performance.

Yet, why did some states develop growth-enhancing institutions but others did not? To answer this question this chapter examines the role played by historical and geographical factors. Colonialism, location and climate have been important to undermining the emergence the institutions that are conducive to growth. For some states, institutions never emerged or were poorly structured, prohibiting growth and keeping them mired in poverty.

In this chapter, we focus on two key factors that stay out of states' control: colonial legacies and geography. States have no control over their colonial history. Yet, although states can implement policies to lessen the impact of colonialism, the reality is that colonial rule created an uphill battle for these states to overcome. It is undeniable that France faced fewer challenges to overcome upon statehood than did some of its former colonies, like Central African Republic and Chad. Moreover, states that experienced particularly exploitative and abusive colonial empires have had more development struggles than those that did not.

A state's geographical location is also a good predictor of its contemporary level of development, yet is also something that is (for the most part) not within a state's control. Geography affects economic performance through a variety of mechanisms, which cumulate to produce a striking relationship: states that are closer to the equator are significantly poorer than states that are far from it.

The first part of this chapter provides an explanation of colonialism, followed by a historical overview. The chapter then reviews how colonialism and geography are strongly correlated with contemporary levels of development. But the story does not end there, of course. Existing research indicates that one of the key mechanisms through which both colonialism and geography have affected economic performance is via their impact on state institutions. After providing a brief explanation of the key concept of geography, the third part of this chapter explains this pathway illustrating how both colonialism and geography affected the types of institutions that emerged in states and, as a consequence, their development. Though both these factors are not sufficient as explanations on their own for the institutional variation we see across states, it is an important part of the story. We close with two brief case studies: the case of Panama, which continues to assert its autonomy with great success, and the case of the Democratic Republic of Congo, which illustrates its devastating effects.

Colonialism

Starting around the 15th century, European powers began to spread their empires overseas to Africa, Asia, the Americas and to a lesser extent the Middle East, claiming land that fell outside of their traditional borders. This process, referred to as colonialism, took a variety of forms. In some places, colonial powers set up governments and established large settler communities, while in others, colonial entrenchment was minimal. Regardless of the scope of colonial activities, the major purpose of these endeavours was the same: to extract resources from newly acquired lands to enrich empires at home.

Though successive waves of independence movements levied by local populations have largely rendered colonialism a relic of the past, its shadow remains. A very clear example of the enduring impact of colonialism can be found in states' linguistic traditions. Former British colonies, ranging from Belize to Ghana to India, continue to this day to maintain English as an official language. Beyond linguistic trends, colonialism also left a lasting impact on the structure of state governments and local markets. While all former colonies faced economic, political and social challenges upon independence as a result of destructive colonial activities, the extent of these challenges varied widely. Some states were able to overcome these challenges relatively quickly, the United States being the prime example, while others found themselves overwhelmed by their magnitude, propelling a seemingly unbreakable cycle of poverty.

Here, we first describe the location of colonial empires and the timing of independence movements. We then discuss patterns of governance by colonial powers, delving into the specific policies that powers enacted and the logic behind them. Lastly, we examine differences in the experience of colonies and their impact on contemporary development patterns.

Historical background

We begin by painting a portrait of the colonial landscape. European colonization began around the 1500s and continued for about the next 400 years. Beginning with the activities of the Portuguese in the late 15th century, European powers launched a number of ventures overseas to acquire new lands. Here, we describe a number of these activities, grouped by the target region.

The Americas

Spain financed missions to the Americas shortly after the Portuguese began their colonial efforts in the 16th century. The Spanish took over most of this region, with the notable exceptions of the eastern coast of North America, which was colonized by the British, present-day Brazil, which was colonized by the Portuguese, and pockets of the Caribbean, which were predominantly colonized by the French.

Independence movements in the Americas started early, with the United States declaring independence in 1776, followed by Haiti in 1804. Brazil secured independence from Portugal two decades later in 1824. In the rest of the Americas, which were dominated by the Spanish, independence movements gained steam about the same time. Spain held onto Puerto Rico (which later fell under US rule), however, until 1897 and Cuba until 1902.

Asia

The British arrived in India in 1612, a territory they would maintain until the mid-20th century, though the Dutch, French, Danish and Portuguese also placed their stamp on India at various junctures. In East Asia, Japan governed present-day Korea and Taiwan from 1895 until the end of World War II. Japan also spread its empire to Manchuria in present-day China, but these activities were halted by war with China in 1937. Europeans first came to Southeast Asia in the 16th century, with the Portuguese arriving in Malacca in present-day Malaysia in 1511, the Dutch taking over in 1641 and the British taking hold of most of Malaysia and Singapore in 1913. The Spanish asserted control of the Philippines in the 1560s, and the United States took over by 1898. Present-day Indonesia was under Dutch control from 1800 through World War II, when it gained independence after a few years of Japanese control. By the early 1900s, Vietnam, Cambodia and Laos were under the control of France and Burma was under the control of the British. France would be driven from the region by 1954 after a difficult war against Vietnam. Britain granted independence to Burma in 1948, to Malaysia in 1957 and Singapore in 1963. Only Thailand escaped European colonization.

Middle East

In the Middle East, the remains of the Ottoman Empire were divided after World War I. Egypt was a British protectorate until the monarchy that was propped up by British rule was ousted in 1952. The British were granted present-day Iraq, Jordan and Palestine, while the French exercised control over present-day Syria and Lebanon. These colonies primarily gained independence in the mid-1900s. Most of North Africa was also under French rule. Algeria fought a bloody war for independence from France from 1954 to 1962, having been ruled by France since 1830. Morocco was colonized by France from 1912 to 1956. Tunisia gained independence from France in 1956 as well, after over eight decades of being a protectorate. The bulk of the Arabian Peninsula, by contrast, fell under the control of Saudi Arabia in 1932.

Africa

No single European power dominated the African continent. Just as decolonization was taking place in the Americas, colonial expansion was intensifying in Africa. From 1870 onwards, colonial powers searched aggressively for new territories. Fierce imperial competition characterized this period, in what has been referred to as the Scramble for Africa. Mediated by the Berlin Conference of 1884, European powers during this time reached an agreement on how to carve up Africa. Kenya and Uganda (named the East African Protectorate), Southern Africa, Nigeria,

Ghana and Sudan fell under British rule; Belgium acquired the Congo Free State; Italy was granted present-day Somalia, Eritrea and Libya; Portugal obtained Mozambique and Angola; and France received most of West Africa. Though influence was exercised over Ethiopia, it was mostly left to its own devices. In total, European powers added almost 8,880,000 square miles to their colonial possessions during the Scramble for Africa.

Independence movements across Africa primarily took place following World War II, given the decrease in European powers' financial and political will to maintain their colonies. Local populations seized this opportunity, such that by the 1970s much of the African colonies had gained independence.

Colonialism and development

Colonial policies

Few would deny that the activities of the European powers during the colonial era were politically, socially and economically destructive to local populations. In fact, many scholars believe that the colonial experience explains a good deal of the poverty that we see in much of the developing world today. European powers nearly always restructured their colonies' economies to meet their own needs, without much care for what was best for local interests. Colonies that were rich in natural resources, for example, were forced to become primary commodities suppliers. At the same time, colonizers often stifled local efforts to industrialize and make manufactured goods, in order to create markets for manufactured commodities from European powers (Frank, 1966; Kohli, 2004). It is for this reason that scholars in the Dependency School (see Chapter 2) emphasized that the history of outside exploitation created the global bifurcation between the 'haves' and 'have-nots'. As Paul Bairoch states, 'there is no doubt that a large number of negative structural features of the process of economic underdevelopment have historical roots going back to European colonization' (Bairoch, 1993, 8). Contemporary research indicates that the mechanism through which colonialism hindered development is through its impact on the formation of state institutions, which we discuss at the end of this chapter. Here, we discuss the specific policies that colonial powers put in place and the ways in which they negatively affected the populations they governed.

Poor educational policies

Educational opportunities for indigenous populations varied widely across the colonies, but in general paled in comparison to those of their colonial peers. In French-controlled Africa, for example, few locals received any education at all. As a reflection of this, by the late 1960s, up to 95% of this population was illiterate (Grier, 1999). Those locals who did receive an education were isolated and alienated from their original culture. Students were required to speak French, and all vernacular languages were forbidden. Most students also boarded and only able to return home for summer vacations, which led to high dropout rates. Teachers were poorly qualified to teach, programmes taught were often irrelevant and most schools were overcrowded (Grier, 1999, 326).

The Belgian colonial educational policies were even worse. Under Belgian colonial rule, students in the present-day Democratic Republic of Congo were not permitted to seek higher education until 1950. Native Africans were also forbidden to receive training as doctors, lawyers or architects, nor were they allowed to study in Belgium (Meredith, 2005, 97).

British colonial educational policies, though flawed in many ways, were quite a bit better in comparison. The British made a conscious effort to avoid alienating the native culture by teaching in the vernacular languages and training teachers from the indigenous tribes (Grier, 1999, 319). However, in some states such as Nigeria, the British failed to implement its educational systems evenly. The South received much better access to education compared to the North, with Southerners being given the opportunity to study in the United Kingdom. Overall, variation in the education policies of the colonizers contributed to an enduring development gap between colonies, despite the fact that post-colonial education rates have largely converged (Grier, 1999, 328). In some cases, the inconsistent education policies within colonies aggravated regional disparities within states, feeding uneven regional development that has often been at the heart of intra-state conflict.

Unfair trade policies

Trade policies of the colonial powers were typically restrictive, preventing colonies from accessing a variety of markets. The Spanish, Portuguese and French, for example, imposed extremely protectionist trade measures. Spanish colonies were only allowed to trade with Spain by law and only permitted to conduct such trade through a single designated port. The French also imposed a strict, mercantilist system. French colonies were forced to import from France, and all exports going to France had to be sold using French ships (Grier, 1999, 320). The United Kingdom again was the exception. By 1830, it employed a free trade policy, opening colonial trade to all foreign states; by 1846, British colonies no longer had to give British goods preferential treatment (Grier, 1999). It is worth noting that monetary policies were equally controlling, in that colonies were denied the autonomy to print and coin their own money (Herbst, 2000).

Unequal land distribution

Colonization also created significant wealth inequality, in part due to the unequal distribution of land and land tenure policies. The land tenure systems exported by Portugal and Spain, for example, have been identified as being particularly problematic for development (Bulmer-Thomas, 2003, 13). Stanley Engerman and Kenneth Sokoloff (2012) argue that Spanish and Portuguese settlers owned a greater proportion of land in their colonies relative to other colonizers, due to the types of natural resources and the labour supply that was present in the states they colonized. In order to capitalize on Latin America's abundant natural resources, the colonizers established large slave plantations in the tropical areas (using both imported slaves and indigenous populations) and cattle haciendas elsewhere. This large concentration of wealth in the hands of a relative few led to the creation of unequal societies where settler elites were able to exploit indigenous and slave populations. Colonial regimes created institutions, in turn, that defended only the property rights of elites. Mexico, for example, emerged from its colonial history with institutions that advantaged elites, giving them preferential access to economic opportunities, which has contributed to the persistence of inequality there (Engerman and Sokoloff, 2012).

Latin America, as a result, has one of the most unequal income distributions in the world. It is not uncommon to find the top 10% of households receiving more than 40% of the total income, whereas the bottom 40% receives less than 15% (Bulmer-Thomas, 2003). In contrast, natural resource endowments in North American colonies, such as New England, led to smaller scale agricultural enterprises and a more equal distribution of wealth and land. Institutions were thus created that secured property rights of broader sectors of the population.

In some parts of Africa, illegal sales of lands help explain why gaps between rich and poor are so pronounced. The settlers expropriated more land than they could effectively use in order to acquire better control over labour. In Rhodesia (present-day Zimbabwe), the expropriation of land resulted in 250,000 wealthy whites controlling half of the most desirable land, while about five million blacks shared the rest. In Kenya in 1952, on the eve of that state's insurrection, some 9,000 settlers had exclusive rights to 16,700 square miles of land, while several million Africans were forced to exist on congested reserves, as contract labourers on white farms and as unskilled workers in the towns.

High levels of inequality that persist in South Africa are also rooted in the colonial policies of unfair land distribution policies. In 1819, 5,000 British immigrants were allowed to settle in South Africa. The 1913 Natives Land Act allocated 87% of the land to white people leaving only 13% for blacks (Acemoglu and Robinson, 2012, 265). Natives served as cheap labour on white land to support industries owned by whites, but few owned land themselves.

Oppressive labour policies

The primary goal of most of the colonial endeavours was enrichment of the colonial power, which was achieved primarily by the exploitation of people. The slave trade had a devastating effect on Africa's development. The only contact that Europe had with Africa from the 16th century to the mid-19th century was through the slave trade. Over 12 million slaves were shipped to the Americas during this time (Lovejoy, 2000). A study by Nathan Nunn (2008) argues that the number of slaves taken during the slave trade is negatively tied to countries' contemporary economic performance. This was certainly the case in Africa. Colonial empires viewed the African population as a cheap labour force and a key asset to colonial development. There were particularly high demands for African labour in the areas of agriculture and mining.

For example, when King Leopold II (1865–1909) of Belgium acquired international approval to add the Congo region (called the Congo Free State and now known as the Democratic Republic of Congo) to his personal empire, it was awash with resources such as ivory, palm oil, timber and cooper. He then commissioned expeditions to strip the Congo's forests of all of their wild rubber, imposing quotas on villagers and taking hostages (Meredith, 2005). He also used a system of slave labour and forced the natives to work the valuable rubber resources. Natives were required to spend 40 hours each month gathering rubber for the colony (Buell, 1965, 567). Those who refused had their hands and feet chopped off, or were tortured and flogged, including women and children. Curfews were enforced and no Congolese were able to travel freely. Thousands were killed for resisting and thousands more fled. The harsh treatment of the natives reduced the Congolese population by 50%, or as many as 10 million people. Meanwhile King Leopold II became one of the richest men in Europe (Meredith, 2005, 96). In Uganda, natives were forced to provide 30 free days of labour a year to help build roads (Buell, 1965, 567), while in Kenya, they were obligated to work 24 days a year unpaid and an additional 60 days a year of compulsory, but compensated, labour (Berman and Lonsdale, 1980, 68).

These labour policies led many to engage in unproductive activities in order to avoid being forced into labour by the Europeans. Some were able to work within the colonial administration, but these individuals were paid so little that they only earned a living by extracting resources from the peasantry. Others escaped by joining rebel armies or armed bandits that did not contribute to production. Guerrilla fighters survived through stealing from the peasant populations (Nunn, 2007).

Box 8.1 Colonialism in the Belgian Congo

The case of the Democratic Republic of Congo (DRC) illustrates how colonial histories can leave very deep wounds. Perhaps no colonial experience was as destructive as the Belgian empire in today's DRC. Belgian exploration of that region started in the 1870s, and its influence there lasted through independence of the DRC in 1960. The leader of Belgium at the time, King Leopold, took control of the Congo and established the Congo Free State from 1885 to 1908, which was the most devastating period of colonial rule. It is possible that during this period only eight million Congolese survived out of the original 30 million.

Leopold resorted to extreme measures to exploit the Congo Free State and maximize the riches he could gain from it. Tactics included murder, torture and human mutilation, all of which were intended to force the Congolese to abandon their traditional way of life and do what was ordered of them by the colonial state. Villages that were not able to meet their daily labour quotas in the supply of rubber and ivory, for example, had their members flogged, imprisoned, raped and killed (Nzongola-Ntalaja, 2002). Raw hide whips were used to flay victims, sometimes to their death (Meredith, 2005, 95). And hostages were even taken on occasion.

After the demise of the Congo Free State in 1908, Belgian Congo emerged, which made the area subject to the rule of Belgian parliament. Economic exploitation continued, though it was less violent in nature. The Belgians joined forces with giant mining and business corporations to govern the area. This exploitation made Belgian Congo incredibly profitable for Belgium. By 1959, it was producing 10% of the world's cooper, 50% of its cobalt and 70% of its industrial diamonds.

At the same time, the Congolese paid a massive price for this success. Congolese were forced to spend 60 days a year working on public construction projects, a number that doubled during World War II. Some were made to work as unpaid labourers and died of starvation. The laws that were implemented disadvantaged locals. Africans were subject to regulations restricting their movement and prevented from owning land (Esterhuyse, 2012, 36).

The Congolese were not allowed to study in Belgium, and the only schools for higher education that existed were Catholic seminaries. They could not become doctors, lawyers or architects, but were instead encouraged to train as clerks, medical assistants or mechanics. In fact, Congolese were prohibited from rising higher than the position of clerk during the Belgian administration. The Belgians cared very little about educating the population and preparing it for the road of self-governance that lay ahead. Even the most elite of the Congolese population lacked education or wealth (Esterhuyse, 2012, 37).

Exploitative taxation

Colonies were also used to generate revenues for the colonial powers. Taxes were levied as an indirect tool of extraction, forcing the African peasantry into extractive employment relations. Annual taxes were equivalent to a month's salary and had to be paid in the currency of the colony. Labour contracts were signed that lasted two years in order to obtain the currency to pay the taxes. Contracts could not be broken once they were signed (Nzula et al., 1979). Peasants were often forced into employment that offered little or no pay.

The European powers sought to make each colony self-supporting, such that growth in government expenditures flowing to the colony had to be offset by financing by the colony. In the case of French colonies in Africa, the French actually received more in taxes from the colonies than they spent or invested. In colonies under British rule in West Africa, an export marketing board accrued surpluses by keeping a large margin between the prices paid to producers and the prices that the boards received for the crop on the world market. These surpluses were kept in London in British government bonds (Rimmer, 1992, 41–42).

In Latin America, Spanish institutions also had negative consequences for the indigenous populations in their colonies, as the major ones erected were meant to exploit indigenous labour and enhance Spain's economy. Spanish elites were legally entitled to labour services from Mexicans and Peruvians, for example. Heavy taxes were imposed on the indigenous populations, which served as a key source of revenues. All surpluses extracted from the peasants remained in Spanish hands. As a result, areas with the largest indigenous populations were the most oppressed and underdeveloped in Latin America (Psacharopoulos and Patrinos, 1994).

Colonial empire strategies for control

European powers enacted a number of policies in their colonial empires that were detrimental to local populations including limiting access to education, imposing unfair trade policies, setting in place unequal distribution of land, exploiting the labour force and using taxation to severely restrict social mobility. Yet, this is the not the only way in which colonialism left its imprint. European powers also *structured* their colonies in ways that had negative (and lasting) consequences.

Many scholars have emphasized the tragedy of colonialism in this regard for Sub-Saharan Africa (from here on referred to as Africa). They point out that colonialism wreaked havoc on the process of state formation that was taking place throughout much of this region, as well as the process of *nation building* (see Box 13.1) – or creating a national identity (Ignatieff, 2002). The colonial experience intensified ethnic identities, which make it more difficult to instil a national identity among native populations.

Borders were drawn arbitrarily, with little care for respecting pre-existing ethnic boundaries. The institutional structure of most colonies was weak, leading to numerous post-independence challenges in governance (Esty et al., 1998). Here, we examine the geographical and institutional structure of the colonies and their legacies. Though we place heavy emphasis on experiences in Africa, we also highlight those in Asia, the Middle East and Latin America.

Geographical borders

Borders in Africa changed constantly until around the 20th century, following the Berlin Conference of 1884. Through the conference, European powers sliced up Africa, putting it under the direct jurisdiction of France, the United Kingdom and to a lesser extent Spain, Germany, Belgium, Italy and Portugal. While these borders often seemed random given the ethnic composition of the territory, the colonial powers designed frontiers to meet their individual needs. They drew borders quickly, regardless of the incompatibility of these lines with the mapping of local groups. The imposed borders split up communities and ethnic groups in an arbitrary manner. Scholars have written that 'little attention was paid to the implications of colonial borders for Africans. They negated the realities of African identities and autonomous African perceptions of the world' (Prah, 2004, 6). Outside of Africa, colonies met similar challenges, including South Asia (India, Pakistan, Bangladesh and Sri Lanka), colonized by the United Kingdom in the mid-19th century until 1947 and Indonesia, colonized by the Netherlands from 1602 until 1945. To meet the wants of colonial powers, different ethnic groups were just thrown together while others were split up.

Though this redrawing of borders occurred in many colonies, it was executed in ways that were particularly ill-suited for local populations in Africa. The experience of Somalia provides an excellent example of this. Somalia itself is ethnically homogenous, comprised predominately of Somalis. Yet, its borders failed to incorporate a multitude of Somalis who lived just outside these lines. As a result, a large number of Somalis today live in present-day Kenya, Ethiopia and Djibouti. Meanwhile, within Somalia itself, the clannish nature of the traditional political system there conflicts with the idea of centralized statehood (Samatar, 1997).

The experience of the Democratic Republic of Congo (formerly Zaire) provides another case in point (see Box 8.1). Its borders are a highly artificial creation derived from Henry Morton Stanley's exploration of the Congo River and King Leopold II of Belgium's search for ivory and wild rubber in the river's basin. The borders drawn uncomfortably bring together different state systems and non-state societies, while splitting important kingdoms and political cultures in areas such as the Lunda and the Bakongo (Hochschild, 1998).

Divide and conquer

Of course, the ways that borders were drawn, though arbitrary on the surface, were part of a larger divide and conquer strategy. The goal of this strategy was to create and heighten ethnic tensions and splinter ethnic identities to ensure outside control over indigenous populations (Horowitz, 1985; Gros, 1996; Esty et al., 1998). This exacerbated social fragmentation to meet the needs of colonial powers.

Examples of the use of the divide and conquer strategy in other domains beyond geography abound. In Sudan, policies were sculpted to trigger tensions between Christians and Muslims. In the south, Christian missionaries were given free rein and offered a Christian education. In the north, by contrast, the activities and influence of the Arab population were curtailed. In Myanmar, as well, the British pitted the Burmese against minority ethnic groups in order to make it easier to control the territory (Smith, 2005, 62). And France did the same in Syria, where colonists emphasized the uniqueness of the Alawites and the Sunnis and structured policies to create political fragmentation, and in Lebanon, where they favoured Christian Maronites over Sunnis and Shiites (Cleveland, 1994).

Groups were deliberately used as tools of the colonial administrations. Belgium manipulated rivalries between the Hutus and the Tutsis in present-day Rwanda to incite tensions between them, while the United Kingdom intensified rivalries in present-day Sri Lanka by favouring the Tamils over the Singhalese. Because a single ethnic group was often encouraged by the colonial power to dominate, groups that were excluded often levied direct challenges against those groups later on (Carment, 2003, 411).

In summary, the colonial experience was mostly destructive for the developing world. Colonial powers stripped states in the developing world of their natural resources, extracted high taxes, unfairly distributed the land, forced indigenous populations to hard labour and enacted ineffective trade and educational policies. Colonial powers also did little to contribute to state building. Geographical borders were drawn up badly and few outside powers invested in institutional infrastructure. States in the developing world emerged from independence without much to work with. Thus the legacy of colonialism for most states in the developing world is still very deep.

Geography

States' geographical locations are not purely independent from colonialism. After all, colonial empires often sought out territories explicitly based on their proximity to valuable goods, like waterways. Though geographical maps often overlap with colonization patterns, the two are not synonymous.

And yet, like the experience of colonialism, a state's geographical location (for the most part) falls outside of its control. Some states have been geographically blessed, while those with more challenging geographical locations have been handed a tougher set of cards. Indeed, geography is another component that is correlated with levels of development.

Geographic factors include many elements such as a country's climate. Countries with tropical climates have been highlighted as more prone to poverty compared to countries in temperate zones. For example, in 1820, the GNP per capita in the tropical regions was roughly 70% of GNP in the temperate zone. By 1992, the GNP per capita in the tropical regions was 25% of that in the temperate zone (Sachs, 2001, 11). Of the 30 richest economies in the world, only Singapore, Hong Kong and Brunei lie in tropical zones (Hausman, 2001, 46). Climate is closely related to the prevalence of certain types of diseases and may affect labour productivity rates as well (Landes, 1999).

In addition to climate, another geographic factor is a country's proximity to oceans and rivers. Landlocked countries face especially difficult economic prospects. Related to this is how mountainous a country is. Though mountains may serve a natural border to protect it from other countries, it may make trade and transport much more difficult. Mountains may also prevent impoverished people from migrating to more productive areas. Geographically trapped people may find it more difficult to move in search of better jobs.

A final geographic factor is a country's soil quality. Soil quality refers to the capacity to sustain plant and animal productivity. Some soils are much less conducive to sustainable development, making agricultural production much more difficult (Herrick, 2000).

Geography and development

Simply put, GDP per capita is higher the farther a state is from the Equator. This is true even if we isolate individual regions. In Latin America, for example, states that are closer to the Equator, like Panama, are poorer than those that are farther from it, like Argentina. It is also true if we look within individual states. The southern part of the United States (which lies in the Northern Hemisphere) is closer to the equator than the northern part; it is also poorer. At the same time, the northern part of Brazil (a state that lies in the Southern Hemisphere) is closer to the Equator than the southern part, and is poorer as well. Moreover, consider that sub-Saharan Africa is the poorest region in the world, and also that 93% of its land area lies between the Tropic of Cancer and the Tropic of Capricorn. The connection is striking.

Because geographical location is so strongly correlated with levels of development, a number of researchers have argued that there is a causal relationship. Specifically, poor geographic conditions are thought to prohibit economic growth, leading to persistent poverty. As Jeffrey Sachs, one of the leading advocates of this argument, writes, 'The proof is on the map' (2012, 148).

According to Sachs (2001) and David E. Bloom and Sachs (1998), the set of states that were never colonized in tropical areas are just as poor as those that were. In addition, there was no reversal of fortunes that took place after decolonization. Geography is the only factor that has remained consistent throughout these periods and across countries. This point is echoed by Fernand Braudel, who writes that 'In understanding Black Africa, geography is more important than history. The geographical context is not all that matters, but it is the most significant' (1995, 120).

This argument has been applied extensively to try to explain Africa's poor growth record. Bloom and Sachs write, for example, 'At the root of Africa's long-term growth crisis is Africa's extraordinary geography' (1998, 214). Africa is by far the most tropical region of the world, and yet in many domains its environment – including climate, soils, topography and diseases – is unrivalled in deterring growth, leading to perpetually low productivity in agriculture, high rates of disease and low trade integration.

There are a number of factors identified in the literature that explain how geography – specifically a tropical location – can negatively impact states. Here, we focus on three: agricultural production, disease and water access.

States in the tropics face greater challenges in producing in agriculture than do states in temperate climates. Part of this is because there are higher average temperatures in tropical states, making the soil–water balance unfavourable to agriculture production (Bloom and Sachs, 1998, 222). According to Bloom and Sachs, 'tropical agriculture, especially food production, is faced with chronic problems of low yields and fragility due to low photosynthetic potential, high evapotranspiration, low and variable rainfall, highly weathered soils, veterinary diseases, and plant and animal pests' (1998, 227). All of this means that states that are in the tropics are going to have greater difficulty excelling in agriculture production than states in temperate zones. Poor agricultural production is harmful to growth, because it lowers an economy's productivity overall and increases the costs of feeding citizens given that food must be imported.

The second mechanism is disease (a topic we return to in greater detail in Chapter 11). There are far higher rates of infectious disease outbreaks in tropical than in temperate states. Because their geographical conditions are breeding grounds for infectious diseases, states in the tropics have more citizens who are sick and/or dying. Think of malaria, a disease that is responsible for the death of millions of people each year, most of whom reside in the developing world (Bloom and Sachs, 1998). Malaria requires a temperature of at least 18°C for the mosquito to be effective. Warm and moist environments are therefore breeding grounds for infectious diseases like malaria. High rates of disease hurt growth because when citizens are sick they are unable to contribute to the economy. In addition, epidemics of disease lower overall life expectancy. As a reflection of this, the average life expectancy at birth of a person in tropical Africa is around 50 years, while it is around 66 years for a person in non-tropical Africa (Bloom and Sachs, 1998). As Bloom and Sachs (1998) show, low life expectancy is associated with lower growth rates.

A third mechanism is water access. Nations that are far from a coastline are poorer and have slower rates of growth than coastal countries. A country whose population is farther than 100 km from the sea grows 0.6% slower per year than nations where the entire population is within 100 km of the coast (Hausman, 2001, 46). Water access is important for growth because it makes it easier for states to engage in trade with one another and at lower costs. Transport costs are often determined by a country's proximity to water. A study found that shipping goods over 1 additional kilometre of land cost as much as shipping them over 7 extra kilometres of sea. Maritime shipping is much cheaper, meaning that countries lacking easy access to water will have a more difficult time entering potential markets. Land transport is especially costly for countries that have to send products across borders. The median landlocked country pays up to 50% more in transport costs than the median coastal nations. It is more than four times as costly to send a container from the Ivory Coast to the Central African Republic than to send the same item from the Ivory Coast to the United States (Hausmann, 2001, 48).

Coastal access also spurs growth by helping states meet the basic needs of citizens (one of which is water), who are better able to contribute in meaningful ways to the economy when they are healthy. Being landlocked and without access to coasts and rivers, then, is a detriment to growth. Not coincidentally, Africa has the highest proportion of landlocked states of any continent in the world and few rivers that are navigable by ocean-going vessels (Bloom and Sachs, 1998).

In sum, some geographical conditions have negatively affected states in the developing world (specifically those located in the tropics) by influencing how productive certain economic activities are going to be (like agriculture), how healthy the population is, and how capable states are of engaging in trade with other states (Sachs, 2012).

Colonialism, geography and the state

Singapore and Cambodia are both tropical states. Yet, unlike Cambodia, Singapore's income per capita level is among the highest in the developing world. The same comparison can be made with the United States and Togo, both of which are former British colonies, but whose development paths have diverged significantly. As we explain here, state institutions are critical to understanding these divergent paths.

Research indicates that both factors – colonialism and geography – affect the development of effective institutions. These institutions, in turn, set states on paths of development that become difficult to deviate from. Institutions, in other words, are the primary path through which colonialism and geography affect economic performance. This is not to say that colonialism and geography exhibit little direct impact on contemporary income levels, but rather that they also have an indirect effect on income levels via their impact on institutions.

Moreover, colonization and geography are closely related, as we mentioned above. Historical records indicate that this overlap is not coincidental; colonial empires sought out specific regions largely based on the types of resources present in those states. The type of natural resources present in a state, in turn, affected the development of institutions (Acemoglu et al., 2001; Engerman and Sokoloff, 2002). In particular, colonizers sought to develop institutions that would maximize their profits, rather than increase the long-term growth of the colony (Acemoglu et al., 2001, 1263). In Africa, Latin America and the Caribbean, for example, studies have shown that the presence of certain types of resources (referred to as endowments) were the key factor shaping the types of institutions developed (Rodrik, 1999; Acemoglu et al., 2004; Isham et al., 2005; Coatsworth, 2008). These endowments include crops, natural resources, labour supply and settler mortality rates. When settler mortality rates were high and natural resources abundant, European powers were more likely to set up extractive colonies, investing little in the institutional development of those states. In contrast, in colonies with low settler mortality rates and few natural resources, colonial settlers were more likely to reside in them, and in turn put in place high-quality institutions.

From this perspective, the quality of institutions was directly affected by the ease with which settlers could make a life for themselves and the extent to which they could pillage resources (Acemoglu et al., 2001; Acemoglu et al., 2004). In places like South Africa, Rhodesia (present-day Zimbabwe) and Botswana, for example, settlers faced comparatively few threats to their survival. They moved to these places in large numbers, establishing property rights and institutions to protect them. This did not occur in colonies where settlers died in large numbers or focused their efforts solely on the extraction of resources. Instead most states in Africa emerged as patron–client fiefdoms. The state was not needed to provide public goods but was used as a fountain of privilege for a small elite. Moreover, the indigenous population was given little opportunity to gain administrative experience.

The types of natural resources present in a state also affected institutional development (for more on this, see Box 10.2 on the *rentier state*). Latin America, for example, was abundant in resources that required high levels of low-skilled labour. Crops such as sugar, coffee and cocoa were grown on large plantations, owned by a few privileged elite and sustained by the importation of slaves. The colonial institutions that were developed were exploitative and protected the rights of a small group of elites, a pattern that persisted after independence. Stanley Engerman and Ken Sokoloff write, for example, that 'the relatively small fractions of their populations composed of whites, as well as their highly unequal distribution of wealth, may have contributed to the evolution of political, legal, and economic institutions that were less favorable toward full participation in the commercial economy by a broad spectrum of the population' (2002, 16). Landed elites in Latin America were able to accumulate personal fortunes and had little incentive to embark on reforms that would threaten their status. To maintain these inequalities, the colonial powers invested very little in Latin American public services or human capital. The administrative institutions were patrimonial during the colonial period and rarely utilized the indigenous population. In contrast, in much of North America, small farms were the norm, which facilitated the development of a large middle class that could pressure for representation and more equitable institutions.

Apart from resources, the identity of the colonizer also appears to have influenced the types of institutions that were implemented (Grier, 1999). In particular, British and Japanese colonization is commonly cited as being less destructive than that of the Spanish, French, Portuguese or Belgians. British colonization, for example, often resulted in greater investment in education, health care, sanitation, roads and law and order (Lange, 2004, 906). Both the British and Japanese focused on constructing a meritocratic civil service, where employees attained positions based on their abilities. A strong legal framework was created to regulate state and society relations, such as in Hong Kong and Singapore (both under British rule). Perhaps for this reason both British and Japanese colonies have performed better after independence. From 1960 to 1988, for example, British colonies grew 1.1% faster per year than colonies that were ruled by other European powers (Bertocchi and Canova, 2002).

In addition, many colonized states saw their customary institutions destroyed by colonizing powers. African societies had developed their own customs, laws, conventions, ethics and rituals to resolve disputes and enforce order (Amin, 1972). Some had even developed formal political systems and legal institutions that resembled modern-day courts (Bohannan and Curtin, 1988). In most cases these laws and customs were eradicated by the colonial power. Yet, in a few instances, such as Botswana, they were left largely intact. In Botswana, the country's traditional cattle-owned hierarchy was left relatively untouched, as was its provision of rights for farmers to own trees they had planted (Swallow et al., 2000). Seemingly inconsequential decisions such as these had positive effects after independence. In places outside of Africa, a similar pattern exists: where well-functioning institutions that existed prior to colonization were allowed to persist, colonies experienced a smooth transition into statehood upon independence (Englebert, 2000).

In summary, the consensus among most researchers is that colonialism and its close cousin, geography, have hurt economic performance. They have done so primarily by impeding the development of growth-promoting institutions (Easterly, 2009). Once adopted, unfortunately, these institutions become difficult to change, setting states on paths of poverty that are difficult to sever (Acemoglu et al., 2002b).

Dealing with a colonial heritage

Dealing with a colonial heritage is difficult because, unlike debt (see Chapter 9), it is not something that can be erased. And for many countries in the developing world, the colonial heritage has had mostly damaging effects on the economic structures and institutions that a country inherits. Though colonialism has had negative effects, it does not mean that colonized countries are destined to live in poverty, while those who were spared enjoy tremendous wealth. The Seychelles and Mauritius overcame their colonial heritages and are two of the most developed countries in Africa, while Ethiopia and Liberia escaped colonization but are two of the poorest countries. In Southeast Asia, Malaysia was colonized, while Thailand was not. Yet, Malaysia's per capita income is $10,000 higher.

Japanese colonies such as South Korea and Taiwan have also been able to overcome the curse of colonialism. Japanese colonialism was characterized as brutal but also productive, as Japan invested heavily in infrastructure and education (Kohli, 2004). Both these country's utilized the investment to build strong and effective administrative institutions. Though the relationships are not without tension, Japan remains South Korea's third biggest export partner while Japan is Taiwan's fourth biggest export partner. Japan also exports high volumes of trade to both countries. Thus, colonial histories can sometimes lead to interdependent relationships that are mutually beneficial.

In particular, countries that emerged with strong leadership committed to the goals of development were able to build strong institutions, in spite of the colonial legacy. Lee Kwan Yew, Singapore's first prime minister, focused more on development than on repeating patterns of colonial development that were inimical to this effort. Botswana's leadership under Seretse Khama was also instrumental in creating a strong state committed to development. But in both these cases, overcoming the colonial legacy required states to pursue institutional reform of possibly all of the state institutions (security, political, administrative and judicial), depending on how dysfunctional the institutions inherited are.

In the next section we offer the case of Panama, which overcame its colonial history and effectively took ownership over its main asset after years of being controlled by the United States. In the case of Panama, administrative institutional reform helped to make the operation of the canal a success.

Case study: Panama and the Panama Canal

In contrast to the DRC (see Box 8.1), Central American countries benefited from achieving independence much earlier (mostly in the early 19th century). In spite of this, many Central American countries have been affected by neo-colonial methods of control by the United States well into the 20th century. This has made asserting independence over their economies challenging at times. As described earlier in the chapter, colonialism often has a negative impact on former colonies fostering the creation of exclusive and poorly managed institutions. As a result, many governments of former colonies have not performed impressively, even after they've been granted autonomy. The case of Panama's management of the Panama Canal, however, illustrates how these challenges can be overcome.

Like most countries in Latin America, Panama was originally colonized by the Spanish in the 16th century. By 1821 it had broken off from Spain to join a union named the Republic of Gran Colombia, putting it under the control of Colombia. With support from the United States, Panama separated from Colombia in 1903. However, this separation enabled the United States to perpetuate a neo-colonial relationship with Panama. On November 18th 1903, Panama and the United States signed the Hay–Bunau Varilla Treaty, which granted the United States the rights to the Canal Zone and gave the United States permission to build, control and manage the Panama Canal. In return, Panama was given a payment of $10 million and an annual rental payment of $250,000. Due to contention over the United States' control of the canal, protests periodically erupted in Panama, resulting in the United States sending troops to suppress them. Increasingly frustrated by the United States' influence over the Panamanian economy, more and more Panamanians wanted revision of the terms of the Hay–Bunau Varilla Treaty. After a series of negotiations, in December of 1999 Panama was officially given control over the Panama Canal.

When Panama was granted control over the Panama Canal in 1999, sceptics predicted that Panama would have difficulty successfully taking over ownership and managing the Canal. In spite of this scepticism, Panama has proven to be a model for successful transitions from neo-colonial control. Its economy has been impressive, having one of the fastest growing economies in Latin America (averaging over 10% from 2006 to 2008) and ranking high in per capita income ($15,000), literacy rates (92%) and life expectancy (76.4 years), with an unemployment rate of 4%.

Since taking responsibility of the canal, Panama has improved its performance. Overall, many scholars have noted that the canal has been better managed under Panamanian control (Montero, 2005). For years the United States had been operating the canal at a loss due to poor management and inefficiency. The Panamanian government decided to turn the canal region from a military zone into a commercialized area, which created further opportunities for employment and profit. The Panamanian government has also strived to achieve high social and environmental standards, with strict ethical codes.

The Panamanian government had already started to dismantle the large patronage system that was associated with the canal and created the Panamanian Canal Authority (ACP), which has been successful in administering and managing the canal (Maurer and Yu, 2010). The ACP has an Advisory Board that meets once a year to discuss its experiences to improve the management of the waterway. All political parties and social groups have taken a view that all issues concerning the canal should be lifted to a legal level, eliminating political interference in the canal (Montero, 2005). This allowed the canal to operate as an independent entity without interference from political parties or former oligarchs. The administration is technocratic and focused on best practices. The ACP has also committed to providing the best services. A merit-based recruitment process has been introduced in order to ensure that the canal has the highest quality personnel, particularly at the managerial level (Rosales, 2007).

As a result of Panama's excellent management, the canal's income has grown, recording an increase of $769 million in 2000 to $1.4 billion in 2006. Traffic also increased from 230 million tons in 2000 to nearly 300 tons in 2006. The safety record has also improved with the number of accidents decreasing from 28 per year in the late 1990s to 12 by 2005. Panama Canal expansion was initiated in 2007, which will double the canal's capacity (Rosales, 2007). Overall, the canal's transition to Panamanian control has been highly successful in spite of many years of being managed by the United States.

Conclusion

The experience of colonialism put many developing states at a serious disadvantage upon independence. Existing societal fabrics were destroyed, cultural groups were split and pitted against one another and economic structures were for the most part erected for exploitation to benefit the empires rather than furthering the welfare of their subjects. Making matters worse, many (though not all) of the states that were colonized happened to be located in the tropics, a region of the world that creates additional challenges for states in terms of agricultural production, disease and water access, to name a few hurdles.

States that were once colonized and/or that happen to be located in the tropics are in many ways victims of bad luck. The colonial experience and bad geography in a number of instances hurt the development of state institutions that are conducive to growth. Such states, through no fault of their own, were confronted with an uphill development challenge after their independence.

Bad luck is undeniably part of the story in explaining why some states have weak state institutions (and as a consequence are poor) and others are not.

Yet, the goal of this chapter is not to attribute low-quality state institutions and continued poverty across the world exclusively to bad luck. Rather, it is simply to point out that it has not been a level playing field. Bad luck does not preclude states from development. As Dani Rodrik et al. write, 'geography is not destiny' (2002, 21). This is because the state is not powerless in all of this. States can and have made choices that redirect their institutional structures in positive ways.

Questions

- In what ways did colonial policies undermine future development of colonized states?
- How did colonial strategies of control undermine nation and state building in Africa?
- According to Sachs and Bloom, why is geography more important than history in explaining Africa's underdevelopment?
- What are endowments and why are they important for explaining variations in development?
- Why was Panama able to manage the Panama Canal more effectively than the United States?

Facts

- African colonies received independence incredibly late, with some not gaining independence until the 1970s.
- Latin America has one of the most unequal income distributions in the world, much of which is due to the land tenure systems that were exported by Portugal and Spain during the colonial period.
- Tropical climates, being landlocked and having poor soil quality are all geographic factors that impact economic development.
- British and Japanese colonization are often cited as being less destructive than Spanish, French, Portuguese or Belgian colonization.
- Since taking over the Panama Canal, Panama has increased its income, increased traffic and improved safety records.

Chapter 9

Debt and Financial Crises

This chapter investigates the challenges posed by debt and financial crises. It explores how developing countries have gotten themselves deep into debt, describing both the international and domestic origins of three of the most significant debt and financial crises, affecting Latin America, Africa and Asia. The chapter also details the consequences of indebtedness for states in the developing world, specifically how this debt hampers economic development and state capacity. The chapter explains how debt has led to more external intervention from international institutions such as the International Monetary Fund (IMF) and what the consequences of this have been. The chapter then explains what has been done to respond to the debt and financial crises, including debt forgiveness, foreign aid and debt restructuring. Finally, this chapter will provide several case studies of how a country lifted itself out of a major economic crisis and used debt relief to encourage institutional reform and development.

Debt

Debts are simply obligations owed to a second party. Internal debt is money that a country's government owes to creditors who are also citizens of the country. Internal debt is not a factor in international debt forgiveness programmes. External debt is either money owed by one government to another, known as bi-lateral debt, or owed to international financial institutions such as the IMF and the World Bank or to private actors, known as multi-lateral debt. Private debt is debt that has accumulated by private actors to another party. Sovereign debt is debt that has accumulated by the state to other actors. The debts of Latin America in the 1980s and Africa in the 1990s and beyond were incurred by governments to private banks and international agencies. The debt in Asia in the late 1990s was primarily incurred by domestic banks to international lending agencies.

In many cases in the developing world, debt can be viewed as illegitimate. This is money owed by corrupt governments for ill-advised purposes that do not benefit their own citizens. This includes debt that is incurred by dictators that do not benefit the ruling class or that are spent on failed projects that are not beneficial to the nation as a whole. This type of illegitimate debt is sometimes referred to as *odious debt*. Odious debt is contracted by a despotic regime, not used in the general interests or needs of the population or the state and, importantly, the lender knew about the first two conditions (Paulus, 2005, 85). Dubious sovereign loans can also fall in this category. For example, Tanzania owed the World Bank over $575 million for 26 failed agricultural projects. Nigeria owed more than $5 billion in loans for projects that never started, let alone failed (Wong, 2012, 78).

The most classic cases of odious debts are debts that were incurred by odious regimes, in that the regime's intentions were to spend lavishly with no intention to pay back the loans. The corrupt and oppressive Duvalier regime in Haiti was responsible for plunging the country into debt. The wedding of Jean-Claude Duvalier reportedly cost more than $2 million and his wife Michele reportedly spent over $20,000 on a weekend shopping trip to Manhattan (Goldstein, 1987; De Côrdoba, 2004). An audit revealed that Jean-Claude Duvalier diverted at least $500 million from 1980 to 1986 (Library of Congress, 2006). Iraq accumulated $125 billion in unpaid debts under Saddam Hussein. When Ferdinand Marcos was ousted from the Philippines in 1986, the country owed foreign creditors over $28 billion and Marcos's personal wealth was more than $10 billion. Anastasio Somoza in Nicaragua left Nicaragua deeply indebted after looting the country of up to $500 million by the time he was overthrown in 1979 (Kremer and Jayachandran, 2002, 7).

Zaire (now the Democratic Republic of Congo), under Joseph Mobutu, represents a classic case of odious debt. While Mobutu was in power from 1965 to 1997, the country accumulated an external debt of $12 billion, while Mobutu and his associates amassed a personal fortune of $10 billion. Meanwhile, per capita income levels declined at an annual rate of 2.2% from 1965 to 1990. From 1979 to 1990 the country's total external debt soared from $4.8 billion to $10.3 billion and the country was virtually bankrupt (Ndikumana and Boyce, 1998, 195–210). By the time Mobutu fell from power, the country's ratio of debt stock to exports stood at 1,200% (Ndikumana and Boyce, 1998, 205). This type of debt is known as *unsustainable debt*. Debt becomes unsustainable when external debt exceeds the value of the country's exports by a ratio of 150% or more or when the ratio of a country's debt to government revenues is above 250%.

While all debt is not a bad omen for the economy, much of the developing world is mired in unsustainable debt. Poor leadership in developing countries and complacency from the international community mostly is to blame. In any event, international debt in the developing world has reached such a scale that some economists are convinced that such debt may be impossible to be erased on its own (Sachs, 1989).

How did the debt and financial crises emerge?

The most notable debt crisis of the last 50 years was the debt crisis that took place during the 1980s. This crisis had global ramifications but most significantly affected the severely indebted middle-income countries (SIMICs) in Latin America. We first focus on the initial crisis that hit Latin America and other parts of the developing world in the 1980s. We then focus on the growing debt that accumulated in severely indebted lower-income countries (SILICs) in Africa in the1990s and later on the financial crisis that hit high- to middle-income countries in Southeast Asia during the late 1990s. States in Asia were fairly capable and were able to bounce back more easily from the financial crisis that cascaded through the region. In contrast, states in Africa are still mired in unsustainable debt. For Latin America, it has only been recently that states have recuperated from the crisis of the 1980s. We now focus on what caused the crisis in Latin America to materialize in the first place.

Latin America

For Latin America, the debt crisis of the 1980s was one of the most traumatic economic events for the region. Known as the 'Lost Decade', per capita income fell from 112% to 98% of the world's average. Collapse of growth, increased poverty and widening income inequality were pervasive. The debt crisis became apparent towards 1980 when borrowers in the developing world resorted to rolling over their debts. In 1970 the total debt was $29 billion. By the end of 1978, total debt was $159 billion, with 80% of this debt being owed by the central government (known as sovereign debt). Between 1975 and 1980, four countries had to postpone amortization payments and service the interest only. Third World debt snowballed from $130 billion in 1973 to some $612 billion in 1982 (Hiatt, 2007). By 1983, there were 21 countries defaulting on their payments.

Prior to 1973, most of the debt was financed through public agencies, which were both bilateral and multilateral. Projects that were often guided by the World Bank supposedly encouraged investment that had some chance of economic success.

The lending climate changed after the oil crisis of 1973–1974. Oil prices quadrupled in 1973–1974. Crude oil prices continued to rise for almost a decade. This caused severe balance of payment problems for developing nations by raising the costs of oil and imported goods. It also caused problems for countries in the developing world by causing a slowdown in demand, which led to a decline in commodity prices by 19% (Ferraro and Rosser, 1994). Many commercial banks found themselves awash with petro-dollars from oil producing states. Oil prices increased the funds available in the Eurodollar market with more dollar-denominated bank deposits from oil exporting countries. Private banks were eager to put this money to use, which led to a lending boom. Banks felt a false sense of security, constantly lending and willing to refinance debt, rolling over debt as the borrower requested (Stambuli, 1998, 20). Changes also took place in how the portfolios of loans in the developing world were structured. Loans moved towards shorter maturities for debt that had been rolled over. Lending became more hectic and individual Third World borrowers were squeezed to make repayments at shorter intervals. Though debt continued to double in Latin America – from $159 billion in 1979 to $327 billion in 1982 – US banks continued to lend more than ever in the crucial years leading to the crisis.

At the same time that loans were being taken out, the international financial climate was very unstable with the unravelling of the Bretton Woods agreement in 1971. Fixed exchange rates dropped in favour of floating exchange rates, which is where the value of all of the main currencies was determined by market trading. Deregulation of currency markets and rules about banking and investment ensued. Greater flows of private money to rich and poor countries helped boost growth but also led to greater instability.

Another problem was that many of the investments that states were making were largely non-productive. In the mid-1970s, a joint venture involving American and French Banks in Gabon opened. By the end of the first year the office had loaned out $600 million in guaranteed export credits and $679 million in syndicated loans. All of the projects were costly and unproductive including building a presidential palace, a series of hotels, jets, government buildings and an incredibly expensive railway (Stambuli, 1998, 20).

Much of the borrowing was also driven by political needs of incumbent governments. Social demands for higher government spending were fed by borrowing rather than extracting high levels of taxes or pursuing money financed deficits that would lead to inflation. Borrowing was particularly high in regions such as Latin America that face high income inequalities because the state was unable to extract revenues from the population and had to borrow instead. Large gaps between rich and poor mean that the size of the class with taxable income is lower. Moreover, the pressures for redistributive policies were strong while the rich were able to resist pressures for higher taxes to help improve the income distribution. Any attempt to practice fiscal restraint was sidelined. For example, in Brazil, Finance Minister Mario Simonsen was fired in 1979 for trying to cut spending. Delfim Netto replaced him and implemented policies that ran the economy further into the debt crisis (Stambuli, 1998, 17).

External policies of the United States in particular were also devastating. Many US policies were framed without thinking through what the international financial implications were. By 1981 interest rates had shot up. Interest payments escalated quickly, from 10% of export receipts in 1977 to 32% in 1983. Interest payments increased from $2.789 billion in 1970 to $36.251 billion in 1987. The increase in interest rates raised the value of the dollar. The dollar increased by 11% in 1982 and by 17% in 1982. This made it even more difficult to meet debt commitments and pay their loans on schedule. Borrowers from the developing world needed to increase their debt or borrow less to avoid high rates of interest. The United Nation Conference on Trade and Development (UNCTAD) calculated that between 1976–1979 and 1980–1982, the rise in interest rates added $41 billion to the stock of debt in the developing world, with interest payments on loans increased by 50% in nominal terms and 75% in real terms (Ferraro and Rosser, 1994).

Compounding this problem, developing countries faced difficulty raising foreign exchange since their exports were selling at reduced rates. Developing countries started to experience a long-term decline in the demand for their products. This upset their balance of trade with other countries, and decreased the demand for their currencies. Foreign exchange shortages led to large devaluations.

From 1979 to 1982, Latin American debt more than doubled, increasing from $159 billion to $327 billion. Yet the biggest economies in Latin America kept on borrowing (Ferraro and Rosser). In February of 1982, Mexico had borrowed another $6.4 billion. By August 12th of 1982, Mexico's minister of finance informed the chairman of the Federal Reserve, the US Secretary of the Treasury and the director of the IMF that Mexico would be unable to meet its August 16th obligation to service an $80 billion debt that was mainly dollar denominated. In a shock to the world, Mexico had defaulted. The results were catastrophic. Private banks stopped lending due to the high risks involved. Governmental and inter-governmental agencies led by the United States stopped to assure the continued repayment of the Mexican loans. All IFIs closed up their financial markets to Mexico. For Mexico, high interest rates coupled with a sudden decline in the price of oil in 1982 made it impossible to pay back its debts (Wood, 1986).

By the end of 1982, 40 nations were in arrears, meaning debt payments were overdue. By October of 1983 the situation worsened and 27 countries owed billions and were forced to reschedule their debts to banks. The four largest countries in Latin America – Mexico, Argentina, Brazil and Venezuela – owed over $176 billion to commercial banks or 74% of the total debt. Of that amount, $37 billion was owed to the eighth largest US bank and constituted 147% of their capital and reserves at the time. Several of the world's largest banks were concerned that they would face major loan defaults and failure. Bank lending declined 20% from 1983 to 1989 as a result and many banks refrained from overseas lending and focused on collecting and restructuring loan portfolios. Virtually overnight, the rules of lending had changed. This made the crisis more severe and protracted. Suddenly Latin American countries had zero access to credit, putting their economies on hold (Sachs and Huizinga, 1987).

The IMF emerged with a more extensive role, becoming the guarantor of creditworthiness for developing countries. In the past, the IMF used its own money to lend to developing countries. Now it was giving private institutions its seal of approval for additional loans of much larger amounts, in exchange for these countries accepting its traditional policies of stabilization and structural adjustment. Instead of emphasizing the need for debt relief, the IMF emphasized the need for improving domestic debt management systems. The assumption was that economic mismanagement was to blame for the debt. According to this view, debtor countries had political constraints and poorly run administrative systems and Structural Adjustment Programs (SAPs) needed to be administered to deal with these problems. Countries were told to reduce food and transport subsidies, layoff public workers, curb government spending and increase taxes and interest rates. All of these policies would affect the poorest people the worst, and many argued that the policies did little to help countries out of debt. Vincent Ferraro and Melissa Rosser claimed that 'the inflows of capital to the IMF from the heavily indebted countries were more than a gross embarrassment; they were conclusive evidence of the IMF's misunderstanding of the causes of the debt crisis' (1994, 355). The IMF also focused very little on preventing capital flight.

Though internal factors were to blame for the debt crisis, global factors were also responsible, and the response of the international community made things even worse. Unfortunately, the response to debt in Africa was not much better. For more on the *Debt trap*, see Box 9.1.

Africa

The debt that was accumulating in Africa first gained global attention in the 1981 World Bank Report. The World Bank report, which was known as the Berg Report because it was written by Elliot Berg, indicated that Liberia, Sierra Leone, Sudan, Zaire and Zambia had experienced problems servicing their debt in the 1970s and were likely to have trouble in the 1980s. According to the report, long-term solutions for debt relief should be sought after.

This debt being acquired in Africa was different from the Latin American debt crisis of the 1980s, where the bulk of the debt owed was to private creditors. In contrast, debt in Africa was owed primarily to multilateral lending institutions, such as the World Bank and the IMF

Box 9.1   Debt trap

The debt trap occurs when it is impossible to repay the debt. Often, even after poor indebted countries have had their debt payments restructured, they are so squeezed in making payments that they become bankrupt again after a few years (Stiglitz, 2013). In many cases this is due to high interest rates (Krumm, 1985). When interest rates are high, paying back debts becomes very difficult. The case of Nigeria illustrates this point. Nigeria borrowed a little over $5 billion, and has paid back about $16 billion but due to high interest rates still owes $28 billion (Okonjo-Iweala et al., 2003, 65). Total interest payments in Indonesia amounted to almost 30% of the government domestic revenue compared to 10% before the financial crisis (Feridhanusetyawan, 2004, 257).

The other issue is the strength of borrowed currencies. When the currency borrowed increases in value compared to the currency of the borrowing nation, this also makes it more difficult to pay back loans. In the case of Mexico, paying back its debts was much harder to do when the dollar was so strong compared to the peso.

The other factor that makes it difficult to pay back debts is the declining worth of commodities, or a deterioration in the terms of trade (Greene and Khan, 1990). For the developing world, many commodities fluctuate wildly in what they are worth. This makes it difficult to gain access to foreign exchange. Declining prices for sugar can make it near-impossible for Haiti to pay back its debts. Debt payment in Nigeria comprises 20–30% of its total exports (Okonjo-Iweala et al., 2003, 8).

Debt service also redirects money that would go towards investment in the economy

In Nigeria before the country had negotiated debt relief (see the case study at the end of the chapter), debt service exceeded $3 billion a year with debt service payments averaging $1.5 billion a year. This was four times the national education budget and nine times the public health budget (Okonjo-Iweala et al., 2003, 8). Thus debt servicing made it difficult to invest in human capital, which can serve as an investment for the economy in the long term.

Some states cannot escape the debt trap because they are saddled with odious debt from a previous corrupt regime. For South Africa under Nelson Mandela, the regime had to face $21 billion worth of debt acquired by the Apartheid regime. Debts that accumulated under Ghana's military dictatorships also made it more difficult for new regimes to generate economic growth.

(Teunissen and Akkerman, 2004). Another big difference is that, unlike their Latin American counterparts in the 1980s, in the 1990s the highly indebted poor countries (HIPC) were much more deeply impoverished. Additionally, the countries in Africa received large positive net transfers from the international donor/creditor community. The median net transfers to HIPCs to relieve the debt were about 11% of GDP on average over the 1990–1994 period (which is calculated after debt service payments). In contrast, the average net transfers to creditors to Mexico were only 5% of GDP over the 1984–1988 period (Kanbur, 2000, 417). Yet, in spite of all of this assistance, little improvement has taken place in alleviating debt.

As stated earlier in the chapter, much of the lending went to odious regimes that creditors knew had no intention or ability of repaying their debts. While in some cases African regimes were borrowing heavily to pay for lavish luxury items, in other cases African governments borrowed heavily from foreign governments and international agencies to pay for a bloated bureaucracy and for overstaffing (Adamolekun, 2002, 381). Overstaffing the state was a means of maintaining patronage networks, but it was not an investment that could lead to future growth.

Meanwhile, the terms of trade for African commodities continued to decrease. This was all the more problematic because Africa is heavily dependent on exporting primary commodities. Adverse decline in the terms of trade cost African countries 25% of their purchasing power of their exports. Cocoa prices fell by 48% from 1986 to 1989. Coffee prices fell by 55% in the same period. Due to declining commodity prices, Africa lost about $50 billion in potential income (Meredith, 2005, 375).

As Africa started to go into debt, the solution to this problem was to dole out development assistance. Nevertheless, much of the high level of development assistance took the form of loans, producing a growing stock of debt – from about $60 billion in 1980 to $230 billion in 2000.

Like Latin American states, African governments also borrowed heavily from private banks at a time when interest rates were rising from 5.5% in 1977 to 9.3% in 1981. Between 1970 and 1980 Africa's external debts rose from $6 billion to $38 billion. By 1982, debts rose to $66 billion and by 1983, they rose to $86 billion. Countries were running up debts that were 40% higher than their annual income. Debt service in Africa increased from an average of $6 billion a year in the early 1980s to about $11 billion a year in the late 1990s. Debt service ratios as a proportion of export earnings rose from 6.5% in 1970 to 28.3% in 1982. As paying back the debt was impossible, governments were forced to simply postpone foreign debt repayments (Meredith, 2005, 282).

Servicing the debt put a strain on African states. Governments ran higher deficits. Hospitals and clinics ran out of medicine and lacked equipment. Schools lacked textbooks and factories needed more raw materials and spare parts of machinery. Electricity and telephone systems broke down. Unemployment levels increased as a result (Meredith, 2005, 283).

Debt service was using up valuable resources that could have been used to tackle more urgent problems. Countries like Zambia were spending over 50% of their export credits on the servicing of debts, seeing no end in sight to paying the debts off.

For African states, while debt service remained high, so did spending. More aid was given to alleviate states from the negative repercussions of the debt crisis, but African governments often used aid resources to delay reform. Government consumption increased and debt was allowed to accumulate more and be rescheduled again. By 1990, 30 countries had negotiated 120 reschedulings (Bjerkholt, 2004).

Rescheduling debts was a ritual that took its toll on the state's development. African countries repeatedly rescheduled their debts, which would reduce debt service payments in the short run, but undermined economic development because most of the state's management resources were completely devoted to rescheduling debt. Most of the best civil servants with financial skills were stuck dealing with debt negotiations. It also hindered development because the constant game of rescheduling created an atmosphere of economic uncertainty. Any new loans to stimulate development were discouraged, since all the lending taking place was focused on paying back debt.

Meanwhile, banks such as Citicorp, Manufacturers Hanover and Morgan Guaranty all saw their profits rise (Danso, 1990). Though only about half of the servicing payments due were actually paid, this outflow exceeded foreign aid and investment. For every British pound given to famine relief to Africa in 1985, the West claimed two pounds in debt payment (Danso, 1990). In the late 1990s, for every $1 the developing world receives in grants, the developing world spends $1.3 on debt repayment (Africa Research Bulletin, 1998). After several decades of debt relief, Africa had little to show for its achievements in development. The average GDP per capita in constant prices was lower in 2000 than it was in 1960.

Southeast Asia

The financial crisis that hit Asia in 1997 is distinct from the debt crises that hit Africa and Latin America for several reasons. In Asia's case, many of the countries involved were rich countries that had experienced uninterrupted growth rates. Additionally, not all of the countries in Asia were mired in debt. The problem in Asia was that both the currency was under attack (the currency was being sold, which caused it to depreciate in value) and the banks had many non-performing loans (loans were given out that were not being paid back). Large levels of capital also left the region in rapid fashion. Thus the crisis is labelled a financial crisis, not a debt crisis per se, because none of the countries defaulted on their sovereign debt.

Nevertheless, all of the countries in Southeast Asia were badly affected: their currencies were attacked, there was a huge loss of capital investment, growth levels had fallen and the banks were not performing.

Until 1996, Asia attracted almost half of the total capital inflow to developing countries. Billions of dollars came into the region and capital movements happened at a staggering pace. Much of this began when Japan was forced to revalue the yen to the dollar in 1985. This forced Japan to seek low-cost production sites away from Japan in order to remain competitive, leading Japan to invest heavily in Southeast Asia, with more than $15 billion flowing into the region from 1986 to 1990. By the early 1990s, however, Japanese investment flows were tapering off and even falling in the case of Thailand.

In spite of this tapering off, by the mid-1990s the countries in Southeast Asia had become addicted to foreign capital. In order to gain funds for the massive investments taking place, a second source of foreign capital was needed. To attract money and investment from elsewhere such as the United States, countries in Southeast Asia devised a strategy that included eliminating foreign exchange and other restrictions on the inflow and outflow of capital. This allowed foreign banks to participate more in domestic banking operations and opened up other financial sectors to foreign players. The other strategy was to maintain high domestic interest rates relative to interest rates in the United States and other global financial centres. This lured speculative capital that would seek to capture the difference from the spread between low rates in New York of 5% to high rates in Manila of 12%. The third strategy was to fix the exchange rate to the dollar in order to reduce risks for foreign investors worried about fluctuations in the region's local currencies.

The IMF and World Bank approved of this formula for attracting investment and early on the strategy was successful in drawing in a foreign portfolio of investment and loans. Thailand, Indonesia and South Korea were particularly exposed to foreign exchange risk and were encouraged to borrow externally. Most of the loans were very short term, known as hot loans with short maturities. Many of the loans being made by domestic banks were questionable, but the banking system was completely unregulated. Many loans were not performing well and the high interest rates made it difficult for loans to be repaid.

Meanwhile, exports in the region became less competitive in comparison to China. China had begun to compete effectively with the other countries in Asia in the 1990s and Western importers sought cheaper manufactured goods from China. While the Asian currencies were pegged to the dollar, China's currency was relatively depreciated compared to the dollar-making their goods that much more competitive. Though wages in Asia went up, output did not increase.

Slowed growth created concerns from creditors about Asian firms being able to pay back their debts. This caused the value of the region's currencies to depreciate due to the relative unattractiveness of their exports compared to China. Meanwhile, as the US dollar rose in value, this made it more difficult to maintain the pegged currency. It also became more difficult to pay back loans. This sparked fear about the region and foreign capital began to leave. The credibility of the exchange rate came into question, and a series of speculative attacks took place that caused the currencies to lose half their value in less than six months. When exchange rates plummeted in mid-1997, this sent the region into a panic.

In response to Thailand's crisis, the IMF responded with a rescue package worth $20 billion in August of 1997. After the rupiah floated in Indonesia, the IMF came through with another package worth $23 billion. South Korea's crisis led to one of the biggest bailout packages from the IMF to date, of over $57 billion (Frontline, 1999). Though these bailouts were significant, the IMF also exacerbated the crisis in the early stages by causing a panic. The IMF thought the problem was that the states were spending more than they were producing. The solution offered by the IMF was to demand that countries in the region balance the budget better by tightening their fiscal and monetary policies. Nevertheless, the austerity programme had the opposite effect and did little to build investor confidence. Domestic banks were also closed too quickly without a comprehensive financial restructuring plan. Without cause, some healthy banks were closed. As a result, the IMF was not able to re-establish market confidence, prevent the collapse of debt servicing or achieve stabilization of exchange rates (Radelet and Sachs, 1998). The policies that were implemented ended up hastening the crisis as policies that attempted to remedy economic problems in one country worsened problems in other countries, known as beggar-thy-neighbour policies.

Even though there was a massive inflow of foreign capital into Thailand, this did not alarm the IMF or the World Bank. Short-term debt accumulated to $41 billion of Thailand's $83 billion of foreign debt by 1995. Then the baht was hit by a massive speculative attack on May 14–15 1997, forcing the currency to float on July 2nd. The baht depreciated severely compared to the dollar, and the stock market in Thailand plunged 75% in 1997. Though Indonesia's banking sector was not performing poorly, when the Thai Baht floated, the rupiah came under a severe attack in August of 1997. The stock market hit a new low. The rupiah was forced to float in August. By November the crisis had hit South Korea. In South Korea the banking sector was overburdened with non-performing loans. The Korean stock exchange dropped by 7% on November 8, 1997, and then fell another 7.2% on November 24 (Action Forex, 2015).

When looking at the causes of the Asian financial crisis, the role of administrative governance was crucial. Business deals were not based on contracts but on personal relationships, cronyism and nepotism. There were information gaps as well, caused by inadequate local government regulation, monitoring and disclosure requirements. The state also pursued policies that satisfied short-term needs, not long-term needs. For example, many states in the region chose to increase spending for patronage purposes and raise interest rates rather than invest. In South Korea, the state stopped investing in the economy and instead relied on Japan for basic machinery and inputs and technology. It never invested in its own work force to help sustain human capital and improve technological proficiency. Instead of putting money into research and development to turn out high-quality and sophisticated technical products, the state encouraged business to improve the profit margins by going into Southeast Asia for cheap and unskilled labour, which then affected the quality of the products being produced.

There was also very little supervision of the financial sector. The financial institutions were poorly developed and borrowed from foreign countries with reckless abandon while relending loans to bad projects that were unable to pay back the enormous interest rates. By 1996, over 75% of the capital inflow of over 97 billion came from loans (Radelet and Sachs, 1998). The government had little control over bad lending or massive short-term borrowing. This led to over-speculation on real estate instead of long-term investment in agriculture, manufacturing, and research and development. There was over $20 billion of residential and commercial properties in the Philippines alone that had not been sold. In Thailand, 40% of loans went to property developers that were non-performing, yet completely unchecked by the government.

The government also did little to control the massive amounts of capital flowing into the region – and did little to prevent rapid capital outflows. The government was also biased towards short-term capital. There was little control or regulation of capital markets. Meanwhile, the banks assumed that their close relationship with the state would lead to a government bailout if loans did not perform well. Thus, the government's close and unprofessional relationship with the banks led to moral hazard – or taking on more risk because you know that you are insured.

The crisis in Asia had global and regional ramifications. Throughout the region, the public made demands for more transparency. The Suharto regime in Indonesia was toppled following protests. Poverty rates increased throughout the region, yet states in Asia were able to bounce back much more quickly.

Debt and development

Unless countries decide to repudiate their debts (to be discussed later in the chapter), debts must be paid back in some fashion. This often results in significant outflows of capital being used to finance the debt. According to the World Bank, 'In 1988, the poorer countries of the world sent out $50 billion to the rich countries, with the cumulative total of these transfers since 1984 is nearly $120 billion', (from the New York Times). By 1987, the IMF had already received about $8.6 billion more in loan repayments and interest charges than it lent out.

The negative impact of unsustainable debt on growth has been noted by many scholars (Cohen, 1993; Fosu, 1999; Clements et al., 2003; Sen et al., 2007). During the debt crisis of the 1980s, per capita consumption of highly indebted countries in 1987 was no higher than it was in the late 1970s. The average growth rate declined from 6.3% a year to 1.7% (UNCTAD, 1988, 101).

Debt servicing also serves as an impediment to economic growth and development because it drastically limits developing countries' participation in the world economy. Debt burdens have led to less accumulation of capital or a depletion of international reserves. Debt servicing has also made it more difficult to finance policies to help consolidate small and medium-sized firms, which has indirect effects on employment and poverty levels (Ayadi and Ayadi, 2008, 237). Debt servicing also limits access to imports. The 17 most heavily indebted nations decreased their imports from the developed world by $72 billion from 1981 to 1986 (Ferraro and Rosser, 1994).

Many scholars concur that debt servicing is not favourable to economic growth because it discourages investment. Known as the *debt overhang thesis* (Krugman, 1988; Sachs, 1989), in the presence of debt overhang, excess debt acts as a distortionary tax. A high debt burden generally means that a significant portion of government fiscal revenue or exports receipts must be devoted to debt servicing (Fosu, 2010, 378). The government has little money to spend on productive public investment, which ends up lowering growth rates. Any new loans serve as debt repayment without any positive impact on growth (Frimpong and Oteng-Abayie, 2006, 124). Actors assume that a share of future output will be used to repay creditors thus decreasing investment and hindering growth, known as the crowding out effect (Degefe, 1992; Elbadawi et al., 1997). These studies confirm that debt overhang has a negative effect on economic growth in developing countries in Africa, Latin America and the Middle East. Studies looking at Ghana and Kenya have also confirmed that debt overhang has led to a negative impact on economic growth and private investment (Were, 2001, 9). Furthermore, for highly indebted countries, per capita investment fell by 40% from 1980 to 1987 (UNCTAD, 1988, 101). For more on the *highly indebted poor countries*, see Box 9.2 and Table 9.1.

Box 9.2   Highly indebted poor countries initiative

The World Bank and the IMF have responded to the issue of debt relief by launching the HIPC initiative in 1996. This aimed to help indebted poor countries make their debts more sustainable. Most of the debt is owed to the major international financial institutions such as the IMF, the World Bank, private lenders and Western governments. Prior to the HIPC initiative, indebted nations could only seek relief from their unsustainable debts through bilateral negotiations with individual creditors or groups of creditors such as the Paris Club. The relief came in the form of rescheduling debt, not relieving the debt. Thus the expectation was that the indebted country would repay the debt at a later date. Prior to the HIPC initiative there was also no forum for debt relief from multilateral lenders or any type of forum to bring together bilateral and multilateral lenders.

The HIPC is a six-year programme for reducing debt to sustainable levels, with the expectation that indebted countries would implement structural reforms that would ensure stability. In order to be a recipient of debt relief, countries qualified that had unsustainable debt in spite of traditional efforts of bilateral debt relief. Debt was considered unsustainable when the ratio of debt to exports exceeded 200–250% or when the ratio of debt to government revenues exceeded 280%.

Critics claimed that the HIPC only reached a limited number of countries (only four countries have received debt relief). The HIPC programme was also criticized for being too long and too inflexible to meet the individual needs of debtor nations. Countries that did not complete the conditions were left with the burden of their debt payments while still struggling to implement the structural reforms. Critics also claimed that the conditions set did not serve the interests of the debtor nations, but only of the creditors. For example, privatization of state industries such as utilities raised costs for citizens who were already deeply impoverished.

In response to these criticisms, the IMF modified the HIPC in several ways in 1999. The minimum requirements for participating were lowered to be more inclusive. The targets for determining sustainability decreased to a debt to export ratio of 150% and a debt to government revenues ratio of 250%. Countries had to be poor enough to qualify for interest-free loans from the World Bank's International Development Association or the IMF's Poverty Reduction and Growth Facility (PRGF). Finally countries had to establish a track record of reforms. The completion point no longer relied on a six-year structure. For countries that could not complete the programme in less than six years, some interim debt relief was administered in the meantime. Additionally, there were fewer conditions from the IMF and the programme encouraged more input from the local community about its design. In 2001, the IMF also decided to provide extra assistance to any country unexpectedly experiencing an economic setback due to external factors such as falling commodity prices or rising interest rates.

Afghanistan, Benin, Bolivia, Burkina Faso, Burundi, Cameroon, Central African Republic, Republic of Congo, Democratic Republic of Congo, Ethiopia, Gambia, Ghana, Guinea-Bissau, Guyana, Haiti, Honduras, Liberia, Madagascar, Mali, Mauritania, Mozambique, Nicaragua, Niger, Rwanda, São Tomé and Príncipe, Senegal, Sierra Leone, Tanzania, Togo, Uganda and Zambia.

Table 9.1   *HIPC countries that have completed the HIPC initiative*

Debt and the state

Debt not only affects investment levels but also affects the capacity of the state because it limits state revenues while also creating more demands for states to attend to. Heavily indebted countries often pursue contractionary fiscal policies in order to gain loans to help pay back their debts. This then can cause the economy to contract as well. Lacking a stimulus, unemployment levels will remain high. Poverty rates will also increase, as the state is less able to provide for its citizens and offer social safety nets (George, 1993).

Thus, the negative effects of debt servicing on the social sector are especially strong. There is nearly a one-third reduction in the social sector's allocation of spending on health and education due to debt servicing (Fosu, 2007, 711; Fosu, 2010, 388). In the case of Africa, over $13.4 billion a year was transferred to external creditors between 1990 and 1993. This is four times as much as governments in the region spent on health services and more than their combined spending on both health and education. It is also much more than the $9 billion a year that UNICEF estimates as the 'total cost of meeting basic human needs for health, nutrition, education, and family planning', (Tarp, 2003, 326). For example, in 2003 Senegal used one-third of its revenues to service foreign debt, which could be used to invest in health care and education (Carrasco et al., 2007). Before a restructuring took place, debt service was particularly hard on Uganda. Uganda spent $3 per person on health care while spending $15 per person on debt service. Many indebted countries in Africa have been obligated to spend more towards debt repayment than on health care (Carrasco et al., 2007).

When countries have been able to restructure their debts, they have invested the reduced debt repayments to pay for education and health-care programmes. Tanzania reduced its annual debt payment by $170 million. The government used the savings to increase spending on education and to eliminate elementary school fees, leading to a 1.6 million student surge in enrolment (Carrasco et al., 2007). Mozambique used the money it saved from debt-relief to invest $13.9 million for child vaccination programmes, $10 million to bring electricity to rural schools and hospitals and to rebuild infrastructure damaged by natural disasters and $3.2 million to build new elementary schools and promote the education of young girls (Nwonwu, 2008, 254).

Dealing with debt

There are three ways for debtor countries to deal with their debts: They can repudiate their debts as was done by Latin American countries in the 1930s; they can make minor adjustments in repayments; or finally they can have their debts reduced. In Latin America several countries opted to repudiate their debts including Bolivia, Brazil, Costa Rica, Dominican Republic, Ecuador, Honduras, Panama and Peru. These countries were able to opt for this step because the Great Depression contrasted with the 1980s in several ways. First, there were absolutely no international institutions to manage the crisis in the 1930s. In contrast, the crisis of the 1980s was managed under an elaborate set-up of institutions. Second, during the Great Depression, Latin American countries put a moratorium on debt repayment, while during the 1990s, Latin American countries made an effort to service their debts under strong international pressure to do so. Efforts to service the debt led to contractionary macroeconomic policies. Spending was decreased, interest rates and reserve requirements were increased and money supply was reduced. The solution for Latin America in the 1930s was to just default on their debt. Countries that declared defaults made partial payments in some years and bought back part of their debt at depressed prices.

Though debt repudiation appears to be an attractive choice, debt repudiation is often not chosen as an option by debtor countries simply because they may fear retaliation from commercial banks. If banks were to cut off non-debt-related activities such as trade credits, the situation for the debtor countries could be made worse. Debtor countries fear retaliation from creditor governments and multilateral lending agencies as well. Refusing to pay back their debt could affect the grants from development banks and trade relations might be disrupted.

Another option for debtor countries is to engage in debt–equity swaps where businesses or properties in debtor countries are purchased at a discount by the banks as partial repayment. Debt for debt swaps involve bonds being offered at discount repayments. There are also cash buy backs where the debtor country buys back its loan at a deep discount. There are also debt-for-nature swaps where the debtor country makes a promise to protect the environment in exchange for the debt to be purchased by outside groups. There are few opportunities for swaps in practice, however. There are few investment opportunities in poorer countries, and the debt crisis has limited these possibilities further. Furthermore, swaps can drain capital, particularly if profit remittances on successful investments are high.

The topic of debt relief continues to be controversial. Critics of debt reduction argue that it reduces incentives for debtor nations to make economic changes that would lead to greater efficiency (Ferraro and Rosser, 1994). Proponents, on the other hand, see debt relief as absolutely critical to lifting states in the developing world out of the vicious cycle of poverty. Debt relief supporters are also opposed to the types of conditions that are applied to highly indebted countries. The structural adjustment policies that are often applied may be inappropriate for highly indebted countries, as they may only work for countries that are dealing with temporary difficulties in maintaining currency values.

While the developed world should work towards creating conditions whereby the poorer countries can generate more income, such as by reducing restrictions on the exports from poor countries and offering support to build up strong financial institutions in the developing world, developing countries also have a responsibility to use the money that they receive more effectively and pursue long-term investments that are more productive.

The following section demonstrates a case where debt relief can be beneficial to administrative institutional reform.

Case study: debt relief and institutional reform in Nigeria

There are many lessons to be learnt from Nigeria's experience with debt relief. In Nigeria's case, debt relief has been used as a platform for public sector reform. Though Nigeria still has tremendous poverty, inequality and corruption, it still offers an example of how debt relief can work to make a positive impact. Heavily reliant on its oil resources, Nigeria now has 6.2% growth rates that are largely driven by the non-petroleum sectors. Nigeria is tapped to have one of the highest growth rates over the next several decades (Weisenthal, 2011). Moreover, Nigeria has embarked on important institutional reforms in the last decade that are very promising for the country's economic development.

Prior to Nigeria's partial debt relief deal, the country was heavily in debt, with Nigeria's external debt standing at $34 billion. Nigeria spent roughly US$1 billion every year on debt servicing, without making an impact on the principal owed. Debt service due in 2000 amounted to $3 billion or 14.5% of export earnings (Ijeoma, 2014, 172). In 2005, Nigeria was able to negotiate one of the largest debt relief deals by the Paris Club (almost 75% of its debt, or $28 billion). The Paris Club bought back the bulk of its debt owed to it for a cash payment of roughly $12 billion. The deal was negotiated on the promise that Nigeria would embark on a series of important economic and political reforms (Dijkstra, 2011).

Prior to even negotiating the debt, Nigeria made several improvements to its government that impacted how successful its debt relief package would be. Nigeria first tackled its debt strategy in 2002 by implementing the Due Process Certification Policy in order to improve the federal procurement process to curb unnecessary spending. This resulted in large savings and more transparency. Every month a publication was issued that presented federal, state and local government revenue allocations. In 2003, under President Olusegun Obasanjo, a strong finance minister, Ngozi Okonjo-Iwela, was appointed, who would be instrumental in negotiating such an impressive debt reduction deal for Nigeria. After Okonjo-Iwela's appointment, Nigeria adopted the Extractive Industries Transparency Initiative in 2003, which allowed for an independent audit of the oil and gas sectors from 1999 to 2004. Nigeria also created a National Economic Empowerment and Development Strategy, which focused on improving public expenditure management, improving its macroeconomic environment, pursuing structural reforms and implementing institutional and governance reforms. Nigeria's government then set up the Federal Government's Debt Management Office (DMO). Resources were then provided to help build the capacity to help the Nigerian government negotiate its debt deal (Alsop and Rogger, 2008).

After Nigeria negotiated its debt deal, the DMO was then used to develop and implement a sustainable borrowing strategy to prevent Nigeria from falling into debt in the future. The DMO was then used to restructure the country's domestic debt stock and develop a domestic bond market, which helped the state meet the government's financial needs. It was critical for Nigeria to set up an autonomous agency that is responsible for managing its debt. Up until 2000, this did not exist in Nigeria.

The government also set up a comprehensive tracking system to monitor and assess the impact of debt relief. Nigeria created a virtual poverty fund (VPF) to provide accounting. This simply entailed providing a coding system that would indicate when certain expenditures by the government were 'poverty reducing' and/or funded by debt relief. The VPF worked within the existing budget structure and did not necessitate setting up a separate institution. This accounting made it clear to see what types of expenditures that were being funded by debt relief were successful in order to ascertain how debt relief is working. The government also developed an Accounting Transactions Recording and Reporting System to produce consolidated reports on debt relief expenditures (Alsop and Rogger, 2008).

According to the World Bank, the activities associated with how debt relief was spent were effectively managed. Debt reduction freed up resources, which could go towards investment in human capital. In addition to a host of projects across many different sectors, the first year resulted in training of 145,000 teachers, building of 166 new primary health centres, distribution of 400,000 insecticide bed nets, purchase of a million doses of anti-malarial medicines and construction of over 4,000 km of rural roads. Additional millions were spent on poverty reduction programmes, such as a social safety net scheme. Grants were also offered to projects that helped achieve the Millennium Development Goals at the state level, by providing matching funds.

There are several important lessons for developing states hoping to make the most of debt relief. First, it is important to implement certain reforms before structuring the debt relief deal. States must first be able to track public spending, and to do so requires making improvements in how public spending is managed. The process needs to be as transparent as possible, with frequent reports revealing how budgets are being spent. Second, the state needs to come up with a sustainable borrowing strategy to ensure that the state does not go back into debt in the future. The commitment to tracking public spending and producing a sustainable borrowing strategy can help states structure debt deals that are more favourable to their needs. After the debt deal has been negotiated, the state needs to create an office to manage debt and public expenditures. This office should be responsible for implementing a tracking system for debt relief expenditures. Having this in place helps understand how debt relief is being spent. It is then important for the office that manages debt to produce a consolidated report that demonstrates how debt relief is working. Finally, debt relief should be used in areas that can help states build social infrastructure that is so necessary for poverty reduction.

The case of Nigeria illustrates that debt relief can act as an 'entry point for improvements in the way that the government worked' by changing the institutions through which public funds are spent (Alsop and Rogger, 2008, 13). Debt relief can help the government introduce sound initiatives and then provide additional funding to reinforce programmes that have proven to be successful (Alsop and Rogger, 2008, 13).

Case study: recovering from the Asian financial crisis in Malaysia

There are few cases of countries being able to completely recover from economic crises. Though the case of Malaysia was not a debt crisis, it does illustrate what the administrative institutions can do to aid in an economic recovery.

Malaysia was not in huge debt when the Asian financial crisis hit in 1997. But it agreed to follow the IMF prescription for facing the crisis, which included raising interest rates, allowing the currency to float and reducing public expenditure by 18% (Lim, 2004, 4). This caused more damage however – and soon after, Malaysia was in the midst of a full-blown economic crisis. By 1998, aggregate demand declined for the first time due to 55% less private investment and 10% less private consumption. The economy contracted by 14% and the GDP growth fell from 7.7% in 1997 to negative 6.7% in 1998. The stock market also fell by over 70% and the ringgit fell to its lowest rate against the dollar (Lim, 2004, 4).

By 1998, it was clear that the policies prescribed were not working. Malaysia set up a National Economic Action Council to help make decisions and policies. In July Malaysia embarked on a National Economic Recovery Plan, which aimed to revitalize the economy and restore confidence. The policies were not implemented overnight, but in stages. The specific goals were to restructure corporate debt, recapitalize and restructure the banking sector, and stabilize the local currency (Lim, 2004, 4).

Rather than be passive, the Malaysian state played a more critical role in steering the country into recovery. First, the state introduced selective capital control measures. Capital control measures had been strongly opposed by the IMF at the time. But Malaysia opted to implement policies that selectively discouraged speculative short-term trading in local shares. Restrictions were also imposed on transferring ringgit funds in outside accounts by non-residents. Though the ringgit was still easily convertible for the purpose of trade, the government worked to discourage short-term speculative portfolios and other investments by foreign residents and the flight of capital by local residents. To do so, measures were implemented to control the conversion of the ringgit to other currencies (Lim, 2004, 5).

The Malaysian government also set up debt restructuring agencies. Instead of closing down fledgling financial institutions, Malaysia consolidated, restructured and recapitalized them. A debt restructuring agency was set up in June 1998 to take over for non-performing loans from banks and to help restructure and manage them. Other agencies were also set up to restructure troubled financial institutions and assist corporations in negotiating and restructuring debt with their creditors (Lim, 2004, 6).

Most importantly, Malaysia decided to halt the contraction of public spending. To revive the economy, the government embarked on an expansionary fiscal policy with a stimulus package of RM 2 billion ($630 million). The state has worked to supervise the banking sector better, help diversify the domestic economy and promote human capital formation and service development (Charette, 2006, 21).

By 1999, GDP growth had rebounded by 5.6% and per capita income levels recovered to the levels of the pre-crisis era. As of 2013, per capita income in Malaysia stands at $17,500 PPP (Ushiyama, 2013). The government's proactive role helped the Malaysian economy recover from the 1997 Asian financial crisis much sooner than its neighbours.

Conclusion

Heavily indebted countries face many obstacles that are difficult to overcome. Though the challenges facing indebted countries are numerous, there are several important lessons for states. The most important lesson is for the state to take an active role in monitoring its own spending. States need to create a sustainable borrowing strategy and track the effectiveness of their spending. Nevertheless, past experience has demonstrated that though it's important to monitor spending, halting state spending completely may have the unintended effect of paralysing the economy.

In addition to focusing on proper spending, it is also important for states to take a role in restructuring their own financial institutions. States should be more involved in supervising their banking sectors to prevent them from performing poorly. In doing so, states may be better equipped to know whether or not to close down poorly performing financial institutions and be better prepared to stave off a crisis.

Finally, developing states that remain passive or uncommitted to reforms will have great difficulty making a recovery. They will also be less likely to receive favourable debt relief packages that can ensure that repayment takes place on their own terms.

Questions

- What is odious debt (offer some examples), and why do some argue that it should be forgiven?
- What is meant by the Lost Decade and what factors contributed to it?
- How was the debt accumulated in Latin America different than the debt accumulated in Africa?
- In what ways did globalization provoke the Asian financial crisis?
- In what ways does debt servicing undermine growth and investment?

Facts

- Unsustainable debt is external debt that has exceeded the value of its exports by a ratio of 150% or more or when the ratio of a country's debt to government revenues is above 250%.
- The debt crisis in Latin American originated when Mexico was unable to pay the interest payment on its loans in August of 1982.
- The Berg Report was written by Elliot Berg of the World Bank in 1981. In it he argued that many countries in Africa would need long-term solutions for debt relief.
- South Korea was the recipient of the largest IMF bailout package at the time when it received over $57 billion in 1997.
- Malaysia was the only country to not accept assistance from the IMF after the Asian financial crisis, and it was also the country to recover most rapidly.

Chapter 10

Natural Disasters and Natural Resources

This chapter looks at environmental curses. Adverse geographical circumstances can be very detrimental for states' economic performance. Though such conditions can put states on institutional paths that are undesirable for growth, they can also hurt states' growth prospects directly. In Chapter 8 we discussed this in depth with respect to how institutions may be shaped by geographical factors. Here, we focus on natural disasters and natural resource endowments.

The first section discusses what natural disasters are, how they affect development and what can be done to mitigate their effects; the second section does the same but focuses instead on natural resource endowments.

Natural disasters

What constitutes a natural disaster? A natural disaster involves an extreme phenomenon that causes significant damage and death, and takes place within a defined location and has a limited endurance (Bankoff, 1999, 383). Nevertheless, many disasters are compound events. For example, an earthquake can trigger a landslide, causing more death and destruction. Since 1950, natural disasters have caused over 4 million deaths and have adversely affected over 4 billion people (Bankoff, 1999, 383). Of all natural disasters, flooding has been the most damaging, killing over 9 million people in the last century (Bankoff, 1999). Natural disasters are also incredibly costly. The average major natural disaster costs around $500 million (Smith, 2013, 31).

Natural disasters occur worldwide, but their effects are more damaging for developing states, where they occur more frequently due to geography and yet where infrastructure is often lacking to withstand them. Not only are developing states located in zones that are more likely to be affected by volcanic activity, seismicity and flooding, but citizens in developing states are more vulnerable to the impact of disasters because their states are poorly equipped to deal with them (Alcántara-Ayala, 2002, 108).

When natural disasters happen, the poorest states are usually the hardest hit (Albala-Bertrand, 1993). The number of deaths, injuries and displacements go down as a state's income level rises (Kahn, 2005). This is also true within states, where the poorest sectors of the citizenry typically suffer the worst outcomes.

Natural disasters do not affect all developing regions equally. Africa experiences the fewest, with 10% occurring there (EM-DAT database, 1900–1999). Asia, by contrast, experiences the most natural disasters, with 42% of all natural disasters occurring in this region, incurring high death tolls. Asia holds 60% of the world's population, but over 80% of the world's natural disaster deaths take place in this region. In the period from 1900 to 2013, over 6.7 million people have been killed in floods due to heavy rains, over 1.5 million have died in earthquakes, 1.2 million have died due to cyclones and over 260,000 have died due to tsunamis. China and India are especially prone to natural disasters with heavy death tolls. In China in the summer of 1931, extreme cyclone activity led to a series of floods that killed possibly as many as four million people, making it the worst natural disaster recorded in history in terms of death toll. The 1976 Tangshan earthquake killed as many as 650,000 people. India has also experienced its fair share of natural disasters, with cyclones being the most damaging. Cyclones in India killed 300,000 people each in 1737 and 1839. More recently, a cyclone hit India's West Bengal and East Pakistan (what is now Bangladesh) in 1970 killing as many as 500,000 people.

Natural disasters have also hit Latin America and the Caribbean particularly hard. In the 20th century, the region was affected by over 1,300 natural disasters, with 972 disasters taking place from 1970 to 2000, or 32 per year. The region has also seen high levels of fatalities due to natural disasters. In the last century there have been over 450,000 fatalities, with over 225,000 fatalities from 1970 to 2000, or an average of 7,500 per year (Charvériat, 2000, 10).

There are many different types of natural disasters that can negatively affect states. Here we focus on three: tropical cyclones (and floods), earthquakes and volcano eruptions.

Tropical cyclones are rapidly rotating storms that contain a low pressure centre, strong winds and heavy rain. They usually originate over tropical oceans, blowing counter-clockwise in the Northern Hemisphere and clockwise in the Southern Hemisphere. Those that occur in the Northwest Atlantic Ocean or Northeast Pacific Ocean are often referred to as hurricanes; those that occur in the Northwest Pacific Ocean are known as typhoons; and those that occur in the Atlantic basin, the Indian Ocean and parts of the Pacific Ocean are simply known as tropical cyclones. Here, we refer to all of these storms as tropical cyclones. In the past 200 years or so, tropical cyclones have killed nearly two million people worldwide, with one million dying in the last century (Bankoff, 1999). In addition to the 1970 Bhola cyclone in what is now Bangladesh mentioned previously, Bangladesh was hit by another tropical cyclone in 1991 that killed nearly 150,000 people. (For more on Bangladesh preparedness programmes, see Box 10.1.) The regions at the greatest risk of tropical cyclones are Asia and Latin America (Kobasa, 2008, 38–39).

Earthquakes are seismic waves that are created when the earth's crusts release energy. Earthquakes with epicentres that are offshore can disrupt the seabed enough to trigger a tsunami. Earthquakes can also stimulate volcanic activity and create landslides. About half a million earthquakes occur annually, of which only one-fifth are actually felt. The combined average death toll may be more than 10,000 people per year, with about a million total deaths taking place in the last century (Alexander, 1993, 42).

Box 10.1 Bangladesh and the Cyclone Preparedness Programme

Bangladesh is a country prone to being hit by devastating cyclones. At the same time, its Cyclone Preparedness Programme exemplifies a successful attempt by the state to buffer citizens from the negative effects of natural disasters. The key to the programme's success is its emphasis on community participation in disaster preparedness.

Following the cyclone in 1970 that killed about a half a million Bangladeshis, it became obvious that the government needed to do more to protect its citizens. The government of Bangladesh, along with the Bangladesh Red Crescent Society, began a project to modernize coastal warnings and evacuations. The Cyclone Preparedness Programme currently covers 11 districts that span 3,500 villages. It focuses on issuing warnings, building shelters and operating relief centres. It also assists in evacuations and search and rescue efforts (Ahrens and Rudolph, 2006, 215).

Part of the reason why the programme works is that it involves local populations. More than 30,000 village volunteers have been organized into teams of 12. Each team has radio equipment to monitor weather reports, sirens, first aid kits and rescue equipment. Though volunteers do not receive payments, they are given some assistance to enable them to attend training sessions (Ahrens and Rudolph, 2006, 215). As a result of the Cyclone Preparedness Programme when another cyclone hit in 1994, around 750,000 people were safely evacuated and the death toll was only 127 (Akhand, 2003). Improvements such as these illustrate how the state can work with society to harness the energy of its population to dampen the impact of natural disasters.

The vast majority (90%) of earthquakes occur in the Pacific Ring of Fire, which is a 40,000 km seismic belt in the Pacific Ocean (National Geographic). China is especially prone to destructive earthquakes. The 1556 Shaanxi earthquake killed as many as 830,000 people. Minor earthquakes are fairly common in places as wide-ranging as the United States, Guatemala, Chile, Peru, Indonesia, Iran, Pakistan, Turkey, New Zealand, Greece, Italy, India and Japan, due to their location near earthquake epicentres, but in reality they can occur anywhere. Like tropical cyclones, earthquakes are very destructive, hurting both people and property, with cities being most at risk.

Earthquakes are particularly damaging to developing countries that are already struggling with poverty. In 2010, an earthquake in Haiti killed an estimated 300,000 people and Haiti is still struggling to rebuild itself from the damage inflicted. That earthquake destroyed hospitals, communications systems and transportation networks making it even more difficult for the state to respond to the crisis. Even worse, the conditions were so poor that they led to a devastating outbreak of cholera, and looting and violence became common. Tsunamis in the aftermath of an earthquake can also be extremely destructive (Hawkins, 2012, 44). The 2004 tsunami in the Indian Ocean, for example, killed about a quarter of a million people and injured many more. Over a decade later, many areas affected are still struggling to bounce back.

Volcano eruptions are ruptures in the crust of the earth that lead to the release of hot lava and volcanic ash. Like earthquakes, the majority of active volcanoes are located in the Pacific Ring of Fire. Latin American and Asian states are typically most frequently affected by volcano eruptions. There are 1,500 active volcanoes worldwide today, with around 50 eruptions each year. In spite of the dangers, volcanoes have attracted human settlement, and more than 10% of the world lives within 100 km of a volcano that was active during historic times. Central America and Southeast Asia are the regions that are highest at risk, with Indonesia facing the greatest threat of volcanoes. In fact, two-thirds of all volcano related deaths have taken place there (Smith, 2013, 177).

Volcano eruptions are the least destructive of the natural disasters discussed here. Though the eruption of Mount Tambora in Indonesia in 1815 killed around 100,000 people, death tolls are still typically quite a bit lower than with tropical cyclones or earthquakes (NPR). One of the more recent devastating volcano eruptions was the 1982 eruption of El Chichón in Mexico, which killed about 3,500 people.

Some earthquakes can be triggered by volcanic activity. Both earthquakes and volcanoes lie on the edges of tectonic plates and because of this earthquakes can sometimes be triggered by the movement of magma from the volcano. Thus earthquakes that are caused by clogged magma are a warning sign of volcanic eruptions. The government in Colombia was well aware that a volcanic eruption was likely prior to the eruption of the Nevado del Ruiz volcano in Tolima, Colombia, in November of 1985, which killed 22,000 people. Reportedly, the government had received multiple warnings from organizations to evacuate the area in September 1985 after a series of earthquakes had taken place, but it refused to do anything about it (Voight et al., 2013).

Natural disasters and development

Natural disasters are very costly to states' economies, both financially and in terms of human life. Developed states, which usually have better systems in place to deal with natural disasters, still experience serious costs when they are hit. Hurricane Katrina, for example, cost the United States over $100 billion in damages in 2005. Yet, developed states' economies are better able to afford these costs (or at least quickly repay the debts incurred by them) because they were in better economic positions to begin with. In addition, because developed states have superior infrastructure and early warning systems in place to minimize the effects of natural disasters, loss of life is less than it would be in other conditions. Economic development typically brings with it improvements in safety (Toya and Skidmore, 2007). The World Disaster Report demonstrated that only 2% of all deaths recorded from natural disasters between 1991 and 2000 took place in countries that score high on the Human Development Index (HDI). More than two-thirds took place in countries with low scores on the HDI, even though more than half of the disasters take place in countries with medium scores on the HDI (Blaikie et al., 2004, 25).

Additionally, one study has shown that if a state with a population of 100 million people increased its GDP per capita from $2,000 to $14,000, it would suffer 700 fewer deaths due to natural disasters per year (Kahn, 2005). In other words, though developed states also suffer significant costs from natural disasters, they are better able to rebound from them and better structured to weather them than are developing states.

The economic consequences of natural disasters in developing states can be truly staggering. Natural disasters can impact industrial output if businesses are destroyed. Trade and commerce can be disrupted when road infrastructure is damaged. Hurricane Mitch, which hit Central America in 1998, killed 9,000 people, affected over three million more, and caused Honduras to lose 80% of its GDP and Nicaragua 49%. The hurricane cost the Central American region as a whole $6 billion. Those numbers, unfortunately, are not atypical. The Mexico City earthquake of 1985, for example, caused between $3 billion and $4 billion worth of damages. In 1988 Hurricane Joan hit Nicaragua and caused it to lose 32.57% of its GDP. Jamaica lost 28.2% of its GDP due to Hurricane Gilbert in 1988.

Disasters are not single discrete events. For developing countries, vulnerable people suffer repeated and mutually reinforcing shocks, which erode their ability to accumulate resources and savings (Blaikie et al., 2004, 5). When household assets and income-generating assets (such as shops, factors, crops, cattle and arable land) are damaged or destroyed, this leads to losses in income. Natural disasters can make land unsuitable for agricultural production. Hurricanes can wash out arable land or permanently affect the salinity of the soil. In Honduras, it took over four years for banana production to return to its normal levels after Hurricane Mitch. This had a strong effect on unemployment and under-employment levels. The rate of unemployment immediately rose to 32% in Honduras (Charvériat, 2000, 13).

Disaster impacts in developing countries are felt within the informal sector where housing, supplies and equipment are uninsured and the result of many years of accumulation. The losses that accrue to informal activities are not included in disaster impact assessments (Pelling, 2003, 32).

With natural disasters the greatest potential for loss of life comes not from the direct impact of the hazard but from the 'everyday health risks following the dislocations caused by a catastrophic disaster such as limited access to clean drinking water, lack of sanitation, insufficient access to food, warmth or shelter and social disorder' (Pelling, 2003, 16). Thus, it is not just the natural disaster itself that leads to high death tolls, but the aftermath. Health conditions worsen for the total population after a natural disaster. Diseases spread more easily due to unsanitary and crowded shelters. Looting and violence are more common.

Frequent exposure to natural disasters can create poverty traps (see Chapter 5) where a previous event reduces the resources that a group or individual has to resist and recover from the next environmental disaster.

Poverty also increases natural disaster vulnerability. Scholars have placed more emphasis on the economic, social and political conditions that make some people more at risk to natural disasters than others. Impoverished people lack access to land that is unexposed to natural disasters, due to high concentration of ownership in the hands of the few. This forces the poor to live in more hazardous locations. Large landowners in Honduras have driven out small farmers forcing peasants to migrate to steep hillsides where agricultural practices caused soil erosion and siltation of rivers. Rural and impoverished population centres are also at risk due to unequal patterns of land ownership, which have forced the rural poor to adopt unsustainable practices of agriculture (such as overusing the land), which in turn makes the land more prone to disasters. In other cases, the rural poor are forced to live in unsafe physical areas. Some populations living on volcanic soil in the Philippines and Indonesia support population densities of more than 1,000 people per square kilometre (Bankoff, 1999, 384).

Impoverished people are also forced to migrate to urban areas and lack access to safe building sites. The poor may have few alternatives but to live in overcrowded slums on steep hillsides, poorly constructed houses or in areas that are prone to disasters (Smith, 2013, 17). The development in urban slopes increases the risk of flooding the lower lying areas, where many of the poor may also reside (Pielke et al., 2003, 111). For example, earthquakes killed 66,000 in Peru in 1970 and 23,000 in Guatemala in 1976 (Charvériat, 2000, 14). Both earthquakes disproportionately affected the poor who did not have the means for self-protection and lived in flimsier houses on steep slopes (Blaikie et al., 2004, 9). Not only does poverty and marginalization cause the poor to be more likely to face a natural disaster but it also means that they are less equipped to deal with natural disasters when they hit.

Making matters worse for the poor, many disasters are compound events. Thus oftentimes states are still recovering from one natural disaster when they are struck by another. Haiti offers a good example of this. The aforementioned 2010 Haitian earthquake not only killed over a quarter of a million people, but it also devastated the Haitian economy. Prior to the earthquake, Haiti was one of the poorest states in the Western Hemisphere. The earthquake did not help matters. After it hit, the capital city, Port-au-Prince, was virtually impassable. Nearly six months after it occurred, only 2% of the rubble from the earthquake had been cleared, making it impossible for economic activities to take place. A year later, things were not much better, with only 5% of the rubble removed.

Haiti's poverty made an adequate response difficult. Insufficient resources were dedicated to rubble collection, and camps for the displaced were erected that had no electricity, running water or sewage systems. Such conditions paved the way for a cholera epidemic later that year (said to be brought in by foreign aid workers). An additional 8,000 people were killed at a rate of 50 deaths per day due to the disease. Crime was also widespread, particularly violence against women and girls. By 2012, about a half a million Haitians remained homeless. This situation made it all the more difficult for Haiti to deal with Tropical Storm Isaac in 2012, which killed 29 people, and Hurricane Sandy, also that year, which killed 55 people. Even though it has been a number of years since the 2010 earthquake, Haiti is still suffering its impact, and the repeated natural disasters that have come its way have just made the situation direr (Berg, 2013).

Natural disaster and the state

Natural disasters such as earthquakes and hurricanes can severely undermine economic development in already impoverished countries. Natural disasters also have calamitous consequences on the state as well. Part of what makes natural disasters difficult for developing states is that they negatively affect the very infrastructure that is needed to help them withstand future ones.

The death toll from the 1985 Colombian volcanic eruption was higher due to the fact that the disaster actually destroyed the state's infrastructure. On the day of the eruption, evacuation attempts were undermined because a severe storm taking place at the same time restricted communication. Roads, highways and bridges were also in ruins. Additionally, the main hospital in Armero was completely destroyed by the eruption. Local towns set up temporary relief clinics, but the inaccessibility of vital antibiotics caused over 150 to die from infections or other complications (Marti and Ernst, 2005, 291).

Haiti's experience with the 2010 earthquake is again also illustrative of how natural disasters can weaken the state. Over 50 health-care centres and hospitals were destroyed, making it more challenging to give medical attention to those in need. The earthquake also ruined a nursing school in the capital and severely damaged the primary midwifery school. Other buildings were also taken out. In towns like Léogâne, 90% of buildings did not survive the earthquake. Even prisons were affected. The Port-au-Prince Prison Civile was ruined, enabling 4,000 inmates to escape. More than half of Haiti's schools and its three main universities were also hit. The Minister of Education at the time, Joel Jean-Pierre, asserted that the education system in Haiti had collapsed (Cawthorne, 2010).

Yet, these types of facilities are important for handling the state's response, both in the short and long term. Education systems, for example, are required to develop the human capital to better implement rapid response systems in the future. In addition, communication systems are vital to getting the word out about a disaster and orchestrating the response. In Haiti, however, they stopped functioning. There was no public telephone system available. Making matters worse, few public officials had working mobile phones prior to the earthquake. Roads were also destroyed. To rebound from such an impact requires significant investment. And yet, natural disasters also make revenue collection difficult. The following section offers an explanation of how states can mitigate against the negative effects of natural disasters.

Dealing with natural disasters

Adequately dealing with natural disasters involves both preparations to minimize their impact and rapid responses once they occur. Though the link between natural disasters and development has been repeatedly demonstrated, governments and lending agencies do not integrate natural hazards into project plans. Most state budgets and international funding for natural disasters come from relief and reconstruction, instead of prevention and preparedness measures. In general, building robust political and administrative institutions, with specific agencies focused on disaster prevention, is critical to dealing effectively with natural disasters.

The first component of prevention and preparedness is an early warning system. Scientists have improved their abilities to track the location of tropical cyclones, but it is still difficult to estimate with much certainty their intensity. Offering an early warning of an earthquake is a tougher task. At best, early warning systems can provide regions with information that one is in progress. With volcanoes, the locations and level of activity is usually known, given that classification systems can rate whether volcanoes are active, dormant or extinct. Alert systems exist that can determine the states of volcanic activity, as well, providing information regarding whether an active volcano's levels are normal or not. Many countries in the developing world do not have the ability to respond to early warnings, however. For example, the 2002 volcanic lava that destroyed 40% of Goma in the Democratic Republic of Congo had been forecast, but Goma lacked the institutional capacity to respond to the predictions made (Pelling, 2003, 34). Early warning systems in all of these areas have become much better overall, such that large death tolls should be preventable through forecasting, preparation and evacuation, but communication systems must be advanced to spread the word about impending disasters.

The state's ability to invest in the infrastructure required to minimize the costs and impact of a natural disaster is also incredibly important. Buildings must be upgraded to help them withstand trauma. For example, in the case of earthquakes, adequate and enforced seismic building codes are the most important factor in preventing high casualties and destruction. The state can also reduce the potential impact of geological or meteorological risks through public engineering projects. The state can reduce geological or meteorological risks through public works such as stabilizing landslides, drilling deep wells to drain or pump water out of soils that are saturated, intercepting debris flows with small dams and directing the run-off from storms into sewers (Davis, 2006, 124).

States can also implement non-structural measures to prevent high casualties, by implementing land use restrictions, building codes and preventing environmental degradation. After Hurricane Gilbert hit Jamaica in 1988, over 30,000 homes were destroyed. The losses were blamed on the lack of preparedness such as poor maintenance of rental property and no compliance with building codes (Blaikie et al., 2004).

Once a natural disaster hits, states need to have modernized health facilities to assist injured people. States also need to be able to respond quickly to a crisis. This requires a sophisticated and professionalized body of state officials who are well-trained and well-organized and modernized health facilities to assist injured people.

An example from Mexico, a state prone to earthquakes, helps illustrate how a proactive state can make a difference. The state's capital, Mexico City, is built on the bed of an ancient lake, making it vulnerable to natural disasters like earthquakes. Sure enough, in 1985, the city experienced a major earthquake that reportedly killed more than 10,000 people. Prior to the earthquake, buildings in the city were constructed using materials of varying quality and type over different periods of time. Some were better built than others; and in a number of places housing standards left much to be desired (Alcántara-Ayala, 2002, 114). Enforcement was lax due to high levels of government corruption. After the earthquake, the government in power at the time, led by the Institutional Revolutionary Party (PRI) and President Miguel de la Madrid, tried to downplay the death toll and even ordered a news blackout. The government did little to address the situation until nearly 40 hours after the earthquake hit.

In the aftermath of the 1985 earthquake, the Mexican government implemented a number of changes to prevent a future one from having such a devastating impact. It put in place an alert system to send electronic messages and an early warning to other areas. It also set up an alarm system to go off in the event of another earthquake hitting the capital. The government created a Civil Protection Committee to organize drills with rescue workers, the police, hospital staff and metro personnel; and evacuation drills are now conducted annually. A number of highly trained specialists are now available for disaster response, and new construction in the city must comply with strict building codes.

Fortunately, Mexico City has not experienced another earthquake of the same magnitude since the 1985 earthquake. However, should one occur, most observers agree that the city is far better prepared to deal with it. Such preparations require an active state willing to and capable of taking action.

As this discussion makes clear, states must be strong and effective to be able to mitigate the effects of natural disasters. Political officials must also have the will to implement the policies necessary for disaster preparedness and a quick response.

Democratic institutions are particularly helpful in this regard. Research indicates that democratic states experience fewer human losses than do non-democratic states in the face of natural disaster (Kahn, 2005). The poorest classes in dictatorships are in fact the most vulnerable to loss of life when natural disasters strike. This occurs because citizens living in democratic states can put pressure on their governments to ensure that they are safe, and governments in turn must adhere to these demands or risk being voted out of power. Citizens can therefore demand that safety standards are enforced and precautionary measures set in place if they live in areas that are prone to natural disasters (Toya and Skidmore, 2007).

Democracies are also less prone to corruption (Nur-tegin and Czap, 2012), which can exacerbate death counts by incentivizing officials not to enforce building codes, infrastructure standards, or zoning requirements (Kahn, 2005, 25–26). Corruption can also serve as a barrier to effective disaster assistance because corrupt governments are less likely to efficiently and fairly distribute payouts. Foreign aid that was channelled to Nicaragua after a devastating earthquake in 1972, ended up in the hands of its dictator Anastasio Somoza Debayle. Additionally, developing countries that rely on patronage can undermine disaster relief efforts. The case of the Philippines with the eruption of Mount Pinatubo in 1991 illustrates this problem. Some members of the congress were accused of politicking for funds and using the disaster as a mean of gaining political capital (Bankoff, 1999, 407).

Even with high-quality political institutions in place to push for the appropriate policies to buffer citizens from natural disasters, as stated above, high-quality administrative institutions are also critical to ensure that these policies are adequately implemented. This requires a well-organized and efficient bureaucracy that can execute public awareness campaigns, devise clear codes for construction, map hazard zones, install early warning systems, and orchestrate the construction of dykes, levees and avalanche barriers. The bureaucratic agency to deal with natural disasters must also be experienced, well trained and already in place before a disaster hits.

The importance of the state's administrative institutions is also illustrated by the series of floods that hit the Rio de Janeiro neighbourhood of Baixada Fluminense in 1988. The floods left 289 dead, 734 injured, 18,560 homeless and caused major damage to infrastructure. In response to the floods, Rio's local government created a special unit to coordinate activities and help receive external funds in the form of a $175 million loan from the World Bank. One of the goals of the World Bank funded project was to help the state and municipal governments develop flood prevention programmes and provide more available funds to maintain environmental infrastructure in Baixada Fluminense, especially given that deforestation of the steep hillsides had increased the risk factors. In spite of the good intentions of these efforts, the objectives of the flood reconstruction project were not realized. The key problem was that Rio's municipality had difficulty in coordinating with the agencies at the national level due to the state's rapid turnaround of management staff, and staff members' overlapping and unclear responsibilities (Pelling, 2003, 35). Because the administrative institutions of the state were not well trained and constantly shifting positions, it was difficult to implement a long-term disaster prevention and response plan that would be helpful.

The Vargas tragedy of 1999 in Venezuela is another example of the importance of having preventive measures such as proper building codes and an effective state agency to deal with disasters already in place that receives societal input. Just north of the capital Caracas, massive floods in Venezuela killed as many as 30,000 in December 1999. Little attention paid to urban planning made the Venezuelan floods incredibly destructive. The poorest quarters were composed of illegal housing that was built on slopes that were unfit for any construction. These illegal homes were very fragile and risk-prone yet little was done to stop continued construction. Land development and environmental policies in Venezuela like many Latin American cities were haphazard, with construction completely unregulated. Minor catastrophes take place every year during the rainy season but the victims are rarely noticed and little is done in terms of prevention.

Though the state was well intentioned, it lacked the organizational capacity to respond effectively. It attempted to create a new institution, Corpo Vargas to respond to the disaster, but it is difficult to create a well-functioning disaster relief agency in the immediate aftermath of a crisis. Recruiting staff, establishing new policies and legal frameworks in an ad hoc manner created major bottlenecks, delays and uncertainty (Clinton, 2006). Thus, though the government was financially equipped to respond (it had allocated over $200 million to restore basic services and benefited from several hundreds of millions in international aid for reconstruction and vulnerability reduction), it took too long to offer compensation and make decisions about urban rezoning. An ad hoc programme was implemented to move victims into homes that were over 400 km away from their original homes. But because victims had not been consulted, this plan was rejected by most victims. The state did not understand that the relocation plan would make it too difficult for the victims to recover financially if they were so far removed from their original homes (Stager, 2009, 96).

In addition to strong administrative institutions, judicial institutions can also play a role in ensuring that there is transparency in the implementation of preventative measures and disclosure of hazards (Raschky, 2008, 629). To detail how the state can proactively tackle the challenge of natural disasters, we offer a case study from the Cayman Islands.

Case study: hurricanes in the Cayman Islands

This discussion has illustrated that the state can play a positive role in shielding populations from the devastating effects of natural disasters, as a number of studies have emphasized (Kahn, 2005; Raschky, 2008). The Cayman Islands offers a nice example of how this can work.

The Cayman Islands is a British overseas territory located in the Caribbean, making it susceptible to hurricanes. It has worked hard to improve governance, however, to reduce the damage incurred by them. It established an early warning system, for example, and promotes self-mobilization of civil society and private corporations. Mechanisms to pursue collective action exist, enhancing citizen involvement in plans to combat climate change (Adger et al., 2005). Because of this disaster preparedness and relief strategies in place there, it has experienced minimal death tolls from hurricanes compared to its neighbours. Hurricane Ivan of 2004, for example, was as strong as Hurricane Katrina (which inflicted serious damage and loss of life in the United States) but only led to two fatalities. In fact, there have only been five fatalities in the past 30 years there due to hurricanes.

There are a number of reasons why the Cayman Islands has been so successful in this regard. First, there is high participation from various stakeholders. A highly committed public and private sector exists that has pushed for reform-minded policies. The National Hurricane Committee (NHC), for example, is both a public and private partnership, and is in charge of all aspects of hurricane preparedness (Tompkins and Hurlston, 2003).

The state institutions that are responsible for disaster management are flexible, enabling them to adapt in response to past successes and failures. At the end of each hurricane season, for example, the NHC puts together a review of the measures that were used and their effectiveness. The national hurricane plan is then revised for the following year, so that mistakes are not repeated again. There are also high levels of accountability and transparency built into this system, such that the population is generally supportive of the NHC's efforts.

This type of learning takes place because the institutional framework allows for innovation and is flexible to changing conditions. Policymakers have discretion to design and implement new initiatives to reduce risk, and decision-makers can make adjustments quickly.

The approaches advocated have a long-term vision. Hurricane preparedness activities are a budget item, for example, in government plans. Budgets are large enough to ensure that qualified staff and sufficient financial resources are devoted to prepare for hurricanes. And long-term risk management is incorporated through integrated land use planning.

The Development and Planning Committee within the government mandates the participation of all government departments to ensure that objectives are clear and that the decision-making process is consultative. Across the Cayman Islands, there are a range of laws and regulations that control and guide different departments to ensure consistency. For example, the Development and Planning Law, along with the Developing and Planning Regulations, stipulate where infrastructure projects should be constructed and how much should be devoted to them (Tompkins and Hurlston, 2003, 11).

In the Cayman Islands, disaster management is more than relief work. It means well-thought-out preventative measures to reduce disaster risk, including the building of flood defences and regulation of land use. In addition to having the capacity to evacuate the public and stockpile and deliver food the state is able to warn and arrange a response (Ahrens and Rudolph, 2006). The Cayman Islands shows that the risks of natural disasters can be mitigated when states take an active role in improving preparation and implementing a plan that has an eye on long-term objectives.

We now turn to a very different type of environmental curse, that of natural resources.

Natural resources

Natural resources are resources that come from the environment. There are essentially two types: diffuse resources and point resources. Diffuse resources are renewable, like forests, fisheries and agricultural crops. They use soil and water and, as the name suggests, are geographically diffuse. Diffuse resources are typically used in the production of crops and livestock; they often require large amounts of labour. Point resources, on the other hand, are non-renewable. Examples, here, include minerals (like copper, diamonds and coltan) and fossils (like oil). Point resources are geographically concentrated and require less labour to extract. In this discussion, we focus primarily on point resources, namely, minerals and oil, given the robust body of literature associating them with negative development outcomes.

Natural resources and development

Kenneth Kaunda, the president of Zambia from 1964 to 1991, once stated with respect to the state's poor performance, 'We are in part to blame, but this is the curse of consensus on the measurement of resource being born with a copper spoon in our mouths' (Ross, 1999, 297). This statement illustrates that natural resources are not always a positive for states. Though they have the potential to enrich states, they often do the opposite, prompting many in the development community and beyond to refer to them as a 'curse'. (Natural resources have also been viewed as a curse for conflict and democratization, but we restrict this discussion to their economic impact.)

Saudi Arabia: 11.7 million

United States: 11.1 million

Russia: 10.4 million

China: 4.4 million

Canada: 3.9 million

Iran: 3.5 million

Iraq: 3.4 million

United Arab Emirates: 3 million

Venezuela: 3 million

Mexico: 2.9 million

Kuwait: 2.7 million

Brazil: 2.6 million

Nigeria: 2.5 million

Norway: 2 million

Algeria: 1.9 million

Angola: 1.8 million

Kazakhstan: 1.6 million

Qatar: 1.6 million

United Kingdom: 1.1 million

Colombia: 1 million

Table 10.1 *Top 20 countries by oil production (barrels a day)*

Source: CIA World Factbook

The evidence supports this, in many ways. Those states that are the richest in natural resources are also among the poorest states in the world. Regions of the developing world that are resource poor, like East Asia, have had strong development records compared to regions of the world that are resource rich, like parts of Africa and Latin America. According to some estimates, just increasing natural resource intensity by one standard deviation reduces annual economic growth rates by 1% (Sachs and Warner, 1997, 2001). If we just look at the states that belong to the Organization of the Petroleum Exporting Countries (OPEC), there is a similar message: the average GDP per capita decreased by 1.3% each year from 1965 to 1998 (Gylfason, 2001). Far from improving economic outcomes, resource income appears to make them worse.

A number of case studies confirm the cross-national evidence too (Gelb, 1988; Karl, 1997; Ross, 1999, 2001). For example, oil-rich Nigeria has proven incapable of translating its oil revenues into economic growth. Since 1971, the state has owned 55–60% of oil operations onshore, earning about 60 billion in revenues in 2005. Though the state has since decreased corruption levels (see Chapter 9), the head of Nigeria's anti-corruption agency estimated that in 2003, 70% of all oil revenues were stolen or wasted (Abrahamsen, 2013, 45). In fact, over $400 billion in revenues have disappeared since 1970. As a result, oil revenues have done little to lift the country out of poverty. Its GDP per capita was a little over $1,000 in 1970; 30 years later it remained at just about the same value. During the same period, Nigeria's poverty rate also more than doubled (from around 35% to around 70%) and inequality worsened considerably. In 1970, the top 2% of the population and the bottom 17% earned the same income, whereas by 2000 the top 2% of the population and the bottom 55% did (World Trade Organization).

Mineral exporters have not fared well either. A 1995 World Bank report for example, found that states with mining sectors comprising more than 50% of exports saw decreases in GDP per capita of a rate of 2.3% per year (Mikesell, 1997, 196; Ross, 2002, 5). These states also have high levels of debt: 12 of the world's most mineral-dependent states and six of its most oil-dependent states are classified by the World Bank as highly indebted (Ross, 2002, 7).

Though researchers debate whether the focal point should be on resource abundance (the amount of natural resource revenues in absolute terms) or resource dependence (the amount of natural resource revenues in comparison to the total economy), the consensus is that natural resources can create obstacles to achieving economic growth and improving human welfare.

What explains this? How is it possible for natural resource endowments to be so destructive to development? Part of the explanation for this lies in a phenomenon referred to as *Dutch Disease*. The concept of Dutch Disease is based on the experience of the Netherlands, a state that saw its manufacturing sector decline since its discovery of natural gas in 1959 (Gylfason, 2001). It captures the paradoxical relationship between natural resource exploitation and manufacturing exports. When states discover natural resources they often neglect other export industries, like manufacturing, in favour of resource extraction. At the same time, once natural resource export income starts flowing in, the windfall profits crowd out other sectors of the economy and discourage entrepreneurship (Sachs and Warner, 2001). To make matters worse, the sudden spike in natural resource exports usually increases the value of the state's currency, making other state exports comparatively seem more expensive and hurting sales. Real wages also go up, further decreasing the competitiveness of other export industries (Frankel and Romer, 1999; Gylfason et al., 1999; Herbertsson et al., 1999). Through all of these mechanisms, states suffering from Dutch Disease see reductions in their total exports as a percentage of their GDP despite the discovery of natural resources. This, in turn, is harmful for development.

Beyond Dutch Disease, there are a number of ways in which natural resources can be a development curse. Point resources, for example, do not require a large labour force. The inputs that are needed for these industries are usually specialized, and therefore imported from other states. This means that there are few linkages in the state between the resource industry and the rest of society: few people receive employment from it and few additional industries are created as a result of it.

Natural resource wealth can also make states vulnerable to fluctuations in prices, leading to greater volatility in the overall economy among resource-rich states. This occurs because world commodity prices are volatile themselves. Crude petroleum prices, for example, fluctuate more than food prices do. The research indicates that states that are dependent on natural resources exhibit greater macroeconomic volatility, which in turn reduces growth (van der Ploeg and Poelhekke, 2009). This volatility is shown to have additional negative effects for investment, income distribution, poverty levels and education (Ramey and Ramey, 1995; Aizenman and Marion, 1999; Flug et al., 1999), a point we return to later in this section.

Beyond this, natural resource income creates opportunities for *rent seeking*. This occurs because resource rents are easily captured by the state, leading to monopolistic behaviour (and where the benefits are not passed on to the public). When resource booms occur, the government may protect and privilege resource producers and/or offer exclusive licenses to exploit and export resources to elites and their cronies. This in turn can prompt would-be entrepreneurs to dedicate their efforts toward getting a piece of the pie, as opposed to engaging in economically productive activities. Those who benefit from rent seeking also rarely use their new riches to invest in the state, which is so critical to generating long-term growth. In Indonesia, for example, in the late 1960s and 1970s, the state-owned oil company Pertamina reportedly created a host of rent seeking opportunities for state officials and their allies. Many of the rents were allegedly used to buy off the Indonesian military. As a result, Indonesia was the first

OPEC member to have to import oil (in 2004) because it had invested so little into energy projects.

There is ample evidence that resource wealth is bad for investment in human capital. In the field of education, for example, school enrolment at all levels declines in conjunction with greater natural resource endowments, as does public spending on education (Gylfason et al., 1999). As a reflection of this, OPEC states send 57% of their children to school, compared to the rest of the world's states, which send 64%. OPEC states also spend less than 4% of their gross national product (GNP) on education compared with the world average of 5%. Resource-rich states opt against investing in education because they do not rely on human capital for income, anticipating that resource rents (which can be acquired with a small labour force) will fund the state for years to come. It is perhaps for this reason that resource-rich states also experience higher child mortality rates. Increases in both mineral and oil dependence are associated with increases in the mortality rates of children under five. Health care is neglected and ignored because such states see little need to invest in their people (Ross, 2001).

Natural resources and the state

The state's ability to eschew investments and other public goods when flush with resource wealth is a reflection of the concept of the *rentier state* (see Box 10.2). Rentier states are states that rely on resource rents as their primary source of revenues. This in turn distorts the types of policies governments pursue. Such states can please their citizens even if they do very little simply because they do not need to rely on taxation to keep the state afloat. They can use resource rents instead. Because citizens benefit from the fact that they are not being taxed, they are less likely to criticize or demand more of their governments. At the same time, there is little pressure for state institutions to be high in quality and the state has incentive to focus on rent distribution instead.

A number of states in the Middle East are illustrative of this. Because many Middle Eastern states are rich in natural resources, they never had to develop the infrastructure to collect taxes (Bellin, 2004). These states also were able to make large investments in state-owned enterprises without having to worry about their levels of productivity. As a result, economic performance in many Middle Eastern states has been underwhelming. Growth rates were above average from 1960 to 1975 in the region as a whole, but then plummeted to the lowest in the world between 1975 and 1990 (Owen, 1992; Said, 2000). The negative consequences of the rentier state were largely to blame.

In addition, resource abundance can also lead to the implementation of poor policies. Politicians can develop a false sense of security due to

Box 10.2   Rentier state

Political scientists, and more specifically area specialists, have argued that certain natural resources undermine administrative capacity and economic development. An abundance of resources may impact the way a state gains revenues. Terry Lynn Karl (1997, 13) argues that the 'revenues a state collects, how it collects them, and the uses to which it puts them define its nature'. States that rely predominantly on resources for revenues are often referred to as rentier states.

Rentier states do not rely on extracting the domestic population's surplus production; instead they're reliant on external revenues known as *rents* (usually derived from oil or the exploitation of other natural resources). These rents are easily captured by the state through exports and because of this, the state makes few attempts to encourage production and manufacturing. Instead the state focuses on allocation and distribution of these rents. Much of this allocation and distribution often comes through patron–client networks, which can give the state a certain measure of stability due to the dependence that forms between the clients and patrons (Smith, 2004). (For more on *clientelism*, see Box 7.2.)

In spite of the appearance of stability, resources affect the quality of state administrative institutions. The rentier state is often bloated and inefficient, as there is little incentive to create successful industries and hire the best and the brightest when the state can rely on rent to keep itself afloat. Rentier states are also 'particularly vulnerable to the problems of patronage and corruption as well as bribery and nepotism' (Gawrick et al., 2011, 6). This again, is due to the lack of incentives to hire individuals to work for the state based on merit, hard work and expertise.

Furthermore, as mentioned before, because rentier states can gain resources from revenues, they do not need to develop extractive institutions. A number of scholars have argued that raising income tax revenues requires more developed administrative institutions (Hydén et al., 2003). The necessity to extract income may force states to develop capable administrative institutions, with a competent, experienced, well-paid and autonomous staff.

Growth rates have been correspondingly unimpressive in the region as a whole. After a better-than-average showing between 1960 and 1975, the Middle East recorded the lowest rate of growth in the world between 1975 and 1990, and lost nearly all the ground that it had gained earlier (Owen, 1992). States in the Middle East with a steady flow of foreign rents have been afforded with the luxury to make huge investments in state owned enterprises with low levels of productivity. The result has been economic underperformance.

the state's resource income, prompting investments in poorly conceived projects (Gylfason and Zoega, 2002). For example, Nigeria's government invested $3 billion in a steel mill in Ajaokuta in the 1970s, yet not a single ton of commercial steel was ever produced (Weinthal and Luong,

2006, 35). The investment was implemented to please government constituents, rather than because it was a sound policy choice. Thus, narrow sectional interests may be promoted in the face of resource wealth, as opposed to diversification of the economy or promotion of competitive industrialization.

Government overconfidence in resource-rich states can lead to other troublesome problems. Governments may start to assume that they will always have steady flows of resource income. Windfalls are treated as permanent and expenditures become incredibly high. When resource prices fluctuate and incomes from resources plummet, states are forced to resort to borrowing, leading to high levels of debt. Mexico, for example, borrowed substantial amounts based on perceived strengths during oil booms, leading to high levels of debt during periods of low oil prices (Sachs and Williamson, 1985)

Rather than dedicate state assets to investments, resource income is instead used by many governments to promote patron–client ties. In Nigeria, for example, oil revenues led to increased spending for northerners. Leaders in resource-rich states fear ouster because the stakes of holding onto power are so high in this environment, prompting them to rely even more so on resource rents to buy off supporters. Mobutu (1965–1997) of Zaire (today's Democratic Republic of Congo), for example, used income from copper, diamonds, zinc, gold, silver and oil to purchase the support of his political challengers, helping to keep him in power for multiple decades despite his autocratic rule. Resource-rich states, in other words, use their sizable resource rents to sustain patronage networks and provide subsidies to key sectors of the populace. In some cases, this can lead to a bloated state in which many unproductive jobs are created just for the purpose of maintaining political support (Robinson et al., 2006). In Kuwait, for example, the government employed 75% of its workforce even though most employees were underutilized and underqualified.

Relatedly, resource dependence is also associated with corruption, which does not bode well for growth (Ross, 2003). Resource-rich states have higher levels of perceived corruption among citizens, for example, than those that are resource poor. This is because the lure of resource riches can trigger *kleptocracy* and the politics of plunder (Acemoglu et al., 2004). State officials devote their work days to finding ways to pad their pockets. In oil-exporting states in Africa, for example, billions of dollars have disappeared from state accounts.

Corruption is easy to get away with because transparency in the management of resource wealth is difficult to ensure. The sheer volume of resource-related transactions can be hard to track and governments can find themselves swamped with more revenues than they have the capacity to manage. The sudden ebbs and flows of revenues can also overwhelm normal budgeting procedures (Ross, 2012). Add to this that state oil companies may try to leverage their access to resource income by managing their receipts through the use of 'opaque offshore accounts' (Ross, 2003, 25). All of these factors make corruption easier to get away with in the presence of resource wealth.

Finally, natural resource wealth is also associated with conflict, as mentioned earlier, which is harmful to growth as well. A number of studies have shown that states whose export earnings are dependent on natural resources are more vulnerable to conflict than are other states. This occurs because the prospects of resource income escalate tensions among rival groups, who seek to claim to it (Reno, 2000). Perhaps more than anything, resource dependence prolongs conflicts by giving rebel groups and/ or government forces a source of funding to prolong their battles. Accordingly, most of the states in Africa that have experienced internal conflict have been dependent on the export of oil or minerals for revenues (Reno, 2000). Angola, for example, which went through a brutal and long-lasting civil war from 1975 to 2002, gets more than 80% of its export earnings from oil. The Democratic Republic of Congo has also suffered from violent internal conflict and it receives nearly 80% of its export earnings from copper and cobalt. Sierra Leone, which had a devastating civil war for many years, has nearly all of its export income coming from titanium, ore and diamonds (Reno, 2000). The message to emerge from this literature is not so much that resources cause conflict, as much as that resources extend conflicts where they already exist (Fearon, 2004; Ross, 2004).

Dealing with natural resources

There are a number of policy initiatives states can pursue to lessen the damaging impact of natural resources on development. For one, they can diversify their export markets. States that export a wide variety of products are better able to deal with fluctuations in the prices of a single industry. Export diversification can also ensure that a broader spectrum of a state's citizens benefit from its natural resources. Oil and mineral exporters, for example, can diversify by developing downstream industries to process the raw materials (Ross, 2003). These industries use large numbers of low-income workers, providing a source of employment for individuals in that income bracket who often see little improvement in their lives on account of natural resources.

States can also create a natural resource fund (e.g. an oil stabilization fund). Such funds have been used in Norway and Alaska, for example, and have been effective. The critical factor here is making sure that the fund is transparent and that allocations are subject to checks and balances, which should prevent government officials from raiding it when they are strapped for cash.

States can also privatize ownership of the resource industry and tax these private companies instead. In Russia, for example, private owner-ship of that country's oil industry led to greater production and increases in profits (Weinthal and Luong, 2006). Russia's gas sector, by contrast, is state-owned, poorly managed and currently in debt. It is important to note that the privatization process works best when it takes place on the state's own terms, so that it can tax the private companies and use the revenues generated for specific sources of investment.

As economist Joseph Stiglitz writes, 'Abundant natural resources can and should be a blessing, not a curse. We know what must be done. What is missing is the political will to make it so' (2004). This statement reflects the critical role that state institutions can play in mitigating the negative effects of natural resource endowments. In fact, states that already have high-quality administrative, judicial and political institutions in place when they discover natural resources are typically better able to withstand the challenges posed by them and even use these resources to their advan-tage (Karl, 1997, 241). Indeed, Chile, a state that has a strong mining industry, particularly in copper, which accounts for over half of its total exports, has achieved remarkable growth rates in the past few decades despite its natural resource riches, primarily because of good governance.

Political institutions play a major role in this. High-quality political institutions are needed to ensure that policies are selected that will protect the state's economy from the resource curse. The research indicates that states with high degrees of personalism, weak political parties, fraudu-lent elections and impotent legislatures are prone to corruption when confronted with natural resource discoveries (Bhattacharyya and Hodler, 2010). The primary reason for this is that in these types of political sys-tems there is less accountability and citizen representation. Political offi-cials need high-quality political institutions that allow for transparency in governance and enable citizen demands to be translated into outcomes. Citizens in democracies can put pressure on government officials to use resource revenues to invest in education, a social safety net, and modern infrastructure, and also to diversify exports and create jobs both in the resource industry and elsewhere.

Other institutional spheres can also be important. High-quality judicial institutions, for example, can help ensure the transparency of stabilization funds and that political officials' actions are kept in check (Gylfason and Zoega, 2002). Independent courts can be used to monitor the behaviour of political officials, while also ensuring that rules and regulations regard-ing the fund's usage are adhered to. Administrative institutions also need to be high in quality to build the capacity for the state to extract resources while also guiding the diversification of the economy and the development of the manufacturing sector.

In sum, with a capable and willing state, natural resources can be a blessing for states rather than a curse.

Case study: resources and development in Trinidad and Tobago

Trinidad and Tobago is one of the wealthiest and most developed nations in the Caribbean. It is also one of the most resource-rich countries per capita, being involved in the petroleum sector for over a century. Trinidad and Tobago is currently the largest oil and natural gas producer in the Caribbean, and these resources account for 40% of its GDP and 80% of its exports. Yet this resource abundance has not hindered its development. It has a per capita income of $28,400, life expectancy of 74.8 years, literacy rate of 98.6% and only 4% of the population lives below the poverty line.

Trinidad and Tobago received independence from the United Kingdom in 1962. Prior to independence, Trinidad and Tobago experienced six years of self-government, which better prepared it for transitioning to self-rule. Trinidad was initially led by Dr Eric Williams, an Oxford-educated scholar and historian whose vision for the country focused on building a strong economy. In order to accomplish this, early on the new government highlighted the importance of creating an efficient and successful public sector.

Often states in resource-rich countries have little incentive to be efficient and productive. Trinidad and Tobago's government resisted the temptation to rest on the wealth of revenues provided by the petroleum industry. The government emphasized public sector reform and wider public accountability, emphasizing 'financial rectitude' (Annisette, 1999, 114). Though government ministers were given autonomy over their departments, they were also expected to be accountable to a Legislative Council. This ensured that decisions being made were concurrent with what was best for the country's development.

Instead of relying on the automatic wealth that resources could generate, the state ensured that the annual budget was sensible and could sustain long-term development plans. This was accomplished in two ways. First, the state emphasized the non-oil sector, and part of its long-term development plans included investing in the country's manufacturing base. To assist with this plan, the state encouraged foreign investment. Plans to diversify the economy were in place by the early pre-independence government.

Second, the state worked to improve the quality and salary of all of its personnel. Civil servants in Trinidad and Tobago are relatively well paid and the state employed a consultant to revise its civil service salary scale (Chaudhry et al., 1994, 126). The government has also focused on utilizing rigorous recruitment methods. In particular, in order to ensure that the state was not reckless in its spending, the state recruited skilled accountants within the state bureaucracy that could assist with ensuring sound budgets (Annisette, 1999, 114). The recruitment of trained accountants within the state to help with budget accounting took place not long after independence was achieved.

Thus the case of Trinidad and Tobago illustrates that states can harness the revenues from resources to build a strong and effective state that can help foster developmental plans. Being democratic and more transparent has also ensured that government spending is kept in check, and clearly earmarked for specific objectives.

Conclusion

States vary dramatically in terms of the types of challenges they face, as this study has illustrated. For some states, these challenges are largely due to their environmental context.

On account of geographical factors, for example, some states are repeatedly struck by natural disasters, including volcanic eruptions, tropical cyclones and earthquakes, which can have devastating tolls on human life and state infrastructure. It can take years and even decades, in some instances, for states to fully recover from major natural disasters. Often, times, before they have had a chance to recover, another disaster has hit.

Yet, at the same time, states are not impotent in the face of natural disasters. Those states that have the institutional capacity and will to orchestrate and implement disaster preparedness strategies and responses suffer far fewer losses than those states that do not. With the right plan in place and infrastructure investments, the damages inflicted by natural disasters can be far lower than they often are in the developing world.

There is a similar story for natural resource endowments. Natural resources are often seen as a curse, despite their potential to make states rich. This occurs because states are typically ill-prepared to deal with natural resource discoveries and the sudden influx of revenues that their exports generate. Natural resource dependence can hurt growth because it has the potential to discourage other export industries, like manufacturing, lower real wages and expose states to the vulnerabilities of price fluctuations in world markets.

Here again, though, the state has the potential to prevent these negative effects from taking shape and even to turn natural resource abundance into a positive for the state's economy. This requires an institutional structure that gives political actors incentives to diversify exports and create natural resource funds and enables other spheres of the state to monitor and ensure compliance in this regard. For this reason, though there are a number of states that have suffered on account of natural resource discoveries, like Angola and Nigeria, there are others that have leveraged them into a positive, like Botswana.

Institutional reforms are not easy to pursue, but they can reap great benefits for states in the developing world challenged by environmental curses like natural disasters and natural resource endowments.

Questions

- Which regions experience the fewest and most natural disasters?
- Why are the poor most badly affected by natural disasters?
- How do natural disasters weaken the state? In what ways can the state mitigate the effects of natural disasters?
- What is meant by 'resource curse' and how does it impact economic and political development, corruption levels and stability?
- Why are institutions important for overcoming the 'resource curse'?

Facts

- Though developed states suffer costs from natural disasters, they are better able to rebound from them. Only 2% of all deaths recorded from natural disasters from 1991 to 2000 took place in countries that score high on the human development index.
- Democracies offer fewer losses than do non-democratic states in the face of natural disasters.
- According to some estimates, just increasing natural resource intensity by one standard deviation reduces annual economic growth rates by 1%.
- Dutch Disease is the phenomenon of neglecting the manufacturing sector after the discovery of a natural resource.
- Growth rates in the oil-rich Middle East states were the lowest in the world between 1975 and 1990.

Chapter 11

Disease Vulnerabilities

Economists have long argued that investing in human capital is critical to long-term economic prosperity. Simply put, to grow an economy requires an able-bodied citizenry that can productively and meaningfully contribute to it. When citizens face repeated battles with infectious disease, losing potential workdays and in some cases their lives, this hurts the state's economy as a whole. In fact, in 2001 alone, around nine million people died of infectious diseases (World Health Organization).

Though the developed world has largely eradicated many infectious diseases due to the success of vaccination programmes, among other things, outbreaks of infectious disease are still fairly common in the developing world, with Sub-Saharan Africa (SSA) being particularly affected. As a sign of this, the life expectancy for a woman in the developed world is 78 years, but for a woman in SSA it is only 46 years. Not only are citizens in poor states more likely to contract infectious diseases, but outbreaks of disease are more likely to keep them poor (World Health Organization).

In the 1960s and 1970s, international financial institutions like the World Bank did not see tackling infectious diseases as a major development problem. Their line of thinking was that a better economy would improve health-care outcomes, not the other way around. By the end of the 1980s, the severity of the problem became more obvious, however, and economists increasingly saw that disease outbreaks were an impediment to prosperity. A 1993 World Bank report announced that it was changing its tune and, consequently, spending on disease prevention increased dramatically in the years to follow reaching over $3 billion by 2003. About the same time, former United Nations secretary general Kofi Annan founded the Global Fund to Fight AIDS, Tuberculosis and Malaria in 2002, which is an international financial institution administered by the World Bank that acts as a clearing house for donor funds with an annual budget of over $1.2 billion (Alilio et al., 2004, 273). In line with these advances, most in the development community are now acutely aware of the dangers of infectious diseases for perpetuating cycles of poverty.

In this chapter, we discuss the problem of infectious disease vulnerabilities. We first explain the key infectious diseases that are pervasive in the developing world and what their consequences are for health. Next, we show how high incidences of infectious disease among the citizenry

234

can hurt development and the state. We close by examining the role state institutions can play in reducing outbreaks of infectious disease and minimizing their impact.

Infectious diseases

There are a plethora of dangerous infectious diseases, but the main diseases that negatively impact people today are HIV/AIDS, malaria and *tuberculosis* (TB), known collectively as the 'big three'. This chapter focuses primary on HIV/AIDS and malaria, though some of the discussion will be relevant to other infectious diseases as well (for more information on TB, see Box 11.2; for neglected tropical diseases, see Box,11.1).

HIV/AIDS

Human Immunodeficiency Virus (HIV) is a sub-microscopic parasite that lives and reproduces in the cells of host organisms (Putzel, 2003). HIV infection makes a person vulnerable to opportunistic infections, such as chronic diarrhoea, persistent fever and pulmonary tuberculosis, as cells that are important for the functionality of the immune system are slowly lost. Over time, HIV disease transitions into Acquired Immune Deficiency Syndrome, typically knows as AIDS. By the time a person has contracted AIDS, the immune system is severely weakened and opportunistic infections take over the body, leading to prolonged illness and eventually death. Since the discovery of AIDS in 1981, more than 30 million people in the world have died of AIDS or AIDS-related diseases (AVERT organization).

The HIV virus spreads from one person to the next through the transmission of contaminated body fluids (as in semen, vaginal secretions or breast milk). The most common mode of transmission is through unsafe sex, followed by the passing of the infection from mother to infant, the use of infected blood and lastly intravenous drug use.

Women are more vulnerable to contracting the disease than are men. There are a few reasons for this. First, there is a greater biological concentration of HIV in semen than in vaginal secretions. In addition, cultural norms often make women even more at risk. Women in many parts of the world often have little say in their sexual practices and due to social and economic disadvantages may have to use sex in return for money, food or shelter. As a sign of this, sex workers are the sector of the female population most at risk of getting HIV. In Nairobi, Kenya, it is estimated that 85% of all sex workers are infected with HIV. Practices such as female circumcision also increase the risk of contracting HIV for women, while male circumcision actually has the opposite effect (Siegfried et al., 2005).

Though women are more at risk of getting AIDS, men are also vulnerable, particularly those who are mobile workers, defined as those who do not return home at the end of a work day. These include truck drivers, construction workers, itinerant traders and soldiers. In the 1980s, for example, a third of Ugandan truck drivers and just about that many Ugandan soldiers were infected with HIV. When mobile workers return home, they spread the virus into their communities, compounding the problem (Gysels et al., 2001).

As of 2011, there are about 34 million people worldwide living with HIV, 90% of them in the developing world and two thirds of them in SSA. In fact, the top 20 states in the world with the highest HIV prevalence are all in Africa. And in at least ten African states, the infection prevalence is greater than 10% of the adult population. This is true even though HIV/AIDS was unknown to Africa just 30 years ago. Swaziland has the highest prevalence of HIV in the world, with 26% of the population infected, followed by Botswana with 23%, Lesotho with 23%, South Africa with 17% and Zimbabwe with 15% (World Health Organization). In terms of the total population infected, South Africa tops the list with 5.6 million citizens living with HIV. Some estimate that due to HIV/AIDS, life expectancy in SSA is 15 years lower than it would have been otherwise (Putzel, 2003, iii).

Ways of addressing HIV/AIDS

There are currently two ways of addressing the HIV/AIDS epidemic: prevention and treatment. It is estimated that an effective prevention programme and treatment for HIV/AIDS would cost about $20 billion per year in SSA (World Bank, 2011). Prevention requires a multifaceted approach, however. First, a state needs to maintain a supply of clean needles in the medical industry so that patients are not mistakenly infected with the disease. States also have to regulate the public health system to ensure that blood banks are regulated and reduce the chances that blood transfusions will transmit the disease. Diagnostic tests need to be accessible to citizens and carried out regularly on the population. This is particularly important for the prevention of the transmission of the disease from mothers to their newborn babies or to the children they breastfeed. Condoms also have to be easily available for citizens to minimize the spread of the disease through sexual activity. Condom use, for example, is said to reduce the chance of HIV infection by 80%, and the risk of infection is less than 1% among monogamous couples who use condoms consistently (Wilkinson, 2002). Prevention can also be encouraged through education, so that individuals know how to protect themselves and others from contracting the disease.

Though treatment for HIV/AIDS also exists, it is a more expensive approach to addressing the disease than prevention. Once diagnosed, HIV-positive individuals must have access to the right drugs to delay the onset of AIDS. There are a number of effective drugs currently on the market for this, though they are expensive. The combination of drugs needed to treat HIV effectively can cost as much as $15,000 per year. Many hospitals in the developing world lack access to these drugs, as well as other drugs that can help combat the opportunistic infections that accompany HIV infection (Bertozzi et al., 2006).

The response so far to HIV/AIDS

Though the HIV/AIDS outbreak is considered a pandemic, it took time for the international community to respond to it. The World Bank even admitted as much, stating that it had 'failed to bring to bear the full weight of our collective instruments, intellect, and influence' (World Bank, 1999; see Putzel, 2003, 2). Partially the problem was that international financial institutions and other public bodies were reluctant to talk about a disease that was largely associated with sexual practices, and partially the problem was that many believed the problem to be a medical issue that the medical profession would find a cure for. Compounding these issues, many state governments were in denial about the extent of HIV/AIDS infection rates among their citizenry. Some even actively blocked an appropriate response. For example, former South African President Thabo Mbeki opposed the use of AZT, one of the most successful drugs for treating HIV/AIDS (Schneider and Fassin, 2002). Developed states often did not improve matters. Andrew Natsios, the then-director of the US Agency for International Development (USAID), for example, told the US House of Representatives that drugs would not work in Africa because Africans would not be able to take drugs in the proper sequence because they did not have watches or a sense of time (Garrett, 2007, 18).

Eventually, governments and the international community got on board with trying to make treatment for HIV/AIDS more accessible to those afflicted with it in the developing world. The statistics show signs of progress. By 2001 less than 40,000 people in SSA were on antiretroviral (ARV) drugs needed to treat the disease even though 25 million were infected (Garrett, 2007, 18). By 2013, 5.3 million were on ARVs and a total of 8 million were receiving treatment of some sort (World Health Organization, 2013b). Efforts to combat the spread of HIV/AIDS have also had some success. The number of people dying of AIDS-related causes fell from 2.2 million in the mid-2000s to 1.7 million by 2011 (World Health Organization, 2013b, 43).

Box 11.1   Neglected tropical diseases

Neglected tropical diseases (NTDs) include bacterial infections (such as trachoma and leprosy), protozoan infections (such as Chagas disease) and helminth infections (such as hookworm and guinea worm). These diseases are common in rural and impoverished areas of low-income countries. They negatively affect childhood growth, intellectual development and education. As a result, they are correlated with poverty and development.

NTDs account for 5.6 million deaths (534,000 each year). The NTDs are the most common conditions affecting the poorest 500 million people living in SSA, and together produce a burden of disease that may be equivalent to up to one-half of SSA's malaria disease burden and more than double that caused by tuberculosis. The greatest number of cases occur in the DRC and Nigeria (Mutero et al., 2006). Approximately 85% of NTDs result from helminth infections. Infections such as hookworm occur in almost 50% of SSA's poorest people, including 40–50 million children and 7 million pregnant women. After hookworm, schistosomiasis (192 million cases) is the second most prevalent NTD (Mutero et al., 2006).

NTDs are often non-lethal but lead to long-term problems. They can persist for years and affect health and performance for decades after an infection has supposedly cleared. For example, trachoma is the leading cause of preventable blindness. Over 130 million people have high-intensity intestinal helminth infections which affect cognitive abilities and leads to dysentery and anaemia. NTDs are also connected to other major diseases. Studies from Malawi showing that women infected with hookworms were at 1.8 times higher risk of having malaria than uninfected women, and studies from Thailand showed an increased susceptibility to malaria in patients with STH infections (Hotez et al., 2006).

Building a more integrated health-care system can help in the delivery of other interventions. It also ensures that health services are delivered to communities that are hard to reach and had lacked health facilities. The Dominican Republic was able to sustain a lymphatic filariasis programme in spite of reduced external funding because it had developed an integrated health system that was able to maintain the programme. Strengthening of primary health-care activities is essential if NTD control is to be integrated into the general health service. General services are more comprehensive and flexible to dealing with the community. General health-care programmes may also be better at pooling resources together to co-implement their activities.

In addition, the development and management of water resources has significant health implications. For example, improving sanitation and irrigation methods could make an impact in preventing the spread of NTDs. Inter-sectoral collaboration is needed to address the challenges of NTDs. Environmental sectors, health sectors and education sectors need to collaborate to come up with a comprehensive approach to dealing with these diseases (Gyapong et al., 2010).

Malaria

Malaria is an infectious disease transmitted through mosquitoes that belong to the genus *anopheles*, which are vectors of the parasite. It is passed through female mosquitoes, which bite humans and transmit infected blood from one person to the next. The female mosquitoes use the proteins from human blood to make a batch of eggs, which are often laid in water, including marshes, puddles and irrigation channels. Malaria is therefore not endemic in places that are dry, cold or high in altitude, given the key role of water for egg laying, as well as the fact that malaria parasites cannot develop at temperatures lower than 16.7 degrees Celsius. Even in warm climates, transmissions are higher during the rainy season.

Eggs will hatch in less than a week, potentially leading to a rapid spread of the disease.

Each year, it is estimated that 3.3 billion people are at risk of contracting malaria (World Health Organization, 2014a). According to the World Health Organization (WHO) as of 2012 there are 207 million cases of malaria worldwide, 80% of which are in Africa. The WHO also claims that there are 627,000 deaths each year due to malaria (though some health journals allege that the number could be as high as a million), 90% of which occur in Africa. For example, countries such as Burkina Faso see 18% of their population die each year due to malaria. Malaria has an especially hard effect on child mortality rates. In fact, 56% of all malaria deaths worldwide are children under the age of five. This number is as high as 85% in Africa. Malaria accounts for upwards of 15% of all deaths in that age group in Africa.

The symptoms of malaria include fever, headache and nausea. Pregnant women who contract malaria can experience spontaneous abortions, while babies born to mothers with the disease often have a low birth weight, which in turn can increase infant mortality. Children with severe incidences of malaria can have lifelong cognitive problems, as well as learning disabilities. Their immune systems are also compromised, making them more susceptible to other illnesses. The type of malaria also affects fatality: the strains in the Americas have lower fatality rates than those in Africa. One of the more serious forms, cerebral malaria, for example, affects over half a million children each year in Africa and kills anywhere from 10% to 40% of patients.

Addressing malaria

The positive news with malaria is that the cycle of transmission between humans and mosquitos can be broken, either through avoiding or killing mosquitoes. Thus, malaria can be eliminated. For example, in the mid-20th century, the United States was able to get rid of malaria by observing successes in parts of Cuba and the Canal Zone of Panama. It launched a public awareness campaign, carried out house spray applications, and engaged in water and larvicide management to try to reduce malarial infections in the southern part of the country, where malaria was a problem. This effort began in 1947, at which point 15,000 malaria cases were reported. By 1951, however, malaria was considered eradicated from the United States (Center for Disease Control).

Eliminating malaria requires more effort than simply controlling it but it is a longer-term solution to the problem. One method of elimination involves larval source management (LSM), which targets the aquatic stage of the problem by reducing vector larval habitats. This can be achieved by draining, removing or filling breeding sites, which kills mosquitoes before they can spread malaria to humans. Larvae, unlike adult mosquitos, are immobile and therefore cannot avoid this type of control strategy by simply changing habitats (Fillinger and Lindsay, 2006). Beyond reducing the number of mosquitoes, LSM also makes it more difficult for female mosquitoes to find sites to lay eggs, also reducing transmission risks (Fillinger and Lindsay, 2006). This method requires monitoring open water sources both inside and outside of households, as well as wetlands and other aquatic areas (Fillinger and Lindsay, 2006). To be effective, irrigation methods also have to be improved in conjunction so that fields are dry enough to disable completion of the larval cycle (Walker and Lynch, 2007).

LSM was an effective approach for many states in the 1930s and 1940s. In Brazil, for example, in the 1930s, a major malaria outbreak killed thousands of citizens in the countryside. In response, the government implemented LSM and eradicated malaria in only two to three years. Egypt adopted a similar approach in the 1940s and eliminated malaria there in only six months. LSM was also used to clear the copper mines of Zambia of malaria, dropping the rate of malaria there by 97% and the malarial mortality rate by 88% from 1929 to 1950 (Killeen et al., 2002).

Though LSM has been successful in dealing with malaria in a number of places, it is less common today. One reason for this is that other methods have emerged that are easier to implement. Many parts of SSA, for example, have far too many small and temporary habitats for mosquitoes for LSM to be feasible. Spraying and treatments can be applied to homes and other areas instead to kill mosquitoes, effectively preventing them from biting and infecting other humans (Curtis and Mnzava, 2000). For example, indoor residual spraying (IRS) entails the application of insecticide to community areas and homes, killing or repelling mosquitoes when they rest on housing fixtures, walls, ceilings and other areas where mosquitoes could potentially come in close contact with humans. The primary insecticide spray used to do this early on was DDT (dichlorodiphenyltrichloroethane), which was discovered in 1941 and is both effective and inexpensive. Such a strategy led to encouraging results in Taiwan, Latin America and the Caribbean, Italy and the Balkans, for example, and most of the time eliminated malaria in less than ten years. Though DDT was later banned in 1972, due to its toxicity for animals, other somewhat more expensive insecticides exist that are also effective.

Environmental methods also exist to naturally reduce larval habitats, such as intermittent irrigation. In Chinese and African rice fields, for example, intermittent irrigation curtailed larval development while at the same time saving water and reducing methane emissions (Mutero et al., 2006). Irrigation infrastructures and management systems can also be designed to lessen the risk of larval development by minimizing incidences of standing and/or slow-moving water. In addition, household wastewater systems can be improved to ensure that water is disposed in ways that reduce the chances of mosquito breeding.

Using approaches like these, there have been a number of successes in malaria elimination. Since 1945, 79 states have got rid of malaria (bringing the total number of malaria free states up to 109), decreasing the proportion of the world's people who live in malaria-endemic regions from 70% to 50%. Of the 99 states in the world that still have problems with malaria, 32 have taken measures to eliminate it (Smith et al., 2013).

Yet, even IRS programmes are not as widespread as would be desired: only 5% of people at risk of contracting the disease are protected by it. Though much of the developed world has concentrated on eradication as the solution to malaria, states in much of the developing world and particularly in SSA have emphasized controlling it.

Simple protective measures like bed nets can make a large difference here. Bed nets treated with insecticides offer individuals protection from the disease in places where window screens do not exist. According to some estimates, a person living in the Kou Valley of Burkina Faso who sleeps without a bed net (a very common scenario there) receives upwards of 150 mosquito bites per night and potentially 35,000 bites per year (Gallup and Sachs, 2001, 89). Bed nets can be very effective at controlling the disease because they irritate and trap mosquitos in search of a human host. In the Sichuan Province of China, for example, over two million treated bed nets were distributed to residents, leading to large declines in malaria infection rates (World Health Organization, 2014a). In the Gambia, it is estimated that a bed net programme reduced child mortality rates by 25% (Alonso et al., 1991, 1501). Each treated net costs around $10 and can cover more than one family member while sleeping.

A final strategy for malaria control involves treatment and testing. There is no vaccine for malaria, but treatments to deal with it have improved dramatically, reducing global mortality rates since 2000 by 25% and by

33% for those in Africa. When treatment and testing for malaria is wide-spread and encouraged, the public health system can quarantine those individuals who have contracted it, to prevent the chances that they will be bitten again by a mosquito carrier, which will then transmit the disease to someone else.

The problem with this strategy is that it requires that states have access to diagnostic tools, as well as low-cost treatments. Much of Africa, for example, does not have rapid diagnosis capabilities for malaria. In the case of Burkina Faso, a 2003 study revealed that 69% of infants of the age of 6–31 months were treated at home and never made it to a clinic (Boelee et al., 2010, 27). Those who can afford anti-malarial drugs may take them even if they do not have malaria to ensure that they do not suffer the negative consequences of the disease. Overuse of these drugs, however, can lead to the parasites becoming more resistant to them. For this reason, rapid and cheap diagnostics are needed in endemic states to conserve the use of those drugs that are the most effective. This situation, though far from ideal, is improving. The number of diagnostic tests from 2010 to 2011 nearly doubled from 88 million to 155 million (WHO, 2013a).

The response so far to malaria

A number of organizations and campaigns have been undertaken in many parts of the world to deal with malaria. One of the founding goals of the WHO, for example, was the global eradication of malaria. From 1955 to 1969, it launched the Global Malaria Eradication Program working with a group of scientists from Europe and the United States. The programme identified states and regions where elimination campaigns would be pursued. Targets included much of Asia and the Americas, though Papua New Guinea and some Indonesian islands were excluded due to administrative, technical and ecological difficulties. Much of tropical Africa was also ignored, though the WHO did support limited anti-malarial efforts in South Africa, Zimbabwe and Ethiopia.

Part of the reason a number of developing states were left out of this programme was that they lacked the health infrastructure necessary to fully eliminate malaria. In addition, many parts of the developing world simply faced too much instability, in the form of civil war and coups, to enable programme implementation. As such, though the Global Malaria Eradication Program initially envisioned the creation of large-scale regional malaria control programmes, this was not possible.

As a result, many observers believe that the WHO programme largely bypassed the African continent. Hospitals were given access to anti-malarial drugs and small eradication programmes were supported, but the overall campaign was minimal there (Finkel, 2007).

Since the Global Malaria Eradication Program ended, the donor, research and policy communities have been more reluctant to pursue elimination, given the strong need for targeted states to have the will and capacity to carry out such a campaign for it to be effective (Feachem and Sabot, 2008).

For this reason, a number of states have focused on controlling malaria. Yet, more needs to be done on this front too. According to the 2009 World Malaria Report, only about one in three African households owns a treated bed net, and only one in four children sleeps under one (Aregawi et al., 2009). Though there were 145 million nets delivered to target populations in 2010, this number dropped to only 66 million by 2012 (World Health Organization, 2012). At the same time, the distribution of bed nets has been shown to dramatically reduce mortality rates, particularly among children. Child mortality rates dropped by about 8% a year in Senegal, Rwanda and Kenya following the widespread distribution of bed nets in those states, and in Vietnam by as much as 37% (Barat, 2006; United Nations, 2012). In Kenya, this involved the government distributing nets free of charge, increasing usage from less than 10% of all households in 2003 to six times that in 2008 (The Economist, 2012).

Disease and development

Though economists now agree that infectious diseases harm growth, for reasons we will address in a moment, the early literature was not always in agreement. In the 1980s, for example, when the HIV/AIDS epidemic gained momentum, a number of researchers believed that its effects would be marginal at best on macroeconomic outcomes. Some researchers even believed that the decreases in population growth on account of HIV/AIDS would lead to increases in GDP per capita. The World Bank's René Bonnel, for example, wrote in a paper on the impact of HIV/AIDS on economic growth, 'In some cases as Botswana, per capita income was projected to increase as a result of HIV/AIDS' (Bonnel, 2000, 2). And as one 1997 study put it, 'there is more flash than substance to the claim that AIDS impedes national economic growth' (Bloom and Mahal, 1997, 120).

Despite these initial assessments, the negative economic consequences of HIV/AIDS, as well as other infectious diseases, are now widely accepted. HIV/AIDS, for example, is estimated to cause declines in per capita income of about 20%. And with malaria, some researchers estimate that per capita growth rates would increase by over 1% in malaria-prone states if health conditions were to improve (Gallup and Sachs, 2001). In SSA, malaria is believed to cost over $12 billion each year and GDP per capita is thought to be about a third less than it would have been had malaria been eradicated in 1960.

Box 11.2 TB

Tuberculosis (TB) is a common infectious disease caused by different strains of mycobacteria that overwhelmingly affects those living in the developing world. Though TB usually attacks the lungs, it can affect other parts of the body as well. The primary symptoms of active TB include a chronic cough, fever, night sweats and weight loss. Once the infection has spread to other organs, this can lead to many other symptoms.

Unlike HIV/AIDS, TB is spread through casual contact, and is transmitted through the air when an individual with an active case of TB coughs or sneezes and the bacterium is inhaled.

Nevertheless, TB and HIV/AIDS are inseparably connected, as 13% of all TB cases are also HIV positive. The HIV infection reactivates latent TB infections and accelerates the progression of any newly acquired TB infections. TB is an illness that expedites the progression of HIV to AIDS. It is responsible for over 30% of all AIDS related deaths, making it the leading cause of deaths for people living with AIDS. TB is more easily contractible in the developing world because of compromised immunity and large rates of HIV infection and AIDS.

In the developing world, TB primarily affects those who are in the most productive years of their lives, adolescents and young adults in Africa. Over 80% of all of those with TB are between the ages of 15 and 49. There are huge costs as a result of low productivity, due to illness, loss of financial support and loss of life. In contrast, in Western countries, TB is a disease that mainly afflicts older people, and those who are immune compromised.

Efforts to combat the disease in the developing world have highlighted the importance of investing in the existing public health-care systems rather than simply relying on vertical programmes. In Tanzania, a new programme launched in 1978 relied on government hospitals and clinics to provide treatment. The programme required that patients were properly registered and the details of those who were cured were recorded so that public health authorities could show health-care workers where TB services were working well and where they could be improved (WHO, 2011b, 105). The programme proved that TB cases could decline in the developing world using the existing public health-care system.

Combatting TB requires a sophisticated health-care system that can diagnose, isolate new cases and properly treat the disease. China has achieved the most progress reducing the TB mortality rate by 80% between 1990 and 2010 by injecting money into its public health-care system for detection, diagnosis and treatment, setting up a better drug supply system and keeping better records of progress (Wang et al., 2007). However, given the strains on already stretched health-care systems in most countries in the developing world, eradicating TB, once a reachable goal, has become much more difficult.

A comparison of the levels of development in states with malaria versus those without it is telling. In 1995, the average GDP per capita of states with malaria was about $1,500; it was more than five times that number in states without it. In fact, in more than a third of states with intense strains of malaria, growth rates were actually negative from 1965 to 1990.

The development trajectories of states that have eradicated malaria are important to point out. The southern region of the United States, for example, has traditionally been significantly poorer than the rest of the country. It was not until malaria was eliminated from the south that it began to catch up. In 1950 when malaria still existed, the South had only 60% of the per capita income of the rest of the United States; this number rose to 68% by 1960 when malaria no longer existed (Barro et al., 1991). Economic performance in both Taiwan and Jamaica began to surpass that of neighbouring states after each got rid of malaria (in 1961 and 1958, respectively). In Nepal, as well, the southern plains called the Terai were uninhabitable until the early 1950s when malaria was eradicated; now that region is the richest and most agriculturally productive part of the country (Gallup and Sachs, 2001, 91).

One of the reasons why infectious diseases are harmful is that they hurt labour productivity, which is critical to economic growth. It has been well-documented, for example, that US efforts to build the Panama Canal in the early 20th century were stalled due to malaria outbreaks and did not gain momentum until malaria became controllable. Diseases like HIV/AIDS and malaria kill or impair individuals who are often in the prime of their lives. Though few adults end up dying from malaria, it is near impossible to work while suffering from the disease. With HIV/AIDS, not only do many adults die from the disease, but it also compromises their immune systems, making them prone to repeated infections. Nearly 80% of those who die from HIV/AIDS, for example, are between the ages of 20 and 50 (World Health Organization).

As a result, infectious disease outbreaks mean more days of the year in which potential workers must stay home. In a sugar mill in South Africa, for example, more than a quarter of all workers tested were HIV positive; these workers took 55 additional days of sick leave during the last two years of their lives than their healthy counterparts (Bollinger and Stover, (1999) CI). Because so many adults die from HIV/AIDS it also reduces the pool of available workers, many of whom only recently entered the work force. Some researchers estimate that most businesses in Africa with more than ten employees have seen at least one employee die of HIV/AIDS or have at least one employee who is infected. Barclays Bank of Zambia, for example, lost more than a quarter of its employees to the disease (Poku, 2002, 541). Beyond the tragic loss of life, the death of so many otherwise able-bodied adults is an investment loss for the state, given the resources that states must devote to develop the human capital of their citizens.

These diseases affect not just those who are infected, but also their care-takers, who are often forced to stay home from work as well to deal with sick relatives. The cumulative effect is that infectious diseases hurt labour productivity and economic output. Some estimate that in Zimbabwe, for example, malaria has led to decreases in the production of maize by 61%, cotton by 47% and groundnuts by 37% (USAID).

Another reason why infectious diseases are economically detrimental is that they decrease investment. Investors tend to avoid putting their resources in places where infectious diseases are endemic. There is simply too much economic uncertainty to make it worth their while. A London-based mining and metal company that opted to invest $1.4 billion to construct an aluminium shelter in Mozambique offers an example of the risks: there were 7,000 cases of malaria among employees and 13 deaths due to the disease in only two years. HIV/AIDS prevalence also deters investment. Businesses have to dedicate more resources to health-care expenses for sick employees, training workers to replace employees on sick leave, and covering sick leave allowances. In fact, there is even a term for the high costs of running a business in HIV/AIDS-endemic areas: the AIDS tax (Rosen et al., 2003).

Tourism also suffers when infectious diseases are widespread, robbing states of reaping the benefits of another source of income. For example, Greece, Spain and Italy now generates significant income from their tourism industries. But this was not always the case. All three states had issues with malaria, with Greece the hardest hit. Prior to the malaria eradication efforts all three undertook in the 1930s and 1940s, their tourism industries were underdeveloped and there were few tourists. Once malaria was eliminated, however, they were able to stimulate demand for tourism and tap into the tourism industry as a revenue generator (Sachs and Malaney, 2002).

Infectious diseases negatively affect economies at the household levels, as well. Households suffer a disease burden, as they must dedicate both time and resources towards dealing with sick family members. In fact, in SSA, anywhere from 70% to 90% of all sicknesses are dealt with at home, and 60% of all deaths (UNICEF, 2002). In other words, infected individuals more often than not are dealing with their illnesses at home, not in the hospital. Family members helping sick relatives lose wages because they cannot attend work, precisely at a time when they have more expenses due to treatment costs. An African family may spend up to 25% of its income on malaria prevention and control, for example (Breman et al., 2004). Similarly, a study on Ivory Coast showed that households with an HIV/AIDS infected family member spend twice as much on medical expenses as other households (Stover and Bollinger, 1999). This leaves households with fewer resources to devote to education costs or investments.

Moreover, infectious diseases lead to slowed growth of human capital, primarily through their impact on the education levels of those affected. Children are at high risk of contracting malaria if they live in areas where it exists, as mentioned earlier. Those who become infected with malaria miss school due to illness. In Kenya, for example, primary school students miss 11% of school days due to malaria and secondary students miss 4% (Lucas, 2010). These effects can cumulate leaving students who have suffered from malaria behind in school and unable to catch up. In addition, because treating malaria can be expensive, some families are forced to forgo sending their children to school because they cannot afford to do so (The state may also lower education investment levels in response to infectious diseases, opting instead to devote resources to public health). Families whose relatives are afflicted by disease may also keep healthy children home instead of at school to put them to work to help pay for costs. At the same time, chronic bouts of malaria negatively affect cognitive development and can lead to anaemia, renal damage and appetite suppression, all of which lower classroom productivity levels and student attendance. High child mortality rates due to infectious diseases also reduce the total number of children attending school. In Swaziland, for example, HIV/AIDS will have reduced the size of the primary school population for each grade by 30% by 2016 (Gachuhi, 1999).

As a contrast to this, states that do not suffer from widespread infectious diseases have better educational outcomes. For example, many states that have been able to eradicate malaria, like Sri Lanka and Paraguay, saw their educational attainment and literacy rates skyrocket afterwards (Lucas, 2010).

States with high levels of infectious diseases also lose their prior investments in human capital (as mentioned earlier) when high-skilled contributors to the economy contract them, lowering their life expectancy. In Botswana, for example, it is estimated that over a third of all teachers are HIV positive. Zambia's Ministry of Education reports that over 2% of its teachers died in 1996 alone (Gachuhi, 1999), a number that was greater than the total number of teachers it produced in its teacher training colleges that year. Experts estimate that this amounts to huge losses, as the death or absence of a single teacher affects the education of anywhere from 20 to 50 children, numbers that are much higher for school administrators. Infections among health-care workers are also problematic. Those in the health-care industry are more susceptible to contracting many infectious diseases due to their increased exposure to them, yet are also vital to helping the population withstand outbreaks. One study from the early 1990s found that HIV prevalence in Zambia's capital, Lusaka, among midwives was 39% and 44% among nurses (United Nations, 2006). State resources that are devoted to the development of human capital reap few rewards when high-skilled workers contract infectious diseases at high rates.

Disease and the state

For these same reasons, infectious diseases also increase government costs. Like with private businesses, in states where diseases are pervasive, states have to spend more on training to deal with absenteeism among employees, sick leave pay and health bills. When government employees face infectious diseases, the state is challenged to provide high-quality services. Some researchers have argued, for example, that in Benin and Mozambique the prevalence of HIV/AIDS among civil servants has hampered the capacity of the bureaucracies there to administer state services (Boutayeb, 2009).

Beyond government employees, overall health-care costs can be higher in disease-ridden states, as states are pressured to devote more resources to dealing with disease. In the case of HIV/AIDS, there are so many orphans due to the disease that states are also strained to increase spending on social welfare programmes to care for them. Infectious diseases place a heavy burden on the public health system, stretching the capacity of already limited health facilities. In Africa, for example, malaria alone accounts for 40% of public health expenditures and 30% to 50% of inpatient admissions (Roll Back Malaria, 2009). A 1996–1997 malaria epidemic in one district in Zimbabwe increased the costs incurred by the Ministry of Health by $290,000 (Bremen et al., 2004). Treatment is even more costly for HIV/AIDS, which in 1995 accounted for 27% of health-care expenditures in Zimbabwe and 66% in Rwanda (Rau, 2003, 6).

Infectious diseases also lead to lost state revenues. HIV/AIDS and malaria lower the size of the workforce, reducing in turn the size of the taxable population. States that are badly affected generate less revenue income, which is precisely what is needed to address health-care costs and offer better assistance. Even those individuals who are part of the workforce have lower wages when they contract infectious diseases due to lost work days, which also decrease the taxes states are able to collect.

In sum, there are a variety of mechanisms through which infectious diseases hurt economic performance and the state. The cumulative effect is that developing states with high rates of infectious disease incidences face serious challenges in getting themselves out of poverty. In the section that follows, we discuss the role that the state can play in helping countries overcome disease vulnerabilities.

Dealing with disease

Experience has shown that there are decisions that states can make that can help them address the developmental challenges posed by infectious diseases, as a number of the anecdotes mentioned earlier indicate. And now that the development community is in agreement that infectious diseases are a major growth killer, a number of efforts have been launched to try to lessen their impact. There are now, for example, over 60,000 non-governmental organizations (NGOs) dedicated to AIDS-related causes! (Garrett, 2007)

Though international organizations can help, experience has also shown that the state must be involved for the effort to be successful in the long term. Combatting infectious diseases primarily requires a state with a government willing and capable to devote resources to administrative institutions – namely a public health-care system in conjunction with specific health-care agencies (such as a malaria control agency) – that can carry out an effective strategy. Here, we discuss the consequences of the top-down approaches (referred to as vertical programmes) to dealing with infectious diseases, which are often supported by the international community.

Disease control programmes spearheaded by those in the development community typically have been vertical in nature, meaning that they operate outside of a target state's existing general health-care structure. They are autonomous from the state's institutions, in that funds are channelled directly to an independent structure that dictates their use; the state's public health-care system has little involvement (Mills et al., 2002; Yamey, 2002). Some of these vertical programmes have been successful, like the WHO's campaign to eliminate smallpox in 1980. Through this programme, millions of children received vaccines leading to the eradication of the disease and saving an estimated three million lives each year since.

The reason a vertical approach worked in this instance, however, is that smallpox is simple to prevent: a safe, effective and relatively cheap vaccine exists that can be administered to children. For many other diseases, including HIV/AIDS and malaria, such an option does not exist.

Donors often support the uses of vertical programmes because they do not trust the state to efficiently use resources, and in many cases, their instincts are correct. As the chapter on corruption made clear, in a number of states in the developing world, the government exists simply to raid states resources. That being said, a top-down approach is a small-picture solution to the problem. Vertical programmes, at best, only address a specific health-care issue and usually operate within a limited time frame. Given the lack of state coordination, they can lead to institutional duplication, as well as inefficiencies because recipients may not know the correct way to use facilities (Pfeiffer et al., 2008). The targeted nature of vertical programmes also means that they are ill-equipped to assist patients with the full range of their health needs. Vertical programmes make little use of local knowledge and specific needs, which can also be critical to a programme's success. Perhaps, most importantly, vertical programmes do little to improve the capacity of the state to meet existing health-care challenges and those that lie ahead. Moreover, they may even disincentivize states to reform their health-care services (Brown et al., 2006). They can divert human and financial resources away from the existing low-quality system and create 'islands of excellence' that do little to fix the long-term problem (Gyapong et al., 2010). Because there is little integration with the state, when international projects leave, the transition can be abrupt making it difficult for countries to manage when assistance programmes leave.

Take the case of Haiti. Due to international efforts, HIV/AIDS prevalence decreased from 6% to 3% from 2002 to 2006, which is a laudable achievement. During the same period, however, Haiti experienced declines in nearly every other health indicator (Garrett, 2007). There were more HIV testing sites than ever before, but the state basically abandoned all other public health programmes. As a result, the effort to fight HIV/AIDS in Haiti 'has not lifted all boats and has not positively impacted public health care' (Garrett, 2007, 23). The overall message is that when donors and development groups work in isolation using vertical programmes to deal with infectious diseases, the results are often not as good as they may appear on the surface.

And yet, the reality is that most disease control programmes have taken this form. The ministries of health in target states have been largely excluded from the process, mainly because experts have assessed that including them will only reduce the efficacy of the programme. The situation is such that in many states in the developing world, the ministries of health face competition from NGOs and relief agencies. As a result, a number of ministries of health have expressed frustration at their inability to monitor the operations of foreign organizations carrying out health programmes in the state, to ensure that these organizations are delivering services that match government policies and priorities, and mitigate duplication of services (Garrett, 2007).

The fact remains that most states in the developing world need better health systems. Improving the health-care system requires investment. Though heads of state in the African Union pledged to devote 15% of their budgets to health services, average health expenditures in SSA rarely exceed 5% of GDP. In fact, most states spend less than $10 per year on health care per person, even though the World Health Organization estimates that three to four times that number is needed (Center for Global Development, 2004). International resources would therefore be better leveraged if they were dedicated to guiding the direction of public health investments and improving the system as a whole. As one researcher puts it, disease control efforts 'should focus less on particular diseases than on broad measures that affect populations' general well-being' (Garrett, 2007, 15).

Integrated programmes, in which state governments work closely with the development community, have been more successful than vertical programmes. Here, the state is involved in the development of targets and resource allocation decisions and disease control specialists are incorporated as technical advisers. Integrated programmes are typically slower in terms of their efficacy, but they lead to longer-term solutions than vertical approaches, by both targeting diseases and delivering better health care more generally (Unger et al., 2003).

With the sufficient resources, there are a number of areas that states (and the development community working with them) can target. These essentially amount to reforms of the state's administrative apparatus, which houses public sector employees, like those in the health-care industry. Here, we list some explicit institutional changes the state could pursue with special attention to the health-care industry specifically.

First, increasing the training opportunities for workers in the health-care industry would help, as would improving the pay and incentive structures in place to encourage individuals to work in the health-care industry and stay there as a career path. Developing states often face difficulties retaining workers in their health-care industries. Many health-care facilities simply lack the labour force to staff them, prohibiting them from providing basic standards of care.

Tanzania, for example, has a health-care workforce of 25,000, though experts estimate it needs at least three times that number to handle its health issues. In developing states, there is often not enough staff trained to handle the population's health issues. Those who do have appropriate training often leave to work in developed states or are lured into working for NGOs and international agencies, who pay as much as a hundred times the government rate (Garrett, 2007). Only about a third of doctors trained in Zimbabwe, for example, actually remain there. Of the 872 medical officers trained in Ghana from 1993 to 2002, only 267 stayed in the country afterwards. An example from Guinea Bissau is particularly striking: though it has received many ARV supplies from donors to combat HIV/AIDS, the drugs remain in a warehouse because it does not have the doctors needed to distribute them (Garrett, 2007).

Beyond improving the training and pay of workers in the health-care industry, the state also needs to devote investment into its health infrastructure to improve surveillance, diagnostics, supplies and information systems (Bryce et al., 2003; Garrett, 2007). Surveillance is important for infectious diseases like malaria to enable the state to recognize where transmissions are taking place. Diagnostic tools are valuable because they provide citizens and health officials with information about infection rates, potentially preventing their spread. Adequate supplies are also critical to preventing the spread of diseases, as reusing needles can transmit them rapidly across a population. For examples, almost 15% of all HIV infections and 25% of all paediatric infections in SSA are due to blood transfusions that were carried out to treat malaria and sickle cell anaemia (Malaney et al., 2004, 144). Improving the health-care industry's information systems is important, too, given that there is often little information available regarding shortages and poor procurement and distribution processes (Lewis, 2006).

All of these changes would result in better treatment availability for citizens suffering from infectious diseases, which in turn would increase their productivity and prevent the disease from spreading further.

To combat infectious diseases, governments must have both the will and resources to do so. Beyond investments in the health industry, however, it is also important for states to maintain and pursue high-quality administrative institutions as a whole. While a well-paid and highly-trained ministry of health and public health sector is one component of a strategy for dealing with disease, a coordinated effort among multiple state agencies is required for such a strategy to be effective, meaning that high-quality administrative institutions are critical. For example, eradicating malaria can involve environmental protection ministries working in conjunction with ministries of health, while spreading awareness about HIV/AIDS prevention can entail collaborative projects with the ministries of education and health. States must have high-quality administrative institutions to pursue the type of comprehensive strategy needed to effectively deal with infectious diseases.

To illustrate that it is possible to effectively combat infectious diseases, we now offer some success stories.

Case studies: HIV/AIDS success stories in Senegal and Uganda

Though HIV/AIDS has had a devastating impact on the quality of life for many living in the developing world, there are a number of success stories, or cases of developing states implementing sound policies to combat HIV/AIDS. Here, we highlight the experiences of Senegal and Uganda.

In Senegal, AIDS was first recorded in 1986, but the state had already taken proactive measures that curbed the spread of the virus. For one, it legalized prostitution so that commercial sex workers would have to register with the state. This led to a general surveillance programme and treatment for sexually transmitted diseases, implemented in the 1970s.

A national programme to fight sexually transmitted diseases was launched in 1978. And as early as 1970, the state has put in place policies to ensure safe blood transfusions to control the spread of infections (Putzel, 2003).

Once AIDS reached Senegal, the government moved quickly to respond to the crisis. It established a surveillance system in 1989, and put forth an aggressive education programme to inform the public about HIV/AIDS. Surveys indicated that over 90% of the public was aware of how to prevent the disease and 70% of respondents reported that they used condoms, which the state had made widely available. Sex workers were also targeted and encouraged to practice safe sex. The government set up a National AIDS Prevention Committee, as well, to coordinate its response. It implemented the usage of systematic HIV screenings of all bags of blood that were used for blood transfusions. All of these factors contributed to the low level of HIV prevalence in Senegal. It is currently around 0.5%, which is one of the lowest rates in Africa.

Uganda was one of the earliest and hardest hit states by the HIV/AIDS epidemic. It has implemented a number of policies to deal with it that have elicited moderate successes, however. The first cases of HIV turned up in Kampala in the late 1970s. At the time, more and more women were turning to the sex trade due to the economic crisis, while increasing numbers of male mobile workers were spending their nights away from home. The jump in interactions between sex workers and male mobile workers that resulted accelerated the spread of the virus. Making matters worse, by the time then-leader Idi Amin fled the country in exile, the health-care system was virtually destroyed, meaning that large numbers of Ugandans were going undiagnosed and untreated. By 1993, HIV prevalence in Kampala hit a high of 30% (Putzel, 2003).

Initially, the government was in denial about the severity of the problem. The Ministry of Health in the 1980s thought that the disease was a wasting disease known as 'slim', for example. By the time Yoweri Museveni came to power in 1985, however, things began to change course. Museveni made fighting the virus one of his main objectives. First, the government had to rebuild its health institutions. Museveni gave his support to the medical community in this effort and made it clear that combatting HIV/AIDS was a major priority. In 1987, the Ministry of Health established surveillance sites in hospitals; in 15 years, the number of sites reached 20. In 1990, Museveni created the AIDS Information Center, which provided voluntary testing and counselling. There were four centres across the country, established in urban areas. By 2000, these efforts had yielded positive results. The Ugandan Blood Transfusions Services claimed that screening was universal and that blood safety was 90%, for example. The HIV prevalence rate has also decreased to around 7% (Putzel, 2003).

Case studies: malaria success stories in Sri Lanka, Zambia and India

A number of developing states have confronted malaria and seen infection rates decline dramatically. Sri Lanka, for example, spearheaded a malaria eradication programme in 1945. It used insecticide sprays every ten weeks, extending to every 12 weeks as the incidence of malaria declined. It also modified irrigation structures and effectively communicated to the agricultural sector that big financial gains could be made from this strategy via water savings. This led to the involvement of non-health sectors, as well, because they stood to benefit from better irrigation (Lucas, 2010). By 1963, malaria had for the most part disappeared. Years of civil war, however, have since brought malaria back. At the turn of the century, Sri Lanka had more than a quarter of a million cases. Today, the Ministry of Health, working with the Global Fund, has taken a multipronged approach, using careful surveillance, vector control, blood testing, treatment and community education. As a result, the disease has been eradicated.

Zambia tackled malaria by using a variety of methods. In the copper belt, it used environmental methods to drain and modify the aquatic habitats of young mosquitoes. It also improved its water management techniques, made housing improvements to reduce standing water, and distributed more bed nets (Utzinger et al., 2001). In the last ten years, it has made great strides to improve access to insecticide treated bed nets (ITNs), in particular. Working with UNICEF, the Global Fund for Malaria, the World Bank and the United States Agency for International Development (USAID), it increased the number of households with access to ITNs from 38% in 2006 to 64% in 2010. It has also reduced the number of deaths due to malaria by 50% from 2000 to 2010. Key to Zambia's success has been the strong and consistent leadership from the Ministry of Health and the Zambia National Malaria Control Center (NMCC). Zambia has been able to track progress using output information on service delivery. Health information systems are now sophisticated enough to report to health facilities across the country in order to track 'fever cases, malaria diagnosis, hospital admissions and treatment activities' (Chizema-Kawesha et al., 2010, 480).

India also embarked on a comprehensive nation-wide programme to deal with malaria, which had once been considered the country's greatest health problem. After India's partition with Pakistan in 1947, there were 75 million cases of malaria and 800,000 deaths. To respond, the National Malaria Programme sprayed insecticide in dwellings and cattle sheds two times a year during peak transmission times. It also sprayed roofs in rural areas. Though India's efforts to control malaria have had their ups and downs, the last five years in particular have seen noticeable improvements. In 2012, there were only 506 deaths to due to malaria and one millions cases of the disease (down from 1.5 million in 2009). India is also projected to see a decrease of at least 50% in its rate of malaria incidences by 2015, according to the World Health Organization (2014b).

Conclusion

In the 1990s, Africa – one of the regions of the world worst affected by infectious diseases – spent less than 3% of state budgets on health care. Spending was so low that in the advent of disease outbreaks, life expectancy rates actually dropped in a number of places since independence. Kenya's life expectancy, for example, was 63 years in 1963 but only 47 years in 2007. Due to a turnaround in health spending, however, Kenya's life expectancy is now rebounding and is up to 57 years (World Health Organization).

And Kenya is not alone in taking steps to improve the health of its citizens. Tanzania, for example, increased its health budget to 13% and saw its life expectancy rates increase by nine years. The Central African Republic, Namibia and Zambia have each tripled the proportion of their budgets they now devote to health care, as well, leading to better health outcomes for their citizens, however marginal.

The message to convey here is that though infectious diseases pose a serious development challenge to many of the world's poorest states, they are surmountable. With the right combination of will and resources, states can eradicate malaria, lesson the incidence of HIV contraction and improve the well-being of their citizens, breaking the cycles of poverty and disease that plague them. Though the road to doing so is not necessarily an easy one, a state-centred approach that draws from past trials and errors in the area of disease control and elimination can save citizens' lives and enable them to be productive participants in the state's economy once again.

Questions

- In what ways is the state critical for controlling malaria?
- Why has Africa been so hard hit by disease? Why has AIDS had the biggest impact on middle income countries in Africa while malaria has affected the poorest countries in Africa?
- What are the ways in which disease impacts development?
- What are the problems with vertical programmes for dealing with disease? What are the benefits of integrated programmes?
- In what ways was the state critical to reducing HIV/AIDS prevalence rates in Senegal and Uganda?

Facts

- The big three diseases are HIV/AIDS, malaria and tuberculosis.
- Swaziland has the highest percentage of HIV/AIDS prevalence in the world with 26.5%, while South African has the largest number of cases with over 5.6 million.
- There are over 207 million cases of malaria worldwide, 80% of which are in Africa.
- Improvements in treatment for malaria have reduced global mortality rates since 2000 by 25% and by 33% for those in Africa.
- In 1947 India had 75 million cases of malaria and 800,000 deaths. Renewed efforts to control malaria by the state-run National Malaria Programme have reduced malaria prevalence to one million cases in 2012 and only 506 deaths.

Chapter 12

Globalization

This chapter examines globalization in the wider context of development, examining the significance of globalization on development and the state. Proponents of globalization claim that the world is becoming smaller and more integrated. Optimists claim that globalization will offer benefits to all who integrate into the global economy and liberalize their economies, with Thomas Friedman (2000) arguing that globalization would simply flatten the world. On the other hand, critics claim that globalization has only increased the gaps between rich and poor. And despite the optimism globalization is not experienced the same way by everyone. Certain parts of the world are more globally connected than others. For example, much of Africa is not well connected to other regions through trade and investment flows. Thus one of the most significant challenges of globalization is that its effects are not evenly distributed. While some states have seen record levels of economic growth, others have seen their economies stagnate. Globalization poses serious challenges to development, even though it also brings great opportunities. This chapter provides an overview of how globalization can be defined, how globalization affects development, and in turn, the state. Additionally, this chapter offers insights to how globalization can be dealt with. Throughout we emphasize that much of this depends on how effective the state is in harnessing the energy of globalization and taking advantage of the possibilities.

Globalization

Globalization is the bringing together of a complex web of people, cultures, markets and practices. Globalization refers to multidimensional and transnational processes that allow the economy, politics and cultures of different countries to penetrate each other (Mittelman, 1995, 273). With globalization, the world is not only more interdependent but is also more compressed. Globalization encompasses a global market, with a free flow of goods, services and information. Globalization is the expansion of economic activities across national boundaries, manifested by international trade, international investment and international finance (Nayyar, 2003, 65). States interact and trade with one another at unprecedented levels, with market forces often making important decisions instead of states. Because of this, some scholars argue that institutional weakness should be considered to be in tandem with globalization.

Globalization has multidimensional components, economic, military, cultural, technological, political and environmental. International networks, associations, institutions, financial markets, MNCs, NGOs, international media, academic circles and IFIs have all become more important in a globalizing world. Globalization is usually measured as integration with the global economy, or trade as a proportion of GDP, trade openness and direct foreign investment. The quality of globalization is often based on the degree to which exports are based on manufacturing rather than resource extraction.

Globalization can be characterized more specifically by seven additional key features, which the following paragraphs will describe in more detail. These features include: increased trade, increased capital and investment movements, rise of multinational corporations, international organizations, migration and movement of people, dissemination of knowledge and threats to state sovereignty.

One of the key aspects of globalization is increased trade and transactions on a global scale. National economies have become more and more integrated into the global economy (Kouzmin and Hayne, 1999a). Globalization features increasing openness of national economies and growing levels of trade. The value of world trade increased 16-fold from 1950 to 1995 with the ratio of exports to GDP more than doubling over the period. Trade liberalization has played an important role in the emergence of the global economy, yet global trade is concentrated between the OECD countries with trade between the North and South remaining surprisingly small.

Globalization also constitutes increased capital and investment movements, such as foreign direct investment (FDI). International capital flows increased 14-fold from 1972 to 1996. There are few domestic barriers to the movement of international capital (Haque, 2002, 105). For example, in the 1990s, the amount of cross border capital flows increased from $536 billion in 1991 to nearly $1.3 trillion in 1995 (Fraser and Oppenheim, 1997). The total amount of FDI increased from $10 billion in 1970 to $349 billion in 1996. By 1996, the total value of cross border mergers and acquisitions had increased to over $274 billion.

There has been a sharp concentration of FDI in developed countries in particular. During the 1980s, Europe, North America and Japan attracted 75% of all FDI, though they account for only 14% of the population.

Ten developing countries received 66% of all FDI to developing countries: Argentina, Brazil, China, Egypt, Hong Kong, Malaysia, Mexico, Singapore, Taiwan and Thailand (European Network on Debt and Development). Most of the FDI flows that have entered developing countries have been in the oil and natural resource industries. The regional distribution of FDI has also been very uneven. For example, Africa has only attracted 6% of the total net FDI to developing countries (Sawkut et al., 2009). Finance is also no longer confined to territories, but has become global. With the ease of cyber banking, by 1995 over '$9 trillion of the world's bank assets belonged to depositors non-resident in the country where the account was held and/or were denominated in a currency issued outside that country' (Scholte, 1997, 439–440).

Globalization also highlights the growing importance of non-state actors such as multinational corporations (MNCs) and international institutions. For more on this, please refer to Box 12.1.

Globalization has also led to the increased importance of international organizations such as the World Bank, the United Nations, the IMF and the World Trade Organization. These organizations have spread liberal ideals and nation-states have been bound to these supra-territorial governance organizations (Korten, 2001). The major international institutions have advocated and in many cases imposed major policy reforms.

Globalization has also led to the increased migration and movement of people and the blurring of cultures and societies. From 1965 to 1990, the proportion of the labour forces migrating to different countries doubled, with most people migrating from developing countries. Anthony Giddens (2002) asserts that globalization can be defined by the intensification of global social relations that link people from far locations closer to each other. Human activity is linked across regions and continents, with more velocity, intensity and impact. Barriers to cross national interaction and exchanges have been reduced. The world appears to be shrinking, distances appear to be shorter and there is increasing ease with which people can interact with one another (Kouzmin and Hayne, 1999a).

Globalization also consists of the wide dissemination of knowledge, and the spread of different beliefs. Globalization also represents the spread of technological expertise and puts a premium on understanding technological knowledge. Technological knowledge is important because high-value manufactured goods require knowledge of intensive methods of production. Proponents of globalization have argued that globalization has facilitated communication among people. With technical innovations such as the internet and mobile phones, globalization has made possible

Box 12.1   What are MNCs?

Globalization highlights the growing importance of non-state actors such as multinational corporations (MNCs) and international financial institutions (IFIs). Critics of globalization have emphasized that the growing prominence of both MNCs and IFIs represents a disturbing trend. In particular, there have been intense debates about the effects of MNCs on the host countries. Dependency theorists (see Chapter 2) argue that MNCs have had little positive effects on the host economy.

Much of the growth of MNCs took place after the 1970s. In 1972 there were only 7,000 MNCs. By 1992 there were already 37,000 MNCs and an additional 200,000 affiliates, 95% of which originated in developed countries; strategic decision-making and research are also linked to the home countries (Abdul-Gafaru, 2006).

With the rise in MNCs, this has enabled a spatial reorganization of production, distribution and marketing of goods and services (Harris, 1993). Multinational corporations (MNCs) began decentralizing the production of goods across the world in the 1970s. Major changes took place in terms of where production took place. Due to the reduced costs, national production was replaced by global production, known as global sourcing. Production companies were able to draw their components and materials from anywhere in the world. There has been a mushrooming of production sites in the developing world for export of manufactured goods worldwide. By the 1980s most developing countries had implemented reforms to allow them to integrate more fully into the global economy.

MNCs are also criticized for taking advantage of lax labour legislation in developing countries. For example, the well-known case of Nike, which has outsourced production to Indonesia, has been heavily criticized. There are no unions and overtime is mandatory, sometimes unpaid. The workers are housed in company barracks and if there is any sort of strike, the military can be called in to break up the strike. In Sukabumi Indonesia, it was alleged that Indonesian military officers were used to intimidate workers to sign a petition that Nike was contractually obligated to pay the newly raised minimum wage. Another Nike factory in Serang Indonesia failed to pay its workers for over 600,000 hours of overtime work for a two-year period (Korten, 2001, 115).

Regardless of the controversial nature of MNCs and the multiple disagreements and debates that they generate, most would agree that their presence and importance in the global economy is unlikely to dissipate any time soon.

the global exchange of ideas. People living in previously remote and inaccessible places have now been given access to information and knowledge. Globalization has also improved connections and coordination among governments, corporations and NGOs.

Finally, for the state, globalization represents a threat to sovereignty, both territorially and concerning the autonomy of the state to pursue its own policies. There has also been a redefinition of the role of the state. State intervention is crucial to reducing uncertainty.

Yet, to some the state has become handcuffed to certain policies that may ignore environmental (for more on this see Box 12.2) and labour regulations. The policy prescriptions imposed on developing countries have advocated reforms that have encouraged the paring down of the state and anti-welfare policies, in efforts to improve efficiency (Haque, 2002, 104). Privatization took place at a rapid pace in the late 1980s and early 1990s. The total number of annual privatization transactions in developing countries went up from only 26 in 1988 to 416 in 1992. Total revenues from privatization increased from $2.6 billion in 1988 to $23.2 billion in 1992 (Cook and Kirkpatrick, 1997). In Mexico for example, the number of state enterprises decreased from 1,155 in 1982 to only 285 in 1990 (Haque, 1999, 205). Overall, globalization has had a major impact on the state. Before going into what the effects have been, we provide an overview of the emergence of globalization followed by the scholarship on globalization and development.

Emergence of globalization

Globalization emerged after the industrial revolution in the 19th century and early 20th century. The first wave of globalization took place during the period of 1870–1913. The global economy became more and more connected and a transition took place from competitive capitalism to late monopoly capitalism. Global trade was highly developed at the turn of the century. Trade and foreign investments grew rapidly. The internationalization of trade, production and finance was high before World War I, but it has decreased severely during the 1930s as a result of protectionism around the world. During the first wave some convergence in per capita and real wages took place within the Atlantic economy.

A second wave of globalization took place after World War II. This period brought many major changes to in the international economy. Major efforts were in place to develop international institutions for financial and trade cooperation. Most profound was the Bretton Woods Conference held in July of 1944 in New Hampshire, which led to agreements by major governments to lay the foundations for international monetary policy, trade and finance. The conference also led to the founding of several international institutions that were created in order to foster economic growth, such as the International Bank for Reconstruction and Development (which would be later known as the World Bank) and the International Monetary Fund (IMF). In 1947, the

General Agreement on Tariffs and Trade (GATT) was signed in Geneva, consisting of a series of agreements that would remove trade restrictions. GATT would eventually become the World Trade Organization, a major institution to manage the global trading system. From here on out, capitalism would enter a more aggressive period. There was much less macro-economic regulations and increasing mobility of private capital. The accumulation of capital accelerated after World War II and reached its zenith in the 1990s. Transaction corporations became much more powerful actors.

Globalization in its most intense form emerged due to two main factors. First, technical innovations have accelerated the process of globalization and have facilitated the growth of global trade. Economies of scale developed due to improvements in technology. Improvements in transportation have also helped generate global trade. Steamships reduced the costs of international transport. Railroads made domestic transport less expensive. In addition to the improvements in transport, with the invention of shipping containers in 1956, more nations were able to trade their goods at lower costs, which helped improve international trade levels (Levinson, 2010). Improvements in aviation and the growth of low-cost communication networks also increased the frequency of global movement and communication. Globalization has been spurred on by technological changes and the spread of information through the press, computers and satellite communication systems. With improvements in communications, the value of technological skills increased.

The second was the rise in importance of neo-liberalism. The term globalization became popularized in the late 1980s in tandem with the emergence of the Washington Consensus, which had emerged as the dominant paradigm. In the 1970s, coupled by the oil shocks, developing countries found themselves in debt with growing balance of payment problems. Assistance to help out with these problems was offered, yet conditional on adopting the tenets of the Washington Consensus. Globalization became a policy choice upon which external finance was contingent. Thomas Friedman refers to this as the 'golden straight jacket' because the application of neo-liberal policies has in some cases led to economic growth, while constraining states politically (Friedman, 2000). Critics of these policies claim that the great powers used their grip over the Bretton Woods institutions to shape the new rules to their own advantage. Former US Secretary of State, Henry Kissinger made this point bluntly in 1999, when he said 'what is called globalization is really another name for the dominant role of the United States'. Thus, the dominance of neo-liberal thinking has been a major feature of globalization.

Globalization and development

Globalization is a powerful force and is an engine of risk creation. It can promote growth but also large inequalities and poverty. It can lead to achievement but also frustration. Globalization can lead to turbulent financial markets and capital flows. It disrupts and undermines traditional economies. It can destroy traditional social structures, and lead to more protests and instability. It can lead to growing unemployment and debt. With globalization, non-state actors (such as multinational corporations) have grown in power (Reilly, 2008, 28). Foreign aid has disappeared, while the prices for global commodities produced in the developing world have decreased (Dorff, 1996). Developing countries have become more integrated into the world trading system, based on their shares of exports in GDP.

There is no shortage of studies that have examined the relationship between globalization and development, though it is difficult to test the relationship between globalization and inequality and poverty directly. Instead most studies have focused on the relationship between globalization and economic growth.

Supporters of globalization argue that trade liberalization policies (or openness to exports, imports and capital flows) encourage exports, which directly contribute to GDP growth. Switching over time from an economy based on import substitution industrialization to opening up the economy to imports would lead to a more efficient allocation of resources, and in turn higher rates of growth. More openness will also lead to increased levels of foreign direct investment (FDI), which then raises the productive capacity of developing countries and helps transfer knowledge and expertise. Financial liberalization will also make new technology more accessible, encourage the development of the domestic financial sector and assist with providing domestic credit.

Intense debate has taken place analysing the relationship between globalization and inequality. Some scholars have demonstrated that there are links between globalization and inequality (Stiglitz, 1998; Birdsall, 2000; Bata and Bergesen, 2002; Talbot, 2002). Both Sen (2002) and Ravallion (2003) note that globalization brings rising disparities in standards of living *within* countries. Empirical evidence has shown that trade openness has contributed to intra-country inequality. For example in China, coastal provinces have grown rapidly, while the inland areas have stagnated. China has lifted 400 million people out of poverty but the progress on poverty reduction has been uneven. In Mexico, while large corn farmers gained as did rural and urban consumers, small and medium farmers saw their incomes fall by 50% in the 1990s. Globalization may also cause explosive social cleavages as the gaps between rich and poor increase (Farazmand,

2001, 440). Globalization may lead to rising expectations and growing frustrations when the results of growth are not felt by everyone. Other studies (Milanovic, 2002) show that the effects of openness on income distribution depend on a country's initial income level. Thus, globalization is generally thought to increase inequalities. However, within countries, the poor living in regions that are highly globalized have fared better in dealing with macro-economic crises compared to those who are more isolated. For example the richest part of Mexico is Northern Mexico, which is also the most globalized.

The case of Chile illustrates the two-sided coin of globalization. Globalization has spurred economic growth, but has also led to growing inequalities. Chile is one of the more liberalized and globalized countries in the world. It embarked on a wide range of neo-liberal policies in the 1970s during the Augusto Pinochet regime (1973–1990), which have mostly remained in place. Chile's administrative welfare state was dismantled in 1973. Many state institutions such as education and health care were privatized. The dismantling of public institutions resulted in the reduction of the number of students to public school by over 700,000 since the policies were implemented, or about 20% of the total. The public system continues to lose tens of thousands of students each year. This has led to student protests to overhaul the system, with over 70% believing that schools should return to the Ministry of Education, which by the 1960s had built a solid national public system that was free of charge. Though the copper industry is state-owned, conglomerates in Chile exploit 70% of the country's copper mines, enjoying profits of around $20 billion in 2007- or about 60% of the total annual state budget and equal to the total spent in public social expenditures (Draibe, 2007, 12–14).

Some other studies have pointed out that inequalities are driven more *between* countries rather than within countries (Lindert and Williamson, 2001; O'Rourke, 2001; Sen, 2002; Ravallion, 2003). Aghion and Williamson (1998) explore the relationship among globalization, growth and inequality, arguing that inequalities can be explained by surges in trade and technology (33). Seshanna and Decornez (2003) demonstrate that though the world economy has become wealthier and more globalized in the past 40 years, it also has become more unequal and polarized. By the 1990s industrialized countries were producing over 80% of the world's GDP and consuming over 80% of the world's goods (Durning and Brough, 1991, 153). Critics charge that globalization has benefited the most powerful industrialized nations while developing countries have become more dependent on these powers. Countries that have been unable to take advantage of technological possibilities have seen the gaps between rich and poor accentuated (Waltz, 1999). However, other scholars contend that globalization is causing growing inequality. Jagdish Bhagwati

(2004) contends that the barriers erected by the developed world pose the bigger problem for the development of developing countries. As he sees it, regions in the developing world such as Africa need less protectionism and more open markets.

Additionally, critics find the global concentration and monopolization of economic, political and organizational power in the hands of a few MNCs to be very alarming. Policy choices that emphasize cushioning the blow of globalization are often impaired because power is concentrated in the hands of global corporations, which are difficult to keep accountable (Held, 1997). David Korten (2001) argues that it is difficult to have equal democratic societies when economic and political power is concentrated in a few large corporations (181).

Other studies demonstrate the ways in which globalization affects the poor in developing countries. Almas Heshmati (2005) underscores that it is difficult to say that trade openness and financial integration will reduce poverty. Scholars (Rogoff et al., 2003) have suggested that the impact of financial integration through growth effects is small. It is difficult to find direct linkages between financial integration and poverty. Overall, Sen (2002) and Ravallion (2003) claim that there is weak evidence that globalization reduces poverty. Extreme poverty rates rose sharply in the developing world during the period from 1980 to 1992. However, since this period extreme poverty rates have decreased. According to the World Bank in 2011, 1.2 billion people lived on less than $1.25 a day compared to 1.91 billion in 1990. Nevertheless, when examining the number of people who live on less than $2 a day, there has been little improvement. About 2.6 billion people live on less than $2 a day in 2011, while this number was 2.59 billion in 1981 (United Nations).

Critics have also claimed that globalization has increased the number of urban poor and rural landless. Over 80% of all the agricultural land in the developing world is owned by only about 3% of all landowners (Haque, 1999, 202). In South Asia, 40% of all rural households are landless. In Africa, 75% do not have access to land. In Latin American, 1% of all landlords own more than 40% of the arable land. Studies in India have demonstrated that the rural poor has gained less from trade reforms than other income groups because they also still face restrictions on labour mobility.

In contrast to these findings, other studies have argued that economic growth is the best anti-poverty measure. Paul Collier and David Dollar (2001) and the World Bank Development Report (2002) have explored the relationship among globalization, growth and poverty, arguing that globalization reduces poverty because more integrated economies tend to grow faster (1). Collier and Dollar (2001) estimate that poverty rates in the developing world may fall by 50% by 2015. Supporters of globalization argue that world poverty rates have fallen from 33% to 17%. East Asia has already achieved the goal of halving poverty by 2015, and South Asia is on target. The global share of people living on less than $1 a day has decreased from 40% to 21% between 1981 and 2001. However, when China and India are taken out of the equation, decreases in poverty rates are minimal. In Latin America, poverty rates rose from 136 million to 266 million. Standards of living also declined due to reductions in social services, decreased access to food, health and education and a decline in wages (Leftwich, 1994). Poverty in Africa has increased both in relative and absolute terms. Africa has seen increases in poverty levels, increasing from 170 million to 310 million in the past two decades. Approximately half of Africa lives in extreme poverty. Africa still only exports unprocessed agricultural products and receives very little foreign investment.

Proponents of globalization argue that it reduces poverty because the faster transmission of knowledge creates an environment that is more conducive to economic growth. Poverty has fallen in countries where exports and FDI are growing. India has opened up to more foreign investment, leading to a decline in poverty. In Zambia, opening up markets has helped poor consumers due to falling prices. In Colombia increases in exports have been associated with increases in compliance with labour legislation and decreases in poverty. Those working in sectors where exports are growing are less likely to be impoverished (Harrison, 2006, 16).

Other scholars (Nissanke and Thorbecke, 2007) have pointed out that openness through trade and financial liberalization increases the flow of goods and capital and can contribute to economic growth. Nevertheless, they caution that though it is likely that the poor benefit from growth, how growth affects poverty reduction depends on the pattern of economic growth, development and income distribution.

Countries in the developing world that are highly integrated and exposed may be more vulnerable to fiscal crises, which can increase poverty rates. Though foreign direct investment is associated with reduced poverty (such as in cases in India and Mexico), unrestricted capital flows are associated with higher rates of poverty (Harrison, 2006, 4). There is a propensity for high levels of capital flight from developing countries to developed countries during periods of instability and crisis. Joseph Stiglitz (2007) echoes this, claiming that capital market liberalization – or where markets are open to the free flow of short term and destabilizing capital – is problematic. World Bank research also showed that this was the case, explaining that capital market liberalization leads to volatility, which is bad for growth. This research was then later finally confirmed by the IMF (Stiglitz, 2007).

Financial crises are particularly hard on the most impoverished, especially if there are few safety nets in place to deal with economic shocks. In Indonesia, the poverty rate increased by 50% after the currency crisis in 1997. Real wages declined by 40%. Household consumption fell by 15%. Mexico has yet to recover from its 1995 peso crisis. Poverty rates in 2000 in Mexico were higher than they had been ten years earlier. By 2003, poverty rates are below what they were at the start of the crisis (Harrison, 2006, 9).

Globalization may spur growth but this will not reduce poverty on its own. Poverty reduction requires both higher levels of growth and pro-poor distribution of the gains from growth (Nissanke and Thorbecke, 2007). How gains from growth are distributed is very important to alleviating poverty. Higher growth rates can often lead to income inequality, which can dampen the positive effects of growth on poverty reduction.

Who benefits from globalization?

Globalization may only alleviate poverty in states that are equipped to benefit from it. Globalization tends to benefit states that already have diverse economies. States in the developing world have smaller and less diverse economies that make them more vulnerable to fluctuations in the economy. States in the developing world must contend with the volatility in the price of their primary products and deterioration in the terms of trade. For example, Senegal produced 141,000 tons of groundnut, which represented 68% of its exports in 1929 and up to 80% of its exports in 1960. Several decades, later groundnut still constituted the principal export for Senegal but the conditions of farmers deteriorated significantly. Countries in the developing world have difficulty diversifying because they lack market power and a domestic resource base to deal with external shocks (Easterly and Kraay, 2000; Armstrong and Read, 2003, 104). Trade may help finance imports that are essential but any gains made through trade may be offset by greater risks from exogenous global shocks (Armstrong and Read, 2003, 111).

Globalization also benefits skilled labour more so than unskilled labour. Proponents of globalization argue that globalization will lead to a demand for unskilled labour in developing countries. However, globalization has been biased towards skilled and educated labour, and recent technological improvements have saved costs on labour. Previous economic theories have postulated that countries with labour abundance can have an advantage. The Stolper Samuelson theorem claimed that countries with labour abundance should see their incomes increase when they open up to trade. Developing countries will benefit from trade reforms because they have a comparative advantage in unskilled labour. However, most jobs today require more skills than the poor in developing countries possess. Moreover, there has been a race to the bottom with wages—and labour unions have been weakened.

Capital and skilled labour do not tend to migrate to poor countries. It is more likely that skilled labour from developing countries will migrate to developed countries, such as the massive migration of skilled health-care workers from Africa migrating to Europe and the United States. For unskilled workers in developing countries, it has become more difficult to migrate abroad. From 1870 to 1914 over 60 million unskilled workers migrated from Europe to North America, whereas today unskilled workers attempting to do the same face many obstacles (Solimano, 2002, 2).

Globalization has also benefited countries with large-scale industries. Countries with smaller economies to begin with have a more difficult time sustaining large-scale high-growth industries. There may not be a wide range of goods available to sustain high-growth industries due to higher transport costs. Communications costs may also be high. Countries such as China, India, Bangladesh and Vietnam have moved from being primarily exporters of primary commodities to focusing on large-scale manufacturing and services.

Globalization improves access to new technologies, which provides unique opportunities for countries in the developing world to raise their incomes. Nevertheless, countries differ widely in terms of their abilities to upgrade and accumulate skills (Mayer, 2000). Research and development is often lacking, which makes it difficult to take advantage of technological progress (Armstrong and Read, 2003, 103). Thus poor states must invest a lot of money in education, training and skills in order to produce higher value added products. Technological diffusion and access to new technology is not universal. The privatization of research in industries such as the bio-tech fields reduce access to new technology in developing countries, leading to widening gaps in productivity. The difficulty for developing countries is that in order to succeed at globalization, you must be able to innovate and produce high-value products. In order to accomplish this, you must have high levels of technological know-how, capacity and human capital.

Globalization also benefits states that were equipped with certain endowments and infrastructure. Low levels of material infrastructure available to the poorest countries do not allow them to 'play on a level playing field with the forces of foreign trade unleashed by globalization', (Ripoll, 2006, 40). For example, in 1994 each person in the industrial countries used 7,514 kilowatt-hours of electricity, compared to 763 per capita in the developing countries. In the poorest countries, the figure was as low as 74 kilowatt-hours per capita, (Ripoll, 2006, 40). Though Africa is a major producer of the world's most important minerals and metal, it is not able to fully take advantage of this potential due to the needs for improvements in physical infrastructure, particularly rail and road. Transport facilities will be crucial to helping Africa take advantage of the opportunities that these resources can offer.

Globalization and the state

Though the modern nation state is not going to wither away because of globalization, for weaker states globalization presents many challenges, demands and causes states to become more vulnerable. Many functions that were traditionally allocated to the state are now moving to a governance network. Governance is needed to manage globalization and how intensely it is pursued (Bhagwati, 2002). The nature of the state has changed due to globalization. The state has been forced to downsize even though, a strong state is needed in order to promote good governance and ensure a stable environment for economic growth to flourish.

Globalization has shrunk the size of the welfare state and has forced the state to do more with less (Farazmand, 1999). Under the guidance of the World Bank and the Asian Development Bank, Malaysia has downsized its public service, the Philippines has reduced its staff by 5–10%, Singapore now practices a strategy of zero manpower growth, aiming to reduce the number of public employees by 10% and Nepal and Thailand have also implemented a freeze in employment and have replaced public employees that are underutilized (Haque, 2002, 109). India has reduced its public employment by 30%. Sri Lanka has introduced an early retirement policy that has affected thousands of government employees (Haque, 2002, 109).

The same freezing of public sector employment has taken place in Argentina, Bolivia, Brazil, Costa Rica, Ghana, Guatemala, Kenya, Mali, Mexico, Senegal and Uganda. Between the 1980s and 1990s, the total number of central government employees decreased from 2.6% to 1.1% of the total population in Asia. The total decreased from 1.8% to 1.1% in Africa and 2.4% to 1.5% in Latin America (Haque, 2002).

The reduced role of the state has led to decreases in government spending on health care and education. In Africa, spending on primary school education has fallen in 21 out of 23 countries (Walton and Seddon, 1994, 138–139). States in the developing world have made little progress in providing health care. Little has been accomplished in decreasing stunted growth rates. Education and health-care cuts have been made in Latin America and Africa. Public spending as a percentage of GDP was very small, falling below 3% in Chile, Colombia, Ecuador, El Salvador, Mexico and Peru and below 2% in Brazil, Guatemala and Paraguay during the period of 1990–1997 (Haque, 2002, 114). Bureaucracies in the developing world have been directly affected by cuts in education as they continue to have a smaller pool of qualified people to select in staffing their agencies (Streeten, 1993).

Globalization squeezes the capacity of states to collect rent. State institutions are important to extract revenues, to ensure that elite remain engaged with society. Without formal institutions, ties become based on

Box 12.2 Globalization, the state and the environment

Globalization presents challenges to the state's ability to protect the environment, including climate change, cross boundary water issues, air pollution, over fishing and the exploitation of natural resources. The state's regulatory powers weaken while economic growth is encouraged. The promotion of economic growth often involves spurring development that is harmful to the environment. Many states are too weak to ensure that growth takes place that considers the environmental impact. For example, increasing production without regulation can worsen problems of pollution. Jamaica was able to increase its production of bauxite and cement, but this led to higher levels of dust pollution (Reed, 1996, 195). The production of manufactured goods without regulations in countries such as Indonesia, Taiwan, Malaysia and Thailand have led to increasing levels of industrial waste, water pollution and deforestation (Devlin and Yap, 1994, 4–55; Haque, 1999, 204). In Mexico, the state is able to do little to prevent environmental damage. As Mexico (along with Canada and the United States) is a member of the North American Free Trade Agreement (NAFTA), there is little it can do prevent a US company from dumping toxic waste, since *Chapter 11* of the agreement restricts the ability of countries to have environmental protections.

Budget cuts lead to major declines in the administrative capacity of environmental agencies in developing countries. For more on globalization and the environment see Box 12.2. Slashed budgets in El Salvador have limited

$\rightarrow$

personal, ethnic or traditional affiliations. Tax revenues in Mexico are only 12% of its GDP, making it almost impossible for Mexico to compete with China, which is using its revenues to invest in education and infrastructure (Stiglitz, 1998).

States also no longer have control over macro-economic policy, having to surrender national policymaking to regional or international organizations. International financial institutions enforce strong measures on both monetary and fiscal policies for countries in the developing world. By 1994, the World Bank had provided $200 billion to the developing world to promote the private sector and in return 'Bank-approved consultants rewrite a country's trade policy, fiscal policy, civil service requirements, labour laws, environmental regulations, energy policy', (Korten, 2001, 165).

Globalization can make it difficult for states in the developing world to manage their budgets. Global firms are able to close their operations overnight and move to more profitable areas. Unless states have ensured the capacity of the state to invest in renewable resources. In Cameroon, budget cuts in the forestry service have weakened the ability of the state to prevent logging and degradation of forests (Reed, 1996, 69). In Jamaica, budget cuts have reduced the state's ability to enforce its environmental standards. Major sectors such as mining and manufacturing have now come under the control of foreign investors in countries such as Tanzania and Zambia. In Costa Rica, it has become more difficult to regulate deforestation and to prevent the use of chemical fertilizers. Timber production is not regulated in Chile or Tanzania. Rubber and cassava production is not regulated in Thailand and foreign companies have encouraged the elimination of virgin forests (Devlin and Yap, 1994; Haque, 1999, 204).

The state is also less able to distribute goods that could be helpful to sustainable development in agriculture. The costs of agricultural inputs such as fertilizer have increased in developing countries and the state is often no longer able to supply farmers with these inputs. This reduces the capacity of small farmers to use these inputs and forces them to 'expand agricultural productivity by cultivating marginal lands' (Haque, 1999, 207).

There is a general consensus that global modes of production and accumulation are linked to environmental degradation. Though globalization may provide opportunities for learning more about how to protect the environment and may facilitate the dissemination of knowledge, globalization encourages the extraction of natural resources and multiple forms of pollution (Jorgenson and Kick, 196). In sum, globalization severely hampers the state's ability to support economic growth that is mindful of the environmental impact.

that there are long-term commitments from global corporations, states' budgets can be very vulnerable.

Dealing with globalization

As the previous section illustrated, globalization has had an impact on the state. Some scholars claim that globalization has made the state powerless, offering states few choices (Murshed, 2002). To critics of globalization, Friedman has responded, that 'globalization isn't a choice, it's a reality' (2000, 113). Joseph Stiglitz (2007) claims that globalization still has tremendous potential, but for developing countries, being able to manage globalization on their own terms is critical. The narrative of the Washington Consensus was that the experience of the developing world with *state-led* economic growth was a disaster. Nevertheless, it was the well-constructed developmental states in East Asia that were able to spur on industrialization using both import substitution and export promotion. Many scholars have contended that it is the countries that have state guided development that have grown the fastest in the developing world (Johnson, 1982; Wade, 1990; Evans, 1995). The following section explains how states can effectively deal with globalization and closes with two case studies of successful performers in Africa – Mauritius and Botswana.

Countries that have benefited the most from globalization have had strong institutions in place to manage global forces. Even the World Bank admits that 'government discretion' is important for a 'wide range of activities that are essential for sustaining growth' (Zagha and Nankani, 2005, 14). Financial openness without institutions will not lead to growth. For example, Haiti is mostly free of tariffs but has not experienced much economic growth (Stiglitz, 2007). Mozambique also liberalized its cashew industry in the early 1990s in response to pressure from the World Bank, but this only led to more poverty and unemployment (Hanlon, 2000). Thus globalization highlights the importance of the state in development discourse. While effective states can harness the energy of globalization to their benefit, weaker states may not be able to take advantage of all of the opportunities that globalization has to offer. In the following section we look at the importance of administrative, judicial, political and financial institutions in helping states navigate the global market (World Bank, 1997; Asian Development Bank, 2000).

The World Bank demonstrates how high-quality public institutions can exceed the impact of good economic policies in explaining development performance (World Bank, 1997). A well-working bureaucracy helps to formulate and implement social and economic policies. It can also help to manage interactions with foreign investment, find new sources of technology, negotiate more favourable trade agreements, come up with smarter ways to protect their populations from instability and manage economic shocks. It may also work with local capital and form close social ties (Evans, 1995). Many scholars have concurred that building a strong bureaucracy is important to explaining economic growth, and the bureaucracy may be particularly helpful in managing globalization (Knack and Keefer, 1995; Campos and Nugent, 1999).

In the case of East Asia, states were able to push domestic firms to compete in the global economy by helping firms upgrade their organizational and technical capacity (Stiglitz, 2003). The state was very selective and very strategic about what type of protection was offered. Industrial subsidies were carefully selected and tied to performance. Close ties were created among financial capital, industrial capital and the state in Japan, Korea and Taiwan. These countries were able to export manufactured goods and improve productivity rates.

Judicial institutions are equally important in helping businesses survive and thrive in a globalized world. Globalization benefits states that have transparency in business and government transactions, control over corruption and have implemented the rule of law. The state must have the capacity to supervise its financial sectors, which is impossible without effective judicial institutions. For example, FDI can only stimulate growth when a strong institutional framework exists such as strong judicial institutions and financial institutions. Togo was not able to create an export processing zone because of the weakness of the judicial institutions in ensuring the rule of law. There was little institutional framework to prevent countless bribes and ensure that legal decisions being made were not arbitrary.

Political institutions can also be important in managing globalization better. States that are able to ensure stable turnover in power and transitions between leaders provide more stability in growth rates over time (Rodrik, 2000). Effective political institutions can also help manage potential social conflicts better (Rodrik, 2000). Institutions need to manage social polarization, enhance social cohesion, allow for some political participation and ensure transparency. In the case of Indonesia, after the Asian financial crisis (see Chapter 9) devastated Indonesia's economy, demonstrations led to the resignation of leader Suharto in 1998. Suharto had been in power for over 31 years and had ruled over a highly corrupt regime. After ousting Suharto from power, Indonesia gradually transitioned into a democracy. As of 2014 it is the second fastest growing economy of the G-20 countries.

Financial institutions are also important for developing countries. Rural banks can play a role in transferring remittances to rural families and channelling current account deposits and savings to urban areas. In many developing countries, the banks lack trained personnel, updated infrastructure and clear accounting standards. There is no effective formal payments system and low depositor confidence. As a result, investing is risky. For domestic entrepreneurs, the banks offer little support.

For globalization to positively impact poverty reduction, public investments in health care and education must be in place. States that have been able to take advantage of globalization have emphasized education. Investments in education improve labour productivity and improve the absorptive technological capacity of an economy (Haggard, 1990; Evans, 1995; Woo-Cumings, 1999). Human capital is especially important in small and poor states to help with comparative advantage and sectoral specialization. Countries in the developing world cannot take advantage of the technological possibilities of North-South technology transfer without establishing institutions with local capacity to absorb technology. Training in technology helps to reduce transaction costs, provide standardization, transparency and provide information. Many states in East Asia were able to develop a comparative advantage in high-value exports. This would not have been possible without a continuous upgrading of human skills.

There must also be collective investments in social insurance to protect workers from volatility. Safety nets can shelter the assets of poor households and prevent the erosion of human capital. Complementary policies must be in place, such as reducing impediments to labour mobility, increasing access to credit, improving technical know-how and providing social safety nets (Harrison, 2006, 4). In Mexico, corn farmers depended upon income support from the government. Without it, their real incomes would have decreased by 50% during the 1990s (Harrison, 2006, 4). In many states in East Asia the emphasis on rural areas is an example of how state expenditures can be pro-poor. The government invested in rural infrastructure, such as roads, irrigation, agricultural support outposts and systems of irrigation. Some scholars have argued that reductions in subsidies and social spending have worsened poverty (Veltmeyer, 1993, 2084). Thus, relying on trade reforms alone will not reduce poverty.

Case studies: globalization in Mauritius and Botswana

Many countries in the developing world may be too impoverished and weak to deal with globalization on their own terms. For many countries in the developing world, the infrastructure, human capital and institutions have been very underdeveloped comparatively speaking. In the case of Africa, it is the states that have the largest public sectors, Botswana and Mauritius, which have also been the best economic performers (Goldsmith, 1999). The activist states have also been able to cushion their populations against the social impact of globalization. The state is also better able to provide social safety nets, establish rules and practices, soften the distributional impact of adjustment, and help develop more equitably. Stronger safety nets also engender greater levels of trust in the government, which builds on social capital that helps ensure stability.

Mauritius has taken advantage of the benefits of globalization, and has stabilized its economy after experiencing economic turmoil in the late 1970s and 1980s. Since 1975 Mauritius has been able to double its GDP per capita. It has improved its position in its global interactions, by making use of its abundant unemployed labour, focusing on labour intensive manufacturing for export. Most importantly, Mauritius worked to improve its human capital, its financial institutions and its regulatory environment. Mauritius has worked to ensure that social safety nets are in place to mitigate globalization's effect on inequality. Finally, Mauritius has effective political institutions, which are more representative of what its citizens want. These factors have been key to the island's success.

Mauritius invested in both its health-care system and its education system. As a result, Mauritius has experienced an increase in life expectancy since 1970 and a decrease in infant mortality rates. Mauritius also offers pre-vocational and vocational training options that focus on providing training in a number of fields for greater employability and career skills enhancement. By investing in human capital, Mauritius has been better prepared to take advantage of technological opportunities. The quality of its educational system has also affected state capacity overall, since the bureaucracy is able to recruit from a broad range of qualified individuals.

Social and political development has also been prioritized. Social justice is managed to help cultivate a stable multi-ethnic society. Mauritius spends 40% of its budget on education, health, pensions, housing, social assistance and food subsidies (Bräutigam, 2000). It also underwrote social security for the population. Mauritius has a compulsory contributory pension system. In 1983, it passed an unemployment act that provided minimum payments to the unemployed heads of households. Political institutions are also much more developed in Mauritius comparatively speaking. Legislative council elections were held in Mauritius as early as 1886. Mauritius has maintained its democracy since it became independent in 1968.

Botswana is another example of a country that has been able to weather the storm of globalization. It has averaged growth rates of more than 5% per year for several decades. Its per capita income (PPP) stands at $17,000, higher than both China and India. Much of its success lies in the fact that Botswana globalized at its own pace and on its own terms, and used an inclusive approach to making big decisions, which relied on local knowledge and technocratic expertise. Finally, when the time came to implement decisions, the bureaucracy was more than capable in doing so (for more on good governance in Botswana, see Chapter 3). Botswana has many different agencies to cover almost every aspect of social and economic life in Botswana (Conteh and Ohemeng, 2009, 64). All of these agencies use a merit-based hiring system that ensures that the most capable personnel are involved in implementing important decisions.

Though Botswana has been privatizing its economy, it has done so at its own speed rather than being quickly directed to do so under a structural adjustment programme (SAP). Botswana embarked on a slow process of privatization but the government still maintained public institutions to provide social and infrastructural services that the country's private sector could not provide. Furthermore, when deciding to privatize, the public sector thoroughly examined the pros and cons of privatization and then engaged in a lengthy debate on how best to proceed to make the public sector more efficient and effective. Technocrats, the private sector and academics as well as politicians were involved in the discussions on privatization plans. The privatization process was entirely internally driven and not developed from the outside. Public sector enterprises were divested slowly to private actors in order to achieve private sector development. Botswana elites also took the initiative to search for ideas about privatization and to engage in policy learning by looking at other countries. The state also invested in Botswana's private sector in order to help develop and diversify the economy (away from cattle and mineral exports).

Conclusion

Globalization represents a major transformation of the global economy, which has had a major impact on issues of development such as economic growth, economic inequality and poverty. In some cases trade has brought great economic benefits with growing possibilities to take advantage of improvements in transportation, communications and technology. At the same time, globalization has also led to economic crises (see Chapter 10) that have had more devastating effects on the developing world, and especially on those who are most vulnerable (Nissanke and Thorbecke, 2006). As social welfare programmes in developing countries declined, this has also had adverse effects on poverty and income distribution (Rudra, 2002). And while some countries have experienced high rates of growth, overall growth rates are still outpaced by the growth of overseas investment and international capital flows.

Globalization has had a major influence on development studies but there is still little scholarly consensus about the effects of globalization. Some scholars have identified globalization as a factor in poverty reduction, while others have argued that reductions in poverty primarily took place in China and India. Globalization supporters argue that the economic gains generated by the free market would trickle down to the poor, but this has not always occurred in practice. For many countries economic growth is not equally distributed, which can worsen the standards of living of the poor. Yet the countries that have grown the fastest have engaged with the global economy. This poses a quandary for states in the developing world. Can developing countries take advantage of globalization without exposing themselves to too many risks? For developing countries, there may not be a choice. Former UN Secretary General Kofi Annan commented that 'arguing against globalization is like arguing against the laws of gravity'. Globalization is clearly a force to be reckoned with, and because of this, it needs to be carefully managed for states to take advantage of what it can offer.

Questions

- When did different waves of globalization emerge? What factors accelerated globalization's intensity?
- Why does globalization exacerbate inequalities both within states and between states?
- In what ways does Chile represent the two-sided coin of globalization?
- What are the characteristics of states that benefit from globalization?
- In what ways does globalization undermine the state?

Facts

- Globalization is usually measured as integration with the global economy, or trade as a proportion of GDP, trade openness and direct foreign investment.
- Globalization has also led to the increased importance of international organizations such as the World Bank, the United Nations, the IMF and the World Trade Organization.
- Though globalization spurs growth, it does not reduce poverty on its own; poverty reduction requires both high levels of growth and pro-poor distribution of the gains from growth.
- Political institutions are important in managing globalization. States that are able to ensure stable turnover in power and transitions between leaders provide more stability in growth rates over time.
- Many scholars have contended that it is the countries that have guided development that have grown the fastest in the developing world, such as Botswana and Mauritius.

Chapter 13

Foreign Aid and NGOs

As the previous chapter highlighted, external actors can play an important role in the development process. In much of the developing world, external actors have attempted to foster development through foreign aid, loans and grants and by providing technical expertise. Though well intentioned, there have been unintended consequences of nongovernmental organizations (NGOs – or organizations that are neither part of the government nor a conventional for-profit business) and foreign aid. Critics have argued that NGOs and foreign aid have created challenges for development and state building, even though their intended effect is to do the opposite. This chapter addresses some of the challenges. Because many scholars have been critical of both foreign aid and NGOs, we treat them as a development hurdle. Nevertheless, that by no means signifies that foreign aid and NGOs cannot be useful in fostering development. Thus the purpose of this chapter is to gain insight into how external actors can help assist the developing world to promote economic development in ways that do not supplant and undermine their state institutions.

An incident in Malawi offers a telling illustration of how external efforts to assist developing states can often fail. Recently an international nongovernmental organization (INGO) launched a project to provide home-based care to patients there dying of AIDS (Barber and Bowie, 2008, 752). Despite good intentions, the project ended up eliciting few results for a number of reasons. Donors frequently engaged in visits to the host sites, but this required nursing staff to spend large amounts of time in hosting-related activities as opposed to attending to patients. Management staff found themselves spending most of their work hours responding to inquiries from the NGO's staff rather than managing the project. Staff members from local institutions were poached by the NGO to work for them, with one officer earning as much as three times the salary after having switched. And after 14 months, the project suddenly came to a halt with no explanation. Because the project was not integrated with the local health apparatus, few lasting gains were made.

Unfortunately, such an experience is not atypical. In this chapter, we offer an analysis of the central issues in foreign aid, as well as some lessons that have been learned from past failures. This chapter addresses the record of foreign aid and identifies ways of moving forward to more efficiently and effectively encourage development and lift people out of poverty.

Foreign aid and nongovernmental organizations

Foreign aid funds are resources that are transferred to countries, often with the aim of promoting development. For more on the top recipients of foreign aid, see Table 13.1. Foreign aid is sometimes referred to as official development assistance (ODA). ODA usually targets developing countries with the funds being provided by governments and donors. Foreign aid either goes directly to recipient countries or is channelled to international organizations (such as the United Nations) or NGOs. In the sections that follow, we provide a history of the aid industry, a brief history of NGOs and an explanation of why foreign aid and NGOs can sometimes be detrimental to development.

Evolution of the aid industry

The contemporary concept of foreign aid sprouted after World War II, with the implementation of the Marshall Plan in 1947. Deeply rooted in the ideas of *modernization theory* (see Chapter 2), the Marshall Plan

---

Afghanistan: $6.725 billion

Vietnam: $4.115 billion

Ethiopia: $3.261 billion

Turkey: $3.0331 billion

Democratic Republic of Congo: $2.859 billion

Tanzania: $2.831 billion

Kenya: $2.654 billion

Ivory Coast: $2.635 billion

Bangladesh: $2.152 billion

Mozambique: $2.097 billion

Table 13.1   *Top recipients of foreign aid*

Source: World Bank Net Official Development Assistance: http://data.worldbank .org/indicator/DT.ODA.ALLD.CD

Box 13.1   Nation building

Nation building is very important to development, both political and economic development. Though nation building is distinct from state building, the two go hand in hand. While the latter entails building the institutions of the state such as the administrative, political, judicial and security institutions, nation building constitutes efforts to build a common identity and a united society. The process of nation building involves developing a common behaviour, values and possibly language. In countries that have multiple ethnicities and religions, nation building necessitates building an identity that can accommodate the various ethnic, linguistic and religious cleavages.

Nation building requires a strong and capable state in order to penetrate society, create cultural symbols and shared histories. Much of nation building takes place within the public educational system. A strong state can create a civic conception of nationalism, where citizens are aware of their responsibilities, are informed about the way the political system works and know how to communicate and voice their opinions to the state. Nation building also takes place through the daily bonds of regular contact between the government and citizens. For example, states that provide generous welfare systems and health care may also be able to create a sense of nationhood.

States in the developing world often have weaker institutions, which are unable to overcome ethnic identities that can be overcome by national identities. Instead the state may choose to promote one ethnic identity over others, leading to a backlash from other ethnic groups. One ethnic group may be economically favoured over others, leading to huge discrepancies between those favoured compared to those left out. The Pashtun identity in Afghanistan had often been promoted by the state instead of a national identity. This had dire consequences for stability and unity in Afghanistan, and has led to low levels of allegiance to the state.

Ethnic divisions are difficult for development because there are low levels of trust between the different groups. Businesses may only choose to work with business partners from their co-ethnic group. Development projects may be undermined by conflict when ethnic identities dictate behaviour. Creating public goods may be undermined by legislation that is more focused on pleasing the whims of a particular ethnic group. For these reasons, it is critical that states with diverse societies, cultivate a national identity that can supersede clan, ethnic or sectarian divisions (Kaplan, 2008).

sought to give large amounts of external assistance to states ruined by the war to spur economic growth (Rostow, 1990). The Marshall Plan was viewed to be a major success. There are a few reasons for this (Bräutigam and Knack, 2004). For one, it provided aid for a limited period of time.

Aid levels also never reached more than 3% of the GDP of the target state. In addition, there was only a single donor helping to minimize confusion and ease coordination barriers.

Because of the success of the Marshall Plan, there was optimism for the potential of foreign aid to help states in need of it. By the 1960s, the amount of foreign aid increased, with more and more developing states included in the set of beneficiaries. At this time, there were few criticisms of the aid industry, which was largely seen as a way of encouraging fruitful partnerships between the international community and recipient states to foster growth.

By the 1970s, however, observers became attuned to the problem of *aid dependence* (Box 13.2). States like Bangladesh, Malawi and Madagascar found themselves highly dependent on foreign aid. And by the 1980s, many developing states were heavily in debt. In response to this, aid allocations became more conditional in the years that followed. Lending and major grant programmes required that recipient states enact desired policy changes. Most of the policies encouraged were in line with the tenets of the *Washington Consensus* (see Chapter 3), with an emphasis on fiscal and monetary discipline, privatization and opening up borders to trade and capital flows.

At the turn of the century, observers grew increasingly aware that policy conditionality was not actually affecting the policy environment among aid recipients (Barder and Birdsall, 2006). Debts among many targeted states were growing yet again and the structural adjustment programmes advocated by the World Bank and International Monetary Fund (IMF) had not elicited the intended results.

The next phase of the aid industry involved an emphasis on good governance, an idea that the 1997 World Bank Development Report helped to make mainstream. The report argued that many states in the developing world were weak and that this was why aid efforts were limited in their efficacy. Development, according to the report, required a strong state with the capacity to implement desired reforms advocated by donors.

This led to a switch among donors from policy conditionality to process conditionality. Today, recipient states no longer have to implement structural adjustment programmes, but they do have to demonstrate some commitment to implementing an appropriate development plan. To assist in this process, NGOs and local communities are now encouraged to work together to discuss a workable strategy. State governments, in turn, must work with donors to produce a strategy paper, which outlines the major features of the approach, which conditions future aid allocations (Barder and Birdsall, 2006).

As a reflection of this philosophical shift, the concept of good governance (see Chapter 3) now pervades the agendas of the major players in the development community. Since 1996, for example, the World Bank has launched over 600 governance-related programmes in 95 states in the developing world (Santiso, 2001, 3). It has been involved in supporting governance programmes and public sector reforms in 50 states, and has focused increasingly on legal and judicial reforms and the fight against corruption. It has also started to devote resources toward building institutions of accountability, like ombudspersons and legislative oversight bodies (World Bank Development Report, 2002). (For more on nation-building, see Box 13.1).

Box 13.2   What is aid dependence?

Aid dependence is a condition caused by the transfers of foreign aid. It is often defined as the 'process by which the continued provision of aid appears to be making no significant contribution to the achievement of self-sustaining development' (Bräutigam and Knack, 2004).

Aid dependence is described as a 'state of mind where aid recipients lose their capacity to think for themselves and thereby relinquish control', (Sobhan, 1996, 122). With aid dependence, the government is unable to perform many of the core functions of government, such as maintaining existing infrastructure or the delivery of basic public services without foreign aid and expertise, provided in the form of technical assistance or projects (Bräutigam and Knack, 2004, 256).

Aid dependency is defined as any state where ODA represents more than 10% of a country's GNP (Goldsmith, 2001). From 1990 to 1997, there were over 30 countries who had ODA averaging more than 10% of their GNPs. The World Bank's Berg Report (1981) claimed that aid starts to have a negative effect on local institutions when aid flows reach 5% of GDP, which would mean that most states in Africa are negatively affected.

Aid dependence is also measured as net aid flows as a percentage of GDP and aid as a percentage of government expenditures. In 1980, 13 countries in Africa were receiving net aid flows, which are aid inflows minus principal repayments at levels well above 10% of GDP. By 1990, that figure had more than doubled to 30 countries. For countries such as Malawi, Ghana and Zambia, aid has funded more than 40% of government expenditures for over 20 years. Today some African states have aid flows that are 75% of government expenditures (Moss et al., 2006, 9).

Aid dependence makes it difficult for developing nations to lift themselves out of poverty on their own terms. Additionally, aid dependent countries may be less accountable to their citizens, making them also less likely to cultivate and invest in effective public institutions. Thus many studies conclude that substantial periods of aid dependence may ultimately have a harmful effect on institutional development (Moss et al., 2006, 1).

Though international financial institutions continue to include economic reforms as a key objective, there is increasing emphasis on strengthening state institutions to encourage development. According to Moises Naim, the first generation of efforts aimed at stabilizing and liberalizing the economy, while the second generation has sought to strengthen governing institutions to improve it (2000).

Beyond the substantive change in the focus of the aid industry, there have also been efforts to increase its effectiveness. In 2005, for example, the Paris Diagnosis was signed by 61 bilateral and multilateral donors and 56 aid recipient states as part of the Paris Declaration on Aid Effectiveness (Fritz and Menocal, 2007). The goal of this agreement was to make the aid industry less fragmented and to improve partnerships. Recipient states are now supposed to take more ownership over development goals and donors are supposed to align their priorities with these goals, as well as streamline their activities (Fritz and Menocal, 2007).

Evolution of NGOs

Though foreign aid can be given directly to the state government (either with or without strings attached), it is often funnelled into the state via NGOs. NGOs are organizations that operate independently from state governments. They vary in terms of the location of their bases, scope, goals and levels of formality. Here, we restrict our discussion to NGOs engaged in development and those that are international in origin. Because of the large presence of NGOs in the developing world, for example, they are now often referred to as the *third sector* (Edwards and Hulme, 1996). We now offer a brief history of NGOs operating in the developing world.

The term NGO was first used after the United Nations was created in 1945 (Davies, 2014). However, prior to the 1970s, NGOs were not viewed as an important component of the implementation of development projects (Banks and Hulme, 2012, 4). At the end of that decade, however, the development landscape had changed. Focus turned to NGOs as arbiters of development in the face of disastrous state economic policies. NGOs were seen as innovative and able to bring new technologies to developing states, many of which had governments that had proven themselves incapable of making the right changes, and in some cases, untrustworthy partners (Banks and Hulme, 2012). In addition, many developing states lacked functional state institutions, prompting NGOs to move in to fill the void. As a result, starting in the 1990s, there was an explosion of NGOs operating in the developing world. Kenya, for example, had around 400 NGOs working inside its borders in 1990, but over 6,000 by 2009 (Brass, 2012). Similarly, Tanzania had about 40 NGOs in 1990, but more than 10,000 by 2000 (Hearn, 2007). Today, there are as many as 40,000 international NGOs operating around the world, with millions more local NGOs. India, for example, has over two million NGOs, while the United States has over one million.

Supporters of NGOs argue that they are organizations uniquely suited to assisting in development and integrating a bottom-up approach (Panda, 2007). They state that NGOs offer social welfare to citizens who are the most vulnerable 'at a lower cost and higher standards of quality than government' (Hearn, 1998, 90). In Haiti, for example, nearly all services are provided by NGOs, after that country's disastrous earthquake in 2010 destroyed virtually all infrastructure. NGOs provide nearly 70% of all health-care services and 85% of all education services in Haiti (Zanotti, 2010). One could argue that Haitians would have endured even more suffering following the earthquake than they already did if it were not for the presence of NGOs. At the same time, NGOs operating in the developing world have been the targets of significant criticism, as has the foreign aid industry more generally. We turn to these critiques in the section that follows.

Foreign aid and development

The relationship between foreign aid and growth has been extremely controversial. Scholars have come to different conclusions about whether or not foreign aid can assist developing countries. Critics of foreign aid have levied a host of complaints about existing and past aid efforts. For example, though Africa has received the largest amount of aid of any region in the world – about $600 billion (Akonor, 2007) – it has had low average growth rates (only around 3.8% from 1996 to 2000, for example) (OECD Observer, 2005). Some assert that external assistance to developing states has not helped growth, while others go even further to say that it has actually harmed it. The foremost critic of the aid industry is economist William Easterly, who writes that 'if all foreign aid given since 1950 had been invested in US Treasury Bills, the cumulative assets of poor countries by 2001 would have amounted to $2.3 trillion' (2002, 15).

According to Easterly, aid recipients have wasted resources. As he sees it, most foreign aid finances consumption in recipient countries, instead of fostering economic growth. Much of the reason for this is that aid often goes directly to finance the projects of corrupt dictatorships. Another problem, however, is that aid is also often tied to require that recipient countries purchase goods from the aid-granting country, which only increases consumption (Easterly and Pfutze, 2008). Easterly is also critical of high overhead costs for foreign aid agencies, which is also wasteful, and at times extravagant.

Easterly's main criticism of foreign aid, however, is that there is no cross-national evidence that aid improves growth records (2003). For example, in the last decade, Haiti has received over $4 billion in aid, yet 60% of Haitians live on less than $2 a day. On the other hand, he argues that the states that have grown the fastest did so with little foreign aid assistance. India and China, for example, are touted as major development success stories, yet each has received little amounts of aid compared to other developing states. He refers to the association between aid and development as 'an integral part of the founding myth and ongoing myth of the aid bureaucracy' (2003, 18). Thus, critics of foreign aid efforts point out a number of serious problems with the contemporary aid industry and the work of NGOs operating within it. Yet, at the same time, there are valuable arguments on the other side.

First it's important to emphasize that some studies simply disagree with the assertion that foreign aid hampers growth (Morrissey, 2001; Sachs, 2005a; Karras, 2006). A study looking at 71 aid receiving countries in the developing world concluded that aid had a positive, permanent and statistically significant effect on growth rate. Every $20 per person donated resulted in a permanent increase in growth rates of real GDP per capita by 0.16%, though the effects of policies were not examined (Karras, 2006).

Proponents of foreign aid also argue that there are number of mechanisms through which aid can contribute to economic growth. Aid can be used to help increase investment in physical and human capital. When foreign aid is simply used to finance the building of schools and health clinics, aid can help developing countries get more out of their population. For countries that are extremely impoverished limited budgets make it difficult to invest in the future (Sachs, 2005a, 85). Aid can also help developing states finance basic infrastructure such as roads, electricity, water and sanitation, which are key components for building economies in the developing world.

Aid can also be used to increase the capacity to import capital goods or technology (Morrissey, 2001). Helping developing countries gain access to important capital goods that are necessary for their economies can be another growth enhancing factor. Others note that foreign aid can help with debt reduction. In a study of Senegal from 1970 to 2000, it was revealed that a 41% of aid was used to finance Senegal's debt (Ouattara, 2006).

Moreover, expectations have probably been too high. Burkina Faso, for example, was once considered to be off track because its primary school enrolment rate was only 35% in 2000. Given its currently modest rate of improvement, it was only expected to reach levels of 59% by 2015, which was seen by the development community as a disappointing increase. Despite perceptions of modest improvement, the actual rate at which Burkina Faso was increasing enrolments was faster than South

Korea's once was during its growth explosion. Expecting Burkina Faso to increase any faster was probably unrealistic (Barder and Birdsall, 2006, 8).

In addition, aid distributions may not be as high as they need to be to make a difference. The cost of putting every child in the world in primary school is estimated to be about $17 billion, for example. Yet there is currently less than $6 billion given by donors for this effort (Barder and Birdsall, 2006, 11). According to Sachs, those states that have not responded well to foreign aid have received less aid compared to other developing states (2005a). In the 1990s, Haiti, for example, received only 10% of the aid that Kosovo received from the United States (Zanotti, 2010).

Moreover, aid allocations are often influenced more by political and strategic considerations than by need. Though the total amount of aid distributed in the world each year has hovered around $120 billion over the past five years, only about a fifth of that has actually gone to the world's poorest states (Organization for Economic Cooperation and Development, 2012).

The amount of aid promised by the developed world is also much larger than actual donations. States in the developed world agreed to give about 0.7% of their national incomes to foreign aid, yet the amount donated typically averages less than half of that (Sachs, 2005a). Scholars have pointed out that aid to Africa, in particular, has decreased significantly from 1960 to 2002 (Addison et al., 2005).

According to Jeffrey Sachs, an economist on the forefront of calls to increase foreign aid to developing states, external assistance is the solution to ending poverty (2005a). Without massive increases in the foreign aid allocated to the poorest states, such states will face enormous challenges growing their economies. The central idea underlying this argument is that many developing states are in the midst of a poverty trap. Their governments cannot provide their citizens with the resources needed to reduce poverty levels precisely because their citizens are too poor to pay taxes. Significant foreign aid allocations are needed, in the eyes of aid proponents like Sachs, to help these states break the vicious cycle.

Nevertheless, Sachs is aware that some governments may not use foreign aid effectively. He argues, however, that the 'biggest problem today is not that poorly governed countries get too much help, but that well-governed countries get far too little' (2005b, 269). In Sachs's view, aid works best when it is part of a comprehensive market-driven strategy for growth, it is distributed selectively, and is only given for a limited duration to remind states that they cannot rely on it forever. In conjunction with foreign aid, Sachs advocates the cancellation of existing debts for developing states to give them a fresh start (see Chapter 9).

Perhaps, the primary reason why foreign aid efforts should not be abandoned, however, is that there have been a few success stories. One could argue that any success is better than zero success, particularly considering how each instance of improved performance means considerable improvements in the lives of the citizens living there. Proponents of aid cite a number of instances in which developing states have prospered precisely because of external assistance. Vietnam, for example, is one of the leading examples. It received significant amounts of foreign aid (According to the World Bank, Vietnam received $14 billion from 1993 to 2004 in ODA, and $4.1 billion in 2012) and used this assistance to lower its inflation and unemployment levels, reduce poverty and disease, and dramatically increase economic growth. Its leadership tailored policies to encourage the manufacturing, information technology and high-tech industries, which quickly became the fastest growing sectors of the economy. It also invested in education and health care for the poorest areas. Vietnam joined the WTO in 2007, as well, because of its commitment to protecting intellectual property rights. Though the state still plays a strong role in the functioning of the economy, compared to other economies in neighbouring states it is one of the most open.

The evidence indicates that foreign aid works best in states that have already developed some institutional foundations (Birdsall, 2007). A number of World Bank studies have concluded that a sound policy environment is also needed for a state to respond well to aid (Isham and Kaufman, 1999; Burnside and Dollar, 2000; Dollar and Levin, 2005). In other words, aid can be effective in boosting growth in countries that followed sound fiscal, monetary and trade policies. Though this may be a disappointing finding, given that aid is not shown to work very well in those places that need it most, it is at least promising for those developing states that have proven capable of engaging in at least some institutional reforms.

Foreign aid, NGOs, donors and the state

The previous section illustrated how controversial the debate on foreign aid is. Proponents claim foreign aid has helped economic development and that the greater problem is that not enough foreign aid has been distributed. Critics of foreign aid have been very vociferous in their condemnation of the aid industry more generally and the NGOs that work within it. In this section we review the central criticisms of foreign aid efforts by donors and NGOs in terms of how it can negatively impact institutions in the developing world.

Too many projects and too many donors

State building efforts have become so numerous in some developing states that it has led to situations of aid abundance, where donors give away aid faster than aid recipients can absorb it (Tendler, 1975). This means that there are often too many projects and too many donors for states to deal with. The average African state, by some estimates, has at least 30 donors working with it, in addition to several dozen international NGOs, leading to a multitude of projects that involve hundreds of different foreign experts (van de Walle, 2001). Yet, the distribution of aid to targeted projects requires government oversight and reporting, as well as the production of strategy papers for donors. Different donors may have different reporting and accounting systems, as well as approaches to ensuring accountability. This can mean that officials become sucked into spending most of their time attending to these tasks as opposed to actually improving conditions for citizens (Bräutigam and Knack, 2004). Many of these states simply do not have the capacity to deal with the administration of the plethora of projects started within them. In addition, having all of these projects that require monitoring and evaluations means that officials are constantly involved in meetings with donors, instead of attending to other important issues (van de Walle and Johnston, 1996). All of this drains state resources and prevents states from providing other services (Barder and Birdsall, 2006).

Tanzania, for example, had to produce more than 2,400 reports a year for donors who had started over 1,000 missions there (World Bank Africa Development Indicators, 2002). Tanzania's government was forced to take a four-month hiatus from tending to donor missions just so the government could have enough time to prepare the budget. In Ghana, as well, senior officials at one point were spending up to 44 weeks of each year fulfilling their duties for donor supervision missions in order to maintain funding (Bräutigam and Botchwey, 1999). In Bolivia, there was once a poverty study funded by five donors that required government officials who were part of the study to spend as much time on the paperwork related to it as on the survey itself (Knack and Rahman, 2007, 178).

Beyond bogging down government officials, having so many donors involved in a state can lead to difficulties in coordination and reduce donor efficiency (Riddell, 2007). Add to this the fact that donors often have conflicting agendas and interests (Zanotti, 2010). Just among the major international financial institutions, like the IMF and the World Bank, there are internal rivalries and differing objectives. All of this can increase the chances that conflicting advice is given and contrasting strategies pursued. Donors often duplicate their efforts due to the lack of coordination, with comparable poverty and governance assessments and financial analyses executed multiple times (OECD, 2003). Multiple donors, for example, have done the same reports on the same topic in the same countries, rather than working together and uniting forces (Easterly, 2003). In fact, many of the aid success stories have actually been those cases in which there was a single or dominant donor involved (Brautigam and Knack, 2004).

This has been part of the problem in Haiti's state building efforts. Even prior to the 2010 earthquake, there were over 8,000 NGOs operating there, all with different agendas, budgets and sponsorships, and bilateral and multilateral partners (Zanotti, 2010). With all of these groups involved, coordination has proven difficult leading to an inefficient external response after the earthquake hit.

In states where there are too many donors and projects, state building efforts are often less effective. Part of the problem is that these groups are not actually competing with one another, leading to a 'cartel of good intentions' (Easterly, 2002). Aid groups are not subject to any competitive pressures to increase their efficiency, given that few states turn them down when they offer assistance. Moreover, because there are so many operating within a country, it is extremely difficult to isolate who is to blame for underwhelming outcomes.

Loss of capable staff in the public sector

Donor projects usually pay far higher salaries than comparable government positions (Zanotti, 2010, 759). As a result, another criticism of state building efforts is that they siphon off the most capable staff from the public sector (Barder and Birdsall, 2006). Organizations like the United Nations, for example, set staff salaries rigidly, making it impossible for them to vary substantially based on the local conditions. Because the salaries paid by donor projects are so high, it increases the bidding price for competent employees. High-level government officials may even leave their positions to create a local NGO so that they can increase their own salaries using external funding. For those individuals who opt to stay working in the public sector, this can decrease morale. It also can decrease the quality of the civil service.

In the 1960s it was not uncommon for NGOs to pay their staff less than the government rate. But international NGOs, in particular, now pay far more than the government does leading to major losses in the civil sector of the most capable employees.

In Kenya, for example, donors pulled seven economists away from the civil service by paying them anywhere from $3,000 to $6,000 per month, compared to the roughly $250 they were making working each month for the government (Knack and Rahman, 2007). In Nigeria, as well, it is five times more lucrative to work at an NGO than to work in a high-level government position (van de Walle and Johnston, 1996). The salary of a janitor working at an international NGO in Mozambique in some places is comparable to that of a national director of the civil service (Fallon and da Silva, 1994).

There have even been some instances of donors paying individuals to attend workshops during the business day. Such workshops typically pay more in one day than a civil servant's monthly salary (Moss et al., 2006). Yet, by incentivizing civil service employees to attend workshops, donors are keeping them from contributing in meaningful ways to the public sector and performing the basic functions of their jobs (Hanlon and Smart, 2008).

Creation of parallel institutions

Another criticism of existing state building efforts is that they often lead to the creation of parallel institutions, which operate within a state but are not part of it. This occurs because donors often prefer to bypass the government and create their own apparatus (Moss et al., 2006). It is often viewed as too risky to have state institutions deal with the flow of aid, so donors instead create their own institutions to process these flows. Yet, according to some observers, these actions have 'contributed to the eroding of both state officials' internal accountability and the possibility of building sound institutions of the state' (Zanotti, 2010, 759).

Instead of encouraging local capacity building, the creation of parallel institutions means that recipient governments are unable to make their own decisions about the types of services that should be provided and how to track expenditures (François and Sud, 2006). Yet, at the same time, governments need to have more authority over budgets so that they can be held accountable for future actions. Governments also gain little experience in how to provide public services when they are left out of the state building process, decreasing their legitimacy in the eyes of citizens (François and Sud, 2006). Moreover, when parallel institutions are in place, any growth that takes place is due to the efforts of the NGO and is therefore not sustainable in the long term once the NGO initiates its exit.

Technical assistance, in particular, has been pursued alongside, rather than with state institutions. Nevertheless, though learning technical skills is a time consuming process for many civil service employees in developing states, it is a necessary one. Government employees have to learn the appropriate skills in order to be effective once the NGO is no longer there. It is only through the practice of how to implement projects that good governance can be achieved (Bräutigam and Knack, 2004).

In Mali, for example, most donors use independent organizations to implement projects rather than working with the state. The Ministry of Planning in Senegal, which is responsible for investment projects, has similarly been bypassed by donors (Bräutigam, 2000, 36). In Haiti, as well, donors have mostly withdrawn any funds that go directly to the Haitian state, out of fears of corruption (Zanotti, 2010). While some of their fears have merit, these activities only prolong the problem of weak institutions in that state. In Kenya, 90% of NGOs are involved in service delivery, bypassing the state altogether (Brass, 2012). And though technical assistance given to African states rose from $1 billion in 1971 to $4 billion in 1995, observers assess that little long-term technology transfer took place during this period due to the creation of parallel institutions (Bräutigam, 2000).

Another implication of parallel institutionalization is that projects are not led by local governments, whose officials are often left out of state building activities. Yet, as a result, local officials do not fully commit to the projects being implemented because they were never a part of them to begin with (Moss et al., 2006). Programmes are instead pre-packaged by donors and far removed from the needs of local populations (Banks and Hulme, 2012, 9).

In contrast, when local officials have ownership over aid projects, they have more incentives to work towards their success. For example, a successful aid effort in the north-eastern region of Brazil came when the World Bank gave a $70 million loan to the Ceara state government. The state was fully committed to the project, leading to land reforms, rural electrification and improved water supply (Easterly, 2002).

Reduced incentives for tax collection

State building efforts have also been criticized because they reduce incentives for states to collect taxes from citizens. The ability to collect revenues is an important indicator of state capacity. Tax revenues are necessary for the state to function and fund services. To be self-sufficient, states must have the ability to tax (Kaldor, 1963). Foreign aid inflows can disincentivize taxation because they enable the state to get by on fewer tax revenues.

This is problematic because it can lead to issues for the state once donor money is no longer flowing freely. States that are dependent on aid, but suddenly no longer receive it, often incur large fiscal deficits because they have not developed the capacity to collect revenues (Ghura, 1998). Aid inflows from one year to the next may be volatile.

This is also troublesome because when states do not have to rely on taxation to stay afloat (but can use aid to do so instead), they do not have to be accountable to their citizens, just foreign donors. International agencies, therefore, become quite powerful (Brautigam, 1992).

The data indicate that taxation revenues in developing states have indeed declined in tandem with increases in aid inflows. In Africa, for example, one study found that 71% of states that received more than 10% of their GDP from aid also had low tax revenues (Ghura, 1998). There was not a single instance of a state with both high aid reliance and high tax revenues. Haiti offers another example. The bulk of Haiti's budget is funded through external assistance (70%), with the rest coming from customs duties. As a result, Haiti has never been forced to develop the capacity to collect revenues through taxation.

Few real policy reforms

Critics of state building also argue that it enables states to put off pursuing the policy reforms they need to get themselves on solid economic footing. Some observers have asserted that governments in the developing world can wait to sell their policy reforms to the highest bidder. States may also engage in zigzag behaviour with their reforms, meaning that they agree to adopt them to get some aid relief and then backslide into old patterns after receiving it. So long as future promises of aid lie in the horizon, developing states have little incentive to change the status quo. Many countries for example, have proven adept in the past at pledging the policy reforms desired by donors and then ignoring them soon afterwards. Right before meetings with donors, governments often agree to specific policies, but then once the aid was pledged backtrack on these agreements (*Economist*, 1995).

The influx of aid can also deter the adoption of policy reforms because it creates a moral hazard, meaning that the state can engage in risky behaviour because an insurance policy (in this case external assistance) is in place. Governments in the developing world can pursue inadvisable policies knowing that they have the chance of getting aid down the road should their efforts fall flat. They have little reason to engage in a meaningful assessment of what they can and cannot afford, nor what the long-term effects might be of reckless choices. All of this discourages the pursuance of the types of policy reforms that are needed for development.

State building efforts can also reduce the state's own incentives to invest – a focal point of any successful development plan – because there is little reason to do so when there is the possibility of receiving more assistance in the future. This problem is referred to as the Samaritan's Dilemma (Gibson et al., 2005). It is particularly troublesome in the area of agriculture. States have little reason to improve their agriculture industry when they know they have access to food aid. This can foster a culture of dependency that can hinder the development of sustainable local agriculture. Food aid distributed in Haiti, for example, decreased Haiti's food production by 66% (Zanotti, 2010, 760).

No exit strategies

An additional critique of the state building is that most programmes do not have an exit strategy. For example, many NGOs play a critical role in providing emergency services, but do little to provide the state with the capacity to handle future emergencies down the road. They come into the country, assist with the crisis bringing in their own personnel, and they leave, without any forethought for how to help the state manage the transition (Easterly, 2003). Exit strategies are basically absent from project planning.

Rather than work in a state until it can easily handle the tasks on its own, NGOs often leave abruptly once funding has dried up. This is particularly problematic when donor states themselves experience a change in government, which can lead to new actors and decisions to abandon development projects. Denmark, for example, experienced a leadership change and, as a consequence, stopped working on a project in Malawi on village health initiatives. Programme beneficiaries were simply left stranded (Barder and Bowie, 2008, 750).

The lack of an exit strategy also leads to problems because states are not given the tools to maintain projects that have been started. Yet, a number of state building efforts entail the creation of public buildings and processing facilities that, once constructed, have high recurrent expenditures (Easterly, 2003). Because there is no exit strategy, when donors head home the state is left with buildings but no means to maintain them. Schools are freshly painted, but there are no teachers to staff them or books and desks to fill them (Brautigam and Knack, 2004).

State building efforts often do not include strategies for the future (Zanotti, 2010). For example, despite the fact that a number of international NGOs have engaged in public health projects in Malawi, not a single one has devoted resources towards funding staff to obtain a Masters in Public Health (Barders and Bowie, 2008, 752). Donors are instead focused on increasing their visibility and giving the impression that their short-term projects were successful, with little attention to their long-term impact (Knack and Rahman, 2007).

No accountability

The state building industry faces very little accountability for its actions (Easterly, 2003). There are few pressures on donors and NGOs to produce results and to assess their successes and failures (Barber and Bowie, 2008). The absence of accountability prohibits learning about how to improve future projects and discourages innovation and efficiency.

Aid agencies, for example, often do not collect case studies of their projects and programmes. Past experiences, therefore, are not used to inform future efforts (Easterly, 2003). And no one is held culpable for disastrous performances.

This would not be a problem if there were never any state building failures. But, instead there have been a plethora of them, often with egregious displays of poor judgment. A project in Lesotho, for example, intended to assist farmers in the mountains with access to markets and better livestock management techniques failed because the beneficiaries were not actually farmers. A project in Sierra Leone, as well, geared towards improving roads there dispersed $45 million to that state even though it was in the middle of a civil war (1998–2001). Nearly a third of all project expenditures had to be dedicated to compensating contractors for their lost time and the destruction of their capital (Easterly, 2003, 36).

The lack of accountability can lead to wastefulness. Critics assert that state building efforts often have huge budgets due to significant overhead costs and excessively high salaries for employees. By some estimates, 84% of USAID funding goes to pay for the salaries of international experts. When donors and policymakers go to visit targeted states, they often stay in luxury hotels, travel in large convoys and attend the diplomatic cocktail party circuit, causing local populations to feel resentment (Tarp, 2003, 322).

Such excessiveness is possible because there is little scrutiny on the performance of state building efforts. The World Bank, for example, only reviews 5% of its loans anywhere from three to ten years later to investigate their impact on development. And data collection that could be used to assess performance is rarely undertaken.

As this discussion makes clear, past and existing foreign aid efforts have been the target of widespread criticism, on a number of grounds. There are too many projects and too many donors, projects siphon away capable local officials, they lead to the creation of parallel institutions, they disincentivize tax collection and real policy reforms, and they lack exit strategies and accountability measures.

The criticism of this industry is so severe that many observers argue that external assistance has only made developing states worse off. In spite of this, we do not argue in favour of abandoning foreign aid. Rather it is important to investigate past cases where foreign aid has been successful and focus on what lessons can be learned from unsuccessful experiences as well. In the next section we offer an explanation of how foreign aid can be used to effectively help states in the developing world achieve their development goals.

Dealing with foreign aid

This chapter has presented the aid industry as a challenge to development. Nevertheless in order to illustrate why foreign aid and the work of NGOs should by no means be abandoned, we highlight the key lessons learnt from cases when foreign aid has been successful.

What are some important lessons about foreign aid and its effectiveness that we can glean from past cases? First foreign aid may be more successful when the goals and targets are very specific so that it is easier to assess their impact. It is very difficult to assess how well foreign aid is working if there are no clear targets. Promoting clear and specific targets may also rectify the problem of foreign aid being used for consumption.

Second, foreign aid is more successful when it is driven by the needs of the recipient countries rather than by the needs of the donors. This is critical to ensuring that aid is used successfully since the recipient country may have more knowledge about the ways in which foreign aid can help foster development. Here it may be especially helpful for both the state and donor agencies to be receptive to the assistance and knowledge from local actors. Moreover recipient countries may be more likely to take ownership in the process and exercise greater will if the aid is being directed towards key goals that recipient states have set out for their development.

Related to this argument, it is also important that foreign aid aligns with pre-existing programmes that may be part of the recipient country's larger long-term strategy. Aid can be used to cover the needs of a plan that is already in motion that may need more funding rather than be used to fund the plans of donors that may not be in sync with the state's objectives. To avoid concurrent aid agencies working against each other and the state, donors should be working under the recipient country's fiscal framework. This ensures that aid is integrated into a long-term plan that the government can oversee more effectively.

Finally, aid projects should have some sort of discussion about whether or not the aid project is working. Aid agencies often have no feedback mechanisms to know what they are doing right or wrong. To ensure that mistakes are not being repeated, it is important for recipient countries to communicate with donors and for those involved in the project to reflect on what has been successful and what needs to be improved.

To illustrate why the aid industry should not totally be abandoned, we offer a success story here on how foreign aid can make a positive impact followed by another success story of how NGOs can be effective. In the following case, foreign aid was used to build strong administrative institutions – namely a viable public health-care system – instead of being used to initiate a project that circumvents and competes against the state. Both cases have been successful because the aim is to create a permanent solution, and the timeframe is not determined by the exigencies of donors.

Case study: Rwanda's success with foreign aid

Rwanda made headlines in 1994 due to the devastating genocide that occurred there, which took the lives of up to one million Rwandans and displaced two million more. Already among the poorest countries in the world, the genocide pushed Rwanda further into economic decline. After the genocide, the health and education systems were destroyed, less than 5% of the population had access to clean water, there was no banking system, and the government did not have the capacity to collect taxes. Add to this that many members of the population were suffering from AIDS, malaria, TB and many different waterborne diseases, which had spread rapidly from one community to the next due to the conflict and were exacerbated by the absence of a health-care system. As a result, Rwanda's life expectancy levels were the lowest in the world from 1994 through 1997 (Logie et al., 2008).

Remarkably, Rwanda has experienced a dramatic turnaround in the years since the genocide. It is now one of the few developing states in the world set to meet most of the millennium development goals by 2015 (Farmer et al., 2013). Indeed, across a broad array of indicators, Rwanda has seen development advances. Since 2005, for example, its GDP has grown at an average rate of 8% per year, lifting more than one million Rwandans out of poverty. The population living under the poverty line was as high as 77% in 1994, but fell to 44% by 2010. In addition, life expectancy at the time of the genocide was 28 years, but as of 2012 is double that number (Farmer et al., 2013).

Due to these dramatic improvements, Rwanda is often touted as a development success story, one that was largely made possible as a result of aid. In particular, Rwanda used donor resources to make large investments in health infrastructure (Farmer et al., 2013), which set in motion positive outcomes in other areas and propelled the economy forward.

After the genocide, the Rwandan government outlined an ambitious plan to improve access to health care. It had few financial resources at the time to implement this plan, however. By the early 2000s, it leveraged a couple of new funding mechanisms to finance its projects, including the Global Fund to Fight AIDS, TB, and Malaria and the United States President's Emergency Plan for AIDS Relief (PEPFAR) (Farmer et al., 2013). Though these programmes were restrictive in terms of how funds could be used, they gave the Rwandan government resources to combat health-care issues.

To increase the efficacy of this effort, Rwanda opted to use an integrated approach in its disease control strategy. Its AIDS control programme, for example, focused not only on prevention but also on dealing with TB and malnutrition. Funds that were intended to be allocated to specific health issues were instead dedicated to strengthening the health-care system as a whole, including rebuilding the health infrastructure and developing a primary care programme (Farmer et al., 2013). The government specified that care needed to be community-based to increase efficiency and ensure delivery to patients with chronic diseases. It also worked to tighten the collaboration between public and private sectors, across a variety of sectors and ministries (Farmer et al., 2013). In addition, Rwanda used assistance from PEPFAR to fund a human resource programme for its health-care system, which entailed the creation of a seven-year plan to increase training levels and access and the initiation of a long-term partnership with US universities (Farmer et al., 2013).

There were a number of additional reforms implemented by the Rwandan government that targeted health-care improvements. Following the genocide, Rwanda faced a serious shortage in human capital. Therefore one of its first steps was to initiate training programmes for doctors and nurses. Health workers were trained to diagnose and provide treatment for the most common diseases and also played a role in family planning, prenatal care and administering childhood immunizations. In 1999, Rwanda pursued a national universal health insurance scheme, known as the *mutuelles de santé*, which was implemented nationwide by the mid-2000s. As of 2012, 90% of the population is enrolled in the programme, with another 7% covered by the civil service, military, or private insurance plans. Preventative interventions, like bed nets and vaccinations, are fully covered, as are treatments for HIV/AIDS, TB and some cancers (Farmer et al., 2013). In conjunction with this plan, the government also used resources from donors to subsidize premiums and co-payments for the poorest 25% of the population (Farmer et al., 2013).

Donor flows to Rwanda increased in the years that followed the genocide, such that they comprise around 40% of the total budget (Logie et al., 2008). In fact, more than half of the health sector's funding comes from donors and NGOs (Logie et al., 2008). The Rwandan government used this funding to invest in an online health management information system and a national AIDS information system. Both systems help to improve the information flows between procurement and distribution divisions of the Ministry of Health, making it easier for officials to manage how efficiently resources are being used (Farmer et al., 2013). The government also introduced a performance-based financing system in 2005, which rewards community health workers, cooperatives, health-care centres and district hospitals that perform well. Those that have better patient follow-up records and improved primary care indicators (like the percentage of women giving birth at health-care facilities and the percentage of children receiving immunizations) are given greater resources. This has helped to increase the quality of facilities, while also motivating staff via the provision of performance-based pay scales (Logie et al., 2008).

The Rwandan government integrated all of its donor funds into one fiscal framework in 2006. This ensured that all of the aid it received was part of a cohesive, long-term strategy. The government has insisted that it has ownership of all development plans and requires donor groups to adhere to these plans. Senior government officials meet with the higher ups of aid organizations to oversee their implementation. Annual meetings are convened, as well, that enable both the government and donors to discuss successes and failures of existing and past efforts (Logie et al., 2008). The Ministry of Health, for example, works directly with foreign aid partners to ensure that the process is transparent, partners are held accountable, and finances are properly managed. NGOs and donors who are unwilling to comply with these policies are asked to leave (Farmer et al., 2013). In addition, rather than creating parallel institutions, donor efforts are aligned with existing government programmes. The Global Fund, for example, now supports Rwanda's health-care system directly by funding the national insurance scheme.

Though Rwanda's situation is not perfect – it has lagged behind in terms of democratic reforms and is still reliant on significant aid flows – its health indicators have improved in dramatic ways due to the government's sound use of aid. By 2012, for example, Rwanda was one of only two states in Africa where citizens have universal access to antiretroviral therapy. It has maintained an HIV infection rate of around 3% in recent years and has seen decreases in HIV/AIDS mortality rates of as much as 80%. In 2011, its success rate for TB treatment was over 90%, and TB mortality rates also plummeted by 77%. In addition, its malaria mortality rates decreased by 87%, maternal mortality rates decreased by 59%, and child mortality rates decreased by 70% (Farmer et al., 2013). These are significant changes that have greatly improved the quality of life experienced by Rwandan citizens. For these reasons, Rwanda offers a telling example of how aid, when used properly, can lead to positive development outcomes.

Case study: Haiti and NGOs

The literature has primarily been critical of NGOs and their effect on development and state building. There are cases, however, where NGOs have contributed to development without simultaneously undermining the state.

As Haiti is one of the poorest countries in the world, it should come as no surprise that there are now over 10,000 NGOs working in Haiti. Though well-intentioned, many of these NGOs have been ineffective in making a long-term impact in Haiti. Terry Buss highlights (2009) why this has been the case. The first problem is that NGOs in Haiti have had a history of starting projects and then pulling out (2009, 105). Thus there has been little focus on creating a sustainable solution. In addition to making quick exits, NGOs did little to involve civil society or the state in their projects. Because of this, the government was indifferent and made no effort to take ownership over these projects to make them sustainable. The NGOs 'welcomed this indifference because it kept them in business' (2009, 119). Moreover, many of the NGO staff members have been inexperienced and have lacked in-depth knowledge of the country. Some NGOs were even accused of being connected to gangs, while other NGOs were becoming increasingly politicized. At the same time, efforts to build capacity in the NGOs created a brain drain in public sector employment. Additionally, because there are so many NGOs, coordination has become difficult. Finally, the parallel delivery of services by NGOs eroded the government's legitimacy and undermined government capacity even further. Simply put, NGOs had no trust that the Haitian government should be allowed to manage projects (2009, 119–120).

In spite of this pessimistic overview, Laura Zanotti illustrates two of the more successful NGOs in Haiti, Partners in Health (PIH) and Fonkoze. PIH has a local origin but is connected internationally, offering free quality health care to over 1.2 million people. PIH has a diverse group of investors and donors, which guarantees its independence from any single donor (Zanotti, 2010, 762). PIH trains local doctors and nurses and links academic research. Its primary focus is on ensuring that everyone has access to quality care and works to alleviate the root causes of diseases. It also provides free health-care education for the poor. It relies on a community partnership and also addresses basic social and economic needs (Zanotti, 2010, 763).

Using a multi-sectoral approach to health care, PIH sees the connection between lack of access to clean water, malnutrition and disease. In 2002 it created clean water and agricultural programmes. That same year, it created Partners in Agriculture (ZA) to tackle issues of malnutrition, treating over 5,000 malnourished children, and providing farmers with the tools and seeds to cultivate their land. It also buys seeds back from farmers, supplying families from cash and any excess seeds are saved and donated to another family for the next season. This helps ensure that the region is as sustainable as possible regarding food (Zanotti, 2010, 762). After several crises hit Haiti and led to rising food prices and starvation, ZA identified crops that would be ready within three months to harvest, planting them on an 80 acre farm. ZA aims to provide agricultural assistance to as many as 5,000 families.

PIH does not charge for its services. Decisions are needs-driven rather than based on the programmatic decisions of bilateral donors or international organizations. PIH brings medical services where they are needed, instead of where they are provided. It runs mobile clinics in four settlements around the capital, which treated 4,200 patients during the first week of operation. PIH also works with the state, and contributes to creating local capacity by working in cooperation with it. It works by paying its workers, helping with local food production, helping build literacy rates and forming local networks. A community-based approach is seen as instrumental to building long-term health-care system (Zanotti, 2010, 764–766).

Health care is also provided with continuity. NGOs are often limited by laws to only perform specific tasks such as emergency relief. Their mandates are defined by donors and their constituencies. Instead of having an exit strategy, PIH has a transition strategy. The goal is not to leave the community quickly but to build up public health-care systems and infrastructure, provide training and support for local medical staff, and employ community health-care workers as agents of change to break the cycles of poverty and disease (Zanotti, 2010, 765).

Another successful NGO has been Fonkoze in Haiti. Fonkoze offers banking and microcredit, and is related to improving literacy of the poor. Fonkoze provides loans giving priority to women, providing training, advice and follow up that is focused on how the loan can benefit the client (Zanotti, 2010, 762, 766).

Fonkoze has 30 branches and 45,000 microcredit borrowers, covering 80% of Haiti, but only 7% of the market. Fonkoze provides savings accounts, currency exchange and remittance services. Fonkoze also provides literacy training, health maintenance and business skills. The loans amount to around $200 and are used to start up and sustain small businesses. Loan participants are then encouraged to simultaneously take part in educational programmes to help loan recipients understand how to run their businesses more effectively. Loans at extremely low interest rates are provided and 80% of loans have been paid back (Zanotti, 2010).

Both these examples illustrate the importance of several factors for NGOs to be most helpful to countries in the developing world. First, NGOs should work closely with the state and the local community, instead of undermining it or supplanting it. This also helps to ensure that decisions are driven by local needs instead of programmatic concerns of donors. Second, NGOs should use a multi-sectoral approach that takes into account not just solving the isolated problem but also other factors that may be contributing to this challenge, such as lack of education and infrastructure. Third, NGOs should have a transition strategy not an exit strategy. Making an impact in developing countries requires a long-term strategy that sees building local capacity and creating a lasting foundation to tackle local challenges as part of its objectives.

Conclusion

Despite these successes, there are far too many underwhelming foreign aid outcomes, particularly considering the vast amount of resources that have been and continue to be devoted to state building. Though foreign aid should not be abandoned, the industry as a whole would probably benefit from paying closer attention to past mistakes in order to increase its effectiveness and reduce the number of its critics.

As the discussion in this chapter illustrates, there are a number of key changes that continue to confront the donor community. First, donors face challenges in coordinating with other donors and in streamlining the number of projects undertaken. Second, they struggle to find the most effective balance between incorporating local actors in meaningful ways – and therefore building local capacity – with taking care not to strip states of their most competent officials or overwhelming them with burdensome administrative functions. Third, donor programmes face challenges of accountability, both in terms of keeping donors in check, as well as the behaviour of state governments.

There remain numerous challenges confronting external actors who desire to improve the situations of citizens in the developing world. Lessons from past foreign efforts and their shortcomings would almost certainly improve future efforts. Though such changes are often difficult to engender, without them foreign aid efforts are unlikely to elicit the types of outcomes that would make life better for the very individuals they seek to assist.

Questions

- What is meant by aid dependence?
- Why is the relationship between foreign aid and growth controversial? What are the two arguments driving the debate about foreign aid?
- In what ways do NGOs and donors undermine state capacity?
- In what instances has foreign aid been successful? Why has this been the case?
- In what ways have Partners in Health and Fonkoze in Haiti contributed to sustainable development? What factors explain their success?

Facts

- The contemporary concept of foreign aid emerged after World War II with the successful implementation of the Marshall Plan in Europe.
- NGOs are often referred to as the third sector; they became increasingly important from the 1970s onward, with more than 40,000 international NGOs operating around the world today.
- More than 70% of Haiti's budget is funded through external assistance.
- Rwanda has used foreign aid to create a public health-care system that reaches 90% of the population.

Part III

The Road Ahead for Development

Chapter 14

Conclusion

Over a billion of the world's people live in poverty (World Bank, 2014). While that statistic alone is certainly daunting, it becomes even more discouraging when we start to consider what it means in practice. Poverty brings with it a host of difficulties, including high infant mortality rates, low literacy levels and low life expectancies. People who are poor are often undernourished, vulnerable to disease, have an increased risk of violence and lack access to basic services like clean water and sanitation. Each of these factors, in turn, presents significant challenges for development, as we have already discussed in this book. For these reasons, poverty has been a major obstacle to development, as underscored by the relatively low levels of progress among the world's poorest countries like Chad, Haiti and Kenya.

Take Haiti, for example, which by some estimates has the highest poverty rate in the world. According to the World Bank's 2012 World Development Indicators, more than half of the population in Haiti lives on less than $1 a day, with nearly 80% living on less than $2. Around 40% of Haitians are unemployed and the average per capita income is somewhere around $750. Nearly 60 infants out of every 1,000 live births die before reaching one year of age. And less than half of the population living in rural areas has access to safe drinking water. These conditions make development hard. Not having access to safe drinking water, for example, uses up valuable productive hours that people must spend carrying and collecting water. Moreover, unsafe water increases the spread of diseases and results in poor sanitation, which exacerbates illnesses and adds an additional strain on development.

In addition, the devastating earthquake that hit Haiti in 2010 destroyed much of the country's already underdeveloped infrastructure. Thousands of Haitians died in the earthquake and many of those who survived found themselves living in squalid camps. The damages incurred by the quake totalled about $8 billion, according to the World Bank, which is around 120% of Haiti's GDP. Making matters worse, UN peacekeepers stationed in the country following the quake brought with them a deadly strain of cholera, which spread so rapidly that Haiti now has the highest number of cholera cases in the world (Randal and Sengupta, 2014).

For some of the poorest states in the world, like Haiti, it can seem near impossible to envision opportunities for positive economic change. Yet, it is important to remember that such changes can occur, as development success stories like those in China and India attest. China had poverty rates of 28% in 1978, but these rates fell to 9% in 1998. India's poverty rates fell from 51% in 1977 to 27% in 2000. Many scholars attributed poverty reduction to high rates of economic growth. In India's case, growth rates had remained very low for a long time and poverty rates, concurrently, remained high. It was not until India achieved higher growth that the country was able to reduce its poverty rates.

Economic growth undoubtedly contributed to poverty reduction in these countries. But such growth was not equally distributed. Although many citizens were lifted out of poverty, economic growth in China and India disproportionately benefitted the rich. Inequality levels increased in China as the country opened itself up to the world economy. The income share of the poorest quintile decreased from 8% to 7% while the share of the richest quintile increased from 30% to 45% (Banerjee et al., 2006, 90). In India after many decades when inequality remained stable, the liberalization years led to an explosion of inequality particularly in urban areas.

So how can we increase the number of development successes? And how can we encourage more equitable growth? We contend that increasing the number of development successes and narrowing the gap between rich and poor requires an informed approach that is empirically grounded.

This study provided a review of what we know about development, with the goal of increasing practitioner awareness of what has worked in the past, what has not, and why. In Chapters 1–3 of this study, we focused on approaches to understanding why some states are rich but others are poor. Here, we discussed the early theories of development, namely modernization theory and the Dependency School, highlighting the contributions and shortcomings of these theories. We then turned to a discussion of the dominant economic philosophical poles that have been advocated to encourage growth, ranging from state-led approaches on one end of the spectrum to neo-liberalism on the other. We identified how these paradigms have affected past approaches to development, and then outlined many of the key economic policies typically supported by economists today.

The empirical record has proven, however, that even some states with the 'right' policies have fallen short of expectations. As the development community is increasingly noting, the quality of a state's institutions significantly affect the utility of economic policies. High-quality state institutions are essential for development because they facilitate the formulation of sound economic policy choices and support their implementation, increasing the efficacy of those choices. Where institutions are absent or are of low quality, not only are effective policy choices less likely to emerge, but even when they do, such choices are likely to be constrained by the inability to effectively execute such strategies. In Chapter 4 of this study, we therefore discussed state institutions. We provided an overview of what state institutions are, how they can be disaggregated, and ways in which we can evaluate their quality with an eye toward enhancing economic performance. Though it is becoming commonplace for members of the development community to state that institutions matter for development, we emphasized the need for a more focused dialogue, which pays close attention to the specific ways in which different types of state institutions can be reformed to encourage growth. We also examined the institutional landscape of developing states today, paying close attention to the ways in which colonial histories and geographical circumstances shaped today's outcomes.

In Chapters 5–13, we turned to an analysis of some of the major development hurdles that states in the developing world confront. We first addressed the major obstacles to development, namely poverty, instability and corruption. We then explained what can be done to reduce poverty, instability and corruption, while also explaining why it's so important to tackle these issues. We then turned to examine the role of colonialism, unsustainable debt levels, environmental curses and vulnerabilities to disease. We showed how these hurdles pose unique challenges for developing states, while also illustrating, where possible, how state institutions can be reformed in ways that enable states to overcome them. We also focused on how globalization and foreign aid can challenge states and complicate the process of development. We then discussed the key critiques levied against these international factors. We argued that though globalization needs to be heavily managed, and the aid industry is in need of reform, there is reason for optimism. Both globalization and foreign aid are two-sided coins; in some cases they can undermine development, but under the right circumstances, they can open up more opportunities for states in the developing world.

We end by underscoring one additional point, and that is the importance of understanding the local context when formulating development strategies. In this study we have highlighted the significance of state institutions for economic development. While there is broad agreement in the development community that institutions matter, the precise form that such institutions should take is less straightforward. We have sought to define, where possible, the general qualities that state institutions should embody in order to effectively encourage development. For example, we highlighted in Chapter 4 that to be effective, a state's administrative institutions should feature meritocratic recruitment and promotion, offer competitive salaries to reduce the lure of bribes, and be autonomous. These are critical institutional features, but the way these criteria are put into practice is likely to be highly dependent on the local context.

Put another way, high-quality institutions can take a multitude of forms and there is no one size fits all solution to designing institutions that facilitate equitable growth. Douglass North (1994, 365) writes: 'economies that adopt the formal rules of another economy will have very different performance characteristics than the first economy because of different informal norms and enforcement... [therefore] transferring the formal political and economic rules of successful Western economies to third-world economies is not a sufficient condition for good economic performance.' Development strategies that take account of domestic strengths and constraints, and also the knowledge of local actors are likely to have the greatest chance of success.

In sum, states in the developing world today face numerous challenges. Yet, they are not powerless in affecting change. Success stories exist, though they may not attract as much attention as the failures. The road to improving economic performance in the developing world is not an easy one, but by identifying how states can shape their institutions to help them overcome development hurdles, and the positive role that external and local actors can play in guiding this process, there is reason for optimism.

References

Abdul-Gafaru, A. (October 19–20, 2006). Are Multinational Corporations Compatible with Sustainable Development in Developing Countries? Paper Prepared for the Conference on Multinational Corporations and Sustainable Development: Strategic Tool for Competitiveness, Atlanta, GA.

Abrahamsen, R. Ed. (2013). *Conflict and Security in Africa*. Rochester, NY: Boydell and Brewer.

Acemoglu, D. & Robinson, J. (2012). *Why National Fail*. New York, NY: Crown Business.

Acemoglu, D., Johnson, S. & Robinson, J.A. (2004) Institutions as the Fundamental Cause of Long-Run Growth. *NBER Working Paper* 10481. Cambridge, MA: National Bureau of Economic Research, 1–111.

Acemoglu, D., Johnson, S. & Robinson, J.A. (2002a). An African Success Story: Botswana. *CEPR Discussion Paper* 3219. London: Centre for Economic Policy Research.

Acemoglu, D., Johnson, S. & Robinson, J.A. (2002b). Reversal of fortune: Geography and institutions in the making of the modern world income distribution. *Quarterly Journal of Economics* 117 (4), 1231–1294.

Acemoglu, D., Johnson, S. & Robinson, J.A. (2001). The colonial origins of comparative development: An empirical investigation. *American Economic Review* 91 (5), 1369–1401.

Acemoglu, D., Verdier, T. & Robinson, J.A. (2004). Kleptocracy and divide and rule: A model of personal rule. *Journal of the European Economic Association* 2 (2–3), 162–192.

Action Forex. (2015). Asian Financial Crisis. http://www.actionforex.com/articles-library/financial-glossary/asian-financial-crisis-20041204325/

Adamolekun, L. (2002). Africa's evolving career civil service systems: Three challenges – state continuity, efficient service delivery and accountability. *International Review of Administrative Sciences* 68 (3), 373–387.

ADB (Asian Development Bank). (2000). *Asian Development Outlook* 2000. New York, NY: Oxford University Press.

Addison, T., Mavrotas, G. & McGillivray, M. (2005). Aid to Africa: An unfinished agenda. *Journal of International Development* 17, 989–1001.

Adelman, I. (1984). Beyond export-led growth. *World Development* 12 (9), 937–949.

Ades, A. & Di Tella, R. (1999). Rents, competition, and corruption. *American Economic Review*, 89 (4), 982–993.

Adger, W. Neil, Hughes, T.P., Folke, C., Carpenter, S.R. & Rockström, J. (2005). Social-ecological resilience to coastal disasters. *Science* 309 (5737), 1036–1039.

Ades, A. & Di Tella, R. (1999). Rents, competition, and corruption. *American Economic Review*, 89 (4) 982–993.

African Development Bank Group. (March 7, 2012). Income inequality in Africa. *Briefing Note* 5, 1–6.

Africa Research Bulletin: Economic, Financial and Technical Series (June 6, 1998). 35 (4). 13423–13454.

Aghion, P. & Williamson, J.G. (1998). *Growth, Inequality, and Globalization: Theory, History, and Policy*. Cambridge: Cambridge University Press.

Aguirre, M. (January 17, 2006). Failed states or weak democracies? The state in Latin America. *Open Democracy*, 1–6.

Agyeman-Duah, B. (June, 1998). Liberia: The Search for a Stable Civil–Military Relations. In Workshop on State Rebuilding after State Collapse in Liberia, organised by the Centre for Democracy & Development, London. June (Vol. 19).

Ahrens, J. & Rudolph, P.M. (2006). The importance of governance in risk reduction and disaster management. *Journal of Contingencies and Crisis Management* 14 (4), 207–220.

Aizenman, J. & Marion, N. (1999). Volatility and investment: Interpreting evidence from developing countries. *Economica* 66, 157–179.

309

Akhand, M.H. (2003). Disaster Management and Cyclone Warning System in Bangladesh. In *Early Warning Systems for Natural Disaster Reduction*, 49–64. Berlin, Heidelberg: Springer.

Akonor, K. (2007). Foreign aid to Africa: A hollow hope. *NYUJ Int'l L. & Pol.*, 40, 1071.

Alagappa, M. & Inoguchi, T. (1999). *International Security Management and the United Nations*. Tokyo, Japan: United Nations University Press.

Alao, C. (1999) The Problem of the Failed State in Africa. In *International Security Management and the United Nations*, edited by Muthiah Alagappa and Takashi Inoguchi, 83–102. Tokyo, Japan: United Nations University Press.

Albadry, A.S.S. & Abdullah, M.K.B. (May 2014). Exploring the key challenges affecting Iraqi parliamentary institution post remove Saddam Hussein's regime. *International Journal of Humanities and Social Science* 7 (4), 203–210.

Albala-Bertrand, J. (1993). *Political Economy of Large Natural Disasters*. New York, NY: Oxford University Press.

Alcántara-Ayala, I. (2002). Geomorphology, natural hazards, vulnerability and prevention of natural disasters in developing countries. *Geomorphology* 47 (2), 107–124.

Alchian, A.A. (2008). Property rights. *The Concise Encyclopedia of Economics*.

Alesina, A. & Perotti, R. (1996). Income distribution, political instability, and investment. *European Economic Review* 40 (6), 1203–1228.

Alesina, A. & Rodrik, D. (May 1994). Distributive politics and economic growth. *Quarterly Journal of Economics* 109, 465–490.

Alexander, D.E. (1993). *Natural Disasters*. Springer.

Aliber, M. (March 2003). Chronic poverty in South Africa: Incidence, causes and policies. *World Development* 31(3), 473–490.

Alilio, M.S., Bygbjerg, I.C. & Breman, J.G. (2004). Are multilateral malaria research and control programs the most successful? Lessons from the past 100 years in Africa. *The American Journal of Tropical Medicine and Hygiene* 71 (2), 268–278.

Almond, G.A. & Powell, G.B. (1978). *Comparative Politics: A Development Approach*. Boston, MA: Little, Brown and Company 1966. Fourth Indian Reprint.

Alonso, P.L., Lindsay, S.W., Armstrong, J.R.M., de Francisco, A., Shenton, F.C., Greenwood, B.M., ... & Hall, A.J. (1991). The effect of insecticide-treated bed nets on mortality of Gambian children. *The Lancet* 337 (8756), 1499–1502.

Alsop, M. & Rogger, D. (2008). *Debt Relief as a Platform for Reform: The Case of Nigeria's Virtual Poverty Fund*. Unpublished manuscript.

Alt, J.E. & Lassen, D.D. (2008). Political and judicial checks on corruption: Evidence from American state governments. *Economics & Politics* 20 (1), 33–61.

Amaghionyeodiwe, L.A. (2009). Government health care spending and the poor: Evidence from Nigeria. *International Journal of Social Economics* 36 (3), 220–236.

Amin, S. (1972). *L'Afrique de l'Ouest bloquée*. Paris: Editions de Minuit.

Anderson, K., Martin, W. & Valenzuela, E. (2009). Long Run Implications of WTO Accession for Agriculture in China. In *China's Agricultural Trade: Issues and Prospects*, edited by I. Sheldon. St Paul, MN: International Agricultural Trade Research Consortium.

Anderson, L. (Summer 2006). The authoritarian executive? Horizontal and vertical accountability in Nicaragua. *Latin American Politics & Society* 48 (2), 141–169.

Andersson, N., Palha da Sousa, C. & Paredes, S. (1995). Social cost of land mines in four countries: Afghanistan, Bosnia, Cambodia, and Mozambique. *BMJ* 311 (7007), 718–721.

Angeles, L. (2007). Inequality and colonialism. *European Economic Review* 51, 1155–1176.

Annisette, M. (1999). Importing accounting: The case of Trinidad and Tobago. *Accounting, Business & Financial History* 9 (1), 103–133.

Aphornsuvan, T. (September 28, 2004). The Search for Order: Constitutions and Human Rights in Thai Political History. Paper presented at Australian National University, 2001 Symposium: Constitutions and Human Rights in a Global Age: An Asia Pacific perspective, 1–10.

Apter, D.E. (1967). *The Politics of Modernization*. Chicago: University of Chicago Press.

Aquino, B. (1997). *Politics of Plunder: The Philippines under Marcos*. Manila, Philippines: University of the Philippines Press.

Arcand, J. (2001). *Undernourishment and Economic Growth: The Efficiency Cost of Hunger* 147. Food & Agriculture Org.

Archibugi, D. & Filippetti, A. (2010). The globalization of intellectual property rights: Four learned lessons and four thesis. *Journal of Global Policy* 1, 137–149.

Ardington, E. (1988). Nkandla revisted: a longitudinal study of strategies adopted to alleviate poverty in a rural community. Rural Urban Studies Unit, Working Paper no. 16. Durban: University of Natal.

Aregawi, M., Cibulskis, R.E., Otten, M. & Williams, R. (2009). *World Malaria Report 2009.* World Health Organization.

Arieff, A. (February 2014). Democratic Republic of Congo: Background and U.S. policy. *Congressional Research Service*, 1–20.

Armstrong, H.W. & Read, R. (2003). The determinants of economic growth in small states. *The Round Table* 92 (363), 99–124.

Asian Development Bank. (2002) Fighting poverty in Asia and the Pacific: The poverty reduction strategy.

Auriol, E. & Warlters, M. (2005). Taxation base in developing countries. *Journal of Public Economics* 89 (4), 625–646.

Austen, R.A. (1987) *African Economic History: Internal Development and External Dependency.* London: James Currey.

Austin, G. (2009) Cash crops and freedom: Export agriculture and the decline of slavery in colonial West Africa. *International Review of Social History* 54 (1), 1–37.

AVERT Organization. http://www.avert.org/worldwide-hiv-aids-statistics.htm

Ayadi, F.S. & Ayadi, F.O. (2008). The impact of external debt on economic growth: A comparative study of Nigeria and South Africa. *Journal of Sustainable Development in Africa* 10 (3), 234–264.

Ayres, R.L. (1998). *Crime and violence as development issues in Latin America and the Caribbean.* World Bank Publications.

Azarya, V. & Chazan, N. (1987). Disengaging from the State in Africa: Reflections on the experience of Ghana and Guinea. *Comparative Studies in Society and History* 29, 106–131.

Azam, J.-P. & Morrison, C., with Chauvin, S. and Rospabé, S. (1999). *Conflict and Growth in Africa, Vol. 1: The Sahel.* OECD Development Centre Studies.

Azfar, O. & Gurgur, T. (2005). Does Corruption Affect Health and Education Outcomes in the Philippines? Available at SSRN 723702. 1–46.

Bairoch, P. (1993). *Economics and World History, Myths and Paradoxes.* Chicago, IL: University of Chicago Press.

Bairoch, P. (1995). *Economics and World History: Myths and Paradoxes.* University of Chicago Press.

Balassa, B. (1971). Trade policies in developing countries. *The American Economic Review*, 178–187.

Ball, N. & Brzoska, M. (2002) Voice and Accountability in the Security Sector. BICC Paper 21.

Banerjee, A., Banerjee, A.V. & Duflo, E. (2011). *Poor Economics: A Radical Rethinking of the Way to Fight Global Poverty.* PublicAffairs.

Banerjee, A.V. & Duflo, E. (2007). The economic lives of the poor. *The Journal of Economic Perspectives: A Journal of the American Economic Association* 21 (1), 141.

Banerjee, A.V., Benabou, R. & Mookherjee, D. eds. (2006). *Understanding Poverty: Poverty and Economic Development.* Oxford: Oxford University Press.

Banerjee, A.V., Gertler, P.J. & Ghatak, M. (2002). Empowerment and efficiency: Tenancy reform in West Bengal. *Journal of Political Economy* 110 (2), 239–280.

Bankoff, G. (1999). A history of poverty: The politics of natural disasters in the Philippines, 1985–95. *The Pacific Review* 12 (3), 381–420.

Banks, N. & Hulme, D. (2012). The role of NGOs and civil society in development and poverty reduction. Brooks World Poverty Institute Working Paper, 171.

Baran, P.A. & Sutcliffe, R.B. (1957). *The Political Economy of Growth.* New York, NY: Monthly Review Press.

Barat, L.M. (2006). Four malaria success stories: How malaria burden was successfully reduced in Brazil, Eritrea, India, and Vietnam. *The American Journal of Tropical Medicine and Hygiene* 74 (1), 12–16.

Barber, M. & Bowie, C. (2008). How international NGOs could do less harm and more good. *Development in Practice* 18 (6), 748–754.

Barder, O. & Birdsall, N. (2006). Payments for progress: A hands-off approach to foreign aid. *Center for Global Development Working Paper* (102), 1–24.

Barnes, D.F. & Binswanger, H. (1986). Impact of rural electrification and infrastructure on agricultural changes. *Economic and Political Weekly* 21, 26–34.

Barrett, R.E. & Whyte, M.K. (1982). Dependency theory and Taiwan: Analysis of a deviant case. *American Journal of Sociology* 87 (5), 1064–1089.

Barrientos, A. & DeJong, J. (2004). Child poverty and cash transfers. *Childhood Poverty Research and Policy Centre Report* No. 4. London: Save the Children.

Barro, R.J. (2000). Rule of law, democracy, and economic performance. *2000 Index of Economic Freedom*, 31–51.

Barro, R.J. (1996). Democracy and growth. *Journal of Economic Growth* 1 (1), 1–27.

Barro, R.J., Sala-i-Martin, X., Blanchard, O.J. & Hall, R.E. (1991). Convergence across states and regions. *Brookings Papers on Economic Activity*, 1991 (1), 107–182.

Basu, S., Andrews, J., Kishore, S., Panjabi, R. & Stuckler, D. (2012). Comparative performance of private and public healthcare systems in low-and middle-income countries: A systematic review. *PLoS Medicine* 9 (6), 1–14.

Basu, D. & Basole, A. (2012). The calorie consumption puzzle in India: An empirical investigation (No. 2012-07). Working Paper, University of Massachusetts, Department of Economics.

Bates, R. (2001). *Prosperity and Violence: The Political Economy of Development.* New York, NY: Norton Publisher.

Bata, M. & Bergesen, A.J. (2002). Global inequality: An introduction (to Special Issue on Global Economy – Part I). *Journal of World-System Research* 8 (1), 2–6.

Beblawi, H. & Luciani, G. (1987). *The Rentier State.* London: Croom Helm, 63–82.

Behrman, J.R. & Deolalikar, A. (1988). Health and nutrition. In *Handbook of Development Economics*, eds. H. Chenery and T.N. Srinivasan. Amsterdam: North Holland.

Behrman, J. & Deolalikar, A.B. (1987). Will developing country nutrition improve with income? A case study from rural South India. *Journal of Political Economy* 95, 492–507.

Behrman, J.R., Sengupta, P. & Todd, P. (2005). Progressing through PROGRESA: An impact assessment of a school subsidy experiment in rural Mexico. *Economic Development and Cultural Change* 54 (1), 237–275.

Belkin, A. & Schofer, E. (2003). Toward a structural understanding of coup risk. *Journal of Conflict Resolution* 47 (5), 594–620.

Bellin, E. (January 2004). The robustness of authoritarianism in the middle east: Exceptionalism in comparative perspective. *Comparative Politics* 36 (2), 139–157.

Bento, J., Silva, A.S., Rodrigues, F. & Duarte, R. (January–February 2011). *Diagnostic tools in tuberculosis. Acta Medica Portuguesa* 24 (1), 145–154.

Berg, A., Ostry, J.D. & Zettelmeyer, J. (2012). What makes growth sustained? *Journal of Development Economics* 98 (2), 149–166.

Berg, R. (2013). Tropical Cyclone Report Hurricane Isaac (AL092012) 21 August–1 September 2012. National Oceanic and Atmospheric Administration/National Weather Service, Miami, FL.

Berman, B.J. & Lonsdale, J.M. (1980). Crises of accumulation, coercion and the colonial state: The development of the labor control system in Kenya, 1919-1929. *Canadian Journal of African Studies*, 55–81.

Bertocchi, G. & Canova, F. (2002). Did colonization matter for growth? An empirical exploration into the historical causes of Africa's underdevelopment. *European Economic Review* 46, 1851–1871.

Bertozzi, S., Padian, N.S., Wegbreit, J., et al. (2006). HIV/AIDS Prevention and Treatment. In *Disease Control Priorities in Developing Countries*, edited by D.T. Jamison, J.G. Breman, A.R. Measham et al. (2nd ed.). Washington, DC: World Bank; Chapter 18. Available from: http://www.ncbi.nlm.nih.gov/books/NBK11782/

Besley, T., Burgess, R. & Prat, A. (2002). *Mass Media and Political Accountability.* World Bank.

Bhagwati, J.N. (2002). *Globalization and Appropriate Governance.* Unu/Wider.

Bhagwati, J.N. (2004). *In Defence of Globalisation.* Oxford, UK: Oxford University Press.

Bhagwati, J.N. & Srinivasan, T.N. (2002). Trade and poverty in the poor countries. *American Economic Review*, 180–183.

Bhattacharyya, S. & Hodler, R. (2010). Natural resources, democracy and corruption. *European Economic Review* 54 (4), 608–621.

Bidani, B. & Ravallion, M. (1997). Decomposing social indicators using distributional data. *Journal of Econometrics* 77 (1), 125–139.

Bienen, H. (1974). Military and society in East Africa: Thinking again about Praetorianism. *Comparative Politics*, 489–517.

Bieri, F. (2010). *From Blood Diamonds to the Kimberley Process: How NGOs Cleaned up the Global Diamond Industry.* Ashgate Publishing.

Biggerstaff, S. (August 2011). Country Profile: Ecuador Strives for a Role in Global Software Near Shore Americas. http://www.nearshoreamericas.com/country-profile-ecuador-strives-role-global-software/

Bird, K. & Shepherd, A. (March 2003). Livelihood and chronic poverty in semi-arid Zimbabwe. *World Development* 31 (3), 591–610.

Birdsall, N. (2007). Do no harm: Aid, weak institutions and the missing middle in Africa. *Development Policy Review* 25 (5), 575–598.

Birdsall, N. (2000). *Why Inequality Matters: The Developing and Transitional Economies.* Washington, DC: Carnegie Endowment for International Peace. Mimeo.

Birdsall, N., Ross, D. & Sabot, R. (1995). Inequality and growth reconsidered: Lessons from East Asia. *The World Bank Economic Review* 9 (3), 477–508.

Bjerkholt, Olav. (2004). New approaches to debt relief and debt sustainability in LDCs. *CDP Background Paper* 5, 1–26.

Blackburn, K., Bosey, N. & Capasso, S. (2008). Living with corruption: Threshold effects in red tape and rent seeking. DES (Department of Economic Studies), University of Naples Parthenope, Italy Working Papers.

Blaikie, P., Cannon, T., Davis, I. & Wisner, B. (2004). *At Risk: Natural Hazards, People's Vulnerability and Disasters.* Routledge.

Bleakley, H. (2010). Malaria eradication in the Americas: A retrospective analysis of childhood exposure. *American Economic Journal Applied Economics* 2 (2), 1–43.

Blomberg, S.B. & Hess, G.D. (2002). The temporal links between conflict and economic activity. *Journal of Conflict Resolution* 46 (1), 74–90.

Bloom, D.E., Canning, D. & Sevilla, J. (2003). Geography and poverty traps. *Journal of Economic Growth* 8 (4), 355–378.

Bloom, D.E. & Mahal, A.S. (1997). Does the AIDS epidemic threaten economic growth? *Journal of Econometrics* 77 (1), 105–124.

Bloom, D.E. & Sachs, J.D. (1998). Geography, demography, and economic growth in Africa. *Brookings Papers on Economic Activity*, 2.

Blunt, P., Turner, M. & Lindroth, H. (2012). Patronage's progress in post Soeharto Indonesia. *Public Administration and Development* 32 (1), 64–81.

Boelee, E., Cecchi, P. & Koné, A. (2010). *Health Impacts of Small Reservoirs in Burkina Faso* (Vol. 136). International Water Management Institute, 1–50.

Bøås, M. (2001). Liberia and Sierra Leone—dead ringers? The logic of neo-patrimonial rule. *Third World Quarterly* 22 (5), 697–723.

Bohannan, P. & Curtin, P.D. (1988). *Africa and Africans.* Prospect Heights, IL: Waveland Press.

Bohlken, A.T. (2010). Coups, elections and the predatory state. *Journal of Theoretical Politics* 22 (2), 169–215.

Bollinger, L., Stover, J., Kerkhoven, R., Mutangadura, G. & Mukurazita, D. (1999). The economic impact of AIDS in Zimbabwe. The POLICY Project—The Futures Group International, Research Triangle Institute, The Centre for Development and Population Activities Funded by USAID.

Bonn International Center for Conversion (BICC). (2006). Security Sector Reform Ghana, 1–11.

Bonnel, R. (2000). HIV/AIDS: Does It Increase or Decrease Growth in Africa? ACT, Africa Department, Washington, DC, World Bank.

Bräutigam, D. (2000). Foreign aid and the politics of participation in economic policy reform. *Public Administration and Development* 20 (3), 253–264.

Boserup, E. (2007). *Woman's Role in Economic Development.* Earthscan.

Bourne, M. (2007) *Arming Conflict: The Proliferation of Small Arms.* London: Palgrave Macmillan.

Boutayeb, A. (2009). The impact of HIV/AIDS on human development in African countries. *BMC Public Health* 9 (1), S3.

Brancati, D. & Snyder, J.L. (2013). Time to kill: The impact of election timing on post conflict stability. *Journal of Conflict Resolution* 57 (5), 822–853.

Brass, J.N. (2012). Why do NGOs go where they go? Evidence from Kenya. *World Development* 40 (2), 387–401.

Brass, W. & Jolly, C.L. eds. (1993). *Population Dynamics of Kenya.* National Academies Press.

Bratton, M. & Chang, E.C.C. (November 2006). State building and democratization in Sub-Saharan Africa: Forwards, backwards or together? *Comparative Political Studies* 39 (9), 1059–1083.

Bratton, M. & van de Walle, N. (July 1994). Neo-patrimonial regimes and political transitions in Africa. *World Politics* 44 (4), 453–489.

Braudel, F. (1995). *A History of Civilizations*. New York, NY: Penguin Books.

Bräutigam, D. & Botchwey, K. (1999). *The Institutional Impact of Aid Dependence on Recipients in Africa*. Bergen: Chr. Michelsen Institute.

Bräutigam, D.A. & Knack, S. (2004). Foreign aid, institutions, and governance in Sub-Saharan Africa. *Economic Development and Cultural Change* 52 (2), 255–285.

Bräutigam, D. & Woolcock, M. (2001). Small states in a global economy: The role of institutions in managing vulnerability and opportunity in small developing countries. No. 2001/37. WIDER Discussion Papers//World Institute for Development Economics (UNU-WIDER).

Brautigam, D. (1992). Governance, economy, and foreign aid. *Studies in Comparative International Development*, 27 (3), 3–25.

Breman J.G., Alilio, M.S. & Mills, A. (August 2004). Conquering the intolerable burden of malaria: What's new, what's needed: A summary. *American Journal of Tropical Medicine and Hygiene* 71 (2).

Brennan, P.J. & Nikaido, H. (1995). The envelope of mycobacteria. *Annual Review Biochemistry* 64, 29–63.

Brett, E.A. (1973). *Colonialism and Underdevelopment in East Africa: The Politics of Economic Change, 1919-1939*. London: Heinemann.

Brinkerhoff, D.W. & Goldsmith, A.A. (December 2002). Clientelism, Patrimonialism and Democratic Governance: An Overview and Framework for Assessment and Programming. *U.S. Agency for International Development Office of Democracy and Governance under Strategic Policy and Institutional Reform*. 1–50.

Brinkerhoff, D.W. & Goldsmith, A.A. (1992). Promoting the sustainability of development institutions: A framework for strategy. *World Development* 20 (3), 369–383.

Brookings Institution. (2010). Governance Matters 2010: Worldwide Governance Indicators Highlight Governance Successes, Reversals, and Failures.

Brooks, J., Cervantes-Godoy, D. & Jonasson, E. (August 2009). Strategies for Smallholders in Developing Countries: Commercialisation, Diversification and Exit. In *EAAE-IAAE Seminar 'Small Farms: Decline or Persistence'*. Canterbury: University of Kent, 26–27.

Brown, T.M., Cueto, M. & Fee, E. (2006). The World Health Organization and the transition from "international" to "global" public health. *American Journal of Public Health* 96 (1), 62.

Brunetti, A. & Weder, B. (2003). A free press is bad news for corruption. *Journal of Public Economics* 87 (7), 1801–1824.

Bryce, J., el Arifeen, S., Pariyo, G., Lanata, C.F., Gwatkin, D. & Habicht, J.P. (2003). Reducing child mortality: Can public health deliver? *The Lancet* 362 (9378), 159–164.

Brzoska, M. (2003). *Development Donors and the Concept of Security Sector Reform*. Geneva: Geneva Centre for the Democratic Control of Armed Forces.

Brzoska, M. (1983). The military related external debt of the third world countries. *Journal of Peace Research*, 271–278.

Buell, R.L. (1965). *The Native Problem in Africa* (Vol. 2). F. Cass.

Buhaug, H., Gleditsch, K.S., Holtermann, H., Østby, G. & Tollefsen, A.F. (2011). It's the local economy, stupid! Geographic wealth dispersion and conflict outbreak location. *Journal of Conflict Resolution* 55 (5), 814–840.

Bulmer-Thomas, V. (2003). *The Economic History of Latin America since Independence* (Vol. 77). Cambridge: Cambridge University Press.

Bunbongkarn, S. (February 1992). Thailand in 1991: Coping with military guardianship. *Asian Survey* 32 (2), 131–139.

Burgoon, B. (2006). On welfare and terror social welfare policies and political-economic roots of terrorism. *Journal of Conflict Resolution* 50 (2), 176–203.

Burnside, C. & Dollar, D. (2000). Aid policies and growth. *American Economic Review* 90 (4), 847–868.

Burton, J. (1987). *Resolving Deep Rooted Conflict: A Handbook*. Lanham, MD: University Press of America.

Buscaglia, E. (2003). Controlling organized crime and corruption in the public sector. *Forum on Crime and Society* 3, 3–34.

Buss, T.F. (2009). *Haiti in the Balance: Why Foreign Aid Has Failed and What We Can Do About It*. Brookings Institution Press.

Byerlee, D., De Janvry, A. & Sadoulet, E. (2009). Agriculture for development: Toward a new paradigm. *Annual Review Resource Economics* 1 (1), 15–31.

Byerlee, D., Diao, X. & Jackson, C. (2005). Agriculture, rural development, and pro-poor growth: Country experiences in the post-reform era. *Agriculture and Rural Development Discussion Paper* 21, 1–72.

Çağatay, N. & Özler, Ş. (1995). Feminization of the labor force: The effects of long-term development and structural adjustment. *World Development* 23 (11), 1883–1894.

Campos, N.F. & Nugent, J.B. (1999). Development performance and the institutions of governance: Evidence from East Asia and Latin America. *World Development* 27 (3), 439–452.

Cardoso, F.H. & Faletto, E. (1979). *Dependency and Development in Latin.* Berkeley, CA: University of California Press.

Carment, D. (2003). Assessing state failure: Implications for theory and policy. *Third World Quarterly* 24 (3), 407–427.

Carothers, T. (1998). The rule of law revival. *Foreign Affairs* 77, 95–106.

Carrasco, E., McClellan, C. & Ro, J. (April 2007). Foreign Debt: Forgiveness and Repudiation. The University of Iowa Center for International Development. http://archive.today/ww57N

Carter, M.R., Little, P.D., Mogues, T. & Negatu, W. (2007). Poverty traps and natural disasters in Ethiopia and Honduras. *World Development* 35 (5), 835–856.

Carter, R. & Mendis, K.N. (2002). Evolutionary and historical aspects of the burden of malaria. *Clinical Microbiology Reviews* 15 (4), 564–594.

Case, A. & Paxson, C.H. (2006). Children's health and social mobility. *The Future of Children* 16 (2), 151–173.

Castro, C. (June 2004). Sustainable development: Mainstream and critical approaches. *Organization and Environment* 17 (2), 195–225.

Cawthorne, A. (January 18, 2010). Haitian Education System "Totally Collapsed" Reuters. http://uk.reuters.com/article/2010/01/18/us-quake-haiti-education-interview-id UKTRE60H12G20100118

Cederman, L., Weidmann, N.B. & Gleditsch, K.S. (2011) Horizontal inequalities and ethnonationalist civil war: A global comparison. *American Political Science Review* 105 (3), 478–495.

Cederman, L., Wimmer, A. & Min, B. (2010). Why do ethnic groups rebel? New data and analysis. *World Politics* 62 (1), 87–119.

Cederman, L., Buhaug, H. & Rød, J.K. (2009). Ethno-nationalist dyads and civil war: A GIS-based analysis. *Journal of Conflict Resolution* 53 (4), 496–525.

Cederman, L., Girardin, L. & Gleditsch, K.S. (2009). Ethno-nationalist triads: Assessing the influence of kin groups on civil wars. *World Politics* 61 (3), 403–437.

Center for Disease Control. Malaria. http://www.cdc.gov/malaria/about/history/

Center for Global Development. (2004). Global HIV/AIDS and the Developing World. http://www.cgdev.org/files/2851_file_GLOBAL_HIV_AIDS1.pdf

Cervantes-Godoy, D. & Dewbre, J. (2010). *Economic Importance of Agriculture for Poverty Reduction* 23. OECD Publishing.

Chang, H.J. (2006). Understanding the relationship between institutions and economic development. Some key theoretical issues. *Revista de Economía Institucional* 8 (14), 125–136.

Chang, H.J. (2003). *Globalization, Economic Development and the Role of the State.* Zed Books.

Charette, D.E. (2006). Malaysia in the global economy: Crisis, recovery, and the road ahead. *New England Journal of Public Policy* 21 (1), 6.

Charvériat, C. (2000). Natural Disasters in Latin America and the Caribbean: An Overview of risk (No. 434). Working Paper, Inter-American Development Bank, Research Department. 1–104.

Chaudhry, S.A., Reid, G.J. & Malik, W.H., eds. (1994). *Civil Service Reform in Latin America and the Caribbean: Proceedings of a Conference (Vol. 23).* World Bank Publications.

Chemin, M. (2009). The impact of the judiciary on entrepreneurship: Evaluation of Pakistan's access to justice Programme. *Journal of Public Economics* 93, 114–125.

Chenery, H.B. & Strout, A.M. (1966). Foreign assistance and economic development. *American Economic Review* 56, 679–733.

Chenery, H.B., Syrquin, M. & Elkington, H. (1975). *Patterns of Development, 1950–1970* (Vol. 3). London: Oxford University Press.

Chesterman, S., Ignatieff, M. & Thakur, R.C., eds. (2005). *Making States Work: State Failure and the Crisis of Governance.* Tokyo, Japan: United Nations University Press.

Chitnis, A., Rawls, D. & Moore, J. (2000). Origin of HIV type 1 in colonial French equatorial Africa? *AIDS Research and Human Retroviruses* 16 (1), 5–8.

Chizema-Kawesha, E., Miller, J.M., Steketee, R.W., Mukonka, V.M., Mukuka, C., Mohamed, A.D., ... & Campbell, C.C. (2010). Scaling up malaria control in Zambia: Progress and impact 2005–2008. *The American Journal of Tropical Medicine and Hygiene* 83 (3), 480–488.

Choi, J.P. & Thum, M. (2005). Corruption and the shadow economy. *International Economic Review* 46 (3), 817–836.

Chong, A. & Calderon, C. (2000). Causality and feedback between institutional measures and economic growth. *Economics and Politics* 12 (1), 69–81.

Christiansen, L. & Demery, L. (2007). *Down to Earth: Agriculture and Poverty Reduction in Africa. Directions in Development*. Washington, DC: World Bank.

Clague, C., Keefer, P., Knack, S. & Olson, M. (1997). Democracy, Autocracy and the Institutions Supportive of Economic Growth. In *Institutions and Economic Development: Growth and Governance in Less-Developed and Post-Socialist Countries*, edited by Christopher Clague. Baltimore, MD: The Johns Hopkins University Press.

Clark, John. (1993). Debt reduction and market re-entry under the Brady plan. *Federal Reserve Bank of New York Quarterly Review* 18 (4), 38–62.

Clements, B.J., Bhattacharya, R. & Nguyen, T.Q. (2003). External debt, public investment, and growth in low-income countries (No. 2003-2249). *International Monetary Fund*. 1–24.

Cleveland, W.L. (1994). *A History of the Modern Middle East*. Boulder, CO: Westview Press.

Clinton, W. (2006). *Lessons Learned from Tsunami Recovery: Key Propositions for Building Back Better. Special Envoy for Tsunami Recovery*. New York, NY: United Nations.

Colclough, C. (1993). Structuralism vs. Neo-Liberalism. In *States or Markets? Neo-liberalism and the Development Policy Debate*, edited by C. Colclough and J. Manor. Oxford: Clarendon Press, 1–25.

Coatsworth, J.H. (2008). Inequality, institutions and economic growth in Latin America. *Journal of Latin American Studies* 40 (3), 545–569.

Cohen, D. (1993). Low investment and large LDC debt in the 1980's. *The American Economic Review*, 437–449.

Cokgezen, M. (2004). Corruption in Kyrgyzstan: The facts, causes and consequences. *Central Asian Survey* 23 (1), 79–94.

Cole, E. & Cook, C. (1998). Characterization of infectious aerosols in health care facilities: An aid to effective engineering controls and preventive strategies. *American Journal Infectious Control* 26 (4), 453–464.

Collins, K. (2009). Economic and security regionalism among patrimonial authoritarian regimes: The case of Central Asia. *Europe-Asia Studies* 61 (2), 249–281.

Collins, K. (2002). Clans, pacts, and politics in Central Asia. *Journal of Democracy* 13 (3), 137–152.

Collier, P. (2007). *Bottom Billion: Why the Poorest Countries Are Failing and What Can Be Done about It*. Oxford: Oxford University Press.

Collier, P. (2008). The politics of hunger: How illusion and greed fan the food crisis. *Foreign Affairs* 87 (6), 67–79.

Collier, P. (2003). *Breaking the Conflict Trap: Civil War and Development Policy*. World Bank Publications.

Collier, P. (1999). On the economic consequences of civil war. *Oxford Economic Papers* 51 (1), 168–183.

Collier, P. & Dollar, D. (2002). Aid allocation and poverty reduction. *European Economic Review* 46, 1475–1500.

Collier, P. & Dollar, D. (2001). Can the world cut poverty in half? How policy reform and effective aid can meet international development goals. *World Development* 29 (11), 1787–1802.

Collier, P. & Gunning, J.W. (Summer 1999). Why has Africa grown slowly? *The Journal of Economic Perspectives* 13 (3), 3–22.

Collier, P. & Hoeffler, A. (2007). Civil war. *Handbook of Defense Economics* 2, 711–739.

Collier, P. & Hoeffler, A. (2002). 'The Political Economy of Secession', manuscript, 30 June, http://www.worldbank.org/ogmc/pdfs/Paul-Collier.pdf

Collier, P. & Hoeffler, A. (2005). Coup Traps: Why Does Africa Have So Many Coups d'état? http://users.ox.ac.uk/~econpco/research/pdfs/Coup-traps.pdf

Concha-Eastman, A. (2002). Urban Violence in Latin America and the Caribbean: Dimensions, Explanations, Actions. In *Citizens of Fear: Urban Violence in Latin America*, edited by Susana Rotker. Rutgers State University Press, 37–54.

Conteh, C. & Ohemeng, F.L. (2009). The politics of decision making in developing countries: A comparative analysis of privatization decisions in Botswana and Ghana. *Public Management Review* 11 (1), 57–77.

Cook, P. & Kirkpatrick, C. (1997). Globalization, regionalization and third world development. *Regional Studies* 31 (1), 55–66.

Coombes, T. (August 4, 2011). *Ghanaian Students Stand Up To Corruption.* Transparency International. http://blog.transparency.org/2011/08/04/ghanaian-students-stand-up-to-corruption/

Cooper, D.A., Krieckhaus, J. & Lusztig, M. (2006). Corruption, democracy, and economic growth. *International Political Science Review* 27 (2), 121–136.

Country Profile Yemen. Global Resource & Information Directory. http://www.fosigrid.org/middle-east/yemen

Court, J., Hydén, G. & Mease, K. (May 2003). The Judiciary and Governance in 16 Developing Countries. *World Governance Survey Discussion Paper* 9 United Nations University. 1–28.

Crafts, N.F. (2000). *Globalization and Growth in the Twentieth Century.* International Monetary Fund.

Cragin, K. & Chalk, P. (2003). *Terrorism and Development: Using Social and Economic Development to Inhibit a Resurgence of Terrorism.* Rand Corporation.

Crouch, H. (1985). *Military Civilian Relations in Southeast Asia.* Oxford: Oxford University Press.

Curtis, C.F. & Mnzava, A.E. (2000). Comparison of house spraying and insecticide-treated nets for malaria control. *Bulletin of the World Health Organization* 78 (12), 1389–1400.

Dahlström, C., Lapuente, V. & Teorell, J. (2011). The merit of meritocratization: Politics, bureaucracy, and the institutional deterrents of corruption. *Political Research Quarterly* 20 (10), 1–13.

Dalpino, C. (Fall 1991). Thailand's search for political accountability. *Journal of Democracy* 2 (4), 61–71.

Daly, H.E. (1994). *For the Common Good: Redirecting the Economy Toward Community, the Environment, and a Sustainable Future* (No. 73). Beacon Press.

Danso, A. (1990). The causes and impact of the African debt crisis. *The Review of Black Political Economy* 19 (1), 5–21.

Datt, G. & Ravallion, M. (1998). Farm productivity and rural poverty in India. *The Journal of Development Studies* 34 (4), 62–85.

Davenport, C. & Armstrong, D.A. (2004). Democracy and the violation of human rights: A statistical analysis from 1976 to 1996. *American Journal of Political Science* 48 (3), 538–554.

Davies, G. (1996). *From Opportunity to Entitlement: The Transformation and Decline of Great Society Liberalism.* St. Lawrence, KS: University Press of Kansas.

Davies, T. (2014). *NGOs: A New History of Transnational Civil Society.* New York, NY: Oxford University Press.

Davis, J. (2004). Corruption in public service delivery: Experience from South Asia's water and sanitation sector. *World Development* 32 (1), 53–71.

Davis, M. (2006). *Planet of Slums.* London and New York: Verso.

Deacon, R.T. (2009). Public good provision under dictatorship and democracy. *Public Choice* 139 (1), 241–262.

Deaton, A. (March 2003). Health, inequality, and economic development. *Journal of Economic Literature* 60, 113–158.

Debiel, T. (September 6–8, 2006) Violent Conflict and State Fragility in Sub-Saharan Africa Trends, Causes and Policy Options. Presentation at the Scribani Conference "Africa and Europe: Cooperation in a Globalized World." 1–14.

Decalo, S. (1989). *Psychoses of Power. African Personal Dictatorships.* Boulder, CO: Westview Press.

Decalo, S. (1985). African personal dictatorships. *The Journal of Modern African Studies* 23 (2), 209–237.

Decalo, S. (1973). Military coups and military regimes in Africa. *The Journal of Modern African Studies* 11 (1), 105–127.

De Côrdoba, J. (January 2, 2004). Impoverished Haiti pins hopes for future on a very old debt. *Wall Street Journal.*

Dedrick, J., Kraemer, K.L., Palacios, J.J., Bastos Tigre, P. & Junqueira Botelho, A.J. (2001). Economic liberalization and the computer industry: Comparing outcomes in Brazil and Mexico. *World Development* 29 (7), 1199–1214.

Deere, C.D. & Meurs, M. (1992). Markets, markets everywhere? Understanding the Cuban anomaly. *World Development* 20 (6), 825–839.

Degefe, B. (1992). Growth and Foreign Debt: The Ethiopian Experience: 1964-86 (No. RP_13).

de Janvry, A., Finan, F., Sadoulet, E. & de la Brière, B. (2005). Evaluating the Implementation of a Decentralised Conditional Cash Transfer Program: A Study of Brazil's Bolsa Escola Program. Unpublished report prepared for the World Bank.

De Janvry, A. & Sadoulet, E. (2010). Agricultural growth and poverty reduction: Additional evidence. *The World Bank Research Observer* 25 (1), 1–20.

de Melo, M., de Macedo-Soares, T. & Pastor-Braga, P.J. (1993). Options for increasing competitiveness, quality and productivity: The case of the Brazilian computer industry. *Technovation* 13 (6), 367–382.

Dercon, S. (2009). Rural poverty: Old challenges in new contexts. *The World Bank Research Observer* 24 (1), 1–28.

De Soto, H. (1989). *The Other Path*. New York, NY: Harper and Row.

Despot's Fall. (August 20, 1979). *Time Magazine*. http://content.time.com/time/magazine/article/0,9171,947351,00.html?promoid=googlep

Devlin, V. & Ffrench-Davis, R. (1995). The great Latin American debt crisis: A decade of asymmetric adjustment. *Poverty, Prosperity and the World Economy*.

Devlin, J. & Yap, N.T. (1994). Sustainable development and the NICs: Cautionary tales for the South in the New World (Dis)Order. *Third World Quarterly* 15 (1), 49–62.

Diamond, J. (1997). *Guns, Germs and Steel: The Fates of Human Societies*. New York, NY: W. W. Norton.

Dianga, J.W. (2002). *Kenya, 1982: The Attempted Coup*. London: Penn Press.

Dickenson, J., Gould, B., Clarke, C., Mather, C., Prothero, M., Siddle, D., Smith, C. & Thomas-Hope, E. (1996). *A Geography of the Third World* (2nd ed.). London: Routledge.

Dijkstra, G. (March 2011). What Did 18 Billion Dollar Achieve? The 2005 Debt Relief to Nigeria. 1–2.

Di John, J. (August 2010). The political economy of taxation and state resilience in Zambia since 1990. *Crisis States Working Papers* 2, 1–25.

Di Puppo, L. (2010). Police reform in Georgia. Cracks in an anti-corruption success story. *U4 Practice Insight* 2, 1–5.

Djalante, R., Holley, C. & Thomalla, F. (2011). Adaptive governance and managing resilience to natural hazards. *International Journal of Disaster Risk Science* 2 (4), 1–14.

Djankov, S., La Porta, R., Lopez-de-Silanes, F. & Shleifer, A. (2002). The regulation of entry. *Quarterly Journal of Economics*, 1–37.

Dollar, D. (2001). Globalization, Inequality, and Poverty since 1980. Background paper, World Bank, Washington, DC. Available at http://www.worldbank.org/research/global

Dollar, D., Fisman, R. & Gatti, R. (2001). Are women really the "fairer" sex? Corruption and women in government. *Journal of Economic Behavior & Organization* 46 (4), 423–429.

Dollar, D. & Kraay, A. (2002). Growth is good for the poor. *Journal of Economic Growth* 7 (3), 195–225.

Dollar, D. & Levin. V. (2005). Sowing and Reaping Institutional Quality and Project Outcomes in Developing Countries. *World Bank Policy Research Working Paper* 3524.

Doornbos, M. (2006). *Global Forces and State Restructuring. Dynamics of State Formation and Collapse*. Basingstoke: Palgrave.

Doornbos, M. (2002). State collapse and fresh starts: Some critical reflections. *Development and Change* 33 (5), 804.

Dorff, R.H. (1996). Democratization and failed states: The challenge of ungovernability. *Parameters* 26, 17–31.

Dornbusch, R. & Edwards, S. (April 1990). The macro-economic populism. *Journal of Development Economics* 32 (2).

Draibe, S.M. (2007). *Latin America: A New Developmental Welfare State Model in the Making?* Palgrave Macmillan.

Dreher, A. (2003). Does globalization affect growth. Evidence from a new index of globalization, forthcoming in *Applied Economics*.

Dreher, A. & Herzfeld, T. (2005). The Economic Costs of Corruption: A Survey and New Evidence. *Public Economics, 506001.* 1–33.

Driscoll, J. (October 18, 2008). Inside the Leviathan: Coup Proofing after State Failure. *Stanford University Working Paper.* 1–56.

Driscoll, W. & Clark, J. (2003). *Globalization and the Poor: Exploitation or Equalizer?* New York, NY: International Debate Education Association.

Drury, A.C., Krieckhaus, J. & Lusztig, M. (2006). Corruption, democracy, and economic growth. *International Political Science Review* 27 (2), 121–136.

Dupuy, A. (1976). Historical stages Spanish colonialism and the origin of underdevelopment in Haiti. *Latin American Perspectives* 3 (2), 5–29.

Durning, A.B. & Brough, H.B. (1991). Taking stock: animal farming and the environment. *Worldwatch Paper* 103, 64–67.

Easterly, W. (May 29, 2009). Geography Lessons: Correcting Sachs on African Economic Development. The Huffington Post. http://www.huffingtonpost.com

Easterly, W. (2005). The Rich Have Markets, the Poor Have Bureaucrats. In *Globalization: What's New*, edited by Michael Weinstein. Columbia University Press, 170–195.

Easterly, W. (Summer 2003). Can foreign aid buy growth? *Journal of Economic Perspectives* 17 (3), 23–48.

Easterly, W. (2002a). The cartel of good intentions: The problem of bureaucracy in foreign aid. *The Journal of Policy Reform* 5 (4), 223–250.

Easterly, W. (2002b). How did heavily indebted poor countries become heavily indebted? Reviewing two decades of debt relief. *World Development* 30 (10), 1677–1696.

Easterly, W. & Kraay A. (2000). Small states, small problems? Income, growth, and volatility in small states. *World Development* 28 (11), 2013–2027.

Easterly, W. & Levine, R. (1997). Africa's growth tragedy: Policies and ethnic divisions. *Quarterly Journal of Economics* 112, 1203–1250.

Easterly, W. & Pfutze, T. (2008). Where does the money go? Best and worst practices in foreign aid. *Journal of Economic Perspectives* 22(2).

The Economist. (May 19, 2012). African Child Mortality: The Best Story in Development.

The Economist. (2009). *Fighting Poverty in Emerging Markets: The Gloves Go On*, www.economist.com, date accessed 26 November 2009.

Education and Training Unit. http://www.etu.org.za/toolbox/docs/development/poverty.html

Edmonds, K. (2011). The Denial of Self-Determination: Haiti and the International Community. 1–5.

Edwards, M. & Hulme, D. (1996). Too close for comfort? The impact of official aid on non-governmental organizations. *World Development* 24 (6), 961–973.

Eigen, P. (2002). Measuring and combating corruption. *The Journal of Policy Reform* 5 (4), 187–201.

Eigen, P. (1996). Field reports: Combating corruption around the world. *Journal of Democracy* 7 (1), 158–168.

Elbadawi, I.A. (1997). Real Exchange Rate Policy and Export Competitiveness in Sub-Saharan Africa. Paper for the WIDER Project on Growth, External Sector and the Role of Non-traditional Exports in Sub-Saharan Africa. WIDER and African Economic Research Consortium, Nairobi.

Elbadawi, I., Ndulu, B. & Ndung'u, N. (1997). Debt Overhang and Economic Growth in Sub-Saharan Africa. In *External Finance for Low-Income Countries*, edited by Z. Iqbal & R. Kanbur. Washington, DC: IMF Institute, pp. 49–76.

Elliott, J. (2012). *An Introduction to Sustainable Development*. New York, NY: Routledge.

Ellner, S. (February 2003). The contrasting variants of the populism of Hugo Chávez and Alberto Fujimori. *Journal of Latin American Studies* 35 (1), 139–162.

Elwan, A. (1999). Poverty and disability: A survey of the literature. Social Protection Advisory Service.

EM-DAT database, 1900-1999.

Emedworld. http://www.emedworld.com/content.php?topic=Tuberculosis

Engerman, S.L. & Sokoloff, K.L. (2012). Five Hundred Years of European Colonization: Inequality and Paths of Development. *Settler Economies in World History.*

Engerman, S. & Sokoloff, K. (2002). Factor Endowments, Inequality, and Paths of Development among New World Economies. *NBER Working Paper* #9259, Cambridge, MA. 1–55.

Engerman, S.L. & Sokoloff, K.L. (1994). Factor Endowments: Institutions, and Differential Paths of Growth among New World Economies: A View from Economic Historians of the United States. 1–54.

Englebert, P. (2000). Pre-colonial institutions, post-colonial states, and economic development in tropical Africa. *Political Research Quarterly* 53 (1), 7–36.

Entwisle, B. & Winegarden, C.R. (1984). Fertility and pension programs in LDCs: A model of mutual reinforcement. *Economic Development and Cultural Change*, 331–354.

Esteban, J. & Ray, D. (1994). On the measurement of polarization. *Econometrica* 62 (4), 819–851.

Esterhuyse, H.W. (2012). A Comparative Study of Governance and State Development in Post-Colonial Botswana and Zaire/DRC. PhD diss., Stellenbosch: Stellenbosch University.

Esty, D.C., Goldstone, J.A., Gurr, T.R., Harff, B., Levy, M., Dabelko, G.D., Surko, P. & Unger, A.N. (July 31, 1998). State Failure Task Force Report: Phase II Findings.

Eswaran, M. (2006). *Fertility in Developing Countries. Understanding Poverty, Part 1.* 143–160.

Eswaran, M. (2002). The empowerment of women, fertility, and child mortality: Towards a theoretical analysis. *Journal of Population Economics* 15 (3), 433–454.

Eswaran, M. & Kotwal, A. (2006). The Role of Agriculture in Development. In *Understanding Poverty*, edited by A.V. Banerjee, R. Benabou & D. Mookherjee. Oxford University Press, 111–123.

European Network on Debt and Development. http://www.eurodad.org/Entries/view/1546154/2014/02/13/Foreign-investment-much-smaller-than-you-might-believe

Evans, P.B. (1995). *Embedded Autonomy: States and Industrial Transformation*. Princeton, NJ: Princeton University Press.

Evans, P.B. (1992). The State as Problem and Solution: Predation, Embedded Autonomy and Structural Change. In *Politics of Economic Development*, edited by S. Haggard & R.R. Kaufman. Princeton, NJ: Princeton University Press, 139–181.

Evans, P.B. (1989). Predatory, developmental, and other apparatuses: A comparative political economy perspective on the Third World State. *Sociological Forum* 4 (4), 561–587.

Evans, P.B. (1986). State, capital, and the transformation of dependence: The Brazilian computer case. *World Development* 14 (7), 791–808.

Evans, P. & Rauch, J. (1999). Bureaucracy and growth: A cross-national analysis of the effects of "Weberian" state structures on economic growth. *American Sociological Review* 64 (5), 748–765.

Ezrow, N.M. & Frantz, E. (2011). *Dictators and Dictatorships: Understanding Authoritarian Regimes and their Leaders*. New York, NY: Bloomsbury Publishing.

Fafchamps, M. & Pender, J. (1997). Precautionary saving, credit constraints, and irreversible investment: Theory and evidence from Semi-arid India. *Journal of Business & Economic Statistics* 15 (2), 180–194.

Fairbanks, C. (October 2001). Disillusionment in the Caucasus and Central Asia. *Journal of Democracy* 12 (4), 49–56.

Fairhead, J. (1992). Paths of authority: Roads, the state and the market in eastern Zaire. *The European Journal of Development Research* 4 (2), 17–35.

Fallon, P.R. & da Silva, L.A.P. (1994). *Recognizing Labor Market Constraints: Government-Donor Competition for Manpower in Mozambique. Rehabilitating Government: Pay and Employment Reform in Africa*. Washington, DC: The World Bank.

Fan, S., ed. (2008). *Public Expenditures, Growth, and Poverty: Lessons from Developing Countries* (Vol. 51). Intl Food Policy Res Inst.

Fan, S., Zhang, L. & Zhang, X. (2002). *Growth, Inequality, and Poverty in Rural China: The Role of Public Investments* (No. 125). Intl Food Policy Res Inst.

Farazmand, A. (2001). Globalization, the state and public administration: A theoretical analysis with policy implications for developmental states. *Public Organization Review* 1 (4), 437–463.

Farazmand, A. (November–December 1999). Globalization and public administration. *Public Administration Review* 59 (6), 509–522.

Farmer, P.E., Nutt, C.T., Wagner, C.M., Claude Sekabaraga, C., Nuthulaganti, T., Jonathan, L., Weigel, J.L. & Farmer, D.B. (2013). Reduced premature mortality in Rwanda: Lessons from success. *BMJ: British Medical Journal* 346.

Fassin, D. & Vasquez, P. (2005). Humanitarian exception as the rule: The political theology of the 1999 Tragedia in Venezuela. *American Ethnologist* 32 (3), 389–405.

Feachem, R. & Sabot, O. (2008). A new global malaria eradication strategy. *The Lancet* 371 (9624), 1633–1635.

Fearon, J.D. (2007). Iraq's civil war. *Foreign Affairs* 86, 2.

Fearon, J.D. (2004). Why do some civil wars last so much longer than others? *Journal of Peace Research* 41 (3), 275–301.

Fearon, J.D. & Laitin, D. (2010). Sons of the soil, migrants, and civil war. *World Development* 39 (2), 199–211.

Fedderke, J. & Klitgaard, R. (1998). Economic growth and social indicators: An exploratory analysis. *Economic Development and Cultural Change* 46 (3), 455–489.

Felbab-Brown, V. (2009). The violent drug market in Mexico and lessons from Colombia. Brookings Institution, 1–29.

Feld, L.P. & Voigt, S. (2003). Economic growth and judicial independence: Cross-country evidence using a new set of indicators. *European Journal of Political Economy* 19 (3), 497–527.

Feridhanusetyawan, T. (2004). *Escaping the Debt Trap.* Southeast Asian Affairs.

Fernández-Kelly, P. & Shefner, J. (2005). *Out of the Shadows: Political Action and the Informal Economy in Latin America.* University Park, PA: Penn State University Press.

Ferraro, V. & Rosser, M. (1994). Global Debt and Third World Development. In *World Security: Challenges for a New Century*, edited by M. Klare & D. Thomas. New York, NY: St. Martin's Press, 332–355.

Fields, G.S. (1980). *Poverty, Inequality, and Development.* CUP Archive.

Fillinger, U. & Lindsay, S.W. (2006). Suppression of exposure to malaria vectors by an order of magnitude using microbial Larvicides in rural Kenya. *Tropical Medicine & International Health* 11 (11), 1629–1642.

Fine, B. (July 2002). Globalisation and Development: The Imperative of Political Economy. In "Towards a New Political Economy of Development: Globalisation and Governance" Conference. Political Economy Research Centre (PERC), University of Sheffield.

Finkel, M. (July 2007). Malaria: Stopping a Global Killer. http://ngm.nationalgeographic.com/ngm/0707/feature1/text4.html

Fleming, M.H., Roman, J. & Farrell, G. (2000). The shadow economy. *Journal of International Affairs* 53 (2), 387–409.

Flug, K., Splilimbergo, A. & Wachtenheim, E. (1999). Investment in education: Do economic volatility and credit constraints matter? *Journal of Development Economics* 55, 465–481.

Fombad, C.M. (2001). The enhancement of good governance in Botswana: A critical assessment of the Ombudsman Act, 1995. *Journal of Southern African Studies* 27 (1), 57–77.

Food and Agriculture Organization of the United Nations: Economic and Social Development (FAO). Agricultural Censuses and Gender Considerations. http://www.fao.org/docrep/003/x2919e/x2919e04.htm

Forex. http://www.actionforex.com/articles-library/financial-glossary/asian-financial-crisis-20041204325/

Forsythe, S. (July 2002). *State of the Art: AIDS and Economics.* 1–129.

Fosu, A.K. (2010). The external debt-servicing constraint and public-expenditure composition in Sub-Saharan Africa. *African Development Review* 22 (3), 378–393.

Fosu, A.K. (2008). Implications of the external debt-servicing constraint for public health expenditure in sub-Saharan Africa. *Oxford Development Studies* 36 (4), 363–377.

Fosu, A.K. (2007). Fiscal allocation for education in sub-Saharan Africa: Implications of the external debt service constraint. *World Development* 35 (4), 702–713.

Fosu, A.K. (1999). The external debt burden and economic growth in the 1980s: Evidence from sub-Saharan Africa. *Canadian Journal of Development Studies/Revue canadienne d'études du développement* 20 (2), 307–318.

François, M. & Sud, I. (2006). Promoting stability and development in fragile and failed states. *Development Policy Review* 24 (2), 141–160.

Frank, A.G. (1969). *Capitalism and Underdevelopment in Latin America: Historical Studies of Chile and Brazil.* New York, NY: Monthly Review Press.

Frank, A.G. (1966). *The Development of Underdevelopment.* New England Free Press.

Franke, A., Gawrich, G. & Alakbarov, G. (2009). Kazakhstan and Azerbaijan as Post-Soviet Rentier States: Resource incomes and autocracy as a double "Curse" in Post-Soviet regimes. *Europe-Asia Studies* 61 (1), 109–140.

Frankel, J.A. & Romer, D. (1999). Does trade cause growth? *American Economic Review*, 379–399.

Frankema, E. & Masé, A. (2014). An Island drifting apart. Why Haiti is mired in poverty while the Dominican Republic forces ahead. *Journal of International Development* 26 (1), 128–148.

Frantz, E. & Kendall-Taylor, A. (2014). A dictator's toolkit understanding how co-optation affects repression in autocracies. *Journal of Peace Research*, 0022343313519808.

Fraser, J. & Oppenheim, J. (1997). What's new about globalization? *McKinsey Quarterly*, 168–179.

Friedman, M. (2009). *Capitalism and Freedom*. University of Chicago Press.

Friedman, T. (2000). *The Lexus and the Olive Tree*. London: HarperCollins.

Friedman, M. (1982). Monetary policy: Theory and practice. *Journal of Money, Credit and Banking*, 98–118.

Friedman, M. (1962). *Capitalism and Freedom*. Chicago: University of Chicago Press (Capitalisme et Liberté, Paris, Robert Laffont, 1971).

Frimpong, J.M. & Oteng-Abayie, E.F. (2006). The impact of external debt on economic growth in Ghana: A cointegration analysis. *Journal of Science and Technology (Ghana)* 26 (3), 122–131.

Fritz, V. & Menocal, A.R. (2007). Developmental states in the new millennium: Concepts and challenges for a new aid agenda. *Development Policy Review* 25 (5), 531–552.

Frontline. (June 1999). Public Broadcasting Service, Timeline of the Panic. http://www.pbs.org/wgbh/pages/frontline/shows/crash/etc/cron.html

Gachuhi, Debbie. (November 1999). The Impact of HIV/AIDS on Education Systems in the Eastern and Southern Africa Region and the Response of Education Systems to HIV/AIDS: Life Skills Programmes. UNICEF. 1–26.

Galbraith, J.K. (2012). *Inequality and Instability: A Study of the World Economy Just Before the Great Crisis*. Oxford: Oxford University Press.

Gallup, J.L., Sachs, J.D. & Mellinger, J.D. (1999). Geography and economic development. *International Regional Science Review* 22, 179.

Gallup, J.L. & Sachs, J.D. (2001). The economic burden of malaria. *The American Journal of Tropical Medicine and Hygiene* 64 (1), 85–96.

Gana, R.L. (1996). Prospects for developing countries under the TRIPS agreement. *Vand. J. Transnat'l L.* 29, 735.

Gandhi, J. (April 2008). Dictatorial institutions and their impact on economic growth. *European Journal of Sociology* 49 (1), 3–30.

Garrett, L. (2007). The challenge of global health. *Foreign Affairs*, 14–38.

Gawrick, A., Melnykovska, I. & Schweickert, R. (September 2011). More than Oil and Geography: Neo-patrimonialism as an Explanation of Bad Governance and Autocratic Stability in Central Asia. *Working Paper Series* 1.

Geda, Alemayehu (2002). Debt issues in Africa: Thinking beyond the HIPC initiative to solving structural problems, WIDER Discussion Papers//World Institute for Development Economics (UNU-WIDER) 35. 1–32.

Geddes, B. (September 2005). Why Parties and Elections in Authoritarian Regimes? In Paper Presented at the Annual Meeting of the American Political Science Association, Washington, DC.

Geddes, B. (2004). Minimum-Winning Coalitions and Personalization in Authoritarian Regimes. Working Paper.

Gelb, A.H. & Associates. (1988). *Oil Windfalls: Blessing or Curse?* New York, NY: Oxford University Press.

George, J.A. (2009). The dangers of reform: State building and national minorities in Georgia. *Central Asian Survey* 28 (2), 135–154.

George, S. (1993). Uses and Abuses of African Debt. Africa within the World: Beyond Dispossession and Dependence. 59–62.

George, S. (1992). The Debt Boomerang: How Third World Debt Harms us All. Trans-National Institute. http://www.tni.org/article/uses-and-abuses-african-debt

Gerschenkron, A. (1962). *Economic Backwardness in Historical Perspective, A Book of Essays*, Cambridge, MA: Belknap Press of Harvard University Press.

Ghani, A., Carnahan, M. & Lockhart, C. (September 2005). Closing the Sovereignty Gap: An Approach to State-Building. *Overseas Development Institute Working Paper* 253. 1–20.

Ghura, M.D. (1998). Tax Revenue in Sub-Saharan Africa-Effects of Economic Policies and Corruption (EPub) (No. 98-135). International Monetary Fund.

Gibson, C.C., Andersson, K. & Shivakumar, S. (2005). *The Samaritan's Dilemma: The Political Economy of Development Aid*. Oxford: Oxford University Press.

Giddens, A. (2002). *Runaway World: How Globalization Is Reshaping Our Lives*. Profile books.

Gini, C. (1921). Measurement of inequality of incomes. *The Economic Journal*, 31 (121), 124–126.

Girling, J. (Autumn 1984). Thailand in Gramscian perspective. *Pacific Affairs* 57 (3), 385–403.

Giustozzi, A. (September 2003). Respectable Warlords: The challenge of state building in post Taleban Afghanistan. *Crisis Research Center Working Paper* 33, 6.

Glaeser, E.L. & Goldin, C. (2004). Corruption and reform: An introduction (No. w10775). *National Bureau of Economic Research*. 1–25.

Glaeser, E.L., La Porta, R., Lopez-de-Silanes, F. & Shleifer, A. (2004). Do institutions cause growth?. *Journal of Economic Growth* 9 (3), 271–303.

Glinkina, S. (1999). Russia's Underground Economy during the Transition. In *Underground Economies in Transition: Unrecorded Activity, Tax Evasion, Corruption and Organized Crime*, edited by Edgar L. Feige and Katarina Ott. Brookfield, VT: Ashgate, 104.

Godnick, W., Muggah, R. & Waszink, C. (October 2002). Stray Bullets: The Impact of Small Arms Misuse in Central America. Occasional Paper 5.

Goel, R.K. & Nelson, M.A. (1998). Corruption and government size: A disaggregated analysis. *Public Choice* 97, 107–120.

Goesling, B. (October 2001). Changing income inequalities within and between nations: New evidence. *American Sociological Review* 66 (5), 745–761.

Goertzel, T.G. (1999). *Fernando Henrique Cardoso: Reinventing Democracy in Brazil*. Boulder, CO: Lynne Rienner Publishers.

Goetz, A.M. (1997). *Getting Institutions Right for Women in Development*. London: Zed Books.

Goldberg, P.K. & Pavcnik, N. (2004). Trade, Inequality, and Poverty: What Do We Know? Evidence from Recent Trade Liberalization Episodes in Developing Countries (No. w10593). *National Bureau of Economic Research*. 1–50.

Goldsmith, A.A. (2004). Predatory versus developmental rule in Africa. *Democratization* 11 (3). 88–110.

Goldsmith, A.A. (2001). Foreign aid and statehood in Africa. *International Organization* 55, 123–148.

Goldsmith, A.A. (1999). Africa's overgrown state reconsidered: Bureaucracy and economic growth. *World Politics* 51, 520–546.

Goldstein, J.L. (1987). Lifestyles of the rich and tyrannical. *The American Scholar*, 235–247.

Goldstone, J. (2008). Pathways to state failure. *Conflict Management and Peace Science* 25, 285–296.

Goldstone, J., Bates, R., Epstein, D., Gurr, T.R., Lustik, M.B., Marshall, M.G., Ulfelder, J. & Woodward, M.A. (2010). Global model for forecasting political instability. *American Journal of Political Science* 54 (1), 190–208.

Goodhand, J. (March 2003). Enduring disorder and persistent poverty: A review of the linkages. *World Development* 31 (3), 629–646.

Goodwin-Gill, G.S. (2006). *Free and Fair Elections*. Inter-Parliamentary Union.

Gorodnichenko, Y. & Peter, K.S. (2007). Public sector pay and corruption: Measuring bribery from micro data. *Journal of Public Economics* 91 (5–6), 963–991.

Gould, D.J. (1980). *Bureaucratic Corruption and Underdevelopment in the Third World: The Case of Zaire*. New York, NY: Pergamon Press.

Gould, D.J. & Amaro-Reyes, J.A. (1983). The effects of corruption on administrative performance: Illustrations from developing countries. *World Bank Staff Working Papers* 580 (7), 1–48.

Gray, L.C. & Moseley, W.G. (2005). A geographical perspective on poverty environment interactions. *The Geographical Journal* 171 (1), 9–23.

Green, R. (1994). The Course of the Four Horsemen: Costs of War and Its Aftermath in Sub-Saharan Africa. In *War and Hunger: Rethinking International Responses to Complex Emergencies*, edited by J. Macrae & A. Zwi. London: Zed Books.

Greene, J.E. & Khan, M.S. (1990). *The African Debt Crisis* (No. 3). Nairobi: Initiatives Publishers.

Grier, R.M. (1999). Colonial legacies and economic growth. *Public Choice* 98 (3–4), 317–335.

Gries, T., Krieger, T. & Meierrieks, D. (2011). Causal linkages between domestic terrorism and economic growth. *Defence and Peace Economics* 22 (5), 493–508.

Gros, J. (1996). Toward a taxonomy of failed states in the new world order: Decaying Somalia, Liberia, Rwanda and Haiti. *Third World Quarterly* 17 (3), 455–472.

Gross, R. & Webb, P. (2006). Wasting time for wasted children: Severe child under-nutrition must be resolved in non-emergency settings. *The Lancet* 367 (9517), 1209–1211.

Gupta, S., Davoodi, H. & Alonso-Terme, R. (2002). Does corruption affect income inequality and poverty? *Economics of Governance* 3 (1), 23–45.

Gurr, T., Marshall, M. & Khosla, D. (2001). *Peace and Conflict 2001. A Global Survey of Armed Conflicts, Self-Determination Movements and Democracy*. College Park, MD: Centre for International Development and Conflict Management, University of Maryland.

Gurtner, F.J. (2003). Currency boards and debt traps: Evidence from Argentina and relevance for Estonia. *The World Economy* 26 (2), 209–228.

Gyapong, J.O., Gyapong, M., Yellu, N., Anakwah, K., Amofah, G., Bockarie, M. & Adjei, S. (2010). Integration of control of neglected tropical diseases into health-care systems: Challenges and opportunities. *The Lancet* 375 (9709), 160–165.

Gyimah-Brempong, K. (2002). Corruption, economic growth, and income inequality in Africa. *Economics of Governance* 3 (3), 183–209.

Gylfason, T. (2001). Natural resources, education, and economic development. *European Economic Review* 45 (4), 847–859.

Gylfason, T., Herbertsson, T.T. & Zoega, G. (1999). A mixed blessing. *Macroeconomic Dynamics* 3 (2), 204–225.

Gylfason, T. & Zoega, G. (April 2002). Inequality and economic growth: Do natural resources matter? *CESifo Working Paper* 712 (5), 1–36.

Gysels, M., Pool, R. & Bwanika, K. (2001). Truck drivers, middlemen and commercial sex workers: AIDS and the mediation of sex in south west Uganda. *AIDS Care* 13 (3), 373–385.

Haggard, S. (1990). *Pathways from the Periphery: The Politics of Growth in the Newly Industrializing Countries*. Cornell University Press.

Haiti Earthquake. 2010. Geo Fact Sheet 285. http://livegeog.files.wordpress.com/2014/05/geofactsheet-haiti-earthquakes-management-two-years-on.pdf

Hall, G.H. & Patrinos, H.A., eds. (2012). *Indigenous Peoples, Poverty, and Development*. Cambridge University Press.

Hall, R. & Jones, C. (1999). Why do some countries produce so much more output per worker than others? *Quarterly Journal of Economics* 114, 83–116.

Hamilton, M.A. (1996). TRIPS agreement: Imperialistic, outdated, and overprotective. *Vand. J. Transnat'l L.* 29, 613.

Hanlon, J. (2000). Power without responsibility: The World Bank & Mozambican cashew nuts. *Review of African Political Economy* 27 (83), 29–45.

Hanlon, J. & Smart, T. (2008). *Do Bicycles Equal Development in Mozambique?* Martelsham: James Currey Publisher.

Haque, M.S. (2002). Globalization, new political economy, and governance: A third world viewpoint. *Administrative Theory & Praxis* 24 (1), 103–124.

Haque, M.S. (1999). The fate of sustainable development under neo-liberal regimes in developing countries. *International Political Science Review* 20 (2), 197–218.

Harris, N. (2003). *AIDS in Developing Countries*. Greenhaven Press.

Harris, R.G. (1993). Globalization, trade, and income. *Canadian Journal of Economics*, 755–776.

Harrison, A. (2006). Globalization and Poverty. No. w12347. National Bureau of Economic Research.

Harrison, D.H. (2003). *The Sociology of Modernization and Development*. New York, NY: Routledge.

Hartlyn, J. (1998). *The Struggle for Democratic Politics in the Dominican Republic*. Chapel Hill, NC: University of North Carolina Press.

Harvey, D. (2005). *A Brief History of Neoliberalism*. Oxford University Press.

Harvey, P. (2005). *Cash and Vouchers in Emergencies: A Discussion Paper*. London: Overseas Development Institute, Humanitarian Policy Group.

Hausmann, R. (2001). Prisoners of geography. *Foreign Policy*, 45–53.

Hawkins, J. (2012). *Earthquake Disasters*. New York, NY: Arcturus Publishing.

Hayami, Y. & Ruttan, V.W. (1971). *Agricultural Development: An International Perspective*. Baltimore, MD: The Johns Hopkins Press.

Hazell, P. & Haggblade, S. (1991). Rural-urban growth linkages in India. *Indian Journal of Agricultural Economics* 46 (4), 515–529.

Hearn, J. (2007). African NGOs: the new compradors?. *Development and Change* 38 (6), 1095–1110.

Hearn, J. (1998). The 'NGO-isation' of Kenyan society: USAID & the restructuring of health care. *Review of African Political Economy* 25 (75), 89–100.

Hegre, H., Ellingsen, T., Gates, S. & Gleditsch, N.P. (2001). Towards a democratic civil peace? *American Political Science Review* 95, 33–48.

Held, D., ed. (1999). *Global Transformations: Politics, Economics and Culture*. Palo Alto, CA: Stanford University Press.

Held, D. (1997). Democracy and globalization. *Global Governance* 3, 251–267.

Heldring, L. & Robinson, J. (2012). *Colonialism and Economic Development in Africa*. Cambridge, MA: National Bureau of Economic Research.

Hendrickson, D. (1999). A Review of Security-sector Reform. Conflict, Security and Development Group. Centre for Defence Studies. King's College, University of London.

Henry, C. & Stiglitz, J. (2010). Intellectual property, dissemination of innovation and sustainable development. *Journal of Global Policy* 1, 237–251.

Herbertsson, T.T., Skulladottir, M.G. & Zoega, G. (1999). Three Symptoms and a Cure: A Contribution to the Economics of the Dutch Disease. Working Paper No. W99:10, Institute of Economic Studies, University of Iceland.

Herbertsson, T.T. & Zoega, G. (1999). Trade surpluses and life-cycle saving behaviour. *Economics Letters* 65 (2), 227–237.

Herbst, J. (2000). *States and Power in Africa: Comparative Lessons in Authority and Control*. Princeton, NJ: Princeton University Press.

Herd, R. & Dougherty, S. (2007). Growth prospects in China and India compared. *The European Journal of Comparative Economics* 4 (1), 65–89.

Herrick, J.E. (2000). Soil quality: An indicator of sustainable land management? *Applied Soil Ecology* 15 (1), 75–83.

Hertz, E., Hebert, J.R. & Landon, J. (1994). Social and environmental factors and life expectancy, infant mortality, and maternal mortality rates: Results of a cross-national comparison. *Social Science & Medicine* 39 (1), 105–114.

Heshmati, A. (2005). The Relationship between Income Inequality, Poverty, and Globalization. No. 2005/37. Research Paper, UNU-WIDER, United Nations University (UNU).

Hewko, J. (2002). Foreign direct investment in transitional economies: Does the rule of law matter. *E. Eur. Const. Rev.* 11, 71.

Hiatt, S.W., ed. (2007). *A Game as Old as Empire: The Secret World of Economic Hit Men and the Web of Global Corruption*. San Francisco, CA: Berrett-Koehler Publishers.

Hochschild, A. (1998). *King Leopold's Ghost: A Story of Greed, Terror, and Heroism in Colonial Africa*. Boston, MA: Houghton Mifflin.

Hochstetler, K. (2006). Rethinking presidentialism: Challenges and presidential falls in South America. *Comparative Politics*, 401–418.

Hodgson, G.M. (March 2006). What are institutions? *Journal of Economic Issues* 60 (1), 1–25.

Hoeckel, K. (2011). Beyond Beirut: Why Reconstruction in Lebanon Did Not Contribute to State-making and Stability. *Crisis States Research Centre*. 1–19.

Höckel, K. (July 2007). Beyond Beirut: Why reconstruction in Lebanon did not contribute to state-making and stability. *Crisis States Research Centre* 1–19.

Hoeffler, A. (2012). On the Causes of Civil War. In *The Oxford Handbook of the Economics of Peace and Conflict*, edited by Michelle R. Garfinkel & S. Skaperdas. Oxford: Oxford University Press.

Hoff, K. & Stiglitz, J. (November 2005). The Creation of the Rule of Law and the Legitimacy of Property Rights: The Political and Economic Consequences of a Corrupt Privatization. *National Bureau of Economic Research Working Paper* 11772. 1–51.

Hofman, A.A. (2000). Economic Growth and Performance in Latin America. 1–43.

Holmberg, S. & Rothstein, B. (2011). Dying of corruption. *Health Economics, Policy and Law* 6 (4), 529–547.

Hopwood, B., Mellor, M. & O'Brien, G. (2005). Sustainable development: Mapping different approaches. *Sustainable Development* 13 (1), 38–52.

Hornbeck, J.F. (2010). *Argentina's Defaulted Sovereign Debt: Dealing with The "Holdouts"*. DIANE Publishing.

Horowitz, D. (1985). *Ethnic Groups in Conflict*. Berkeley, CA: University of California Press.

Hotez, P.J., Molyneux, D.H., Fenwick, A., Ottesen, E., Sachs, S.E. & Sachs, J.D. (2006). Incorporating a rapid-impact package for neglected tropical diseases with programs for HIV/AIDS, tuberculosis, and malaria. *PLoS Medicine* 3 (5), 102.

Howe, H.M. (2001). *Ambiguous Order: Military Forces in African States*. Boulder, CO: Lynne Rienner Publishers.

Hrituleac, A. (December 2001). The Effects of Colonialism on African Economic Development. Aarhus University. 1–77.

Huang, Q., Rozelle, S., Lohmar, B., Huang, J. & Wang, J. (2006). Irrigation, agricultural performance and poverty reduction in China. *Food Policy* 31 (1), 30–52.

Hulme, D. (March 2003). Chronic poverty and development policy: An introduction. *World Development* 31 (3), 399–402.

Hulme, D. & Shepherd, A. (2003). Conceptualizing chronic poverty. *World Development* 31 (3), 403–423.

Huntington, S.P. (1996). *The Clash of Civilizations and the Remaking of World Order.* Penguin Books.

Huntington, S.P. (1991). *The Third Wave: Democratization in the Late 20th Century.* Norman, OK: University of Oklahoma Press.

Huntington, S.P. (1968). *Political Order in Changing Societies.* New Haven, CT: Yale University Press.

Huntington, S.P. (1957). *The Solider and the State: The Theory and Politics of Civil-Military Relations.* Cambridge, MA: Harvard University Press.

Hurtado, P. & Benson, D. (March 28th, 2012). Argentine Funds Can't Be Seized by Bond Holders, Judge Says. Bloomberg News. http://www.bloomberg.com/news/2012-03-28/u-s-judge-vacates-2-2-billion-order-in-argentine-bond-case.html

Husain, A.M.M., ed. (1998). *Poverty Alleviation and Empowerment: The Second Impact Assessment Study of BRAC's Rural Development Program.* Dhaka: Bangladesh Rural Advancement Committee.

Hutchcroft, P.D. (April 1991). Oligarchs and Cronies in the Philippine State: The politics of patrimonial plunder. *World Politics: A Quarterly Journal of International Relations* 43 (3), 414–450.

Hutchful, E. (1997). Military policy and reform in Ghana. *The Journal of Modern African Studies* 35 (2), 251–278.

Hydén, G., Court, J. & Mease, K. (July 2003). The bureaucracy and governance in 16 developing countries. *World Governance Survey Discussion Paper* 7, 1–27.

Ibhawoh, B. & Dibua, J.I. (2003). Deconstructing Ujamaa: The legacy of Julius Nyerere in the Quest for social and economic development in Africa. *African Journal of Political Science* 8 (1), 59–83.

Ignatieff, M. (Winter 2002). Intervention and state failure. *Dissent* 49 (1), 114–123.

Ijeoma, N.B. (2014). An empirical analysis of the impact of debt on the Nigerian economy. *AFRREV IJAH: An International Journal of Arts and Humanities* 2 (3), 165–191.

Illife, J. (2006). *The African AIDS Epidemic: A History.* Athens, OH: Ohio University Press; Oxford: James Currey; Cape Town: Double Storey Publishers.

IMF. (2013). Factsheet: Debt Relief under the Heavily Indebted Poor Countries (HIPC) Initiative - accessed January 13, 2010. http://www.imf.org/external/np/exr/facts/hipc.htm

IMF (International Monetary Fund). (2009). *Regional Economic Outlook: Sub-Saharan Africa – Weathering the Storm.* Washington, DC: IMF.

Indrawati, S.M. (May 16, 2013). Op-ed: No end to poverty without better governance. http://www.worldbank.org/en/news/opinion/2013/05/16/op-ed-no-end-to-poverty-without-better-governance

Isham, J. & Kaufman, D. (1999). The forgotten rationale for policy reform: The productivity of investment projects. *Quarterly Journal of Economics* 114 (1), 149–184.

Isham, J., Woolcock, M., Pritchett, L. & Busby, G. (September 28, 2005). The varieties of resource experience: Natural resource export structures and the political economy of economic growth. *The World Bank Economic Review* 19 (2), 141–174.

Islam, N. (1989). Colonial legacy, administrative reform and politics: Pakistan 1947–1987. *Public Administration and Development* 9 (1989), 271–285.

Islam, R., Banerji, A., Cull, R., Demirguc-Kunt, A., Djankov, S., Dyck, A., Kraay, A., McLiesh, C., Pittman, R. (2002). *World Development Report 2002: Building Institutions for Markets.* World Development Report. Washington, DC : World Bank Group.

Janowitz, M. (1988). *Military Institutions and Coercion in the Developing Nations: The Military in the Political Development of New Nations.* Chicago, IL: University of Chicago Press.

Jaquette, J.S. & Wolchik, S.L., eds. (1998). *Women and Democracy: Latin America and Central and Eastern Europe.* JHU Press.

Jenne, E.K. (2007). *Ethnic Bargaining: The Paradox of Minority Empowerment.* Ithaca, NY: Cornell University Press.

Jenne, E.K., Saideman, S.M. & Lowe, W. (2007). Separatism as a bargaining posture: The role of leverage in minority radicalization. *Journal of Peace Research* 44 (5), 539–558.

Johnson, C. (1982). *MITI and the Japanese Miracle: The Growth of Industrial Policy, 1925-1975*. Stanford, CA: Stanford University Press.

Johnson, S., Kaufmann, D. & Zoido-Lobatón, P. (1998). Regulatory discretion and the unofficial economy. *American Economic Review* 88 (2), 387–392.

Johnston, B.F. & Mellor, J.W. (September 1961). The role of agriculture in economic development. *American Economic Review* 51 (4), 566–593.

Johnston, M. (1996). The search for definitions: The vitality of politics and the issue of corruption. *International Social Science Journal* 48 (149), 321–335.

Jones, B. & Chandran, R. (2008). *Concepts and Dilemmas of State Building in Fragile Situations: From Fragility to Resilience*. Paris: Organization for Economic Cooperation and Development.

Jones, P. (2013). History matters: New evidence on the long run impact of colonial rule on institutions. *Journal of Comparative Economics* 41, 181–200.

Jorgenson, A.K. & Kick, E.L. (2003). Globalization and the environment. *Journal of World-Systems Research* 9 (2), 195–203.

Kahn, M.E. (2005). The death toll from natural disasters: The role of income, geography, and institutions. *Review of Economics and Statistics* 87 (2), 271–284.

Kaldor, N. (1963). Taxation for economic development. *The Journal of Modern African Studies* 1 (1), 7–23.

Kanbur, Ravi. (2000). Aid, Conditionality and Debt in Africa. Foreign Aid and Development: Lessons Learnt and Directions for the Future. 409–422.

Kaplan, S. (2008). *Fixing Fragile States: A New Paradigm for Development*. London: Praeger.

Karl, T.L. (1997). *The Paradox of Plenty: Oil Booms and Petro-States* (Vol. 26). Berkeley, CA: University of California Press.

Karras, G. (2006). Foreign aid and long-run economic growth: Empirical evidence for a panel of developing countries. *Journal of International Development* 7 (18), 15–28.

Kaufmann, D. (2004). Governance Redux: The Empirical Challenge. Chapter in Global Competitiveness Report 2003-2004. In World Economic Forum.

Kaufmann, D., Kraay, A. & Mastruzzi, M. (2010). The Worldwide Governance Indicators: A Summary of Methodology, Data and Analytical Issues. World Bank Policy Research Working Paper, 5430.

Kauffman, D., Kraay, A. & Zoido-Lobatón (1999). *Governance Matters*. World Bank Policy Working Paper No. 2196. Washington, DC: World Bank.

Keefer, P. & Knack, S. (1997). Why don't poor countries catch up? A cross-national test of an institutional explanation. *Economic Inquiry* 35 (3), 590–602.

Keet, C.M. (2002). Agriculture and Development. Transcript of Presentation. University of Limerick, 2002.

Kennemore, A. & Weeks, G. (2011). Twenty-first century socialism? The elusive search for a post-neoliberal development model in Bolivia and Ecuador. *Bulletin of Latin American Research* 30 (3), 267–281.

Khan, M.M. (1998). Political and administrative corruption: Concepts, comparative experiences and Bangladesh case. *Transparency International*, 1–20.

Killeen, G.F., Fillinger, U., Kiche, I., Gouagna, L.C. & Knols, B.G. (2002). Eradication of Anopheles gambiae from Brazil: Lessons for malaria control in Africa? *The Lancet Infectious Diseases* 2 (10), 618–627.

Kirkpatrick, C. & Barrientos, A. (2004). *The Lewis Model after Fifty Years*, no. 30550. University of Manchester, Institute for Development Policy and Management (IDPM).

Kissinger, H. (October 12, 1999). Lecture delivered at Trinity College Dublin.

Knack, S. & Keefer, P. (1995). Institutions and economic performance: Cross-country tests using alternative institutional measures. *Economics and Politics* 7 (3), 207–228.

Knack, S. & Rahman, A. (2007). Donor fragmentation and bureaucratic quality in aid recipients. *Journal of Development Economics* 83 (1), 176–197.

Kobasa, P.A. (2008). *Library of Natural Disasters-Hurricanes, Typhoons, and Other Tropical Cyclones*. World Book. Chicago Press.

Kohli, A. (2004). *State-Directed Development: Political Power and Industrialization in the Global Periphery*, Cambridge: Cambridge University Press.

Kolstad, I. & Wiig, A. (2009). Is transparency the key to reducing corruption in resource-rich countries? *World Development* 37 (3), 521–532.

Koonings, K. & Kruijt, D. (2004). *Armed Actors: Organized Violence and State Failure in Latin America*. London: Zed Books.

Korten, D.C. (2001). *When Corporations Rule the World*. Bloomfield, CT: Berret-Keohler Publishers.

Kouzmin, A. & Hayne, A., eds. (1999a). *Essays in Economic Globalization, Transnational Policies and Vulnerability* (Vol. 9). IOS Press.

Kouzmin, A. & Hayne, A. (1999b). Globalization: Rhetorical trends and unpalatable realities for public sectors. *Essays in Economic Globalization, Trans-National Policies and Vulnerability*, 1–12.

Kramer, J.J. (August 1997). Political corruption in post-Communist Russia: The case for democratization. In XVIIth World Congress of International Political Science Association (IPSA) held in Seoul, Korea on August (pp. 17–21).

Krasner, S.D. (2011). Review article: Foreign aid: Competing paradigms. *Journal of Intervention and Statebuilding* 5 (2), 123–149.

Krasner, S.D. (1984). Approaches to the State: Alternative Conceptions and Historical Dynamics.

Kremer, M. & Jayachandran, S. (2002). Odious debt (No. w8953). *National Bureau of Economic Research*. 1–44.

Krueger, A.B. & Malečková, J. (2003). Education, poverty and terrorism: Is there a causal connection? *The Journal of Economic Perspectives* 17 (4), 119–144.

Krugman, P. (1988). Financing vs. forgiving a debt overhang. *Journal of Development Economics* 29 (3), 253–268.

Krumm, K.L. (1985). *The External Debt of Sub-Saharan Africa: Origins, Magnitude, and Implications for Action*. Washington, DC: World Bank.

Kudamatsu, M. (2009). Ethnic Favoritism: Micro Evidence from Guinea. 1–36.

Kukhianidze, A. (2009). Corruption and organized crime in Georgia before and after the "rose revolution". *Central Asian Survey* 28 (2), 215–234.

Kumar, V., Abbas, A.K., Fausto, N. & Mitchell, R.N. (2007). *Robbins Basic Pathology* (8th ed.). Saunders Elsevier, 516–522.

Kurer, O. (2005). Corruption: An alternative approach to its definition and measurement. *Political Studies* 53 (1), 222–239.

Kuznets, S. (March 1955). Economic growth and income inequality. *American Economic Review* 45, 1–28.

Lal, D. (1983). *The Poverty of "Development Economics"*. London, UK: Institute of Economic Affairs.

Landes, D.S. (1999). *The Wealth and Poverty of Nations: Why Some Are So Rich and Some So Poor*. WW Norton & Company.

Lange, M. (June 2004). British colonial legacies and political development original research. *World Development* 32 (6), 905–922.

Lange, M., Mahoney, J. & Vom Hau, M. (2006). Colonialism and development: A comparative analysis of Spanish and British colonies. *American Journal of Sociology* 111 (5), 1412–1462.

La Porta, R., Lopez-de-Silanes, F., Shleifer, A. & Vishny, R. (1998). Law and finance. *Journal of Political Economy* 106, 1113–1155.

La Porta, R., Lopez-de-Silanes, F., Shleifer, A. & Vishny, R. (1999). The quality of government. *Journal of Law, Economics, and Organization* 15, 445–470.

Larrea, C. (2006). Neoliberal Policies and Social Development in Latin America: The Case of Ecuador. In *Congress of Social Sciences and Humanities*. New York, NY: CERLAC.

Larsson, T. (2001). *Race to the Top: The Real Story of Globalization*. Cato Institute.

Lau, L.J., Qian, Y. & Roland, G. (2000). Reform without losers: An interpretation of China's dual-track approach to transition. *Journal of Political Economy* 108 (1), 120–143.

Lawn, S.D. & Zumla, A.I. (July 2, 2011). Tuberculosis. *The Lancet* 378 (9785), 57–72.

Le Billion, P. (2005). *Geopolitics of Resource Wars: Resource Dependence, Governance and Violence*. London: Frank Cass.

Lederman, D., Loayza, N.V. & Soares, R.R. (2005). Accountability and corruption: Political institutions matter. *Economics & Politics* 17 (1), 1–35.

Lee, T. (October 2005). Military cohesion and regime maintenance: Explaining the role of the military in 1989 China and 1998 Indonesia. *Armed Forces & Society* 32 (1), 80–104.

Lee, Y.C.A., Tang, C.S., Ang, L.W., Han, H.K., James, L. & Goh, K.T. (2009). Epidemiological characteristics of imported and locally-acquired malaria in Singapore. *Annals Academy of Medicine* Singapore 38(10), 840–849.

Leftwich, A. (2006). What are institutions? *IPPG Briefing* 1, 1–4.

Leftwich, A. (2000). *States of Development: On the Primacy of Politics in Development*. Cambridge: Polity.

Leftwich, A. (1994). Governance, the state and the politics of development. *Development and Change* 25 (2), 363–386.

Lehoucq, F. & Pérez-Liñán, A. (2014). Breaking out of the coup trap political competition and military coups in Latin America. *Comparative Political Studies* 47 (8), 1105–1129.

Lele, S.M. (1991). Sustainable development: A critical review. *World Development* 19 (6), 607–621.

Lemarchand, R. (1972). Political clientelism and ethnicity in tropical Africa: Competing solidarities in nation-building. *The American Political Science Review*, 68–90.

Lenski, G.E. & Lenski, J. (1987). *Human Societies: An Introduction to Sociology*. New York, NY: McGraw Hill, Inc.

Leon, G. (February 2012). Loyalty for Sale? Military Spending and Coups d' Etat. CWPE 1209. 1–49.

Leslie, W.J. (1987). *The World Bank and Structural Transformation in Developing Countries: The Case of Zaire*, Boulder, CO: Lynne Rienner Publishers.

Levin, M. & Satarov, G. (2000). Corruption and institutions in Russia. *European Journal of Political Economy* 16 (1), 113–132.

Levinson, M. (2010). *The Box: How the Shipping Container Made the World Smaller and the World Economy Bigger*. Princeton, NJ: Princeton University Press.

Levinson, M. (2008). Freight pain: The rise and fall of globalization. *Foreign Affairs*, 133–140.

Lewis, M. (2006). *Governance and Corruption in Public Health Care Systems (No. 78)*. Washington, DC: Center for Global Development.

Lewis, A. (1955). *The Theory of Economic Growth*. Homewood, IL: R.D. Irwin.

Light, M. (2014). Police reforms in the Republic of Georgia: The convergence of domestic and foreign policy in an anti-corruption drive. *Policing and Society* 24 (3), 318–345.

Lim, J.A. (2004). Macroeconomic Implications of the Southeast Asian Crises. After the Storm: Crisis, Recovery and Sustaining Development in Four Asian Economies. In *After the Storm: Crisis, Recovery and Sustaining Development in Four Asian Economies*, edited by J.K. Sundaram. NUS Press, 40–74.

Limongi Neto, F.P., Cheibub, J.A., Alvarez, M.M. & Przeworski, A. (1996). What makes democracies endure? *Journal of Democracy* 7 (1), 39–55.

Lindert, P.H. & Williamson, J.G. (2001). *Globalization and Inequality: A Long History*. World Bank.

Linz, J.J. & Stepan, A. (1996). *Problems of Democratic Consolidation*. Baltimore, MD: Johns Hopkins University Press.

Lipset, S.M. (1963). *Political Man: The Social Bases of Politics* (Vol. 330). Garden City, NY: Doubleday.

Lipset, S.M. & Lenz, G.S. (2000). Corruption, Culture, and Markets. In *Culture Matters: How Values Shape Human Progress*, edited by L.E. Harrison & S.P. Huntington. Basic Books, 112.

Lipton, M. (1977). *Why Poor People Stay Poor: A Study of Urban Bias in World Development*. London: Temple Smith.

LoGerfo, J. & King, D. (1996). Thailand: Toward democratic stability. *Journal of Democracy* 7 (1), 102–117.

Logie, D.E., Rowson, M. & Ndagije, F. (2008). Innovations in Rwanda's health system: Looking to the future. *The Lancet* 372 (9634), 256–261.

Londegran, J. & Poole, K. (1990). Poverty, the coup trap and the seizure of executive power. *World Politics* 92, 1–24.

López-Calva, L.F. & Lustig, N., eds. (2010). *Declining Inequality in Latin America: A Decade of Progress?* Brookings Institution Press.

Lovejoy, P.E., ed. (2000). *Identity in the Shadow of Slavery*. New York, NY: Bloomsbury Publishing.

Lucas, A.M. (2010). Malaria eradication and educational attainment: Evidence from Paraguay and Sri Lanka. *American Economic Journal. Applied Economics* 2 (2), 46.

Lundahl, M. (1997). Inside the predatory state: The rationale, methods, and economic consequences of kleptocratic regimes. *Nordic Journal of Political Economy* 24, 31–50.

Luttwak, E. (1979). *Coup d'etat*. Wildwood House.

MacDonald, B. (1997). *Military Spending in Developing Countries*. Montreal, QC: McGill Queen University Press.

MacGaffey, J. (1991). *The Real Economy of Zaire: The Contribution of Smuggling & Other Unofficial Activities to National Wealth.* University of Pennsylvania Press.

Machethe, C.L. (October 2004). Agriculture and Poverty in South Africa: Can agriculture Reduce Poverty. Paper presented at the Overcoming Underdevelopment Conference held in Pretoria.

Macintyre, B. (2010). The Fault Line in Haiti Runs Straight to France. *The Sunday Times*, 21.

Magaloni, B. (2006). *Voting for Autocracy.* New York, NY: Cambridge University Press.

Magnussen, L., Ehiri, J. & Jolly, P. (2004). Comprehensive versus selective primary health care: Lessons for global health policy. *Health Affairs* 23 (3), 167–176.

Malan, M., Rakate, P. & McIntyre, A. (2002). *Peacekeeping in Sierra Leone: UNAMSIL Hits the Home Straight* (Vol. 68). Pretoria: Institute for Security Studies.

Malaney, P., Spielman, A. & Sachs, J. (2004). The malaria gap. *The American Journal of Tropical Medicine and Hygiene* 71 (2), 141–146.

Marinov, N. & Goemans, H. (2013). Coups and democracy. *British Journal of Political Science*, 1–27.

Marti, J. & Ernst, G.J. (eds). (2005). *Volcanoes and the Environment.* Cambridge: Cambridge University Press.

Martinussen, J.D. (1997). *Society, States and Market: A Guide to Competing Theories of Development.* London: Zed Kooks Ltd.

Matshediso, I.B. (2005). A review of mineral development and investment policies of Botswana. *Resources Policy* 30 (3), 203–207.

Marx, K. (1875a). Manifesto of the Communist Party (1848), "Preface" to the Contribution to the Critique of Political Economy (1859). *Critique of the Gotha Programme.*

Marx, K. (1875b). Part I. *Critique of the Gotha Program.*

Marx, K. & Engels, F. (1848). *The Communist Manifesto.*

Matin, I. & Hulme, D. (March 2003). Programs for the poorest: Learning from the IGVGD Program Bangladesh. *World Development* 31 (3), 647–665.

Maurer, N. & Yu, C. (2010). *The Big Ditch: How America Took, Built, Ran, and Ultimately Gave Away the Panama Canal.* Princeton University Press.

Mauro, P. (1998). Corruption and the composition of government expenditure. *Journal of Public economics* 69 (2), 263–279.

Mauro, P. (1995). Corruption and growth. *Quarterly Journal of Economics* 110, 681–712.

Mayer, J. (2000). Globalization, technology transfer and skill accumulation in low-income countries. *Globalization, Marginalization and Development.*

McGowan, P.J. (2003). African military coups d'état, 1956–2001: Frequency, trends and distribution. *The Journal of Modern African Studies* 41 (3), 339–370.

McGowan, P. & Johnson, T.H. (1986). Sixty coups in thirty years-Further evidence regarding African military coups d'État. *The Journal of Modern African Studies* 24 (3), 539–546.

McIntyre, D., Thiede, M., Dahlgren, G. & Whitehead, M. (2006). What are the economic consequences for households of illness and of paying for health care in low-and middle-income country contexts? *Social Science & Medicine* 62 (4), 858–865.

McMillan, M., Rodrik, D. & Welch, K.H. (2002). When Economic Reform Goes Wrong: Cashews in Mozambique (No. w9117). National Bureau of Economic Research. 1–69.

Mehta, A.K. & Shah, A. (March 2003). Chronic poverty in India: Incidence, causes and policies. *World Development* 31 (3), 491–511.

Meier, G.M. & Stiglitz, J.E., eds. (2001). *Frontiers of Development Economics: The Future in Perspective.* World Bank Publications.

Mellor, J.W. (1999). Pro-poor Growth: The Relation between Growth in Agriculture and Poverty Reduction. Prepared for USAID/G/EGAD. http://agronor.org/Mellor1.htm

Meredith, M. (2005). *The State of Africa: A History of Fifty Years of Independence.* London: Free Press.

Messick, R.E. (1999). Judicial reform and economic development: A survey of the issues. *The World Bank Research Observer* 14 (1), 117–136.

Mezey, M.L. (March 1973). The 1971 coup in Thailand: Understanding why the legislature fails. *Asian Survey* 13 (3), 306–317.

Midgley, J. (2014). *Social Development: Theory and Practice.* London: Sage Publications.

Mikesell, R.F. (1997). Explaining the resource curse, with special reference to mineral-exporting countries. *Resources Policy* 23 (4), 191–199.

Milanovic, B. (2002). Can We Discern the Effect of Globalization on Income Distribution? World Bank, Poverty Team, Development Research Group.

Milliken, J. & Krause, K. (2002). State failure, state collapse, and state reconstruction: Concepts, lessons and strategies. *Development and Change* 33 (5), 753–774.

Mills, A., Brugha, R., Hanson, K. & McPake, B. (2002). What can be done about the private health sector in low-income countries? *Bulletin of the World Health Organization* 80 (4), 325–330.

Milman, C. & Lundstedt, S.B. (1994). Privatizing state owned enterprises in Latin America: A research agenda. *International Journal of Public Administration* 17 (9), 1663–1677.

Mitra, S. (May 2005). Disability and social safety nets in developing countries. World Bank 509. 1–45.

Mitra, S., Pošarac, A. & Vick, B. (2011). *Disability and Poverty in Developing Countries: A Snapshot from the World Health Survey.* World Bank.

Mittelman, J.H. (1995). Rethinking the international division of labour in the context of globalisation. *Third World Quarterly* 16 (2), 273–296.

Mo, P.J. (2001). Corruption and economic growth. *Journal of Comparative Economics* 29, 66–79.

Montalvo, J. & Ravallion, M. (2009). The Pattern of Growth and Poverty Reduction in China. *Policy Research Working Paper* 5069, The World Bank.

Montero Llácer, F.J. (2005). Panama canal management. *Marine Policy* 29 (1), 25–37.

Moore, B. (1966). *Social Origins of Dictatorship and Democracy: Lord and Peasant in the Making of the Modern World.* Boston, MA: Beacon Press.

Moore, D. (1999). 'Sail on, O Ship of state': Neo-liberalism, globalisation and the governance of Africa. *The Journal of Peasant Studies* 27 (1), 61–96.

Moore, M. (2004). Revenues, state formation, and the quality of governance in developing countries. *International Political Science Review* 25 (3), 297–319.

Moore, M. (2001). Political underdevelopment: What causes bad governance? *Public Management Review* 3 (3), 385–418.

Moore, S. & Buscaglia, E. (1999). *Judicial Corruption in Developing Countries: Its Causes and Economic Consequences,* 88. Stanford, CA: Hoover Institute Press.

Morrison, D.G. & Stevenson, H.M. (1971). Political instability in independent black Africa: More dimensions of conflict behavior within nations. *Journal of Conflict Resolution,* 347–368.

Morrissey, O. (2001). Does aid increase growth?. *Progress in Development Studies* 1 (1), 37–50.

Moser, C.O. (1989). Gender planning in the Third World: Meeting practical and strategic gender needs. *World Development* 17 (11), 1799–1825.

Moss, T., Pettersson, G. & Van de Walle, N. (2006). An Aid-Institutions Paradox? A Review Essay on Aid Dependency and State Building in Sub-Saharan Africa 74.

Moustafa, T. (2003). Law versus the state: The judicialization of politics in Egypt. *Law & Social Inquiry* 28 (4), 883–930.

Moyo, D. (2009). *Dead Aid: Why Aid Is Not Working and How There Is a Better Way for Africa.* New York, NY: Macmillan.

Muller, E. & Seligson, M. (1987). Inequality and insurgency. *American Political Science Review* 81 (2), 425–452.

Murshed, M., ed. (2002). *Globalization, Marginalization and Development.* Routledge.

Mussa, M. (2002). *Argentina and the Fund: From Triumph to Tragedy.* Peterson Institute.

Musungu, S.F. & Oh, C. (August 2005). The Use of Flexibilities in TRIPS by Developing Countries: Can They Promote Access to Medicines? Commission on Intellectual Property Rights, Innovation and Public Health (CIPIH).

Mutero, C.M., McCartney, M., Boelee, E., Hawkes, C. & Ruel, M.T. (May 2006). Understanding the links between agriculture and health. Understanding the links between agriculture and health. *International Food Policy Research Institute* (IFPRI) 13 (6), 1–2.

Myrdal, G. (1970). The Soft State in Underdeveloped Countries. In *Unfashionable Economics: Essays in Honour of Lord Balogh,* edited by P. Streeten. London: Weidenfeld and Nicolson, 227–243.

Naim, M. (2000). Washington consensus or Washington confusion? *Foreign Policy,* 87–103.

Nasuti, P. (2011). The Determinants of Anti-Corruption Reform in the Republic of Georgia. 1–4.

National Geographic. http://www.nationalgeographic.com/features/04/forcesofnature/resources/

NationalMedia.http://www.nationmultimedia.com/breakingnews/Abhisit-apologises-for-failing-to-protect-democrac-30234577.html

National Public Radio. http://www.npr.org/templates/story/story.php?storyId=15691309

Nayyar, D. (2003). *Globalization and Development. Rethinking Development Economics.* London: Amthem Press.

Ndikumana, L. & Boyce, J. (1998). Congo's odious debt: External borrowing and capital flight in Zaire. *Development and Change* 29 (2), 195–217.

N'Diaye, B. (2005). Mauritania, August 2005: Justice and democracy, or just another coup? *African Affairs* 105 (420), 421–441.

Ndulu, B.J. & Mutalemwa, C.K. (2002). *Tanzania at the Turn of the Century: Background Papers and Statistics.* Washington, DC: World Bank.

Needler, M.C. (1975). Military motivations in the seizure of power. *Latin American Research Review*, 63–79.

Neher, C.D. (July 1992). Political succession in Thailand. *Asian Survey* 32 (7), 585–605.

Neher, C.D. (Summer 1970). Constitutionalism and elections in Thailand. *Pacific Affairs* 43 (2), 240–257.

Neuman, W. (February 17, 2013). President Correa handily wins re-election in Ecuador. *New York Times.* http://www.nytimes.com/2013/02/18/world/americas/rafael-correa-wins-re-election-in-ecuador.html?_r=0

Newman, B.A. & Thomson, R.J. (1989). Economic growth and social development: A longitudinal analysis of causal priority. *World Development* 17 (4), 461–471.

New York Times. (September 18, 1989) p. DI.

Nissanke, M. & Thorbecke, E. (2007). Linking Globalization to Poverty. United Nations University, World Institute for Development Economics Research.

Nissanke, M. & Thorbecke, E. (2006). Channels and policy debate in the globalization-inequality-poverty nexus. *World Development* 34 (8), 1338–1360.

Nordlinger, E.A. (1977). *Soldiers in Politics: Military Coups and Governments.* Englewood Cliffs, NJ: Prentice-Hall.

North, D.C. (June 1994). Economic performance through time. *American Economic Review* 84 (3), 359–367.

North, D.C. (1990). *Institutions, Institutional Change and Economic Performance.* Cambridge: Cambridge University Press.

North, D.C. (1981). *Structure and Change in Economic History.* New York, NY: WW Norton.

North, D.C. & Thomas, R.P. (1970). An economic theory of growth of the Western World. *The Economic History Review* 23 (1), 1–17.

Ntoumi, F., Djimde, A.A., Mbacham, W. & Egwang, T. (2004). The importance and future of malaria research in Africa. *The American Journal of Tropical Medicine and Hygiene* 71 (2), 0v–0.

Nunn, N. (2008). The long-term effects of Africa's slave trades. *The Quarterly Journal of Economics* 123 (1), 139–176.

Nunn, N. (2007). Historical legacies: A model linking Africa's past to its current underdevelopment. *Journal of Development Economics* 83, 157–175.

Nur-tegin, K. & Czap, H.J. (March 2012). Corruption: Democracy, autocracy, and political stability. *Economic Analysis & Policy* 42 (1).

Nwonwu, F. (2008). The role of universal primary education in development. *Africa Insight* 37 (4), 137–147.

Nzongola-Ntalaja, G. (2002). *The Congo from Leopold to Kabila: A peoples history.* London: Zed Books.

Nzula, A.T., Potekhin, I.I. & Zusmanovich, A.Z. (1979). *Forced labour in colonial Africa.* Edited by Robin Cohen. No. 2. Zed Press.

O'Donnell, G. (January 1994). Delegative democracy. *Journal of Democracy* 5 (1), 55–69.

O'Donnell, G. (August 1993). On the state, democratization and come conceptual problems: A Latin American view with glances at some post-communist countries. *World Politics* 2 (8), 1355–1369.

O'Driscoll Jr., G.P. & Hoskins, L. (2003). Property rights: The Key to Economic Development. *The Cato Institute Policy Paper* 482.

OECD. http://www.oecd.org/investment/stats/

O'Kane, R.H. (1989). Military regimes: Power and force. *European Journal of Political Research* 17 (3), 333–350.

Okonjo-Iweala, N., Soludo, C.C. & Muhtar, M., eds. (2003). *The Debt Trap in Nigeria: Towards a Sustainable Debt Strategy.* Africa World Press.

Olken, B.A. (2005). Monitoring corruption: Evidence from a field experiment in Indonesia (No. w11753). *National Bureau of Economic Research.*

Olken, B.A. (2006). Corruption and the costs of redistribution: Micro evidence from Indonesia. *Journal of Public Economics* 90 (4), 853–870.

Olken, B.A. & Pande, R. (2012). Corruption in developing countries. *Annual Review of Economics* 4, 479–509.

O'Meara, W.P., Mangeni, J.N., Steketee, R. & Greenwood, B. (2010). Changes in the burden of malaria in sub-Saharan Africa. *The Lancet Infectious Diseases* 10 (8), 545–555.

Omololu, O.T. (2007). Corruption, governance and political instability in Nigeria. *African Journal of Political Science and International Relations* 1 (2), 28–37.

Organisation for Economic Co-operation and Development. (2003). *Harmonising Donor Practices for Effective aid Delivery*. OECD.

Organization for Economic Cooperation and Development. (2012). http://www.oecd.org/dac/stats/.

O'Rourke, K.H. (2001). *Globalization and Inequality: Historical Trends (No. w8339)*. Cambridge, MA: National Bureau of Economic Research, 1–44.

O'Rourke, K.H. & Williamson, J.G. (2001). *Globalization and History: The Evolution of a Nineteenth-Century Atlantic Economy*. MIT Press.

Osei, B. (1995). *Ghana: The Burden of Debt-Service Payment under Structural Adjustment*.

Osoba, S.O. (1996). Corruption in Nigeria: Historical perspectives. *Review of African Political Economy* 23 (69), 371–386.

Organization Economic Cooperation Development. (2010). http://www.oecd.org/dev/asia-pacific/1823686.pdf

Østby, G. (2008) Polarization, horizontal inequalities and violent civil conflict. *Journal of Peace Research* 45 (2), 143–162.

Osuorah, D.C., Ezeudu, C.E., Onah, S.K. & Anyabolu, O.T. (2013). Household bed net ownership and use among under-5 children in Nigeria. *Research & Reports in Tropical Medicine*, 4.

Ouattara, B. (2006). Aid, debt and fiscal policies in Senegal. *Journal of International Development* 18 (8), 1105–1122.

Owen, R. (1992). *State, Power and Politics in the Making of the Modern Middle East*. New York, NY: Routledge.

Palmer, M., Ali, L. & Yassim, E. (1988). *The Egyptian Bureaucracy*. Syracuse, NY: Syracuse University Press.

Panda, B. (2007). Top down or bottom up? A study of grassroots NGOs' approach. *Journal of Health Management* 9 (2), 257–273.

Parra, F. (2004). *Oil Politics: A Modern History of Petroleum*. IB Tauris.

Parris, T.M. & Kates, R.W. (2003). Characterizing and measuring sustainable development. *Annual Review of Environment and Resources* 28 (1), 559–586.

Pastor, Jr., M. & Zimbalist, A. (1995). Waiting for change: Adjustment and reform in Cuba. *World Development* 23 (5), 705–720.

Paulus, C.G. (2005). Odious debts vs. debt trap: A realistic help. Brook. *J. Int'l L.*, 31, 83.

Pausewang, Siegfried, Cheru, Fantu, Brüne, Stefan & Chole, Eshetu. (1990). *Ethiopia: Rural Development Options*. London: Zed Books.

Payne, K., Warrington, S., Bennett, O. & van der Gaag, N. (2009). *High Stakes: The Future for Mountain Societies*. Panos Ltd.

Peet, R. & Hartwick, E. (1999). *Theories of Development*. New York, NY: Guildford Press.

Pelling, M. (2003). *The Vulnerability of Cities: Natural Disasters and Social Resilience*. Earthscan.

Perez-Lopez, J.F. (August 2003). The Cuban Economy in 2002–2003. In Annual Meeting of the Association for the Study of the Cuban Economy, Coral Gables, FL.

Pérez-López, J.F. (2003). Waiting for Godot: Cuba's stalled reforms and continuing economic crisis. *Cuban Communism 1959-2003*. 176–197.

Persson, T., Tabellini, G. & Trebbi, F. (2003). Electoral rules and corruption. *Journal of the European Economic Association* 1 (4), 958–989.

Peters, B.G. (2011). *Institutional Theory in Political Science: The New Institutionalism*. New York, NY: Bloomsbury Publishing.

Peters, D.H., Garg, A., Bloom, G., Walker, D.G., Brieger, W.R. & Hafizur Rahman, M. (2008). Poverty and access to health care in developing countries. *Annals of the New York Academy of Sciences* 1136 (1), 161–171.

Pfeiffer, J., Johnson, W., Fort, M., Shakow, A., Hagopian, A., Gloyd, S. & Gimbel-Sherr, K. (2008). Strengthening health systems in poor countries: A code of conduct for nongovernmental organizations. *American Journal of Public Health* 98 (12), 2134.

Piazza, J.A. (2011). Poverty, minority economic discrimination, and domestic terrorism. *Journal of Peace Research* 48 (3), 339–353.

Pielke, Jr., R.A., Rubiera, J., Landsea, C., Fernández, M.L. & Klein, R. (2003). Hurricane vulnerability in Latin America and the Caribbean: Normalized damage and loss potentials. *Natural Hazards Review* 4 (3), 101–114.

Piketty, T. & Sanz, E. (2006). The Evolution of Top Incomes: A Historical and International Perspective. No. w11955. National Bureau of Economic Research.

Pilster, U. & Bohmelt, T. (2011). Coup-proofing and military effectiveness in interstate wars, 1967–99. *Conflict Management and Peace Science* 28 (4), 1–20.

Pion-Berlin, D. (1992). Military autonomy and emerging democracies in South America. *Comparative Politics* 25 (1), 83–102.

Plott, C. (1979). The Application of Laboratory Experimental Methods to Public Choice. In *Collective Decision Making: Applications from Public Choice Theory*, edited by C.S. Russell. Baltimore, MD: Johns Hopkins University Press, 137–160.

Poku, N.K. (2002). Poverty, debt and Africa's HIV/AIDS crisis. *International Affairs* 78 (3), 531–546.

Popova, M. (April 15, 2014). Ukraine's legal problems: Why Kiev's plans to purge the judiciary will backfire. *Foreign Affairs*.

Pope, J. (May 31, 1996). National Integrity Programs. Partnership for Governance Conference, Copenhagen, Denmark. 23–26.

Posen, B. (1993). The security dilemma and ethnic conflict. *Survival* 5, 27–47.

Powell, J. (2012). Determinants of the attempting and outcome of coups d'état. *Journal of Conflict Resolution*, 1–24.

Powell, J.M. & Thyne, C.L. (2011). Global instances of coups from 1950 to 2010: A new dataset. *Journal of Peace Research* 48 (2), 249–259.

Prah, K.K. (2004). African Wars and Ethnic Conflicts Rebuilding Failed States. *Human Development Report Occasional Paper* 10.

Prebisch, R. (1950). *The Economic Development of Latin America and Its Principal Problems*. New York, NY: United Nations.

Presbitero, A.F. (2008). The debt-growth nexus in poor countries: A reassessment. *Economics: The Open-Access, Open-Assessment E-Journal*.

Prillaman, W.C. (2000). *The Judiciary and Democratic Decay in Latin American: Declining Confidence in the Rule of Law*. Westport, CT: Greenwood Publishing.

Pritchett, L. & Kaufmann, D. (1998). Civil liberties, democracy, and the performance of government projects. *Finance and Development* 35, 26–29.

Przeworski, A. (April 12, 2011). Afronline interview. www.afronline.org

Przeworski, A., Alvarez, M.E., Cheibub, J.A. & Limongi, F. (2000). *Democracy and Development: Political Institutions and Well Being in the World, 1950-1990*. Cambridge: Cambridge University Press.

Psacharopoulos, G. & Patrinos, H.A. (1994). *Indigenous People and Poverty in Latin America: An Empirical Analysis*. World Bank.

Putzel, J. (2003). Institutionalising an emergency response: HIV/AIDS and governance in Uganda and Senegal. London School of Economy and Political Science, Department for Internat. Development.

Putzel, J. (April 2001). Research in Latin America. *Crisis States Research Programme Working Paper* 4, 1–16.

Quah, J.S.T. (April 2008). Curbing corruption in India: An impossible dream? *Current History* 240–259.

Quah, J.S.T. (April 2006). Curbing Asian corruption: An impossible dream? *Current History* 105 (690), 176–179.

Quaye, R. & Coombs, H. (2011). The implementation of anti-money laundering, terrorist finance and corruption laws in Ghana. *International Journal of Government Financial Management* 11 (2), 50.

Radelet, S. & Sachs, J. (August 1998). *The Onset of the East Asian Financial Crisis* (No. w6680). Cambridge, MA: *National Bureau of Economic Research*, 1–57.

Rahman, M. & Giasuddin, R.S. (2012). Tuberculosis. *AKMMC Journal* 3 (2), 1–5.

Ramey, G. & Ramey, V.A. (1995). Cross-country evidence on the link between volatility and growth. *American Economic Review* 85, 1138–1151.

Ramsbotham, O., Miall, H. & Woodhouse, T. (2011). *Contemporary Conflict Resolution*. Cambridge: Polity.

Randal C.A. & Sengupta, S. (April 20, 2014). U.N. Struggles to Stem Haiti Cholera Epidemic. *The New York Times.* http://www.nytimes.com

Raschky, Paul A. (2008). Institutions and the losses from natural disasters. *Natural Hazards and Earth System Science* 8 (4), 627–634.

Rau, B. (2003). HIV/AIDS and child labour: A state-of-the-art review with recommendations for action. *International Labour Organization* 6, 1–76. http://www.ilo.org/wcmsp5/groups/public/@ed_protect/@protrav/@ilo_aids/documents/publication/wcms_119222.pdf

Ravallion, M. (2003). The debate on globalization, poverty and inequality: Why measurement matters. *International Affairs* 79 (4), 739–753.

Ravallion, M. (2001). Growth, inequality and poverty: Looking beyond averages. *World Development* 29 (11), 1803–1815.

Ravallion, M. (1997). Can high-inequality developing countries escape absolute poverty? *Economics Letters* 56 (1), 51–57.

Ravallion, M. & Chen, S. (2007). China's (uneven) progress against poverty. *Journal of Development Economics* 82 (1), 1–42.

Ravallion, M. & Datt, G. (1996). How important to India's poor is the sectoral composition of economic growth? *The World Bank Economic Review* 10 (1), 1–25.

Ray, D. (1998). *Development Economics.* Princeton University Press.

Reames, B. (2003). *Police Forces in Mexico: A Profile.*

Reed, D. (1996). *Structural Adjustment, the Environment, and Sustainable Development.* London: Earthscan.

Reilly, D.A. (2008). The two-level game of failing states: Internal and external sources of state failure. *The Journal of Conflict Studies* 28.

Regan, P.M. (2009). *Sixteen Million One: Understanding Civil War.* Boulder, CO: Paradigm Publishers.

Reno, W. (2000). Shadow States and the Political Economy of Civil Wars. In *Greed and Grievance: Economic Agendas and Civil Wars,* edited by M. Berdal and D. Malone. Boulder, CO: Lynne Rienner, 43–68.

Rhodes, R.A.W., Binder, S. & Rockman, B.A. (2006). *The Oxford Handbook of Political Institutions.* Oxford: Oxford University Press.

Riain, S.O. (2000). States and markets in an era of globalization. *Annual Review of Sociology* 26 (1), 187–213.

Ricardo, D. (1817). On the Principles of Political Economy and Taxation. In *Works and Correspondence of David Ricardo, Volume I,* edited by Piero Sraffa. Cambridge University Press, 1951.

Riddell, R.C. (2007). *Does Foreign Aid Really Work?* Oxford University Press.

Riker, W.H. (1982). Implications from the disequilibrium of majority rule for the study of institutions. *The American Political Science Review,* 432–437.

Riley, S.P. (1999). Petty corruption and development. *Development in Practice* 9 (1–2), 189–193.

Rimmer, D. (1992). *Staying Poor: Ghana's Political Economy, 1950-1990.* Oxford: Pergamon Press and the World Bank.

Ripoll, J. (2006). Globalisation: A curse or a blessing on the road to the millennium development goals? Documentos CIDOB. *Desarrollo* 1, 1–49.

Robbins, R.H. (2007). *Global Problems and the Culture of Capitalism.* Boston, MA: Allyn & Bacon.

Roberts, K.M. (October 1995). Neo-liberalism and the transformation of populism in Latin America: The Peruvian case. *World Politics* 48 (1), 82–116.

Robertson-Snape, F. (1999). Corruption, collusion and nepotism in Indonesia. *Third World Quarterly* 20 (3), 589–602.

Robinson, J.A. (2009). *Botswana as a Role Model for Country Success.*

Robinson, J.A. (2004). Squaring the circle? Some thoughts on the idea of sustainable development. *Ecological Economics* 48 (4), 369–384.

Robinson, J.A. & Parsons, Q.N. (2006). State formation and governance in Botswana. *Journal of African Economies* 15 (1), 100–140.

Robinson, J.A., Torvik, R. & Verdier, T. (2006). Political foundations of the resource curse. *Journal of Development Economics* 79, 447–468.

Rodgers, D. (November 2004). Old wine in new bottles or new wine in old bottles? Conceptualizing violence and governmentality in contemporary Latin America. *Crisis States Research Center Discussion Paper* 6, 1–22.

Rodrik, D. (2008). *One Economics, Many Recipes: Globalization, Institutions, and Economic Growth.* Princeton, NJ: Princeton University Press.

Rodrik, D. (2005). Growth strategies. *Handbook of Economic Growth* 1A, 967–1014.

Rodrik, D. (2004). Getting institutions right. *CESifo DICE Report* (2), 2–4.

Rodrik, D. (2000). Institutions for high-quality growth: What they are and how to acquire them. *Studies in Comparative International Development* 35 (3), 3–31.

Rodrik, D. (1999). Where did all the growth go? External shocks, social conflict, and growth collapses. *Journal of Economic Growth* 4 (4), 385–412.

Rodrik, D. & Alesina, A. (1994). Distributive Politics and Economic Growth.

Rodrik, D., Subramanian, A. & Trebbi, F. (November 2002). Institutions Rule: The Primacy of Institutions over Geography and Integration in Economic Development. *The National Bureau of Economic Research, Working Paper* 9305.

Rogoff, K., Shang-Jin, W. & Ayhan Kose. M. (2003). *Effects of Financial Globalization on Developing Countries: Some Empirical Evidence* (Vol. 17). Washington, DC: International Monetary Fund.

Rola-Rubzen, M.F., Hardaker, J.B. & Dillon, J.L. (2001). Agricultural economists and world poverty: Progress and prospects. *Australian Journal of Agricultural and Resource Economics* 45 (1), 39–66.

Rosales, M.R. (2007). *The Panama Canal Expansion Project: Transit Maritime Mega Project Development, Reactions, and Alternatives from Affected People.* University of Florida Press.

Rose-Ackerman, S. (2002). When Is Corruption Harmful. Political Corruption. In *Concepts and Contexts* (Vol. 3), edited by Arnold J. Heidenheimer & Michael Johnston. New Brunswick, NJ: Transactions Publishers, 353–371.

Rose-Ackerman, S. (1999). *Corruption and Government: Causes, Consequences, and Reform.* Cambridge: Cambridge University Press.

Rose-Ackerman, S. (1996). Democracy and "grand" corruption. *International Social Science Journal* 48 (149), 365–380.

Rose-Ackerman, S. (ed.). (2007). International Handbook on the Economics of Corruption. Cheltenham: Edward Elgar Publishing.

Rosen, S., Simon, J., Vincent, J.R., MacLeod, W., Fox, M. & Thea, D.M. (2003). AIDS is your business. *Harvard Business Review* 81 (2), 80–87.

Rosenzweig, M.R. & Wolpin, K.I. (1993). Credit market constraints, consumption smoothing, and the accumulation of durable production assets in low-income countries: Investments in bullocks in India. *Journal of Political Economy*, 223–244.

Ross, M.L. (2012). *The Oil Curse: How Petroleum Wealth Shapes the Development of Nations.* Princeton, NJ: Princeton University Press.

Ross, M.L. (2004). What do we know about natural resources and civil war? *Journal of Peace Research* 41 (3), 337–356.

Ross, M.L. (2003). The natural resource curse: How wealth can make you poor. *Natural Resources and Violent Conflict: Options and Actions,* 17–42.

Ross, M.L. (December 2002). Natural Resources and Civil War: An Overview with Some Policy Options. Draft Report Prepared for The Governance of Natural Resources Revenues Conference, Sponsored by the World Bank and the Agence Française de Développement, Paris.

Ross, M.L. (2001). Does oil hinder democracy? *World Politics* 53 (3), 325–361.

Ross, M.L. (1999). The political economy of the resource curse. *World Politics* 51 (2), 297–322.

Rostow, W.W. (1960/1990). *The Stages of Economic Development: A Non-Communist Manifesto.* Cambridge: Cambridge University Press.

Rotberg, R. (2003). *State Failure and State Weakness in a Time of Terror.* Washington, DC: Brookings Institute Press.

Rotberg, R.I. (1988). Haiti's past mortgages its future. *Foreign Affairs,* 93–109.

Ruby, T.Z. & Gibler, D. (2010). US professional military education and democratization abroad. *European Journal of International Relations* 16 (3), 339–364.

Rudra, N. (2002). Globalization and the decline of the welfare state in less-developed countries. *International Organization* 56 (02), 411–445.

Rugege, S. (2006). Judicial independence in Rwanda. *Pacific McGeorge Global Business & Development Law Journal* 19, 411–425.

Rukuni, M. & Eicher, C.K. (1994). *Zimbabwe's Agricultural Revolution.* University of Zimbabwe Publications Office.

Rustow, D.A. (1970). Transitions to democracy: Toward a dynamic model. *Comparative Politics*, 337–363.

Sachs, J.D. (September/October 2012). Government, geography, and growth. *Foreign Affairs* 91 (5), 142–150. www.foreignaffairs.com

Sachs, J.D. (2005a). The development challenge. *Foreign Affairs*, 78–90.

Sachs, J.D. (2005b). *The End of Poverty: Economic Possibilities for Our Time*. New York, NY: Penguin Books.

Sachs, J.D. (2001). Tropical underdevelopment (No. w8119). National Bureau of Economic Research. 1–34.

Sachs, J.D. (1989). Conditionality, Debt Relief, and the Developing Country Debt Crisis. In *Developing Country Debt and Economic Performance, Volume 1: The International Financial System*. University of Chicago Press, 255–296.

Sachs, J.D. & Huizinga, H. (1987). US commercial banks and the developing country debt crisis. *Brookings Papers on Economic Activity* 2, 555–606.

Sachs, J.D. & Malaney, P. (2002). The economic and social burden of malaria. *Nature* 415 (6872), 680–685.

Sachs, J.D. & Warner, A.M. (2001). The curse of natural resources. *European Economic Review* 45 (4), 827–838.

Sachs, J.D. & Warner, A.M. (1995). Natural resource abundance and economic growth. *National Bureau of Economic Research* 5398, 1–45.

Sachs, J.D. & Warner, A.M. (1997). Fundamental sources of long-run growth. *The American Economic Review*, 184–188.

Sachs, J.D. & Williamson, J. (1985). External debt and macroeconomic performance in Latin America and East Asia. *Brookings Papers on Economic Activity*, 523–573.

Sadasivam, B. (1997). The impact of structural adjustment on women: A governance and human rights agenda. *Human Rights Quarterly* 19 (3), 630–665.

Said, M.E. (2000). Egypt: The Dialectics of State Security and Social Decay. IPG. 5–18.

Saith, A. (2007). Millennium development goals and the dumbing-down of development: Goals set for the poor, goalposts set by the rich. *International Institute of Asian Studies Newsletter* 45, 12–13.

Samatar, A.I. (1999). *An African Miracle: State and Class Leadership and Colonial Legacy in Botswana Development*. Portsmouth: Heinemann.

Samatar, A.I. (1997). Leadership and ethnicity in the making of African State models: Botswana versus Somalia. *Third World Quarterly* 18 (4), 687–708.

Sanchez, P.M. (2002). The end of hegemony? Panama and the United States. *International Journal on World Peace*, 57–89.

Santiso, C. (2001). World Bank and good governance: good governance and aid effectiveness: the World Bank and conditionality. *Geo. Public Pol'y Rev.* 7, 1–137.

Sarigil, Z. (2011). Civil-military relations beyond dichotomy: With special reference to Turkey. *Turkish Studies* 12 (2), 265–278.

Sawkut, R., Boopen, S., Ramessur-Seenarain, T. & Vinesh, S. (2009). Determinants of FDI: Lessons from African economies. *Journal of Applied Business and Economics*. Also fromvi. unctad.org/files/wksp/iiawksp08/docs/.../sannrojidpaper.doc

Schiff, M.W. & Valdes, A. (1992). *The Plundering of Agriculture in Developing Countries*. World Bank Publications.

Schifferes, S. (March 1, 2004). Haiti: An Economic Basket-Case. BBC News.

Schneckener, U. (2006). Fragile Statehood, Armed Non-state Actors and Security Governance. *Private Actors and Security Governance, Berlin*. 23–41.

Schneider, G. & Wiesehomeier, N. (2008). Rules that matter: Political institutions and the diversity – conflict nexus. *Journal of Peace Research* 45 (2), 183–203.

Schneider, H. & Fassin, D. (2002). Denial and defiance: A socio-political analysis of AIDS in South Africa. *AIDS* 16, 45–51.

Scholte, J.A. (1997). Global capitalism and the state. *International Affairs* (Royal Institute of International Affairs 1944-), 427–452.

Schubert, B. & Goldberg, J. (2004). *The Pilot Social Cash Transfer Scheme: Kalomo District, Zambia*. Lusaka: GTZ.

Schultz, T.P. (2007). Population policies, fertility, women's human capital, and child quality. *Handbook of Development Economics* 4, 249–303.

Schultz, T.P. (2006). Fertility and Income. In *Understanding Poverty*, edited by A.V. Benabou & D. Mookherjee. Oxford University Press, 125–142.

Schultz, T.W. (1980). Nobel lecture: The economics of being poor. *The Journal of Political Economy*, 639–651.

Schultz, T.W. (1964). *Transforming Traditional Agriculture*. New Haven, CT: Yale University Press.

Schultz, T.W. (1962). Reflection on investment in man. *Journal of Political Economy* 70, S1–S8.

Schuurman, F.J., ed. (2001). *Globalization and Development Studies: Challenges for the 21st Century*. Sage.

Scobell, A. (1994). Politics, professionalism, and peacekeeping: An analysis of the 1987 military coup in Fiji. *Comparative Politics*, 187–201.

Sebudubudu, D. (2010). The impact of good governance on development and poverty in Africa: Botswana: A relatively successful African initiative. *African Journal of Political Science and International Relations* 4 (7), 249–262.

Sebudubudu, D. (2005). The Institutional Framework of the Developmental State in Botswana. The Potentiality of Developmental States in Africa: Botswana & Uganda Compared, Dakar, CODESRIA.

Sebudubudu, D. & Molutsi, P. (2008). Botswana's democracy: Explanations for success? *Politeia* 27 (1), 47–64.

Seers, D. (1972). What are we trying to measure? *The Journal of Development Studies* 8 (3), 21–36.

Seers, D. (1969). *The Meaning of Development*. New Delhi.

Sen, A. (2002). Globalization, inequality and global protest. *Development* 45 (2), 11–16.

Sen, A. (1999). Commodities and Capabilities. *OUP Catalogue*.

Sen, A. (1992). *Inequality Re-examined*. Oxford: Oxford University Press.

Sen, A. (1983). Development: Which way now? *Economic Journal* 93 (372), 745–762.

Sen, S., Kasibhatla, K.M. & Stewart, D.B. (2007). Debt overhang and economic growth-the Asian and the Latin American experiences. *Economic Systems* 31 (1), 3–11.

Seshanna, S. & Decornez, S. (2003). Income polarization and inequality across countries: An empirical study. *Journal of Policy Modeling* 25 (4), 335–358.

Shaban, R.A. (October 1987). Testing between competing models of sharecropping. *The Journal of Political Economy* 95 (5), 893–920.

Sharp, P.M. & Hahn, B.H. (2011). Origins of HIV and the AIDS pandemic. *Cold Spring Harbor Perspectives in Medicine* 1 (1), a006841.

Shelley, L. (1999). Identifying, counting and categorizing transnational criminal organizations. *Transnational Organized Crime* 5 (1), 1–18.

Shelley, L., Scott, E.R. & Latta, A., eds. (2007). *Organized Crime and Corruption in Georgia*. Routledge.

Siegfried, N., Muller, M., Deeks, J., Volmink, J., Egger, M., Low, N. & Williamson, P. (2005). HIV and male circumcision—A systematic review with assessment of the quality of studies. *The Lancet Infectious Diseases* 5 (3), 165–173.

Sindzingre, A.N. (2004). Bringing the Developmental State Back in: Contrasting Development Trajectories in Sub-Saharan Africa and East Asia. Document Presented at the 6th Annual Society for the Advancement of Socio-Economics (SASE), University of George Washington, Washington.

Sindzingre, A. (2007). Financing the developmental state: Tax and revenue issues. *Development Policy Review* 25 (5), 615–632.

Singer, H.W. (1982). *Terms of Trade Controversy and the Evolution of Soft Financing: Early Years in the UN, 1947-1951*. IDS Publications.

Skocpol, T. (1985). Bringing the State Back in: Strategies of Analysis in Current Research. In *Bringing the State Back*, edited by P.B. Evans, D. Rueschemeyer & T. Skocpol. Cambridge University Press, 3–37.

Skolnik, R. (2011). *Global Health 101* (2nd ed.). Burlington, MA: Jones & Bartlett Learning, 253.

Smart, T. (2008). *Do Bicycles Equal Development in Mozambique?* Boydell & Brewer Ltd.

Smith, A. (1937). *The Wealth of Nations* [1776].

Smith, B. (2004). Oil wealth and regime survival in the developing world, 1960–1999. *American Journal of Political Science* 48 (2), 232–246.

Smith, D.L., Cohen, J.M., Chiyaka, C., Johnston, G., Gething, P.W., Gosling, R., ... & Tatem, A.J. (2013). A sticky situation: The unexpected stability of malaria elimination. *Philosophical Transactions of the Royal Society B: Biological Sciences* 368 (1623), 120-145.

Smith, K. (2013). *Environmental Hazards: Assessing Risk and Reducing Disaster*. Routledge.

Smith, M.T. (2005). Ethnic politics and regional development in Myanmar. *Myanmar: Beyond Politics to Societal Imperatives.*

Sneddon, C., Howarth, R.B. & Norgaard, R.B. (2006). Sustainable development in a post-Brundtland world. *Ecological Economics* 57 (2), 253–268.

Sobhan, R. (1996). Aid Dependence and Donor Policy: The Case of Tanzania with Lessons from Bangladesh's Experience. In Sida, 1996, Aid Dependency: Causes, Symptoms and Remedies; Project 2015.

Sohail, M. & Cavill, S. (2008). Water for the Poor: Corruption in Water Supply and Sanitation. *Global Corruption Report 2008: Corruption in the Water Sector*, 44–52.

Sokoloff, K.L. (2000). Institutions, Factor Endowments, and Paths of Development in the New World. Villa Borsig Workshop Series 2000 on the Institutional Foundations of a Market Economy.

Solimano, A. (2002). Globalization, History and International Migration: A View from Latin America. In workshop for the World Commission on the Social Dimensions of Globalization, 16–17.

Solimano, A. & Soto, R. (2005). *Economic Growth in Latin America in the Late 20th Century: Evidence and Interpretation* (Vol. 33). United Nations Publications.

Southall, R. (2006). Troubled visionary: Nyerere as a former president. *Leadership Change and Former Presidents in African Politics*, 233–255.

Stager, H. (2009). Post-disaster Opportunities: An Assessment of Reconstruction Activities following the 1999 Debris Flows in Vargas State, Venezuela.

Stambuli, P.K. (1998). Causes and Consequences of the 1982 World Debt Crisis? Pre-Doctoral Research Paper. Department of Economics, University of Surrey, Guildford. 1–35.

Stigler, G. (1987). *The Theory of Price* (4th ed.). New York, NY: The Macmillan Company.

Stiglitz, J. (June 2007). The Post Washington Consensus. Initiative for policy dialogue. Task Force on Global Governance. Working Paper Series. http://www2.gsb.columbia.edu/faculty/jstiglitz/papers.cfm

Stiglitz, J.E. (September 4, 2013). The Vultures' Victory. http://www.project-syndicate.org/commentary/argentina-s-debt-and-american-courts-by-joseph-e--stiglitz

Stiglitz, J.E. (2012). *The Price of Inequality.* Penguin.

Stiglitz, J.E. (2007). *Making Globalization Work.* WW Norton & Company.

Stiglitz, J.E. (August 18, 2004). We Can Now Cure Dutch Disease. *The Guardian.*

Stiglitz, J.E. (2003). Globalization and growth in emerging markets and the new economy. *Journal of Policy Modeling* 25 (5), 505–524.

Stiglitz, J.E. (1998a). Distinguished lecture on economics in government: The private uses of public interests: Incentives and institutions. *The Journal of Economic Perspectives*, 3–22.

Stiglitz, J.E. (October 1998b). Towards a New Paradigm for Development. United Nations Conference on Trade and Development.

Stohl, R. (September/Fall 2005). Reality check: The danger of small arms proliferation. *Conflict and Security*, 75.

Stone, D.L. & Wright, C., eds. (2006). *The World Bank and Governance: A Decade of Reform and Reaction.* New York, NY: Routledge.

Stover, J. & Bollinger, L. (March 1999). Economic Impact of AIDS, Policy Project. 1–14.

Strauss, J. (1986). Does better nutrition raise farm productivity? *Journal of Political Economy* 94, 297–320.

Streeten, P. (1993). The special problems of small countries. *World Development* 21 (2), 197–202.

Streeten, P. (1989). Basic needs: Premises and promises. *Journal of Policy Modeling* I, 136–146.

Sukma, R. & Prasetyono, E. (2003). Security Sector Reform in Indonesia: The Military and the Police. Netherlands Institute of International Relations "Clingendael" Working Series Paper, 9.

Sumbadze, N. (2009). Saakashvili in the public eye: What public opinion polls tell us. *Central Asian Survey* 28 (2), 185–197.

Sung, H.E. (2004). State failure, economic failure, and predatory organized crime: A comparative analysis. *Journal of Research in Crime and Delinquency* 41 (2), 111–129.

Suryadarma, D. (2012). How corruption diminishes the effectiveness of public spending on education in Indonesia. *Bulletin of Indonesian Economic Studies* 48 (1), 85–100.

Swamy, A., Knack, S., Lee, Y. & Azfar, O. (2001). Gender and Corruption. In *Democracy, Governance and Growth*, edited by Stephen Knack. 191–224.

Swallow, B., Kirk, M. & Hazell, P. (2000). *Property Rights, Risk, and Livestock Development in Africa*. IFPRI.

Sweig, J.E. & Bustamante, M.J. (July/August 2013). Cuba after communism. *Foreign Affairs*.

Talbot, J.M. (2002). Information, finance and the new international inequality: The case of coffee. *Journal of World-Systems Research* 8 (2), 214–250.

Tamada, Y. (1995). Coups in Thailand, 1980–1991: Classmates, internal conflicts and relations with the government of the military. *Southeast Asian Studies* 33, 317–339.

Tanzi, V. & Davoodi, H. (1997). Corruption, public investment, and growth. *IMF Working Paper* 139, 1–23.

Tarp, F., ed. (2003). *Foreign Aid and Development: Lessons Learnt and Directions for the Future*. London: Routledge.

TB In the News 2012: Price for Rapid TB Test Slashed. (August 8, 2012). http://www.cabsa.org.za/book/export/html/7204

Tendler, J. (1975). *Inside Foreign Aid*.

Teubal, M. (2004). Rise and collapse of neoliberalism in Argentina. The role of economic groups. *Journal of Developing Societies* 20 (3–4), 173–188.

Teunissen, J.J. & Akkerman, A., eds. (2004). *HIPC Debt Relief: Myths and Reality*. Fondad.

Thomas, T.S. & Kiser, S.D. (2002). *Lords of the Silk Route: Violent Non-state Actors in Central Asia*. Boulder, CO: Diane Publishing.

Tilak, J.B. (2007). Post-elementary education, poverty and development in India. *International Journal of Educational Development* 27 (4), 435–445.

Tilak, J.B.G. (December 1999). Education and poverty in South Asia. *Prospects* 29 (4), 517–533.

Tilak, J.B.G. (1994). *Education for Development in Asia*. New Delhi: Sage Publications.

Timmer, C.P. (1988). The Agricultural Transformation. In *Handbook of Development Economics* (Vol. 1), edited by H. Chenery & T.N. Srinivasan. Amsterdam: North Holland.

Tompkins, E.L. (2005). Planning for climate change in small islands: Insights from national hurricane preparedness in the Cayman Islands. *Global Environmental Change* 15 (2), 139–149.

Tompkins, E.L. & Hurlston, L. (2003). Report to the Cayman Islands' Government. Adaptation Lessons Learned from Responding to Tropical Cyclones by the Cayman Islands Government, 1988–2002. 35. Tyndall Working Paper.

Tompkins, E.L., Lemos, M.C. & Boyd, E. (2008). A less disastrous disaster: Managing response to climate-driven hazards in the Cayman Islands and NE Brazil. *Global Environmental Change* 18 (4), 736–745.

Townsend, Peter. (1993). *The International Analysis of Poverty*. London: Harvester Wheatsheaf.

Toya, H. & Skidmore, M. (2007). Economic development and the impacts of natural disasters. *Economics Letters* 94 (1), 20–25.

Transparency International. (2013). Corruption Perceptions Index 2013. www.cpi.transparency.org

Transparency International. (2008). http://www.transparency.org/whatwedo/pub/global_corruption_report_2008_corruption_in_the_water_sector

Transparency International. (2007). http://www.transparency.org/whatwedo/publication/global_corruption_report_2007_corruption_and_judicial_systems

Transparency International Annual Report, 2012. 1–78.

Treisman, D. (2000). The causes of corruption: A cross-national study. *Journal of Public Economics* 76 (3), 399–457.

Ugur, M. & Dasgupta, N. (2011). Corruption and economic growth: A meta-analysis of the evidence on low-income countries and beyond. MPRA Paper No. 31226, 1–43. Mundial, B. (1997).

Ullah, A.A. (2004). Poverty reduction in Bangladesh: Does good governance matter? NAPSIPAG 423–442.

UNDP. (November 12, 2013). Human Development Report for Latin America 2013–2014. http://www.undp.org/content/undp/en/home/librarypage/hdr/human-development-report-for-latin-america-2013-2014/

Unger, J.P., De Paepe, P. & Green, A. (2003). A code of best practice for disease control programmes to avoid damaging health care services in developing countries. *The International Journal of Health Planning and Management* 18 (S1), S27–S39.

UNICEF. (2002). Annual Report. http://unicef.dk/sites/default/files/mediafiles/UNICEF_Annual_Report_2002.pdf

United Nations Conference on Trade and Development. (1988). *Trade and Development Report, 1988*, UNCTAD/FDR/8. New York, NY: United Nations.

UN declaration at World Summit on Social Development in Copenhagen in 1995.

United Nations. (2013). *Inequality Matters: Report of the World Social Situation*. New York, NY: United Nations.

United Nations. http://www.un.org/en/globalissues/briefingpapers/food/vitalstats.shtml

United Nations Department of Economic and Social Affairs/Population Division. (July 2006). The Impact of AIDS: Impact on the Health Sector. 75–79. http://www.un.org/esa/population/publications/AIDSimpact/90_CHAP_VII.pdf

United Nations Department of Economic and Social Affairs (UNDESA). (2014). International Decade for Action: Water for Life, 2005-2015. http://www.un.org/waterforlifedecade/sanitation.shtml

United Nations Development Programme. (1995). *Human Development Report 1995*. New York: Oxford University Press.

United Nations Institute for Disarmament. (September 2006). Scoping Study on Mine Action and Small Arms Control within the Framework of Armed Violence and Poverty Reduction. 1–30.

United Nations Millennium Report. (2012). http://www.un.org/millenniumgoals/pdf/MDG%20Report%202012.pdf

UNODC Homicide Statistics.

United Nations, Religions for Peace. (2008). Small Arms and Light Weapons, Africa. 1–28.

The United States Library of Congress – Federal Research Division Country Profile: Haiti (May 2006).

Uphoff, N.T. (1992). *Local Institutions and Participation for Sustainable Development*. Sustainable Agriculture Programme of the International Institute for Environment and Development, London, UK.

Urra, F.J. (2007). Assessing Corruption An Analytical Review of Corruption Measurement and Its Problems: Perception, Error and Utility. Edmund A. Walsh School of Foreign Service (May), 1–20.

USAID. (June 2009). Reducing Corruption in the Judiciary. 1–47.

USAID. (March 2014). Zimbabwe Food Security Brief. 1–35.

Ushiyama, R. (2013). Malaysia Aims to Become a High-Income Country. Japan Center for Economic Research. 31–46.

Utzinger, J., Tozan, Y. & Singer, B.H. (2001). Efficacy and cost-effectiveness of environmental management for malaria control. *Tropical Medicine & International Health* 6 (9), 677–687.

Valenzuela, E. & Anderson, K. (2008). Alternative Agricultural Price Distortions for CGE Analysis of Developing Countries, 2004 and 1980-84. Research Memorandum, 13.

van de Walle, N. (October 5–6, 2000). The Impact of Multi-Party Politics in Sub-Saharan Africa. Paper Prepared for Delivery at the Norwegian Association for Development Research Annual Conference, "The State under Pressure", Bergen, Norway.

van Rijckeghem, C. & Weder, B. (2001). Bureaucratic corruption and the rate of temptation: Do wages in the civil service affect corruption, and by how much? *Journal of Development Economics* 65, 307–331.

Van de Walle, D. & Cratty, D. (2004). Is the emerging non-farm market economy the route out of poverty in Vietnam? *Economics of Transition* 12 (2), 237–274.

Van de Walle, N. (2001). *African Economies and the Politics of Permanent Crisis, 1979–1999*. Cambridge University Press.

Van de Walle, N. & Johnston, T.A. (1996). *Improving aid to Africa* (No. 21). Washington, DC: Overseas Development Council.

Van der Ploeg, F. & Poelhekke, S. (2009). Volatility and the Natural Resource Curse. Oxford Economic Papers 27.

van Rijckeghem, C. & Weder, B. (2001). Bureaucratic corruption and the rate of temptation: Do wages in the civil service affect corruption, and by how much? *Journal of Development Economics* 65, 307–331.

Veltmeyer, H. (1993). Liberalisation and structural adjustment in Latin America: In search of an alternative. *Economic and Political Weekly*, 2080-2086.

Vietor, R.H. (2005). Globalization and Growth. Case Studies in National Economic Strategies.

Voight, B., Calvache, M.L., Hall, M.L. & Monsalve, M.L. (2013). Nevado del Ruiz Volcano, Colombia 1985. *Encyclopedia of Natural Hazards*, 732–738.

Vollrath, D. (2007). Land distribution and international agricultural productivity. *American Journal of Agricultural Economics* 89 (1), 202–216.

Vreeland, J. (2008). The effect of political regime on civil war: Unpacking Anocracy. *Journal of Conflict Resolution* 52 (3), 401–425.

Wade, R. (1990). *Governing the Market: Economic Theory and the Role of Government in Taiwan's Industrialization.* Princeton, NJ: Princeton University Press.

Wade, R.H. (2003). What strategies are viable for developing countries today? The world trade organization and the shrinking of "development space." *Review of International Political Economy* 10 (4), 621–644.

Walker, K. & Lynch, M. (2007). Contributions of Anopheles larval control to malaria suppression in tropical Africa: Review of achievements and potential. *Medical and Veterinary Entomology* 21 (1), 2–21.

Wallerstein, I., ed. (1979). *The Capitalist World-Economy* (Vol. 2). Cambridge University Press.

Walter Solutions Energy Group. http://www.walterenergy.info/page-ogf/Worldwide_EP_and_Oil_Shortage_Trends.html

Walton, J. & Seddon, D. (1994). *Free Markets & Food Riots: The Politics of Global Adjustment.* Cambridge, MA: Blackwell Publishers.

Waltz, K.N. (1999). Globalization and governance. *PS: Political Science & Politics* 32 (4), 693–700.

Wang, L., Liu, J. & Chin, D.P. (2007). Progress in tuberculosis control and the evolving public-health system in China. *The Lancet* 369 (9562), 691–696.

Wang, T.Y. (1998). Arms transfers and coups d'état: A study on sub-Saharan Africa. *Journal of Peace Research* 35 (6), 659–675.

Webb, P. & von Braun, J. (1994). *Famine and Food Security in Ethiopia: Lessons for Africa.* Chichester (UK): John Wiley and Sons.

Webber, D. (2007). Good budgeting, better justice: Modern budget practices for the judicial sector. *Law and Development Working Paper Series* 3, 1–76.

Weber, M. (1994). The profession and vocation of politics. *Weber: Political Writings*, 309–369.

Weber, M. (1978). *Economy and Society* (Vol. 1). Berkeley, CA: University of California Press.

Weidmann, N.B. (2009). Geography as motivation and opportunity: Group concentration and ethnic conflict. *Journal of Conflict Resolution* 53 (4), 526–543.

Weingast, B.R. (March 2002). Institutions and Political Commitment. 1–224.

Weinthal, E. & Luong, P.J. (2006). Combating the resource curse: An alternative solution to managing mineral wealth. *Perspectives on Politics* 4 (1), 35–53.

Weisenthal, J. (February 22, 2011). Forget the BRICs: Citi's Willem Buiter Presents: The 11 "3G" Countries That Will Win The Future" Business Insider. http://www.businessinsider.com/willem-buiter-3g-countries-2011-2?slop=1&IR=T

Welch, C.E. (1972). Praetorianism in commonwealth West Africa. *The Journal of Modern African Studies* 10 (02), 203–222.

Welch, C.E. & Smith, A.K. (1974). *Military Role and Rule: Perspectives on Civil-Military Relations.* North Scituate, MA: Duxbury Press.

Were, M. (2001). The Impact of External Debt on Economic Growth in Kenya: An Empirical Assessment (No. 2001/116). WIDER Discussion Papers//World Institute for Development Economics (UNU-WIDER).

What Are Intractable Conflicts? Beyond Intractability, 2003. http://www.beyondintractability.org/essay/meaning-intractability

Widner, J.A. (2001) *Building the Rule of Law: Francis Nyalali and the Road to Judicial Independence in Africa.* London: WW Norton.

Wilkinson D. Condom effectiveness in reducing heterosexual HIV transmission: RHL commentary (last revised: 11 November 2002). The WHO Reproductive Health Library; Geneva: World Health Organization. http://apps.who.int/rhl/hiv_aids/dwcom/en/

Willett, S. (2009). Defence expenditures, arms procurement and corruption in Sub-Saharan Africa. *Review of African Political Economy* 36 (121), 335–351.

Wong, Y. (2012). *Sovereign Finance and the Poverty of Nations: Odious Debt in International Law.* Cheltenham: Edward Elgar Publishing.

Woo-Cumings, M., ed. (1999). *The Developmental State.* Ithaca, NY: Cornell University Press.

Wood, G. (March 2003). Staying secure, staying poor: The "Faustian Bargain". *World Development* 31 (3), 455–471.

Wood, R.E. (1986). *From Marshall Plan to Debt Crisis: Foreign Aid and Development Choices in the World Economy* (Vol. 15). Berkeley, CA: University of California Press.

World Bank. http://data.worldbank.org/indicator/DT.ODA.ALLD.CD

World Bank. (2013a). Democratic Republic of Congo Overview. www.worldbank.org

World Bank. (2013b). *Remarkable Declines in Global Poverty, But Major Challenges Remain*, www.worldbank.org, date accessed 7 April 2013.

World Bank. (2014). *World Development Indicators.* www.worldbank.org, date accessed 7 May 2014.

World Bank. (2014). Poverty Overview. http://www.worldbank.org/en/topic/poverty/overview
World Bank. (2012). *World Development Indicators 2012*. World Bank Publications.
World Bank. (2011). HIV/AIDS Regional Update – Africa. http://web.worldbank.org/WBSITE/ EXTERNAL/COUNTRIES/AFRICAEXT/EXTAFRHEANUTPOP/EXTAFRREGTOPHIV AIDS/0,,contentMDK:20415756~menuPK:1830800~pagePK:34004173~piPK:34003707 ~theSitePK:717148,00.html
World Bank. (2007). *World Development Report 2008: Agriculture for Development*.
World Bank. (2003). *Rural Poverty Report*. Washington DC: The World Bank.
World Bank. (2002a). *Treasure or Trouble? Mining in Developing Countries*. Washington, DC: World Bank Group.
World Bank. (2002b). World Bank Group Work in Low Income Countries Under Stress.
World Bank. (June 2, 1999). http://www.worldbank.org/aids-econ/africa/fire.htm
World Bank. (1998). Fighting Systemic Corruption: Foundations for Institutional Reforms. 1–10.
World Bank. (1997). *World Development Report 1997: The State in a Changing World*. Oxford University Press.
World Bank. (1995). *World Development Report*. Washington, DC: World Bank.
World Bank. (1990). *Evaluation Results for 1988: Issues in Policy Study*. Washington, DC: The Operations Evaluations Department, the World Bank.
World Bank. (1975). *The Assault on World Poverty*. Baltimore, MD: Johns Hopkins University Press.
World Bank Development Indicators. (2013). http://data.worldbank.org/data-catalog/world-development-indicators; http://www.worldbank.org/en/topic/poverty/overview
World Development Report 1997: The State in a Changing World. Washington, DC: The World Bank.
World Commission on Environment and Development. (1987). *Our Common Future*. Oxford: Oxford University Press.
World Health Organization. (2014a). Malaria Control: The Power of Integrated Action. http://www.who.int/heli/risks/vectors/malariacontrol/en/index6.html
World Health Organization. (2014b). Malaria Factsheet 14. http://www.who.int/mediacentre/ factsheets/fs094/en/
World Health Organization. (March 2014c). Ten Facts about Malaria. http://www.who.int/ features/factfiles/malaria/en/
World Health Organization. (September 2013) Women's Health. http://www.who.int/ mediacentre/factsheets/fs334/en/
World Health Organization. (2013a). 2001-2010: Decade to Roll Back Malaria in Developing Countries, Particularly in Africa. http://www.who.int/malaria/publications/atoz/UNGA_ malaria_report_2013_English.pdf
World Health Organization. (June 2013b). Global Update on HIV Treatment 2013: Results, Impact and Opportunities. 1–126.
World Health Organization. (2012). New Report Signals Slowdown in the Fight against Malaria. http://www.who.int/mediacentre/news/releases/2012/malaria_20121217/en/
World Health Organization. (2011a). The Sixteenth Global Report on Tuberculosis.
World Health Organization. (2011b). Tuberculosis, *Bugs, Drugs and Smoke*. http://www.who .int/about/bugs_drugs_smoke_chapter_6_tuberculosis.pdf
World Health Organization. (November 2010). Tuberculosis Fact sheet N°104.
World Health Organization. (2009). Epidemiology. Global Tuberculosis Control: Epidemiology, Strategy, Financing, 6–33.
World Hunger Organization. http://www.worldhunger.org/articles/Learn/child_hunger_facts.htm
World Trade Organization. www.wto.org/english/tratop_e/tpr_e/s147-1_e.doc
Wulf, H. (July 2004). Security Sector Reform in Developing and Transitional Countries. *Berghof Research Center for Constructive Conflict Management*. 1–20.
Yamey, G. (2002). Why does the world still need WHO? *BMJ* 325 (7375), 1294–1298.
Zagha, R. & Nankani, G.T., eds. (2005). *Economic Growth in the 1990s: Learning from a Decade of Reform*. World Bank Publications.
Zanotti, L. (2010). Cacophonies of aid, failed state building and NGOs in Haiti: Setting the stage for disaster, envisioning the future. *Third World Quarterly* 31 (5), 755–771.
Zartman, W. (1995). *Collapsed States: The Disintegration and Restoration of Legitimate Authority*. Boulder, CO: Lynne Rienner.
Zimmerman, E. (Spring 1979). Toward a Causal Model of Military Coups d'Etat. *Armed Forces and Society*.

Author/Scholar Index

Index

Bold terms are terms that are most frequently mentioned in the book.